PENGUIN HANDBOOKS

THE COMPETITIVE RUNNER'S HANDBOOK

BOB GLOVER is founder and president of Robert H. Glover and Associates, Inc., a fitness consulting firm serving a variety of corporate and community clients. He is also director of educational programs for the 25,000-member New York Road Runners Club. He is the former fitness director of New York City's West Side YMCA, where he developed and led one of the nation's largest fitness programs, with over 5,000 participants. He is also the founder and coach of several running teams, including the elite women's team, Atalanta New York, who have won several national championships in both the open and masters categories and have won the New York Marathon three times and the Avon International Marathon Club Championship four times. Glover has more than ten years' experience coaching all levels of runners, but he achieves his greatest satisfaction from helping the back-of-the-pack male and female runners increase their enjoyment of the sport. Over 50,000 of these "athletes" have participated in his programs.

PETE SCHUDER was the 1968 "Athlete of the Year" at Rutgers University, where he was the school record holder in six events and an NCAA finalist in the quarter-mile event. He was a three-time All-American in AAU indoor competition at 600 yards and the mile relay. He also competed for the powerful Sports International running club coached by Brooks Johnson, the 1984 U.S.A. Women's Olympic Track Coach. Schuder has been a professional coach for 15 years at the high school, college and club level. He has coached track and cross-country at Columbia University since 1972. At Columbia he has coached four NCAA All-Americans, and in 1979 his cross-country team won the Ivy League Championship and the Heptagonal Games for the first time in over 40 years.

Glover and Schuder met as graduate students at Columbia University in 1976 and over the years have blended together their combined experiences of more than 40 years in running—Schuder as a track runner and coach, Glover as a road racer and coach—to produce the program detailed in this book.

Also by Bob Glover

The Runner's Handbook
by Bob Glover and Jack Shepherd

The Runner's Handbook Training Diary
by Bob Glover and Jack Shepherd

The COMPETITIVE RUNNER'S Handbook

Bob Glover and Pete Schuder

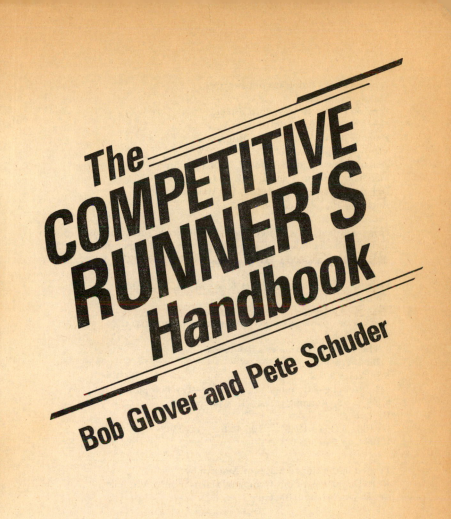

PENGUIN BOOKS

Penguin Books Ltd, Harmondsworth,
Middlesex, England
Penguin Books, 40 West 23rd Street,
New York, New York 10010, U.S.A.
Penguin Books Australia Ltd, Ringwood,
Victoria, Australia
Penguin Books Canada Limited, 2801 John Street,
Markham, Ontario, Canada L3R 1B4
Penguin Books (N.Z.) Ltd, 182–190 Wairau Road,
Auckland 10, New Zealand

First published in the United States of America in simultaneous hardcover
and paperback editions by The Viking Press and Penguin Books 1983

This paperback edition reprinted 1983

LIBRARY OF CONGRESS CATALOGING IN PUBLICATION DATA
Glover, Bob.
  The competitive runner's handbook.
  Bibliography: p.
  Includes index.
  1. Running—Training. 2. Running—Psychological
aspects. 3. Running races. I. Schuder, Pete.
II. Title.
GV1061.5.G54 1983   796.4'26   83-2302
ISBN 0 14 046.565 0

Printed in the United States of America by
R. R. Donnelley & Sons Company, Harrisonburg, Virginia
Set in Videocomp Baskerville

Text design: Levavi & Levavi

DEDICATION

To Christopher Ross Glover, my son; Virginia, Wife and Mommy; and Corinne and Ross Glover, my parents

Dear Christopher:

Happy Birthday! Today, as this book crosses the finish line, you are one year old. The book began its life when you did—what a long, eventful year. Remember your first race? Father's Day in Central Park when you were only one month old. Daddy and Grandpa Glover ran with you, pushing the carriage, and you were the star of the day. You were even interviewed on television. Mommy and Daddy ran a lot of miles with you over the weekends. It sure got people excited to see the three of us running together. Mommy made a lot of sacrifices so Daddy could finish this book. We both love her very much. Although you were running all by yourself by eleven months, Mommy says you don't have to be a runner if you don't want to be. I hope you run, but if not, at least be sure to do some kind of exercise. It's good for you. Daddy and Mommy love you very much, and Chrissy, I forgive you for eating page 81—I know you thought you were helping.

Bob Glover
New York City
May 23, 1982

To my two families, who are my strength:

Laurie, Matthew and Tabitha Ann, our newborn, who have touched my soul and allowed me to respond.

My parents, Ed and Gertrude, and my brother and sister, Ricky and Monica, who gave me support during my early years.

Pete Schuder
Teaneck, New Jersey
August 30, 1982

IN MEMORY

On April 12, 1983, Bill "Coach" Coughlin went out for his daily training run in Jackson, Michigan. He was run down by a car and tragically taken away from all his friends. For several decades he was a highly respected high school track coach and athletic director in Rome, New York. Only a few weeks before his death he retired, married, and started a new life with his wife, Dee. He planned to use this book as an aid to a marathon class that they would teach together. Coach was my professional adviser, my training partner, my friend. He was the perfect role model for athletes who sought discipline and dedication. He was a coach's coach. His inspiration will live on in the hearts of thousands of runners and friends.

—Bob Glover

CONTENTS_____

Acknowledgments   *11*

Preface   *17*

Introduction: You Are an Athlete!   *19*

Part I: TRAINING   **27**

 1. Categories of Runners   *29*

 2. Basic Training Principles   *39*

 3. Three Basic Questions: How Far? How
    Fast? How Often?   *56*

 4. The Distance Workout: Endurance-
    Training Runs   *74*

 5. Playing with Speed   *81*

 6. The Speed Workout: Strength-Training
    Runs   *98*

7. The Speed Workout: Rhythm-Training Runs   *108*

8. The Speed Workout: Power-Training Runs   *124*

9. The Training Schedule   *135*

10. How to Write Your Own Training Schedule   *152*

Part II: SPECIFIC TRAINING   **165**

11. Your First Race   *167*

12. Your First Marathon   *176*

13. The 10 km–Half Marathon   *187*

14. The Marathon   *201*

15. The 5 km–4-Mile Race   *229*

16. The Mile   *240*

17. Cross-Country   *254*

18. Beyond the Marathon—The Ultra   *269*

Part III: RACING   **279**

19. Goal Setting and Race-Time Prediction   *281*

20. Mental Preparation for Racing   *292*

Part IV: TECHNIQUE   **313**

21. Running Form   *315*

22. Running with Style   *336*

23. Racing Technique   *342*

Part V: INJURY AND ILLNESS   **359**

24. Twenty-four Causes of Injury and
    Illness   *361*

25. Prevention and Management of Injury
    and Illness   *394*

Part VI: SUPPLEMENTAL EXERCISES   **415**

26. Weight Training and Supplemental
    Exercises   *417*

27. The Warm-Up and Cool-Down Routines *431*

Part VII: FOOD, DRINK AND WEIGHT   **443**

28. Eating and Running   *445*

29. Drinking and Running   *458*

30. Running and Your Body Weight   *472*

**Part VIII: BALANCING THE STRESSES
IN YOUR LIFE**   **489**

31. The Runner's Triangle   *491*

APPENDICES   **499**

  Basic Physiology Terms   *501*

  Rhythm and Power Workout Guides   *504*

  90% Effort Guide   *509*

  Race-Time Comparison and Predictor
  Chart   *510*

Pacing Charts 512

Pace Chart for Track Races and Workouts 524

Mile-Kilometer Time Comparisons 526

Racing-Distance Conversions 527

Recommended Reading 528

Running Organizations 532

INDEX 535

ACKNOWLEDGMENTS

Both of us have been involved with competitive running for more than 20 years. During those two decades, many individuals have helped us in our careers as competitive runners and as coaches. They contributed greatly to this book.

Bob Glover especially wishes to thank his first three bosses during his years with the YMCA: Bob Elia, executive director of the Enterprise, Alabama YMCA; George Goyer, executive director of the Rome, New York YMCA; and Alexander Melleby, director of health and physical education of the West Side YMCA in New York City.

Al Melleby, now director of the National YMCA Healthy Back Program, and author of *The Y's Way to a Healthy Back*, taught Glover the basics of physical fitness and hired him as his right-hand man at the largest YMCA fitness program in the United States, that of the West Side Y.

Dr. George Sheehan and Dr. Richard Schuster freely offered medical advice (way before the running boom) that often kept Glover and his team and class members on the road to better racing. Joe Henderson, "Mr. Bubbles," encouraged Glover as a novice writer and fitness specialist and edited Bob's first published piece, and has alwa available with helpful encouragement. Dr. Hans Kraus, founder of the President's Council on Physical Fitness and Sports, has also helped Glover with medical advice, and his guidance in physical fitness helped him form his foundation as a professional. Richard Traum and John Eisner gave valuable business and legal advice in the founding and growth of Robert H. Glover and Associates, Inc., a corporate fitness consulting firm, and were available for suggestions on this book, too. Finally, Fred Lebow, director of the New York Marathon and the New York Road Runners Club, encouraged Bob to develop his running classes and clinics through the club, and also encouraged the development of his championship women's teams that won the women's division of the 1976, 1977 and 1978 New York Marathons as well as club championships in the 1979, 1980, 1981 and 1982 Avon International Marathons. Fred also turned Bob loose as a writer, encouraging him to write feature articles for the club newsletter after moving the Road Runners' headquarters from Fred's apartment to a closet in the back of Bob's fitness lab.

From these writings came collaboration with Jack Shepherd, author of nine books (three national best-sellers) and coauthor, with his coach as a beginner runner, of *The Runner's Handbook*. A quarter of a million readers later that book was a national best-seller, and Shepherd's professional writing skills make both this book and *The Runner's Handbook* enjoyable reading.

There are also many coaches and runners whose experience and expertise Glover has drawn on. To list them all is to risk missing one or two. But those from upstate New York need a special thanks for their contributions to his early career as a coach and road racer: Roman Runners Al Stringham, Bill Coughlin, Carl Eilenberg and Dr. Fred Grabo; Utica Pacemakers Joe Ficcaro, Sam Gratch, Tom Hovey and Syl Pascale; Syracuse Chargers Arnie Briggs, Kathy Switzer, Al Bonney and Chuck Wiltse.

The vast New York Road Runner community has also helped Bob, and includes the veterans Joe Kleinerman,

Harry Murphy, Kurt Steiner, Ted Corbitt, Dr. Norb Sander and Gary Muhrcke. Special mention must go to the pioneer of women's long-distance running, whose advice as a runner and a friend have always been valued: Bob Glover's heroine, Nina Kuscsik. Three other runners helped Bob advance from an average racer to a respectable local class competitor: Mike Cleary and Vince McDonald, who with Bob pioneered the George Washington Bridge Run, and Jim Ferris, the former University of Oregon runner and "upstater" who pushed Bob into a "new dimension" during workouts and challenged him to be daring during races.

The five teams that Bob Glover founded and coached— the Roman Runners, the West Side YMCA Runners Club, Greater New York Athletic Association, the elite Nike-sponsored women's team, Atalanta, and the Achilles Track Club for the physically handicapped—have included more than 500 men and women runners whose experiences shaped this book. In particular, Bob learned much as a coach of 18 sub-three-hour women marathon runners: Lauri McBride and Jane Killion Reagan (New York City's first sub-three-hour women), Sharon Barbano, Marilyn Hulak, Marcy Schwam, Angella Hearn, Chris Hearn, Maddy Harmeling, Kathy Naughton, Suzanne Hoppinthal, Robin Ladas, Diane Israel, Kathy Horton, Trish Smith, Vivian Chang, Toshika d'Elia, Sharon Given and Linda Jannelli. The national class masters runners from Atalanta have taught Glover that you don't get old, you get better: Toshika d'Elia, Patty Lee Parmalee, Nancy Tighe and Alicia Moore.

Sharon Barbano and Marcy Schwam get special thanks. Sharon was the number one guinea pig for Glover's training methods since 1978 and was a high-scoring member for four successive Avon International Marathon club championships. Marcy, the invincible world class ultramarathoner, inspired the team; her advice forms the basis for the section of this book on the ultramarathon.

Many thanks go to 5,000 men and women who have participated in various New York Road Runners classes since 1977. The Road Runners coaching staff also contributed their experiences and questions to this book. Special thanks to staff members Ann Rugh, Lisa Eben, and Bill Whiston, and national class Irish runner Jean Whiston.

Pete Schuder wishes to thank Les Wallack and Art Gulden, his first coaches on the college level, who taught him the basics and inspired him to become a national class runner and a professional coach. John Novak deserves special mention as Pete's roommate, teammate and partner during Schuder's high school coaching career at Metuchen High School in New Jersey. Their endless discussions on coaching principles and philosophies pushed Pete to search for answers to the many questions of training and racing, and helped shape this work.

Brooks Johnson taught Pete to analyze and evaluate the technical aspects of running. He also made him believe in his talents as a track coach. All of these friends and mentors contributed to Pete's knowledge of running.

Desi Foynes, Paul Heck and Charles Allen were Pete Schuder's first All-America track and field athletes at Columbia University. They gave him the confidence to continue growing and experimenting as a coach. Members of Columbia's league championship cross-country team of 1979 also must be thanked, particularly Charlie Miers, Paul Loomie, Wally Collins, Paul Hofmann, Jim Hannon and Rich McNally.

Outside of college track, there were others who contributed to Pete's knowledge and therefore to this book. Cheryl Norton taught Pete how to train women runners. The New York Road Runners classes gave him experience with the average adult runner. Thanks also go to the North Jersey Masters Track Club which Pete coaches, especially Dick Suggs, Ann Morris, Fred and Toshi d'Elia, Laurie Schuder—she married the coach—and national class masters runners Anne Bing and Helene Bedrock, who expressed their appreciation in so many ways for his coaching.

The authors also thank Dr. Murray Weisenfeld and Dr. Edward Colt who reviewed key medical sections of this book, and sports psychologist Dr. Andrew Gentile who offered helpful advice on the mental preparation for racing section.

Finally, we want to thank Martha Kinney for her professional editing of this challenging, marathon project.

PREFACE

This is not merely another book to read. It is a running book to use—to help you coach yourself. And once you have read it and tried it, keep this coach handy on your bookshelf.

The idea that running was a fad of the 1970's "Me Decade" has been left in the dust at road races around the world. In a column in *New York Running News*, Fred Lebow, the irascible guru of the international marathon and president of the 25,000-member New York Road Runners Club, asked, "Has the Running Boom Hit the Wall?" His own statistics provided the answer: more than 45,000 people—almost double the number of two years earlier—entered and finished races sponsored by the NYRRC in 1981. And more than 60,000 people applied for the coveted 16,000 openings in the 1982 New York Marathon.

"Marathon fever" has now hit Europe and spread even as far as China. At the First Annual London Marathon in 1981, 7,000 runners competed while a million spectators watched. The following year 80,000 applied for entry forms! The First Annual Rome Marathon (1982) attracted 4,000 runners and drew another 40,000 for a simultaneous 11 km event. In 1982, a half-marathon event in Milan drew

50,000 runners; a race in New Zealand attracted 60,000, and the Australian Sydney-to-Surf race drew over 50,000 runners. Some 30,000 to 50,000 runners compete in Atlanta's Peachtree 10 km and San Francisco's Bay-to-Breakers race, and 5,000 women compete in the L'Eggs Mini-Marathon in New York City. The running boom has switched gears from beginner to competitor. This book provides the training guidelines for these thousands of runners ranging in ability from ten-minute milers to five-minute milers.

Today runners are savvy, road smart. They know how to run, but more and more are starting to race and want to improve their performance. They want to know how to train for the marathon, how to improve their race times, what type of speed work to use, how to improve their running form, and what to eat before racing. These questions are asked every day by runners we train. We have written this book in response to questions like these.

The Runner's Handbook, by Bob Glover and Jack Shepherd, was a national best-seller and was called "the best technical work available for the beginner and intermediate runner." *The Competitive Runner's Handbook* takes up where the first book ended. It is a baton passed in the race toward your best times and best running.

Our goal here is to take the established runner, the man or woman entering racing or wishing to improve race times, and coach him or her to higher levels of performance. Most runners want to improve their times, but few have access to qualified coaching. Most coaches are too busy teaching the elite runners to respond to the questions of the average runner. We have coached every level of competitive runner from beginner to elite. Working with our classes and teams, we have trained several thousand athletes of every size, shape, age, and ability. This book comes from their questions and our experiences.

INTRODUCTION: YOU ARE AN ATHLETE!

Yes, you! Whether you are 15 or 70, tall or short, man or woman, fast runner or slow, novice or veteran racer—you are an athlete. Anyone who competes and has the desire to improve is an athlete. While elite athletes are the winners of competitive races, the rest of us are winners too. Each of us runs against himself or herself. Our "competition" is against the clock and our "old" selves—what we were a year ago. In other sports, there are losers as well as winners. But in running, we competitive runners are all "players" who stand together at the starting line and then strive to excel *for ourselves*. At the finish, we are all winners.

In our competitive running classes at the New York Road Runners and the North Jersey Masters Track Club, we coach runners whose racing pace per mile ranges from five to ten minutes. We treat them all the same. They all get pushed through vigorous workouts. Indeed, since 1976, when Bob Glover first started his "competitive running classes" for New York Road Runners Club members, he treated each runner like an athlete. Even Club President Fred Lebow thought Glover was crazy. But Glover argued that every man and woman runner wanted to compete and improve, and to do this they would need to find their limits, just like the elite runner.

If you race and you want to get better, you are a competitive runner. To reach your full potential, you must take a positive attitude toward your training and running. Do not worry about things you cannot control. A major part of athletic ability is inherited. C. T. Davis, professor at the London School of Hygiene and Tropical Medicine, states that an athlete is one who makes maximum use of his or her genetic endowment by training in his or her environment. By that he means: Go with what you've got. It's too late to be born an elite runner. But you can gain much satisfaction by running your best with what skills you have. Believe in yourself. Hard, consistent work pays off. Work to the best of your ability. You will feel better about yourself—and you will improve athletically as your self-esteem and confidence grow.

As a competitive runner, you place a high priority on running. The better you perform, the higher up running is on your list of priorities. Your improvement is relative to the time and energy you put into running. Some of you may wish to improve modestly, with slowly growing commitment and gains. Others may wish to reach out and challenge themselves to the fullest. Both must have a positive attitude in order to succeed. You must see yourself as an athlete and an achiever, not just as a participant. Dream about running with smooth, effortless rhythm and strides. Picture yourself passing other runners and winning races. Feel good about your accomplishments.

Who knows what your potential may be? Bob Glover has an uncanny knack of picking top women competitors out of the pack. Many times he has watched an unknown runner in a race, or run with her, and known that she had that little special extra. Usually it's a blend of athletic ability combined with a strong desire to succeed. Patty Lee Parmalee, for example, got lost during her first Road Runners Club speed class and ended up with the fastest group of men. Glover let her suffer, and watched. She wouldn't give up, and when she finished, he told her, "You can be a national class masters runner."

"OK," she replied, "let's do it." And Patty Lee, age 42, has become one of the best after joining the rigorous Atalanta team workouts. In fact, she won in her age division in the 1982 L'Eggs Mini-Marathon.

But while some runners are discovered, others discover themselves. They are the runners who, in any race, cross the finish line and jump up and down in joy with a new PR (personal record). We are all winners in this race. And in our classes, and in this book, we treat the fast and the slow the same: we push them, encourage them, and they get better. You can do this too. All you have to do is plan your training carefully, be patient, and understand that today and forever you are an athlete.

EXCUSES, EXCUSES!

We have heard them all: "I'm too old. I'm too far out of shape. I'm too big, too small, too fat, too skinny. I don't have the time. Running isn't for women." We accept none of them. And there is no reason why every runner cannot improve and become a better athlete. The key is commitment and training. You hold in your hand a proven guide to get you down that road.

● "I'm too old." Mary Rodriguez is more than 60 years old. She works at a school for underprivileged youth in the South Bronx—and often runs to work. In the spring of 1977, Mary was 40 pounds overweight. She attended one of our New York Road Runners Club clinics for beginner runners. She wanted to start running to inspire her husband, who had recovered from a heart attack, to start exercising. During one of Glover's pep talks she sat in the front row and afterwards tapped him on the shoulder: "I'm going to do it!" She started the following Saturday, and within three months Mary had completed her first race, a 10 km. The next year she improved her time for the L'Eggs Mini-Marathon by 15 minutes and then completed the 1978 New York Marathon in 4:31. She had also lost 42 pounds. But perhaps best of all, Mary Rodriguez is now a competitive athlete and wins many trophies in her age division.

• "I'm too busy." Toshi d'Elia started running in her late thirties because she was getting fat. She entered her first race as a favor to her daughter, who wanted someone who would finish last, behind her girl friends. Toshi, however, finished third, won a trophy—and never looked back. She's been winning ever since. In 1978, Toshi went to Bob Glover with a problem: she couldn't break the three-hour marathon barrier. No wonder. She was running more than 100 miles a week, in addition to her family responsibilities and a demanding job as a teacher of deaf children. Glover told her to cut back on her mileage and add two days a week of speed workouts: once a week on a track and once on hills. In 1979, Toshi at age 49 became the oldest woman to break three hours for the marathon—in the Boston Marathon—an achievement that was reported in *Sports Illustrated*. In 1980, at the World Masters Championship in Glasgow, Toshi set a world record for the 50+ age division with an outstanding 2:57:21. In 1981, her autobiography, *Running On*, became a hit in her native Japan and a TV movie was filmed of her life. And it all started when she *cut back* her mileage because she was, indeed, too busy.

• "I can't run that far or that fast." Marcy Schwam started running to keep in shape for tennis. In 1975, she went to Glover for help in breaking 3:30 so she could qualify for the Boston Marathon. She made slow but steady progress over the next few years and then won the women's division in the first race up the stairs of the Empire State Building. She ran a race up Pike's Peak. Marcy went on to win ultramarathon runs, and she set the American women's road record for 100 km and the world record for 48 hours of running on a track. In 1981, she dedicated herself to improving her speed, and by running track workouts with her Atalanta teammates, Marcy ran a five-mile race averaging under six minutes per mile. Before she started the speed workouts, she couldn't run a single mile under six minutes. During a 24-hour race, Marcy also set women's world records for 50 miles (6:43), 100 km (8:46) and 100 miles (15:44). Then in 1981, Marcy ran a six-day race on a quarter-mile track. She hit the marathon mark in 3:20, broke her own 48-hour mark with 158 miles, and went on to become the first woman ever to complete this event, covering 384 miles in a six-day race. In 1982, she set a world record and became the first woman to break the six-hour barrier for 50 miles with a time of 5:59:25. Three weeks later she improved her marathon PR to 2:48:17. In 1980, 1981 and 1982, to no one's surprise, Marcy Schwam was named the woman ultramarathoner of the year and received the Nurmi Award. For most of 1981, Marcy would run at 5 a.m., then go to work as a construction worker—carrying around heavy bags of cement with the best of the men. After work she would run more miles or do a team speed workout. And you can't get your mileage in?

• "I'm handicapped." Mort Schlein started in the New York Road Runners beginner's class at the age of 45. He was just like any other sedentary, overweight, middle-aged runner—except that Mort is blind. Using a series of friends who run with him, holding his elbow or a short rope tied to his arm, Mort built his mileage to include 10- to 12-mile runs. A running friend even made him a raised map of Central Park so he could get a better feel for his training route. When he couldn't find a partner, he ran up the stairs in his apartment building. Mort decided that he wanted to become an athlete, and enrolled in the competitive class. Glover showed no mercy, and sometimes grabbed Mort's guideline and yanked him up the hills on sprints. Mort went on to complete the 1981 New York Marathon. Mort insists that he is no different from any of us who run. And he isn't—except he has disciplined himself to be a better athlete than he was.

Still have excuses? We all know the story of Terry Fox, who in 1980 ran 3,339 miles—a "Marathon of Hope"— across Canada to raise money for the Canadian Cancer Society. The 22-year-old Canadian had lost his right leg at the knee to cancer in 1977. Just before this very athletic young man had his leg removed, a friend had given him a copy of the January 1977 *Runner's World* article about a one-legged marathon man—Dick Traum. Encouraged and inspired, Terry vowed to run across Canada to raise money to fight this affliction he faced. Then, in June 1981, two-thirds of the way across Canada, Terry Fox lost his life to the dreaded disease.

Dick Traum had lost his right leg above the knee in 1965 as the result of a freak automobile accident. In 1975, at the age of 34, Dick found that his company, Personnelmetrics (which now handles the computer scoring for the New York Marathon), was growing rapidly, and with it his weight and blood pressure. He needed help and went to see Bob Glover, then fitness director at New York City's West Side YMCA.

When Traum hopped into Bob's office on one leg, Bob jumped out of his chair and candidly asked, "Can you run?"

"Sure," Traum lied. He hadn't run a step. But that evening he practiced in the hallway of his apartment until he got the skill of hopping along. "I don't run," Dick now explains, "but hop, swing my artificial leg, and take a step."

Dick Traum quickly progressed through the beginner, intermediate and advanced levels of the Y fitness program, and Glover challenged him to enter a five-mile race in Central Park. Dick finished last, in 72 minutes, but as he crossed the line the other runners loudly cheered him. He went on to run a half marathon and a 30 km. Then he started training for the marathon. He worked out three times a week, with two two-hour runs of nine miles each and one five-hour run of 18 miles—all on the 23-laps-per-mile indoor Y track. Dick's training was estimated to be the equivalent of 60 miles a week for the average runner. (Traum needed the days off to allow the welts to heal on his stump.)

In 1976, Dick completed the New York Marathon in 7:24, which included an extra couple of miles because he got lost. The next year, he lowered his time to 6:44. But in

1978, Dick had trouble with his knee and ran little. He started indoor biking at his coach's insistence and worked out for an hour, three times a week. In late May 1979, Traum nonchalantly plunked down $10 for the New York Marathon entry fee. Then, investment made, he turned to Glover for coaching. Glover decided that Dick should train on a stationary bike, with a minimum of actual running, and on race day cover the course with a run/walk style. Dick built up to one day of running (up to five miles), one day of indoor biking for two hours, and one day of biking for four hours. He often did "pickups" of two to three minutes on the bike to relieve boredom. He ran a five-mile race, and a 20 km to test the knee, before completing the New York Marathon comfortably in 8:04. He skipped the 1980 event, but the marathon addiction made him come back for more.

In 1981, Dick continued working out on the bike—his longest time was while watching Saturday night television, 6 to 11:30, covering 110 km. After running back-to-back 10 km's for Terry Fox's charity in Toronto, Dick completed the 1981 New York Marathon in 7:21.

Next time you have an excuse, think of these runners who through dedication overcame obstacles to become better athletes. You can do it too!

KEY INGREDIENTS TO SUCCESSFUL RUNNING

Each runner has two levels of running potential—ideal and realistic. Ideally, you should maximize your abilities by spending enough time and effort on all aspects of training. Realistically, you do your best and recognize that you are not a full-time runner. Being totally committed to running takes time. Bill Rodgers once remarked: "No one who works a forty-hour week will ever beat me." He's right—and we working stiffs should accept that.

This book explains the key aspects of successful running. Don't let them overwhelm you. Budget your time and energy to become a better runner within the limits of your realistic goals. Don't let anyone push you beyond tnese goals. Some ingredients are more important than others. A breakdown in one area, however, may cause you to fail in other areas and result in less than optimal performance. The key ingredients of competitive running are detailed in the following chapters.

Before you proceed to Chapter 1, review the list of physiology terms on pages 501–503. A basic understanding of key terms is essential to proper training.

Part I
TRAINING

1. CATEGORIES OF RUNNERS

There are four categories of competitive runners: novice, basic, advanced and champion. By identifying your level, you can use this book to structure your own training program and fit it to your needs. You can set approximate goals for your weekly mileage, long runs, speed workouts, training schedule, and races.

Obviously, these categories are only approximate guides to help you determine what program is best for you. In many cases, a runner may be putting in less or more mileage than that indicated for his or her racing time. Young, fast runners will get away with less mileage. Older runners often run somewhat less mileage than indicated for their category; this is especially true for those runners age 50 or older. One of our women runners in that age group logs only 50 miles a week, rather than 70 as called for, but her times place her at the champion level. Generally, most runners fit into one of these categories and are training to move into the next level. We have adjusted the categories for age and sex. The racing time range for your age group can be used to help you set racing goals and to predict your race times for all racing distances.

OLDER RUNNERS

Most races categorize runners in different age groups for awards. Thus, as you get older you still compare yourself to your peers. Eventually, however, times slow. The peak age for endurance activity is 26–30, according to a study reported in the *British Medical Journal* (1973) by Dr. L. E. Bottinger of Stockholm. Runners who start late in life may not peak until much later; however, all runners have their best chance for optimal race times between the ages of 26 and 30. A long-term study being conducted at Washington University in St. Louis involving competitive runners aged 50 and older reports encouraging news: People don't slow down with age as fast as many have believed. That research shows only a 5 percent per decade decrease in performance after the age of 30 if training is steady. As you move into an older age group, you can adjust your race time goals using our category guidelines. You may find that you can move up a category just by getting older. Aging does bring some rewards.

YOUNGER RUNNERS

The "open" division is the youngest group on the charts and starts at age 18. We do not encourage children age 12 and younger to compete in long-distance running. Rather, we prefer to have them experience the joys of running for fitness and racing for fun. We suggest they limit their mileage to runs of 1 to 4 miles and races up to 2 miles. Young children should be encouraged to let their bodies fly, their legs run. But they must be harnessed so that growing bones and growing minds are not damaged. Parents are cautioned: don't push them too soon; let your children *choose* to run—for themselves, not for you.

Teenage runners should learn how to run fast over short distances and have fun. They should concentrate on the distances run in their schools—up to 5 km, and if they wish, on road races up to 10 km. As runners mature at this age, their stamina increases and they can run faster over longer distances. We do not recommend marathon running until an adolescent is capable of handling both the training and the racing physically and emotionally. Junior high school and high school track programs are excellent starting points.

WOMEN RUNNERS

Physical characteristics make women runners different from men. Women have only 85 to 90 percent of the heart size of men, and they also have smaller lungs. They have more body fat, but smaller bones and less muscle. Women generally weigh less than men of the same height and have less power to propel the mass.

According to Dr. Ernst van Aaken, a long-time promoter of women's running in Germany and throughout the world: "Women are born with greater natural stamina. Men, on the other hand, will always throw farther, jump higher, run faster for shorter stretches. Forty percent of a man's body weight is muscle; in women, muscle amounts to only twenty-three percent. Instead of this, women have more hypodermal fatty tissue—and that is the source of energy for hours' long exertion." Women runners, Dr. van Aaken suggests, may become competitive with men at long distances. Indeed, we often find that women in our programs can't beat a man for a shorter distance of 5–10 km, but will easily beat him for the marathon. At shorter distances, men have more power for speed and run away from most women. A study by K. J. Cureton at the University of Georgia concluded that "the additional sex-specific essential fat of women" could not be eliminated by diet or training, and provided justification for separate distance-running performance standards for men and women. In running, biology is indeed destiny.

In this book, and in our classes and teams, we coach women in the same way as we coach men. We have adjusted our race time categories to compensate for the physiological differences between men and women. For more information on the physiological, psychological and sociological aspects of running for women, we recommend *Running Free* by Dr. Joan Ullyot.

NOVICE COMPETITOR

This runner has raced little or lacks the time or ability to improve and move into the next level.

Experience: Has been running at least six months and just started racing, or has been racing only a few months, or may be an experienced runner who hasn't trained seriously.

Mileage: 15 to 30 miles per week, and moves into the 40 to 50 range for a marathon.

Frequency: Runs 5 to 6 days per week.

Long runs: 4 to 12 miles every 2 to 3 weeks, and will move into the 15- to 20-mile range for marathon training.

Speed work: 1 day a week or less, *after* experiencing a few races.

Races: 1 to 10 times per year, usually 10 km or less.

Race times: See Chart A below and at top of opposite page.

CHART A   NOVICE COMPETITOR—
RACE-TIME RANGES FOR MEN

DISTANCE	(OPEN)	(40–49)	(50–59)	(60–69)
5 km	23:30 +	25:30 +	27:30 +	29:30 +
10 km	48:00 +	52:00 +	56:00 +	60:00 +
15 km	75:00 +	81:00 +	87:00 +	93:00 +
10 miles	80:00 +	86:40 +	93:20 +	1:40 +
20 km	1:42 +	1:51 +	1:59 +	2:07 +
Half marathon	1:50 +	2:00 +	2:10 +	2:20 +
25 km	2:10 +	2:20:30 +	2:31:30 +	2:42:30 +
30 km	2:38 +	2:51:30 +	3:04:30 +	3:17:30 +
Marathon	3:50 +	4:10 +	4:30 +	4:50 +

Note: Times for the novice competitor reflect a wide range of performance, from being able to just finish the distance to running near the basic competitor times. For example, 48:00 + for an open man for 10 km means his time would be more than 48 minutes, and thus this runner is a novice competitor. For example, his time could be 50 or 60 minutes. His goal would be to move up to the basic competitor category by improving his time in order to break 48 minutes.

CHART A NOVICE COMPETITOR—
RACE-TIME RANGES FOR WOMEN

DISTANCE	(OPEN)	(40–49)	(50–59)	(60–69)
5 km	25:30 +	27:30 +	29:30 +	31:30 +
10 km	52:00 +	56:00 +	60:00 +	64:00 +
15 km	81:00 +	87:00 +	93:00 +	99:00 +
10 miles	86:40 +	93:20 +	1:40 +	1:46:40 +
20 km	1:51 +	1:59 +	2:07 +	2:15 +
Half marathon	2:00 +	2:10 +	2:20 +	2:30 +
25 km	2:20:30 +	2:31:30 +	2:42:30 +	2:53:30 +
30 km	2:51:30 +	3:04:30 +	3:17:30 +	3:30:30 +
Marathon	4:10 +	4:30 +	4:50 +	5:10 +

Note: Times for the novice competitor reflect a wide range of performance, from being able to just finish the distance to running near the basic competitor times. For example, 52:00 + for an open woman for 10 km means her time would be more than 52 minutes, and thus this runner is a novice competitor. For example, her time could be 55 or 60 minutes. Her goal would be to move up to the basic competitor category by improving her time in order to break 52 minutes.

BASIC COMPETITOR

This is the majority of the runners in the middle of the pack and back. They run half marathons and shorter races well. They can finish a marathon with their heads up in a respectable time. These runners do some speed work to improve their times. They may be first-time marathon runners, and train more than the novice competitor to run that race in reasonable time.

Experience: Has been running at least 2 years, racing at least 1 to 2 years.

Mileage: 25 to 60 miles a week.

Frequency: 5 to 7 days per week.

Long runs: 10 to 20 miles, once every other week.

Speed work: 1 day a week when preparing for races, two if experienced.

Races: 5 to 12 a year, usually from 10 km to a half marathon; typically, no more than one marathon a year.

Race times: See Chart B on following page.

CHART B BASIC COMPETITOR—RACE-TIME RANGES FOR MEN

DISTANCE	(OPEN)	(40–49)	(50–59)	(60–69)
5 km	19:30–23:30	20:30–25:30	21:30–27:30	22:30–29:30
10 km	40:00–48:00	42:00–52:00	44:00–56:00	46:00–60:00
15 km	63:00–75:00	66:00–81:00	69:00–87:00	72:00–93:00
10 miles	66:40–80:00	70:00–86:40	73:20–93:20	76:40–1:40
20 km	1:25–1:42	1:29–1:51	1:34–1:59	1:38–2:07
Half marathon	1:30–1:50	1:35–2:00	1:40–2:10	1:45–2:20
25 km	1:46–2:10	1:53–2:20:30	1:59–2:31:30	2:05–2:42:30
30 km	2:12–2:38	2:18–2:51:30	2:25–3:04:30	2:32–3:17:30
Marathon	3:10–3:50	3:20–4:10	3:30–4:30	3:40–4:50

Note: A runner may qualify as a basic competitor in one distance, such as the 5 km, but because of a lack of mileage or experience be classified as a novice competitor in another distance, such as the marathon.

CHART B BASIC COMPETITOR—RACE-TIME RANGES FOR WOMEN

DISTANCE	(OPEN)	(40–49)	(50–59)	(60–69)
5 km	21:30–25:30	22:30–27:30	24:30–29:30	26:30–31:30
10 km	44:00–52:00	46:00–56:00	50:00–60:00	54:00–64:00
15 km	69:00–81:00	72:00–87:00	78:00–93:00	84:00–99:00
10 miles	73:20–86:40	76:40–93:20	83:20–1:40	90:00–1:46:40
20 km	1:34–1:51	1:38–1:59	1:46–2:07	1:54–2:15
Half marathon	1:40–2:00	1:45–2:10	1:55–2:20	2:05–2:30
25 km	1:59–2:20:30	2:05–2:31:30	2:15–2:42:30	2:26–2:53:30
30 km	2:25–2:51:30	2:32–3:04:30	2:45–3:17:30	2:58–3:30:30
Marathon	3:30–4:10	3:40–4:30	4:00–4:50	4:20–5:10

Note: A runner may qualify as a basic competitor in one distance, such as the 5 km, but because of a lack of mileage or experience be classified as a novice competitor in another distance, such as the marathon.

ADVANCED COMPETITOR

This is the highest level of competition most runners can achieve, due to limited natural ability, lack of time, or family responsibilities. This runner is serious about the sport, and races well at the marathon distance and under, usually placing in the top 10 to 25 percent of the field and winning awards in local races.

Experience: Has been running at least 4 years and racing for at least 2 years.

Mileage: 40 to 80 miles per week.

Frequency: 6 to 7 days a week; perhaps a few two-a-days.

Long runs: 10 to 20 miles, once every 2 weeks, or 2 out of every 3 weeks.

Speed work: 1 or 2 days per week while preparing for races.

Races: 10 to 20 times a year at a variety of distances. Runs no more than 2 or 3 marathons per year.

Race times: See Chart C below.

CHART C   ADVANCED COMPETITOR—RACE-TIME RANGES FOR MEN

DISTANCE	(OPEN)	(40–49)	(50–59)	(60–69)
5 km	16:30–19:30	17:30–20:30	18:30–21:30	20:30–22:30
10 km	34:00–40:00	36:00–42:00	38:00–44:00	42:00–46:00
15 km	53:00–63:00	56:00–66:00	59:00–69:00	66:00–72:00
10 miles	56:40–66:40	60:00–70:00	63:20–73:20	70:00–76:40
20 km	1:12–1:25	1:16–1:29	1:21–1:34	1:29–1:38
Half marathon	1:15–1:30	1:20–1:35	1:25–1:40	1:35–1:45
25 km	1:31–1:46	1:37–1:53	1:42–1:59	1:53–2:05
30 km	1:51–2:12	1:58–2:18	2:04–2:25	2:18–2:32
Marathon	2:40–3:10	2:50–3:20	3:00–3:30	3:20–3:40

CHART C   ADVANCED COMPETITOR—RACE-TIME RANGES FOR WOMEN

DISTANCE	(OPEN)	(40–49)	(50–59)	(60–69)
5 km	18:30–21:30	20:30–22:30	22:30–24:30	24:30–26:30
10 km	38:00–44:00	42:00–46:00	46:00–50:00	50:00–54:00
15 km	59:00–69:00	66:00–72:00	72:00–78:00	78:00–84:00
10 miles	63:20–73:20	70:00–76:40	76:40–83:20	83:20–90:00
20 km	1:21–1:34	1:29–1:38	1:38–1:46	1:47–1:54
Half marathon	1:25–1:40	1:35–1:45	1:45–1:55	1:55–2:05
25 km	1:42–1:59	1:53–2:05	2:05–2:15	2:15–2:26
30 km	2:04–2:25	2:18–2:32	2:32–2:45	2:45–2:58
Marathon	3:00–3:30	3:20–3:40	3:40–4:00	4:00–4:20

CHAMPION COMPETITOR

This level is achieved by those with the time, talent and energy to reach at least the top local class. This runner often competes at the edge of national class. This is a serious level of competitive training. The champion usually places in the top 10 to 20 runners overall in local races, or in the top five in the masters age groups. These runners are also very often race winners.

Experience: Has been running at least 5 years, and racing at least 4 years.

Mileage: 60 to 100 miles per week.

Frequency: Runs 7 days a week, with several two-a-days.

Long runs: 12 to 20 miles, 2 out of 3 weeks or 3 out of 4 weeks.

CHART D   CHAMPION COMPETITOR—RACE-TIME RANGES FOR MEN

DISTANCE	(OPEN)	(40–49)	(50–59)	(60–69)
5 km	14:30–16:30	15:30–17:30	17:00–18:30	19:00–20:30
10 km	30:00–34:00	32:00–36:00	35:00–38:00	39:00–42:00
15 km	46:00–53:00	49:00–56:00	55:00–59:00	61:00–66:00
10 miles	50:00–56:40	53:20–60:00	58:20–63:20	65:00–70:00
20 km	1:03–1:12	1:07–1:16	1:14–1:21	1:23–1:29
Half marathon	1:06–1:15	1:10–1:20	1:17:30–1:25	1:27:30–1:35
25 km	1:20–1:31	1:25–1:37	1:34–1:42	1:45–1:53
30 km	1:37–1:51	1:44–1:58	1:54–2:04	2:08–2:18
Marathon	2:20–2:40	2:30–2:50	2:45–3:00	3:05–3:20

CHART D   CHAMPION COMPETITOR—RACE-TIME RANGES FOR WOMEN

DISTANCE	(OPEN)	(40–49)	(50–59)	(60–69)
5 km	17:00–18:30	19:00–20:30	20:30–22:30	23:00–24:30
10 km	35:00–38:00	39:00–42:00	42:00–46:00	47:00–50:00
15 km	55:00–59:00	61:00–66:00	66:00–72:00	73:00–78:00
10 miles	58:20–63:20	65:00–70:00	70:00–76:40	78:20–83:20
20 km	1:14–1:21	1:23–1:29	1:29–1:38	1:40–1:47
Half marathon	1:17:30–1:25	1:27:30–1:35	1:35–1:45	1:47:30–1:55
25 km	1:34–1:42	1:45–1:53	1:53–2:05	2:07–2:15
30 km	1:54–2:04	2:08–2:18	2:18–2:32	2:35–2:45
Marathon	2:45–3:00	3:05–3:20	3:20–3:40	3:45–4:00

Speed work: 2 to 3 days per week when preparing for a key race.

Races: 10 to 20 times a year at a variety of distances. Runs no more than 2 or 3 marathons a year.

Race times: See Chart D, on the opposite page.

NATIONAL CLASS AND ELITE RUNNERS

Beyond these four categories are the national class and elite runners. Since some of the champion runners may aspire to the national class level, we have included racing times (Chart E, below) for this category. In fact, several of the runners we coach ranging in age from 25–55 have entered this level.

We do not set specific training guidelines for national

CHART E   NATIONAL CLASS COMPETITOR—RACE-TIME RANGES FOR MEN

DISTANCE	(OPEN)	(40–49)	(50–59)	(60–69)
5 km	14:30	15:30	17:00	19:00
10 km	30:00	32:00	35:00	39:00
15 km	46:00	49:00	55:00	61:00
10 miles	50:00	53:20	58:20	65:00
20 km	1:03	1:07	1:14	1:23
Half marathon	1:06	1:10	1:17:30	1:27:30
25 km	1:20	1:25	1:34	1:45
30 km	1:37	1:44	1:54	2:08
Marathon	2:20	2:30	2:45	3:05

CHART E   NATIONAL CLASS COMPETITOR—RACE-TIME RANGES FOR WOMEN

DISTANCE	(OPEN)	(40–49)	(50–59)	(60–69)
5 km	17:00	19:00	20:30	23:00
10 km	35:00	39:00	42:00	47:00
15 km	55:00	61:00	66:00	73:00
10 miles	58:20	65:00	70:00	78:20
20 km	1:14	1:23	1:29	1:40
Half marathon	1:17:30	1:27:30	1:35	1:47:30
25 km	1:34	1:45	1:53	2:07
30 km	1:54	2:08	2:18	2:35
Marathon	2:45	3:05	3:20	3:45

class runners, who include, for example, a sub–2:20 male marathoner and a sub–2:45 female marathoner. Runners at this level would follow the same general guidelines as the champion competitor.

The elite runner was made in heaven and seldom runs in hell. They are the big guns: Rodgers, Salazar, Shorter, Waitz, Roe, Catalano. There is little anyone can teach them except, perhaps, to remind them that they wouldn't be at the top if the rest of us weren't behind them.

2. BASIC TRAINING PRINCIPLES

This book is for men and women who see themselves as athletes and wish to *train*—not just go for a run each day—in order to race longer distances and faster times. You may be a ten-minute-per-mile or a five-minute-per-mile runner, but you seriously want to improve by following a well-organized training program. You hold that program in your hands.

According to Joe Henderson, "Running is an end in itself, while training is a means to an end." The competitive runner plans his or her runs and develops a training schedule directed toward a key race or races several weeks ahead. Running is still enjoyable, but involves more dedication, structure, regularity and work. Some of these runs, particularly long runs and speed sessions, carry a different kind of reward. You learn the satisfaction of completing hard workouts that help you accomplish training and racing goals. You learn what it means"to pay your dues," and see a new PR on the clock at the finish line. Training teaches both the body and the mind to meet racing's many challenges.

Our training methods are based on established principles. Every coach and every athlete "steals" hints from this person or that person, and processes them through the trial and error of personal experience. The result is different applications of the same basic knowledge. We do not pretend to have invented competitive training. We are greatly indebted to those pioneer coaches, runners and scientists who have contributed to the resource bank we draw on. Other coaches may tell you to train differently; they are neither right nor wrong. They have interpreted the basic training principles in a different way.

The following ten principles form the backbone of our training program for the competitive runner:

I. THE PRINCIPLE OF FOUNDATION TRAINING AND SHARPENING

When you construct a house, you start with the foundation and build on that. The same is true of competitive running.

You must build a *foundation* of aerobic endurance. You do this by progressively increasing your work load and then, as you approach your race target, you *sharpen* your training with specific speed workouts designed so that you peak for your race or series of races. Then you recover and rebuild with foundation endurance running.

This basic principle is used by two types of runners:

1. The runner "on the way up"—the beginner racer or marathoner—slowly develops a foundation of endurance before adding miles to his or her schedule. For the true beginner, this means building to a base of 30 minutes of running five times a week before building toward the first race. The novice marathoner builds to a foundation of 30 to 40 miles a week and then adds to this base.

The mileage foundation for this type of runner is essential. Sharpening means increasing the number of miles with more foundation endurance work in order to have the stamina to complete the aimed-for event. After the goal (race) is reached, the runner cuts back on mileage, recovers, and then rebuilds a foundation at a higher level of mileage for the next challenge, and either improves time or increases the distance raced. For the first one to two years of running and racing, the novice puts in almost exclusively foundation aerobic runs at a conversation pace.

2. The experienced competitor wants to improve his or her time. To do this, he or she expands from a foundation of endurance and sharpens for the race with speed workouts. Having peaked for a race, the competitive runner needs a period of decreased activity to rebuild the foundation and sharpen again to reach an even higher level of performance.

In other sports this principle is applied as a seasonal approach. Professional teams have spring training or summer camps and preseason workouts and games. High school and college track teams have well-defined seasons: cross-country in the fall, indoor track in the winter, and outdoor track in the spring. The average competitive road racer has neither well-defined seasons, nor a coach to develop him or her, following the principle of foundation training and sharpening.

A training program for competitive runners consists of three parts: the off-season (rebuilding—light running), the preseason (progressive foundation endurance running), and the competitive season (specific training to sharpen and build to peak performance). Some competitive road racers only "peak" once a year. For the average competitive runner, this may mean an increase in mileage and workouts leading to a popular mass marathon. For others, it may mean building up for key races two or three times a year. Some elite runners spend six months to a year building toward one key race, perhaps to run a fast time or qualify for the Olympic team. Most runners, however, have varying peaks and valleys in their running year.

The average competitor follows a two-season approach. He or she may back off during the cold weather and then build for a spring race—perhaps the Boston Marathon. Then he or she may back off during the hot summer to build for the fall races—maybe the New York Marathon. Most popular races are held in the spring and fall, when the weather is cooler.

Foundation training is done year-round. During the off

season, it is used for recovery and maintenance running. During the build-up period, it increases progressively to improve aerobic and muscular endurance. During the sharpening periods of the competitive season, foundation endurance runs form the backbone of a weekly schedule. Remember, the better the base developed through foundation training, the more hard work your body will be able to do as you prepare for your big race, and the more likely you are to become a successful competitive runner.

II. THE PRINCIPLE OF CONSISTENCY

Foundation training is based on steady, *consistent* work. Constant training—52 weeks a year—is necessary for the competitive runner. You run when it's hot or cold, when you are high or low, alone or with friends, when aiming toward a big race or when your goal has been achieved.

Joe Henderson comments in his book *Run Farther, Run Faster*: "A runner adapts slowly to his work. He has to sneak up on bigger loads by taking many small, quiet steps instead of making explosive leaps at them. But the little gains add up to more in the long run than do the sporadic lunges. It's the old tortoise-and-hare principle of 'steady pace wins the race.' It's a matter of consistency."

You must train all week—not just on Saturday and Sunday. Even small amounts of running on a regular basis are better for you than sporadic hard days followed by days of inactivity.

If you decide to cut back for a change of pace, replace the aerobic exercise with another. Develop a minimal fitness base of running—anywhere between 50 to 75 percent of your peak mileage—and don't fall below it except in case of injury or illness. For example, if you normally build to 60 miles a week for a marathon, don't fall below a base of 30 to 45 miles a week during your lull in training. If you do, it will be too hard to build back up. Train consistently all year in order to grow stronger year after year. "Put miles in the bank."

Consistency requires discipline. Force yourself out the door. An advanced competitor puts in some mileage every day; novice and basic competitors run six days a week. Log your runs in your diary. It is easy to fall into the habit of taking a day off when things get a little tough. Instead of not running at all, cut back your mileage on days when you are faced with obstacles; force yourself to do a minimal amount to keep the habit of consistency alive. To succeed as a runner, you must be a little crazy about getting in your daily run. Schedule your run for the same time every day; make it an important appointment with yourself. Remember: it is better to do something each day—"packing in the miles"—than nothing at all.

When you build to your intended mileage level for base training for a big race, try to stay consistent. In 1978, Bob Glover ran exactly 100 miles each week for 12 consecutive weeks of foundation work. This consistency seemed fanatical even to other runners. After lowering his mileage to 80–90 miles a week and doing some quick speed work with Pete Schuder yelling at him, Glover enjoyed two months of racing times he had never before dreamed he could accomplish, peaking with a 1:43 30 km race.

On the other hand, consistent training needs to be practical. If your body asks for a day off—take it. But only sound reasons like physical fatigue, injury or major travel conflicts should excuse you. The training diary helps here. By logging miles in it and keeping a record of daily, weekly and monthly totals, you are forced to be consistent and disciplined. Count your weekly mileage from Monday through Sunday, so that you have the full weekend at the end of your training week and can make up a few miles on those days. Also, since many races fall on Sundays, you can plan your weekly training going into a race.

Consistency in mileage is best measured by counting your monthly mileage. For example, if your goal is 10 miles a day, that would be about 280 miles a month (count your running month as having 28 days). You may log 65, 75, 68, 72 miles during the four weeks and still be very consistent. This allows you flexibility as you taper for races or take days off. When training seriously, set a range limit on your weekly and monthly goals and record it. For example, you should run not less than 60 miles in a single week, but not more than 70 miles; that would mean 65 miles on the average as a consistent foundation.

If you miss a day or two, don't try to make it up all at once. Add a mile or two a day, or forget the missed mileage. Consistency means training daily in manageable amounts. Running twice as far one day to make up for a lost day is not consistent training; it's overtraining. Forget the lost day and continue the next day at the *rate of training* you would normally have followed for the week. If you run 60 miles instead of 70, you are still training at a 10-mile-per-day rate. Also, the day off may have been necessary to prevent injury from stress.

Unfortunately, your body builds fitness slowly and loses it quickly. It takes only a few weeks to lose most of the adaptation to training that you have worked so hard to achieve. It takes less time to get out of shape than to get into shape—unfair, but true. You can maintain fitness with consistency on a year-round basis, avoiding injury by avoiding the causes and listening to the warning signals.

III. THE PRINCIPLE OF ADAPTATION TO PROGRESSIVE STRESS

The body—and mind—gradually adapts to increasing levels of stress. The body is a remarkable organism, and will surprise you in its ability to get stronger in order to adapt to stress. But it can also surprise you by breaking down if you overstress it. The stress shouldn't be either too little or too much. It must be intense enough and regular enough to promote adaptation to a higher level of racing fitness—the "training effect." On the other hand, if the stress is too much (overtraining), you overtax the adaptation system, causing fatigue, injury or poor performance. "Train, don't strain" is the rule to follow. You train hard enough to improve, but don't strain so much that you defeat the improvement. More—faster and longer—isn't always better.

Thus you apply a training stress in the form of your *hard* workouts (or gradually increased mileage) and balance it with easy days to allow for *recovery* between, and you do this for a training season followed by a rest season. If the stress is applied regularly and is nearly equal to your body's capacity to handle the work (harder than your normal easy run, but not all out), your body will adapt by increasing its capacity. As the body becomes accustomed to handling a specific amount of work, the work load should be increased slightly until the body can adapt to running with the same effort as before. As your fitness improves, you should be able to handle a greater training load with the same effort. The progress continues until you reach your ultimate capability, the limit of your body's ability to adapt without breaking down.

For the beginning runner and racer, progress comes fairly rapidly with visible results: improved finishing times for races. Novice and basic competitors in our classes often see their times improve by several minutes. But as you approach your maximum potential, progress becomes less dramatic. The more you improve, the harder it is to continue improving. Some runners make a major jump in progress and then level out for a long time. Plateaus are a natural part of progress. Expect them. You can't keep on improving your time at the same rate; rather, you'll improve and then level off, and then improve again. Little by little your performance base will increase. These improvements, especially at the longer distances, will be greatest for the least experienced runners; elite runners measure improvements in seconds.

Runners at all levels successfully apply the principle of progressive stress. The best evidence of this is in the Boston Marathon, where in 1975 excellence for the average male and female runner was measured by the qualifying time of 3:30. Within five years, however, that standard was raised by 40 minutes—these men had to improve their times to 2:50 (women with a 3:20, 3:10 for men over 40). Few athletes dreamed of a sub-three-hour marathon in the early 1970's. Now many runners are achieving that time. In 1972, the qualifying time for the U.S. Men's Olympic Marathon trials—the standard of excellence—was 2:30. By 1984, it will be approximately ten minutes faster. That is a significant improvement at that level of competition. Athletes at all levels are finding that by pushing themselves progressively farther and faster, they are reaching performances they never dreamed possible.

The danger here is overloading your body. You can avoid that by following the ten-percent rule: never increase your mileage or speed by more than ten percent from one week to the next, or one month to the next. Also, do no more than ten percent of your running as racing.

IV. THE PRINCIPLE OF RECOVERY

It is essential to alternate stress and recovery periods. Here are some basic rules:

1. In your day-to-day schedule, you should precede and follow each hard day (speed workout, race or long run) with one or more easy days (of short or medium runs, or time off). It usually takes 48 hours to recover from hard runs, and 72 hours or more from races. Light running the day after a hard session helps prevent injury and circulates blood to fatigued muscles, helping remove accumulated waste products and getting them ready to work again. Consider active rest after hard runs or on the day following; this includes stretching, swimming, walking, massage, warm baths, etc.

2. During your speed workout, you should rest following each repetition or hard run.

3. Rest (taper) before a race, and slowly rebuild following the race. A common mistake is to rush back into training.

4. For your yearly schedule, you should build your foun-

dation and then sharpen for a few races, followed by several weeks of recovery running. You can't train hard year-round.

When scheduling your daily, weekly or seasonal routine, you should alternate stress with recovery. Your body responds best to stressful hard work if it's also given the chance to recover and repair itself. Stress applied on top of stress equals breakdown; stress followed by recovery equals progress. If sufficient recovery does not occur, then the body's resources are depleted. The concept of alternating work and rest is popularly called the "hard-easy method."

What is easy for one runner, however, may be difficult for another. Also, it may take some runners longer to recover after certain runs. Perhaps you ran your workout too hard, your course was unusually hilly, it was a very hot day, or you were short on sleep and long on stress. Listen to your body and learn to recognize its warning signs—sore muscles, fatigue. Sometimes your body tricks you. After a hard workout or race you may feel very strong the next day and be tempted to run hard. Don't! Often "the two-day lag" occurs—you feel fine the day after your hard day, but are wiped out the following day.

If you ignore this principle of recovery, you can dig yourself into a very deep hole. One of Atalanta's top runners ran an "easy" 20-miler on a Thursday, 10 miles on Friday, and then on Saturday ran a team workout of 20 miles which included a 4-mile race. (The plan also included going into the workout well rested and coming off it easy. She failed on both counts.) The day following this workout, she went for an easy run, but met Odis Sanders, the 2:14 marathoner and 1981 New York Road Runner of the Year, who was out for *his* easy run of 12 miles. The two ran on together at a 6-minute-per-mile pace. The following day, the Atalanta runner couldn't go to work; she was totally depleted of energy reserves. Glover made her go "cold turkey": not a step of running for three days. Luckily, she recovered fully.

Some runners alternate weeks of hard-easy training. Jeff Galloway, former Olympic marathoner, values this schedule. After every three weeks of normal training, he takes a week of rest—no speed work, no long runs, and only 50 percent of his normal mileage. This system is especially good for the runner who has a tendency to overtrain, since it has its own built-in physical and mental relief.

The hard-easy concept is perhaps the most difficult principle to teach in our running classes. Runners want to run a hard or long race on Sunday, and go for a 10-miler on Monday, and then on Tuesday, they wonder why they are outsprinted by the grandmothers in our class. *You must rest before and after all long runs, speed workouts and races.* The average working man or woman must be careful not to try to squeeze in hard days on both Saturday and Sunday—the result can be total fatigue by Monday or Tuesday, or worse, an injury.

Do not train the same number of miles every day. Run slow some days, and vary your mileage. Some runners actually need to be taught how to run slowly. Coaches should be as concerned about holding back their athletes as pushing them.

Hard-easy training involves mixing the distance and speed of your runs in such a way as to induce the right amount of stress, and the needed types of both stress and recovery, that will help you in your running. We will teach you how to plan your training schedule safely and wisely by balancing speed, distance and rest. The formula is easy: hard work + rest = faster times.

V. THE PRINCIPLE OF SPECIFICITY OF TRAINING

You will train differently for a 5 km race and a marathon, to run on a fast, flat course or a rugged, hilly one, to race in cool weather or in the heat. After building your foundation of endurance, and as you sharpen for your race, you need to train your body and mind for the specific demands of the race or series of races you plan to enter.

When you run different types of races over varying terrains in varied weather conditions, you ask your body to work differently from your normal training runs. You should alter your training so that the speed, distance, resistance, form and temperature conditions will be as nearly as possible the same as for your race. Specific training will allow your body to adapt to the specific stresses it will encounter on race day.

The best way to train your body for running is by running. No matter how many hours you spend swimming or biking, you still won't be using the same muscles the same way as you do in running. Running consists of several types of runs. With running itself, you must choose the specific types of endurance and speed runs and apply them in your training to help you prepare for particular races. You need to practice certain skills of running so that you become good at them, feel comfortable with them, and your body adapts physiologically to them. A sprinter's success depends largely on his or her ability to contract muscles powerfully and run in oxygen debt. The marathon runner needs a well-developed cardiorespiratory system and muscular endurance—strength over distance. The 5 km–10 km runner is somewhere in between, and needs the capacities of both the marathoner and the sprinter. If you are increasing your distance, you need to do more specific training for endurance. If you are decreasing your distance, you need to develop more specific training for speed.

Do not, however, become obsessed with this training. You shouldn't run long every day in preparation for a marathon, nor run only uphill for a hilly event. Most of your training sessions should be the same, except that for one to three days a week (from a few weeks for shorter races to a few months for longer ones), as you sharpen you should also alter your training.

Specific training should be used in five basic areas:

Distance

You need to train your muscles, mind and cardiorespiratory systems to handle the stress of fatigue associated with running long distances. The longer the race, the more important it is to train with higher mileage and longer single runs. Any increase in the distance of your usual race (such as from one mile to 10 km) and any training for the marathon distance or beyond require two specific changes in your training: increases in total mileage and increases in long runs.

Speed

You need to train yourself to be comfortable at your race pace. Do some training at race pace or faster. The miler would do specific training much faster than the 10 km runner since, obviously, the required pace is much quicker. The marathoner would run many workouts slower and over longer distances than the 10 km runner.

It makes sense that if you do most of your daily running at 7:30 per mile and the fastest you have ever run a single mile is 5:50, you are going to be uncomfortable if you start a race at a six-minute-mile pace. Thus, you need to improve your speed so that you can be comfortable at the early brisk pace and can generate speed for tactical bursts during the race and at the finish.

Racing Form

You should practice the biomechanics of racing form at race pace or slightly faster so that your body feels comfortable at this pace. This includes uphill and downhill form.

Terrain

If you are planning to run a flat, fast course on a track or road, you should prepare yourself by doing some quick track or roadwork at race pace or faster. The race pace will be quicker than what you are used to. A hilly course requires some hill running in your normal training, and some hill speed sessions. In brief, train for the course you will run.

Heat

Avoid training in the heat, but if you usually run in the early morning or late evening and your race starts at noon, you must also do some running at that time of day. Be sure to slow the training pace and drink plenty of fluids, even when you're not thirsty. If you plan to race in hot weather but must train in cool weather, you have three options: move into the climate zone of the race for one to two weeks to allow yourself to acclimatize; artificially simulate heat conditions by running with extra clothing for a few days a week; get into the best shape you can, and pray for clouds and rain.

VI. THE PRINCIPLE OF INDIVIDUALITY AND FLEXIBILITY

All training must be flexible, adapting to the needs of the individual runner. A coach shouldn't establish a single training schedule for all athletes; each runner has personal likes and dislikes, strengths and weaknesses. Your ability level and training goal are unique to you. Use the guidelines in this book to write your own training program—a program that will change as your individual needs change.

Find out what training works best for you. Some runners will thrive on a steady diet of high mileage and weekly 20-milers, while others would break down physically or mentally following this program. Some benefit most from one-mile speed workouts, while others feel they race better at all distances by doing shorter, faster 440's. Some need more rest than others after races and between hard workouts.

Learn to "go with your strengths." If you can pound out high mileage and have lots of endurance for long races, you are a natural endurance runner. You may find that no matter how much you train to improve your speed, you make only minimal gains at best. We can't make a sprinter out of a turtle. But by "going with your strengths" you can train with high mileage and concentrate on longer speed workouts—such as one- or two-mile rhythm workouts or quick tempo runs of five to ten kilometers. You work on improving your speed over longer distance, rather than for a shorter sprint. Try to improve in the areas you have less talent in, but don't waste a lot of time on them if you will get better results by maximizing your natural ability in other areas.

Your training program must be flexible. You should be prepared to adapt to weather conditions, available facilities, your health, and family obligations. Alter your training to fit your needs—be practical, not stubborn. On the other hand, don't be so flexible that you lose consistency and discipline. Include variety in your training program. Don't run the same distance every day over the same course at the same time of day with the same people at the same pace. Vary your training and speed workouts. For the most part, the competitive athlete in training should pick a few basic courses of varying lengths and stick to them. Putting in high mileage is often an unglamorous robotlike task, and being familiar with the terrain is quite helpful when you are tired and just want to push automatic and cruise without thinking. Save the joys of exploring for when you are especially bored or when traveling. Having a trusty course is a kind of security blanket—you feel comfortable with it. And it is safer—you make friends along the route who will help take care of you and offer you encouragement. If a group of runners meet to run, chances are that the pace they will run will be too fast for some and too slow for others—just as in a race. You must be willing to compromise a little, but in general find training partners who will help you—neither pushing you too hard nor holding you back too much.

To vary your racing distances, try cross-country in the fall, shorter races, maybe even track, in the summer. Take time off between racing seasons; perhaps try an alternative like cross-country skiing. Don't train only for marathon races all year long.

VII. THE PRINCIPLE OF CONFIDENCE BUILDING

Confidence comes with experience and the triumph of progressive training workloads and improved race performances. If you believe in yourself and know you have a strong foundation of training, success is only a few miles down the road.

As you approach big races, use key workouts and smaller races to increase your confidence and mental toughness. Surviving long runs and speed workouts and pushing yourself in training toughens you and builds confidence that you can meet a challenge and not quit.

Some highly trained runners will toughen themselves by "pulling a max." This means that about two or three weeks before a big race they will run a much harder workout than usual. Bob Glover's all-time "max workout" was twenty 440's at hard pace with little recovery on a hot day. To make it worse, Pete Schuder yelled at him the whole time and clocked the recovery to the second so that Glover couldn't cheat. He rested for several days, and then two weeks later went out confident on a hot day and ran one of his best races. Other coaches use such a method, commonly known as "callousing." They want their runners to experience stress in workouts so they will be tougher on race day. Obviously, this practice should be limited to those more experienced runners who are very fit.

Every runner can increase his or her toughness and confidence by applying a little more stress in order to "enter a new dimension" on race day. We all have more physical potential than our minds allow us to use. The trick is to reach down deep, run through those psychological barriers, and maximize our potential as athletes.

VIII. THE PRINCIPLE OF PATIENCE AND EXPERIENCE

Successful racing doesn't happen overnight. For the competitive runner, success is measured in years, not weeks. Each day you put more miles in the bank and build for the future. With increased experience as a competitor, you become a wiser and more efficient racer. You *experience* your first marathon, for example, then *race* the next. Important lessons have to be learned: dressing for races, drinking on the run, handling heat and cold, pacing and race strategy. No matter how many times you have read what to do, until you have experienced it and learned by doing—possibly learned through error—you won't be a skilled competitor. You will learn more from every race you run—even after years of competition. Take your time and be patient as you progress slowly but steadily. Learn from your racing experience over the years so that you will be able to get more out of your body with every race and every year of racing. The more years you log in your diary, the better competitor you will be.

IX. THE PRINCIPLE OF EXTENDED GOALS

Competitive running offers the average athlete a never-ending finish line. There seem always to be new challenges—longer distances to conquer or more minutes and seconds to knock off the clock. Even as we slow down with age, we are presented with new opportunities as we move into new age classifications, with new standards of excellence. You may remember when your goal was only to run a mile or complete a local 10 km race or a marathon. After you conquer the distance goals, you can establish time goals for each distance—breaking 3:30 for the marathon, then 3:15, and so on.

Our sport gives us a tremendous incentive to keep improving—the extended goal. No matter how fast you run a race, once it is over you can plan to improve on that effort.

But progress comes slowly. You should always set your goals—reasonable ones—for a full year ahead. This way you won't be in a rush and overdo it.

X. THE PRINCIPLE OF MODERATION AND BALANCE

Too much of anything—food, drink, parties, training miles, speed work, races, even sex—isn't good. You need to take a moderate approach to your life. Balancing the major stresses of your life—career, family and running—is as important as balancing the individual parts of your training program.

3. THREE BASIC QUESTIONS: HOW FAR? HOW FAST? HOW OFTEN?

Three of the most common questions about running are: How far should I run? How fast should I run? How often should I run? The answers are determined by two other questions: What is the purpose of your training? and, How much can you tolerate physically and mentally? You may not be able to attain certain running goals because your body or the environment won't allow it. But most often, you fail as a competitive runner because you want too much too soon and do not respond to warning signals of injury and overtraining.

HOW FAR SHOULD I RUN?

This depends upon how much mileage you need to meet your realistic goals and how much mileage you can tolerate physically and mentally. Unfortunately, what you need and what you can do are not always the same. Mileage is the backbone of every runner's program. Each of us needs first to develop a base of endurance, and then, following the principle of foundation training, to build up that base for the race or season of races. In our early running years, our most important task is simply to increase that base of endurance with aerobic training.

Getting to the finish line in reasonable health is enough of a goal for most of us. Later you may wish to run faster, and you will need to increase your mileage to do so. Here the mileage treadmill begins: you need more mileage to run faster. Too much mileage will defeat you mentally and physically: you may never get to the starting line. With too little mileage, however, you'll have trouble getting to the finish line.

Ken Young, director of the National Running Data Center, theorized in *The 1974 Marathon Handbook* that every runner can predict his or her "collapse point" and thus determine how much mileage he or she needs to run well. Young said: "What is the collapse point? In simple terms, it is the maximum distance a runner can expect to go before the urge to slow down overwhelms him. More commonly, the collapse point is called 'The Wall.' . . . [It] is characterized by a sudden decrease in performance, often occurring within a single mile. Pace may drop by two or three minutes per mile or more." Sound familiar?

"The collapse point," Young continued, "appears to be determined almost entirely by training mileage. The simple rule of thumb is to take the maximum mileage for two consecutive months, determine the daily average over these two months and triple it. . . . In order to extend one's collapse point, then, it is clear that the total mileage must be increased over a time span of two or more months. . . . The collapse point can be extended markedly through proper training." To illustrate, if you averaged 49 miles a week (7 miles a day), your collapse point would be 3×7 or 21 miles.

Any training theory, particularly one based on statistics, doesn't fit all runners. You must modify these theories to fit your own experience. We have found, after working with a wide range of runners of all abilities, that the collapse-point theory can be adapted somewhat. First, you can survive a race on less training mileage than Young indicates if you are willing to run a slow pace and take short walk breaks if necessary. You may need as much mileage as Ken indicates, however, if you wish to *race* the distance successfully and not shuffle through it.

The box below indicates the minimum mileage you will need. Some may run well on less, but be cautious. To race well, you will need more mileage, longer runs and eventually speed work. A minimum mileage base should get you to the finish line—but you will probably experience a taste of the Wall in longer races and the marathon event. Higher mileage will help you run through the Wall and maintain your pace in the late stages of the race.

The following formulas will guide competitors through their survival training for a specific race. Running much more mileage than is indicated may harm your performance. You may not be ready to handle that much. Start from a sound fitness base, and increase gradually.

The first-time racer and novice competitor should use the minimum mileage guideline in the specific ways outlined in the chart "B. Suggested Weekly Mileage Totals for the Novice Competitor," at the top of the opposite page.

A. MINIMUM WEEKLY MILEAGE GUIDELINES FOR RACE "SURVIVORS"

For up to the half marathon:	Minimally two times the race distance, preferably three times or more; *and* complete at least two or three long runs of at least two-thirds the race distance or slightly longer.
Half marathon to the marathon:	Minimally 1.5 times the race distance, preferably two times the race distance; *and* complete at least two or three long runs of at least two-thirds the race distance, up to 20 miles.

Note: You should average the mileage indicated for 6–8 weeks before tapering for the race.

B. SUGGESTED WEEKLY MILEAGE TOTALS FOR THE NOVICE COMPETITOR

RACE DISTANCE	WEEKLY MILEAGE	LONG-RUN MILEAGE
5 km–4 mile	10–20	3–4
10 km	15–20	4–6
15 km–half marathon	25–40	8–10
Marathon	40–50	16–20

Note: These mileages should be averaged for 6–8 weeks prior to tapering for your race. You should complete two or three long runs in this 6–8-week period.

As you work to improve your race time, you will also need to increase the minimal mileage in order to race successfully. Most competitive runners fit into our recommended minimum and maximum mileages (see below). You do not need to maintain this mileage year around. Take a break after the big race, and lower your mileage level.

C. SUGGESTED WEEKLY MILEAGE TOTALS FOR EXPERIENCED COMPETITORS

RACE DISTANCE	BASIC COMPETITOR		ADVANCED COMPETITOR		CHAMPION COMPETITOR	
	Weekly	*Long run*	*Weekly*	*Long run*	*Weekly*	*Long run*
5 km–4 mile	25–40	8–10	30–50	8–12	40–70	12–16
10 km	30–55	8–12	45–75	10–18	60–90	15–20
15 km–half marathon	45–60	15–20	60–70	15–20	70–90	20
Marathon	50–65	18–20	60–85	18–20	70–100	20–23

Note: These mileages should be averaged for 8–12 weeks prior to tapering for your race. The suggested long runs should be completed two to three times per month depending on your fitness level and racing schedule.

Age and Experience

Teenage and younger runners should not run more than 40 miles a week, for doing so may contribute to injury or "burnout." Runners above the age of 40 may be able to run less, especially if they have faithfully put a large reservoir of miles in the bank. Runners who have accumulated many miles for several years often find that they can race well at a lower mileage level than in previous years. Because older runners don't recover as fast from injuries and previous runs, it is often wise for them to run less mileage than their younger friends do.

Time on Your Feet

Elite male runners average about six minutes per mile for a 10-mile training run. Thus, they log about 10 miles per hour on the road. An elite female runner and many elite masters runners may cover the same distance at 6:30 to 7:00 per mile. The average runner will take from 7:00 to 9:00 per mile. That is a time range of from one hour for the elite runner to one-and-a-half hours for some average runners on a 10-mile run. Obviously, it takes a lot longer to cover the same mileage at nine minutes per mile than at six.

The average nine-minute-per-mile runner who attempts to match the high mileage of the six-minute-per-mile superstar will actually spend 50 percent more time on the road than the elite runner. The elite runner would have to cover 150 miles to put in the same training time as the runner who covers 100 miles. Be careful when comparing mileage figures—no matter what the numbers. The slower you run compared to the average runner, the more you should consider time rather than mileage in setting your daily and weekly goals. In fact, some runners prefer to log their training by minutes run rather than mileage because for these it more accurately reflects their training. That makes sense, but since races are held over mileage distances and most training information is expressed in mileage, we'll stick to this system for this book.

Runners, regardless of age or sex, who train and race at approximately the same pace can handle similar weekly mileage work loads. Our fitness category system, adjusted for age and sex, recommends a wide range of racing and training paces within each category. Within each racing distance chapter, we recommend flexible weekly mileage goals to adjust for the differences in the amount of time you spend training and your age and running experience. The slower runner should run fewer miles than a faster competitor within the same fitness category, because a slower runner covering the same distance would spend more time training. This additional effort could create a higher risk of injury or fatigue. These adjustments are most critical when doing high-mileage marathon training.

Here are some other points about mileage:

It is harder to keep your mileage up if
- you are running over very hilly terrain;
- you must combat extremes of heat or cold, or snow and ice;
- you are running in the reduced light of early morning or late evening;
- you are carrying extra pounds;
- you are running on business trips or on vacation;
- you just don't enjoy running long and slow, but prefer to run shorter and faster;
- you have achieved your goal and do not have a goal to aim towards;
- you don't have training partners to help you along, especially on long runs;
- you have an inflexible work schedule, or many career and family responsibilities;
- you don't have a coach and teammates to support you.

You must lower your mileage if
- you increase the pace significantly for training runs;
- you add more hard speed work as you sharpen for a race;
- you are tapering for a race, or recovering from a race;
- you are racing very often;
- you are recovering from an injury;
- warning signs of injury or illness, and thus overtraining, appear;
- you have completed your racing season or big race— take a break!

Guidelines for Increasing Mileage

We have found that by applying these simple rules you can progress safely with little worry of overtraining:

• How you increase your mileage depends first on how often you are running now. If you are running less than six days a week, gradually add more days per week until you are running six to seven days consistently. Don't add too much mileage on the new days at first. Later, you may wish to continue taking a rest day, or you may choose to run seven days per week.

• Once you get up to your maximum number of training days per week, stay at that level for a few weeks. First increase the distance of your long run, and then of your medium run. Gradually lengthen all your runs while maintaining a balance of effort. Be sure to alternate hard (long or fast) days with easy days as you build up your mileage.

• Avoid any sudden changes. Avoid dramatic increases in mileage from day to day, week to week, month to month, even year to year. Don't increase your weekly mileage or long runs by more than five to ten percent; you will invite injury if you do. Be patient, not *a* patient. A common mistake is to increase mileage quickly when you feel good or are in a hurry to build up for a race. The usual result of increasing your work load too rapidly is either fatigue or injury. It may not seem like much if you jump your mileage from 20 to 40 miles per week when you compare yourself to friends who run 70 to 80 miles a week. But don't be fooled into thinking that you are running only 40 miles a week. You have *doubled* your work load, and your body isn't ready for it. A ten percent increase can range from two miles a week (for the 20-mile-per-week runner) to ten miles a week (for the 100-mile-per-week runner). This is a safe way to progress. A conservative program for the novice competitor wishing to move from 20 to 40 miles a week would be to add two miles a week up to 40, and then level off. This progress would take fourteen weeks, and you would be gradually tricking the body into handling more mileage.

A typical 14-week progression, starting with 20 miles per week, may look like this: 20, 22, 24, 26, 26, 28, 30, 30, 32, 34, 36, 36, 38, 40, 40. This program increases your mileage by a total of 20 miles a week, but your body can safely handle this increase, since it is gradual.

• Don't continuously move your mileage upwards. Here's a math riddle for you: Add ten percent each week, week after week, until you're running 24 hours a day. How long will this take you? Get the message?

Every few weeks, "level off" for a week or two before adding more mileage. Then reach a planned level that you can handle—such as 40 or 50 miles a week—and stay there for a few weeks or months. Increase slowly, taking a few breaks along the way. Periodically "plateau" for a while so you can regenerate physically and mentally for another upward push. These plateaus of mileage may increase only from year to year, and are determined by what you can safely handle as you strive to meet your training goals. Rest breaks along the way, or even periods of decreased mileage—planned or unplanned—will help reduce the pressure of constantly building up mileage. You do not have to increase every week. Your goal is long term, not short term.

• Back off occasionally, especially after big races and when warning signs of overtraining appear. Progress regularly, and if you find it difficult, back off and choose a more gradual course of build-up.

• You don't *have* to move up the ladder. You can get off the mileage treadmill any time. More isn't necessarily best for you. If you are happy with the level you are now at and have achieved a comfortable balance between running and the rest of your life, don't let peer pressure or your inner guilt feelings drive you to do more. Maintain your present program and be happy with it. You can always move up later if the urge strikes.

• Determine the upper limits of mileage you have time

for and can handle physically and mentally at this stage of your running career. If you are not careful about realistic limits, you are going to reach a point where you can no longer increase your mileage without incurring injury. You may be too tired all the time and not looking forward to running. Each of us must determine our own upper limits. Don't compare yourself to a runner with more experience and talent. And your limits can be flexible; you may be able to handle more in the good training months of spring and summer than you can in the dismal winter. After several years of running, you may have built to an upper limit of 40 miles a week which is comfortable for you. The next year, however, you may find that due to accumulated miles in the bank and experience, you can safely handle 50 miles a week—a figure that would previously have wiped you out. The important thing to remember is that you should be aware of your limitations and not force yourself to go beyond these realistic boundaries.

Tips for Managing Your Miles

• Some runners prefer alternating longer weeks with shorter weeks. For example, 50-60-50-60 is an average of 55 miles for the month. By setting *monthly* goals rather than weekly ones, you can be more flexible with your training week and won't be as obsessed with trying to make up miles lost due to a few days off.

• Don't try to make up mileage. You can make up some mileage gradually over a period of weeks, but generally it is better to forget the lost miles and concern yourself with continuing at the rate of so many miles per day on the average.

• Don't count "junk" miles. Running a mile to the subway and then a mile to the office, for example, may save time and may even be enjoyable, but it isn't part of your training. Training mileage shouldn't be logged unless you run at least four miles at a time and are running in your training heart-rate range (except for the novice competitor, for whom two- or three-mile runs can represent a workout). Don't look for every excuse to put miles in your diary. It is more important that the miles you claim are of reasonable quality.

• Don't be a slave to your training diary. You should plot your mileage regularly in advance—this gives you the motivation to keep it up. But don't feel you absolutely have to run once more late on Sunday night in order to reach your goal so you can record it. Diaries are great coaches—they can make you keep going. They are also lousy coaches—the obsession to write down mileage sometimes causes the runner to lose sight of the quality of his training. In the end, it is the blend of quantity and quality mileage that will help you improve times, not how many miles you write into your diary.

• Measure training by miles or minutes. If you don't know exactly how long your course is, estimate it—on the conservative side. If you are traveling over unknown terrain, estimate mileage by your pace. For example, if you feel you are running 7:30 a mile, that equals eight miles in an hour. Run up the road for a half hour and return, and log eight miles in your diary. That is close enough. You don't have to be exact.

• How do you "count" mileage if you did a hard speed workout which didn't cover much mileage? Cheat! The easiest solution if you are obsessed with mileage totals is to credit yourself with whatever mileage you would have run in the time you took to do your speed workout, including the recovery time between runs. For longer speed sessions such as one-mile workouts, you'll get in adequate mileage. Also, always run before and after each speed workout and race. It'll help you keep your mileage up.

• Establish a realistic range of mileage. If you want to average 75 miles a week, don't go over 80–85, but try not to go under 65–70. Thus, you can adjust for the weather and other variables.

Getting By on Less

It is possible, but not advisable, for some runners to get by on less mileage than we recommend, and still race well. But not everyone can do it. It takes careful planning and a certain amount of raw talent. Here are some guidelines to follow if you do not have the time, desire or ability to handle high mileage. For example, you may follow this system to run 50 miles a week instead of 70:

1. Alternate easy days with brisk days. In general, you need to go faster in your training runs more often.

2. Run hills regularly in endurance runs and speed sessions.

3. Do regular speed work—at least twice a week.

4. Do one long run per week, but not too long relative to your total weekly mileage.

5. Back off regularly and don't race, run long or run fast for a few weeks.

6. Race often when you want to race well—two or three times per month.

7. Find your mileage peak and then concentrate on quality. Remember, you are taking a shortcut. If you don't succeed, don't blame us. Novices need the minimal mileage figures. These guidelines are for the more experienced competitive runner.

Advantages of High Mileage

Beyond the minimum goal of finishing, you may benefit from increased mileage as long as it is tied realistically to your racing goal and to what you can tolerate. What is high mileage for one may be excessive for another.

Besides training your body to become more efficient at burning fat for fuel, thus sparing glycogen, high-mileage runners feel that they have a great psychological advantage. You feel strong when you come down off high mileage for an important race (often you "train through" lesser races and keep the mileage up). With rest, your legs don't seem as tired, and mentally you just *know* you are strong.

Atalanta's scoring trio for their club championship title in the 1981 Avon International Marathon in Ottawa—Marilyn Hulak, Sharon Barbano and Marcy Schwam—all came down off 100-mile weeks and felt mentally prepared for the race. This was a needed edge, as they had to call upon this extra toughness to combat the effects of the hot weather.

Hal Higdon, a national class masters runner, observed in *The Runner*: "Successful running at any level does come from a blend of quantity and quality, a continuous shifting of training mileage and method over the years. High mileage is the answer for some runners, but it is not the only answer. Ultimately, you have to consider the many different reasons why you enjoy running and determine how much racing performance means to you."

HOW FAST SHOULD I RUN?

The quality of your runs—the pace—is determined by your goals. We run for two reasons: fitness and racing. Running for fitness means running aerobically within your training heart-rate range and at a comfortable pace. Training for racing includes both aerobic and anaerobic runs. Anaerobic runs make you train at or above the upper limits of your training heart-rate range. This is what is required on race day.

Your pace determines not only how fast you run, but also how hard your heart works. The faster you run, the faster it works; the more fit you are, the more efficiently it pumps oxygen-enriched blood to the muscles. Runners are concerned with four types of heart rates or pulse:

Resting Heart Rate (Base Pulse)

The average resting heart rate for men is 60 to 80 beats per minute, and for women, 70 to 90. A very fit person's heart rate will be around 60 or below, and a serious runner may reach the 40- to 50-beat range. Check your rate in the morning when you first wake up. One easy way is to press your index and middle fingers of one hand against the up-turned wrist of the other. Count the beats for ten seconds and multiply by six. Record this pulse rate in your running diary. If your base pulse is ten or more beats per minute higher than normal for you, it may be a sign of overtraining.

Maximum Heart Rate

This is the point at which your heart "peaks" out. It can't satisfy the body's increased demand for oxygen and cannot beat any faster. Maximum heart rate is at or near the point of exhaustion.

Training Heart Rate

This is your aerobic heart rate. Running at this level provides sufficient training effect for your cardiovascular system. This "target zone" of safe, beneficial training falls between two numbers, 70 to 85 percent of your maximum heart rate. (The 85 percent is the approximate border between aerobic and anaerobic states.)

Calculate your estimated maximum heart rate by subtracting your age from 220. Your training heart-rate range for aerobic endurance runs is 70 to 85 percent of this number. Here is a chart to save you the math:

TRAINING HEART-RATE RANGE

AGE	70%	85%
20–25	140	167
26–30	134	163
31–35	131	159
36–40	127	155
41–45	124	150
46–50	120	146
51–55	117	142
56–60	113	138
61–65	110	133
66–70	106	129

` The pulse rates are based on a predicted maximum, and yours may not precisely correspond. You may exceed your cutoff without hard breathing, or you may feel tired at the lower level. For all terrains and in all climates, the "talk test" is a good measure; if you are running so fast that you can't carry on a conversation, slow down.

Your training pulse and pace are particular to you. A comfortable six-minute pace for an elite runner may only be 70 percent of his maximum, whereas a basic competitor would be out of breath trying to keep up. Conversely, at an eight-minute pace, which may be a basic competitor's 70-percent level, the elite runner would be below his training range. Be careful when running with others that you don't run too fast or too slow; set your own pace for maximum benefit.

Stop and take your pulse periodically during your run or at the end of an evenly paced run. With practice you will be able to guess it, just as you can guess your per-mile pace pretty accurately. Judge by perceived exertion and forget the numbers. If you can talk comfortably and are running fast enough to perspire, you are training aerobically (70–85 percent). If you can talk, but not easily, you are at the aerobic-anaerobic borderline (85 percent). If you are out of breath, straining and unable to talk, you are in oxygen debt (over 85 percent). Many experienced runners prefer to do much of their training at a faster pace—around 80 percent—rather than 70 percent. They feel they get more for the miles by running shorter distances faster.

Recovery Heart Rate

Your recovery heart rate is your post cool-down pulse. After training runs, following 15 to 20 minutes of walking and stretching, your pulse rate should be below 100 beats per minute. If it isn't, either you didn't cool down properly, or you ran too hard.

Training Pace

In deciding how fast to run, most runners think in terms of pace per mile, and not pulse rate. But your pulse rate will reflect factors such as heat and fatigue which would be neglected if you measured only your exertion at pace per mile. The safest bet is to learn what your pulse feels like at various paces and to adjust to environmental conditions and other stresses.

Most advanced and champion marathoners train at about one minute per mile slower than their marathon pace, or about one-and-a-half minutes per mile slower than their pace for the 10 km race. For example, elite marathoners race at five minutes per mile and train at six minutes per mile. Obviously these paces would slow in the extremes of heat and cold and over arduous terrain. Within each major racing distance chapter, we recommend flexible guidelines for your training pace per mile.

As you become more fit, the pace of your training runs will naturally become faster. For example, Charles Miers began his career as an eighteen-year-old college freshman at Columbia under the guidance of Pete Schuder. Miers's distance training consisted of doing a majority of his running at 7:00+ per mile pace. Five years later, Miers has matured into an excellent distance runner, recording times of 2:20 for the marathon, and 29:17 for the 10 km on the track. His distance runs are now very rarely slower than a 6:30 pace; most of them are run at around a 6:15 pace. Even at these fairly fast paces, Miers is doing aerobic endurance training. He has increased the pace of his training runs to keep up with his development as a distance runner.

HOW OFTEN SHOULD I RUN?

To maintain mileage and fitness, you need to run several days a week. To progress from a fitness runner to a racer, you should run four to six times a week. The basic competitive runner will run five or more times a week, and the advanced and champion runner will run six to seven days. Few elite runners skip a day; most run twice a day. For your first few *years* of running, take off a day or so per week. As you become fitter and wish to increase your mileage, short runs (five to ten miles) will come to feel like days off to your highly conditioned body. Which days to take off will be determined by your own schedule—when you do your long runs and speed work, and when you race. Monday is often a preferred rest day following a long weekend of training or racing.

Should I Run Twice a Day?

No! Unless you are:

1. Running through an injury, or recovering from an injury when two four-mile runs (for example) may be less stressful than one eight-miler.

2. Running in difficult footing—on an indoor track or in the snow—that will tire out your muscles. You are more prone to injury the longer you run under such conditions. You might run two five-miles runs, or run one indoors and one outdoors instead of a single longer run. Remember this rule of thumb: to avoid muscle strain or injury, don't run more than 45 minutes in difficult footing.

3. Running in rain, extreme cold or heat. Two short runs are better than risking your health for a longer time. No matter how hot or cold it is, you won't get too uncomfortable for the first 30 to 45 minutes.

4. Running with a busy schedule. You may have to break up your runs into two-a-days occasionally to have time to meet the demands of family and job. Some runners choose to save time and money by running to and from work.

5. Running for recovery. In the day or days following a hard race, you may find it beneficial to run two short workouts; two light miles with a morning swim and an evening three-miler may speed recovery.

6. Running before a speed workout. If your workout is in the evening, a short run in the morning or at noon will loosen you up.

7. Running with high mileage. The high-mileage runner can increase his or her mileage by adding a few extra morning or evening runs a week of about five miles each.

One of the problems of high mileage is that you run more slowly because of fatigue. Also you may pick up bad habits, such as altered form. You may not even run fast enough to improve your fitness level. For this runner, two-a-days are essential.

Most runners need not run twice a day. Medical researchers haven't decided which is more beneficial—a single ten-miler or two five-milers. Certainly you shouldn't eliminate the single long run. Unless you are a top runner wanting to move up to a more competitive level, you should run only once a day. The runner averaging more than ten miles a day almost has to use two-a-days. If you decide to use this method, experiment with it to see if it agrees with your body and mind.

Start with a few two-milers in the morning in addition to your evening run. Make the morning runs slow and easy. Later, move up to four- or five-milers. When doing two-a-days, any run below four miles won't improve your aerobic fitness.

Two-a-days also take time. You may feel as if you do nothing all day but stretch, run, shower, eat and sleep. Running once a day gives you the most miles per hour of time invested. Since you must warm up and cool down twice for two-a-days, beware of shortchanging yourself in that important area. Forcing two-a-days will increase your risk of injury.

What Time of Day Should I Run?

Most runners do the bulk of their training on weekdays in the evening. Most also run on weekend mornings. Our bodies have their own individual cycles, and most of us run when it feels best for us and when we enjoy it most. Some prefer the morning—to wake up and get the run behind them. Others enjoy a break at the noon hour or in the afternoon, to ease away the tensions of the day.

Morning runs may start your day on a pleasant note and leave you the rest of the day free. Even if you plan a second run, you start out with miles in the bank; if you miss the second run, you're still ahead. If you're a morning runner, you'll know it when you hit the road; and if you're not, you'll feel that too.

Running in the morning is difficult in the winter, when it gets light later. It's also easy to skip the stretching then. Instead, try a little walking first, and then stretch lightly for a few minutes to limber up. Morning runs should be slow and easy. But since most races are held in the morning, you should also do a few hard runs and some long runs (before eating breakfast some days, to practice depletion). The easy morning run can also help you recover from the previous day's workout and get you ready for your second, more vigorous run of the day.

Noon runs are better in winter than in summer, when the day is hottest. Most runners who run mornings do not also run at noon, but some two-a-day runners will put in a few miles during their lunch hour.

Evening is when most runners are on the road. The pressures of the day are left behind, and you come home refreshed and—unless you've taken a very hard, long run—ready for the evening. These runs, however, are most likely to interfere with the rest of your social life, and dinners and evenings out often have to be rescheduled to accommodate the evening runner. Also, running too hard late in the day may make it hard for you to relax and get to sleep.

4. THE DISTANCE WORKOUT: ENDURANCE-TRAINING RUNS

Endurance runs are one of the four types of runs used as workouts in our program. The other types of runs are speed workouts for strength, rhythm and power. Endurance runs are the basic foundation training and are used all year by all levels of runners. They are continuous distance runs done within your training heart-rate range at conversational pace. The intensity of the run is light enough to allow you to train aerobically and not go into oxygen debt; yet it is quick enough to provide a training effect. If you are very fit, you will be able to run at a fairly fast pace and still train aerobically. Many elite runners can train aerobically at a running pace of approximately 5:00 to 5:15 per mile. For most runners, endurance runs are done at speeds between 7:00 and 9:00 per mile. The following chart lists the various types of endurance-training runs you will use.

ENDURANCE TRAINING RUNS	DISTANCE
1. Long Slow Distance	10–23 miles
2. Medium Slow Distance	4–15 miles
3. Short Slow Distance	2–10 miles

Endurance training used as foundation work produces the following physiological benefits:

- increases the efficiency of your heart
- increases your coronary blood supply
- increases the efficient use of oxygen
- improves your respiratory system
- increases the strength and endurance of your leg muscles
- brings about increased neuromuscular efficiency

THE LONG-DISTANCE RUN

This aerobic run is considered a *hard* workout. A long, easy run may not seem to be placing much resistance on your body, but staying on your feet this long will significantly tire muscles and drain your body of glycogen reserves. It takes one-and-a-half to three-and-a-half hours to complete the long run. The average runner shouldn't attempt to go beyond three-and-a-half hours, no matter how many miles have been covered. Ideally, you cover at least two-thirds or more of the time period that you'll be racing. The distance covered ranges from ten miles for novice competitors or short-distance specialists (even four to six miles may be long for some) up to 20 miles. Bob Glover has his elite At-alanta marathoners do a few 22–23-mile runs going into major marathons because the runners have to be on their feet for about three hours—at their training pace—which is as long as, or longer than, they will be racing. Thus, they call upon energy sources similar to those they will use on marathon day, and it gives them tremendous confidence as well that they can last the distance, even though they will be taking a risk by starting at an ambitious pace. The small differences between a 20-miler and a 23-miler is quite significant at that distance, but this should be used by only experienced marathoners capable of running sub-three-hours. Most long runs by experienced competitors are 15–20 miles. The veteran ultramarathoner may go as high as 30- to 50-mile training runs.

It must be stressed that the long-distance training run ideally should be no longer than one-third of your weekly mileage and shouldn't be done more than once per week. It should be used no more than twice a month for novice and average competitors, and no more than three out of four weeks for serious competitors and elite runners. It may be used less or not at all between racing seasons. Many experienced runners alternate 15-mile runs with 20-mile runs either every week or every third or fourth week. Long runs are usually done at a pace somewhat slower than that of the medium-distance run. Most long runs are done on weekend mornings, when they don't interfere with work or social life or require running in the dark.

Start the run slowly, and build to a steady pace. Finish the run over the final half mile with a fairly brisk pace to help stretch out and to minimize leg fatigue. Do not sprint. If you are feeling fatigued or your form is getting sloppy, slow down or walk rather than risk injury. But keep plugging away, building "character" that will help you endure long races. Although this is a continuous run, take some breaks to drink fluids, to go to the bathroom or to stretch. Don't stop for too long, however, or your legs may tighten and it will be difficult to continue. To avoid this, keep moving by walking around; you don't have to jog in place while waiting for the streetlight. Don't worry about the lost time, either; if you are that compulsive, turn off your stopwatch. Slow the pace on hot days or when footing is difficult.

Be sure to warm up and cool down properly for all runs, especially the long, tiring ones. This is important. Stretch gently after your long runs, and relax in a tub, take a walk or swim to help you recover. Take it easy for the next day or two. Drink plenty of fluids.

Here are some general points about long-distance runs:

• Run on a fairly flat or gently rolling course to prevent overtraining. Don't search out the hilliest course you can find—long runs are tough enough as it is.

• If you are new at the distance, it's OK to take a few walk breaks.

• Gradually increase the distance of the long runs, following the guidelines of the previous chapter.

• Experienced runners may occasionally run the last three to five miles at marathon pace or faster to get the feel of finishing strong.

• A few pickups (short brisk runs) now and then in the run will use different muscles and rest tired ones. This is especially helpful if the course is quite flat.

• You can use your prerace jog and postrace cool-down to complete a long run. For example, for a low-key four-mile race, highly trained runners will run four miles for warm-up, run the race and then do an easy 12-miler for a total of 20 miles. Even for a 10-mile race, they will run a total of 15 for that day. This enables them to get in a long run and race while trying to maintain high mileage. They then take it easy the next two days. Otherwise, they would be forced to attempt to get in a long run during the week.

> *Safety Note:* Combining speed work or races with long runs on weekends for the sake of convenience should be avoided if possible, but may be OK for high-mileage runners who know how to listen to their body. The average person should *never* attempt such combinations—always follow long runs, races and speed work with at least one easy day.

• Sometimes you can use a long race as a long training run. Just don't get caught up in the race and go too fast. For example, a 20-mile training run during a race at close to your training pace of 8:00 is fine, but at 7:15 pace is too fast—even if you would normally race at sub-7:00 and were holding back. Think of it this way: How tired would you feel if you went out and ran that long and fast by yourself? This applies even for shorter distances of ten miles. If you can't trust yourself to hold back, don't wear a number, or wait until the other runners are a few minutes up the road before you start. Often runners will say they are going to run only 20 miles of a marathon as training, and then they get caught up in it and finish—that's a long training run that results in lost days due to fatigue. And a slow marathon time isn't worth the effort.

• Try to make an appointment with another runner or group of runners so that you are forced to get out (many clubs have regular long runs once a week and people show up whenever they please). It is so easy to cut your run short when you run alone, or not even start. If you find yourself going too fast, drop back and look for a slower partner when running with a group. On long runs, the rule is that it is far better to go with someone slower and complete the run than with someone faster who will wear you out. Don't turn group runs into a race.

• To make the run easier to complete, try to avoid going past your home or the finishing point until the very end. Otherwise it is too easy to drop out. Try running out for half the distance, then return home, and you will get in the distance with less thought about dropping out.

• It is not necessary to go the race distance on long runs. *Never*—unless highly, highly conditioned—go 26.2 miles. Some novices feel that they have to go the distance prior to the marathon to prove they can do it. Save those last six miles or so for race day when the other runners and the crowd will cheer you on. If you're an average runner, anything beyond 20 miles will greatly fatigue you and ruin your training.

Long runs:

• Condition the body to burn a higher percentage of fat with glycogen—"sparing glycogen"—thus leaving more glycogen available for later in the long race. The Wall is pushed back. This is why long runs of 18 miles or more are essential to marathon training. Once glycogen reserves are used up, fat is burned and your body adjusts to using this alternate source of fuel.

• Help develop your muscular capacity and enable you to continue running for longer periods of time without your legs weakening.

• Improve your aerobic capacity, which in turn helps you run longer without feeling tired.

• Increase your capillary formation in the muscles, some

doctors believe, thus supplying more oxygen to the leg muscles.

● Help boost your total mileage for the week, and thereby raise your "Collapse Point."

● Burn lots of fat and thus help reduce your weight.

● Make the short and medium runs during the week seem much easier to handle.

● Discipline your mind to running, and train it to become a long-distance mind by gradually increasing your weekly mileage and conditioning your body. Become convinced that you can go the distance. Runners often believe that long runs are more valuable mentally than physically. The long run conditions the mind to run through fatigue and boosts your confidence. Long runs are essential in conditioning you to the mental and physical stresses of the road. You become used to holding a reasonable pace and form for long periods of time, which you will have to do for the long races.

THE MEDIUM-DISTANCE ENDURANCE RUN

This relaxed run takes about 30 minutes to 1½ hours to complete, depending upon your level of fitness and the pace that you run. The distance covered ranges from 4 miles for novice competitors to as much as 15 miles for elite runners. A single medium-distance run will be about 15 percent of your total weekly mileage. Your average miles per day for the week will fall within the range of this category, but don't run this distance every day. Balance it with long runs and short runs. The medium run is used one to four times per week and is done over a variety of terrain—mostly flat or moderately hilly.

The primary goal for running medium-distance runs is to "pack in the miles" without placing great stress on your body and mind.

THE SHORT-DISTANCE ENDURANCE RUN

Easy days are well earned. Enjoy them. This run lasts from about 20 minutes to one hour—the range for an easy recovery day for novices up to elite runners. The distance stretches from two miles to ten miles, or about five to ten percent of your weekly mileage. The short-distance run is used once or twice a week over even terrain with few hills included. The emphasis is on staying relaxed and comfortable. Always run well within your capacity. Use the short run to accumulate weekly mileage and for fun; it is a time to run with friends, recover from hard or long workouts, or run for solitude and exploration.

There are alternatives to doing a short-distance run that will also serve as recovery or easy days: an off day; a long walk, or swimming or biking for up to an hour.

The short-distance run or easy run is used primarily as a recovery run or as an easy training day. It usually precedes or follows long runs, speed workouts and races.

5. PLAYING WITH SPEED

The earliest days of road racing saw runners favoring long, slow distance training. Then, spurred by the success of Emil Zatopek, the great Czech runner who dominated the 1952 Olympic Games and ran large quantities of speed workouts on a track, runners shifted to speed training, the new formula for success. In the 1970's, runners shifted back to long, slow distance running (now called LSD). By the 1980's, however, track-trained stars like Allison Roe of New Zealand, Grete Waitz of Norway and Craig Virgin and Alberto Salazar of the U.S. took over the road-running events. Many American runners agreed that "long, slow running only teaches you to run slow," and they took off for the track. Speed training again became the secret formula for success.

We believe that neither long, slow runs nor speed training alone is a successful training formula. The key is blending them together into a balanced training schedule. A base of endurance running should be followed by speed workouts on a track, hills, trails and roads to sharpen for key races. Although some runners may avoid speed work and still race well, most will benefit if it is done properly.

Generally we recommend that 80 to 90 percent of your

training be endurance work, and only 10 to 20 percent be speed. The first-time racer and first-time marathoner should do only endurance training. The competitive marathoner runs 90 percent endurance training and 10 percent speed as he or she sharpens for a race. Experienced racers preparing for a 10 km or less may do 25 percent speed work; the average racer will do no more than 10 percent. All runners do fewer speed workouts during their training lulls between races. The shorter the race, the more speed workouts you need. The less experienced you are, the fewer speed workouts you should do.

Safety Note: We do not recommend that you begin to add speed work to your training until you (1) have been running *at least* one year, (2) have completed *at least* two races, (3) run *at least* 20 miles a week, and (4) can race 10 km at a faster pace per mile than your daily training pace for 5 km–4 miles. Runners who are susceptible to injury when doing speed work must be conservative with their workouts or avoid speed work altogether. It is better to enjoy racing at less than optimal conditioning than to be injured and not able to participate.

Here are some guidelines for the experienced racer for blending endurance runs and speed workouts:

RACE	ENDURANCE	SPEED
1500 m-1 mile	60%	40%
5 km-4 miles	75%	25%
10 km-half marathon	85%	15%
Marathon	90%	10%

By increasing mileage, without speed work, the average runner finds that he or she can race faster and faster for the first few years of running. Endurance training gets these runners to the finish line comfortably. Eventually, however, as they try to race at a faster pace, they begin to struggle, especially in the 10 km-and-under races. Now, with a solid endurance base, these runners are ready for speed work.

Generally, you can benefit from speed work if:

- It is difficult for you to hold a fast pace during a race, but you finish feeling as though you could have run farther at the same pace: "If only the race had been longer."
- You feel uncomfortable with the pace at the start of or during the race, or cannot generate a "kick" at the end.
- You lack the strength to generate power during a race, especially up hills.
- Your racing form needs improvement.
- You need to improve your race pace judgment.
- You want to "sharpen" for a key race or series of races.
- You want to test your limits in a nonracing situation.

Your goal, at all levels, is to improve your stamina: the ability to run a fast pace over long distances. To increase your stamina, you will need to work on three areas: strength, speed and endurance.

Strength in running means training that increases your muscular strength and endurance and improves your ability to hold a fast pace. Strength workouts include weight training and continuous speed runs: rolling hills runs, fast continuous runs, tempo runs, and *fartlek* (a Swedish word meaning "speed play").

Speed work means training to run faster. We break speed work into three categories: strength-training runs, rhythm-training runs (to improve pace, racing form and aerobic conditioning), and power-training runs (to improve speed, strength and anaerobic conditioning). Each of these speed workouts overlaps with and complements the others.

Strength speed workouts, except for *fartlek,* are run at a steady, continuous pace. *Fartlek* workouts are a combination of strength-training runs and rhythm and power runs. They are run continuously with intermittent bursts of speed at race pace or faster over a set distance, with recovery at a moderate pace.

Rhythm and power workouts are run in bursts, with recovery periods between them. Speed workouts may be run on a track, roads or trails. They are often done up hills, and are called "speed work in disguise," because you work very hard without having to run as fast as you would on a track. The training results of these short, fast runs with brief rests are well established. Intermittent speed workouts, run at a fast, even pace, not only condition you to run faster, but also enable you to improve form and style, since they are often run in contained areas (a track or hill) which allow a coach to monitor your technique. Since they are run over measurable distances, you can control the workout better and measure progress. These workouts get the most out of you in the least amount of time and bring rapid improvements in your fitness level after only a few weeks. You can do much more work at a fast pace than would be possible with continuous running.

THE SPEED WORKOUT: 1-2-3 APPROACH

Speed workouts are tough. They will benefit you—and they can also injure you. Minimize the risk of injury with intelligent use of speed work.

Don't just put on your running shoes and go out for a workout. Plan. Speed training is intense, and poor habits surface quickly and can cause loss of training time from soreness or injury. By following a proper speed-training routine, you should complete a good workout and still feel like running the next day. Analyze your body's training needs, and plan your speed workout program to safely meet those needs.

All workouts—both endurance and speed—should follow this 1-2-3 step approach:

Step One. The Warm-Up lasts about 15 minutes for endurance runs, 30 minutes to one hour for speed work and races.

Step Two. The Workout lasts from 30 minutes to one-and-a-half hours.
Step Three. The Cool-Down lasts from 15 minutes to 30 minutes or more.

Allow enough time to do all three steps carefully. If you skip one step, you may get injured. See Chapter 27 for a sample warm-up and cool-down routine to use for speed workouts.

The Workout

The workout consists of running a set distance at a certain pace, or at various paces. The variables of these runs can be manipulated to control the workout:

Quantity is the number of repetitions you run, the distance. For a workout of 440 yards, for example, you may do ten repetitions (or reps) as a rhythm workout, but six repetitions as a power workout. More reps are done for rhythm than power because they are less intense.

Intensity is the speed at which you run each repetition. Rhythm runs are done at or near race pace, power runs are done very fast. Rhythm runs are done aerobically or at your aerobic-anaerobic borderline. Power runs are run in oxygen debt, anaerobically. Strength runs combine aerobic and anaerobic running, mostly along the borderline.

Rest is the amount of recovery time between each repetition. For rhythm runs this varies from 30 seconds to 3 minutes, an incomplete recovery in which your heart rate drops to the bottom of your training range (approximately 120 beats per minute). For power runs the rest is longer; you want—and will beg for—complete recovery so you can run hard again. This will take 5 to 15 minutes.

Rest breaks are either walking or jogging—or a combination of both. Walking is preferred for all rhythm runs by novices because they cannot recover fast enough with jogging. But jogging is preferred for most runners doing rhythm work because it keeps them loose. Veteran runners develop their own preferences. For power work, most people will walk—usually they have no choice—or walk until they get their breath back and then jog. But either way, keep moving. Whether you run or walk has nothing to do with the benefits of your workout. Benefits come from the hard running, not the recovery method.

Intermittent speed workouts are controlled by three variables: quantity, intensity, rest. To make the workout harder, increase the number of reps, increase your speed, decrease your rest time. *Do not* change more than one variable at a time. In the following chapters we will give you guidelines for controlling these variables during rhythm and power speed workouts.

The Track Workout Language

All speed workouts are written to include the three variables. For example, a rhythm workout would be indicated: 10 × 440 at 10 km pace, 2 min. jog. This shorthand means that your track workout will be 10 repetitions of 440 yards in length (quantity), at your 10 km pace (intensity), with a two-minute recovery jog (rest) between each repetition.

FACTORS INFLUENCING YOUR SPEED WORKOUTS

The quantity (distance), intensity (pace) and frequency of your speed runs depend upon two essential factors: (1) the purpose or goal of your training and (2) what you can tolerate in terms of your fitness level, experience, and environmental, physical and psychological limitations.

1. Goals

For all speed levels, you should have speed workout goals.

Your goal for each speed workout relates specifically to your racing goal and your present phase of training. If your goal is to build strength and staying power, you may want to run strength speed workouts. If your goal is to develop a sense of pace, improve your race form, or build for longer races, you may select a rhythm workout. If you wish to improve your raw speed and strength or your ability to run in oxygen debt, or to sharpen skills for a short race, you may choose a power workout.

Some runners choose training specific to a course. They prepare for hilly races by running hills. Sharon Barbano, for example, after moving to Boston, started running speed workouts over the "Heartbreak Hills" portion of the Boston Marathon route near her apartment. On Marathon day, she tore up those hills with confidence and strength. Power and rhythm workouts over the finishing stretch of a course are also good to give the runner a feeling of confidence for kicking to the finish line. *Fartlek* runs over parts of the course will give you a sense of the battle at strategic points and prepare you for an upcoming race by giving you a feel of landmarks along the way.

2. Fitness and Experience Levels

Your fitness level, training and racing experience determine how much speed work you can handle. Here are guidelines for our four categories of runners:

The Novice Competitor. This runner has a base of 20 miles per week and has run several races. Don't attempt any speed work until you reach this minimal level. Then safely learn the fundamentals of competitive speed training: how to run a workout, what proper form is, and so forth. The goal is to learn and to get a feel for your running potential rather than to train hard. This runner does fewer repetitions, runs no faster than present race pace, and takes plenty of rest between hard workouts.

To start, we recommend that you try a few quick—but not all-out—"pickups" of about 50 to 100 yards to get the feel of running fast. Do this once or twice a week during your regular training runs; try it only after at least two miles of easy jogging, and follow the speed workout with another slow, cool-down jog.

Do about six pickups, and then, over time, gradually extend the distance. This is a modified *fartlek* workout. Next, you may be able to add conservative, slow-paced rhythm workouts to your program. Races, of course, are considered speed training for you.

The key words here are caution and patience. Start carefully and allow your body to adapt to the new stress. If possible, start speed work under the supervision of a coach who understands runners at your level.

Safety Note: We recommend that at this level—20–30 miles per week, new to racing and speed work—you run only one speed session per week and that you limit it to a modified *fartlek*, rolling hills or rhythm run. Save the long, continuous strength runs and the faster power workouts for later when you have become more fit and more experienced.

In classes, we find that by improving runners' judgment of pace—of their knowledge that they can run with some discomfort and with improved form—they can within a few weeks achieve dramatic improvements in race times. But remember: You didn't reach your present level in a month; don't speed through your speed work.

The Basic Competitor. This runner can safely handle one—perhaps two—speed workouts per week. If just starting speed work, follow the guidelines for the novice competitor. With experience, this runner can benefit from the full range of speed work by adding tougher strength-training runs and faster rhythm and power runs.

After adjusting to one hard speed workout per week, add a second, light one, perhaps a modified *fartlek*, rolling hills or conservative rhythm run, before going into key races. You should keep the speed work within your limitations. Most speed work-related injuries come in this group: the runner wants to progress quickly but hasn't the experience or the "speed miles in the bank." Slow progression is important in both mileage and speed accumulation.

The Advanced Competitor. This runner is experienced at speed work and racing. He or she benefits from speed work one or two times a week. Some runners may do three speed workouts preparing for shorter races. This runner's biggest problems are finding the time to do all this running and balancing higher mileage with the quality of the speed work.

The Champion Competitor. This runner may run two to four speed workouts a week, depending on the distance of the upcoming race and whether or not he or she is sharpening for it. This runner, benefiting from experience, knows what is best for a champion effort for each race.

Safety Note: All runners must ease back into speed work after a layoff. Don't fool yourself into thinking that you are still in good shape. "Memory training"—remembering how well you ran in the past and thinking you still can do it now—leads to shattered egos and injury. Return slowly, step by step.

---

3. Environmental Limitations

Speed workouts will be influenced by your environment: the weather, altitude, hills, your equipment, the time of day, and the running surface.

Hot Weather. If you train outdoors, weather may be the most important factor. If you train in hot weather, remember the following guidelines:

• The best temperature for running is 45° to 70°F. As temperature and humidity increase, you work harder. You should adjust your goals and your workout accordingly.

• *Continuous runs* should be shortened in the heat. Slow your pace. Take breaks to drink, and drink plenty of fluids.

• For *intermittent workouts* take longer recovery breaks. Walk instead of jog, drink fluids and pour them over yourself while recovering. Stay in the shade until ready to run again. Recovery is a battle to bring your heart rate and temperature down. Power workouts may be preferred for hot days since the workout is shorter, recovery time longer, and your muscles looser.

• Don't compare hot-day run times with those run in

cool weather. In fact, we seldom time hot-weather work-outs; they are meaningless compared to the effort. Make other adjustments: run slower, do fewer reps; change clothing if the weather changes.

• In group workouts, remember not all runners react the same way to heat.

• Be sure you have access to water, shade and other comforts. Bring your own water and sponges if necessary, or plan your workouts on tracks that have access to water or along roads or in loops where water is available. Never run a speed workout on a hot day without fluids and shade handy.

• Warm up and run the workout in the shade if possible. Run a course near a lake, stream or pond, so you can jump in after finishing. To avoid the heat altogether, schedule your workouts for early morning or the evening, when it's much cooler.

• Remember, drink plenty of fluids *after* the workout.

Cold Weather. Cool, crisp weather allows you to run fast and recover fast. Below 32°F, however, speed work can become dangerous. If you train in cold weather, observe these guidelines:

• Do not attempt short, fast speed workouts, especially power workouts, when it is extremely cold. The cold weather will cause your muscles, ligaments and tendons to remain very tight—you won't be able to loosen up adequately—resulting in lack of efficiency in your motion and possible injury.

• Do light rhythm runs or brisk strength-training continuous runs to keep moving—and warm.

• If you try to run very hard, your lungs will feel scorched, your throat sore and raspy.

• Cooling occurs very quickly between sessions. Be prepared to put on a warm-up suit or more clothing between work loads, and towel off to keep from getting cold and wet.

• Adjust your time goals. You are forced to go slower,

since your body can't go all out in the cold and the extra clothing slows your pace.

- The key is to keep moving and slow the pace. Don't overdress or you'll overheat, even in the coldest of weather. Attach hat, gloves and windbreaker to your body so you can keep adjusting to the conditions. Don't underdress, or you will be very uncomfortable.

- Take extra time to warm up. Jog three or four miles before doing anything hard, and then do your first few work loads conservatively to further ease into hard work.

- As soon as you are finished—just as when finishing a race in the cold—take off your wet shirt and put on a dry one; add extra clothing if needed. Keep jogging to prevent tightening up, and then head for a warm place. Remove all wet clothing and replace it with dry things if you are not going home immediately. As soon as possible, take a warm bath or shower, but not until your body has fully recovered from the workout and your heart rate is back to its normal level.

Wind, Rain, Lightning, Snow and Ice. If you try to train in inclement weather, remember these guidelines:

- A strong wind can ruin rhythm workouts. First it blows you faster, then slower; you fatigue more quickly. You should just run at your intended effort level and forget time goals.

- In cold, steady rain, stick to a steady, brisk strength run at a moderate pace. If the track is slippery or full of water, try finding a dry run on hills or along roadways.

- Don't cancel workouts, just modify them. But don't mess with those speedy bolts from the sky. Lightning kills. Get off the track or road.

- Ice and snow can be fun to run in, but risky. Never attempt to run hard on ice or snow; you may get injured. Adjust your workout by running a slower, steady pace so you can be sure of a strong foot plant. Look for bare spots on the course and pick it up on them. Or look for dry hills and do your workout there. You may want to wait for better weather, or run a modified speed session on an indoor track, indoor bike, treadmill or in the pool.

Altitude. There is less oxygen at higher altitudes, and you can go into oxygen debt faster. If you are traveling and run in an altitude much higher than the one you live in, skip your speed work unless you will be there for a week or longer. Slowly adjust; allow for a slower pace and a longer recovery period.

Hills. Running a rhythm or power workout on a very steep hill may be counterproductive. The hill must be challenging, but not so steep that good racing form is impossible. It's good to include a few steep hills on strength-training runs, but in all cases watch out for the downhills, where injury is possible.

Safety Note: Running downhill is more dangerous than running uphill when doing several repetitions up and down a hill. Be careful to use good form and relax—not brake—when coming downhill. It is better to walk down a steep hill than risk injury.

Shoes. Training shoes are the only equipment most of you need. If you are above the level of basic competitor, you may want racing flats. If you plan to race in racing flats, use them in most of your speed workouts. Do your warm-up in them; don't just switch for the hard work. Racing flats have a lower heel; therefore, do extra stretching for your Achilles tendon and calves. Stick with your training shoes if you are bothered by injuries or if you are doing speed training on hard surfaces. Extra padding in your training shoes will also help. After your speed workout, put on your training flats for the cool-down run.

Do not experiment with spikes in speed sessions or races unless you are used to them and will really benefit from using them for several races on the track or for cross-country. Few road runners should ever use spikes; the risk of injury caused by their flimsy support and low heels is too great.

Time of Day. You run faster during daytime because you see better. If you must run after dark, either select a well-lighted route or slow down. The New York Road Runners classes train in Central Park, and during the winter when the lighting is poor, they modify their workouts by slowing down. In summer, when it is lighter, they run faster.

Running Surfaces. For continuous speed runs, just charge along your normal flat or hilly training courses. For intermittent speed work, the best setting is a good hill or your local track.

Most outdoor tracks are 440-yard ovals; newer ones may be 400 meters. The track is ideal for speed workouts since times and splits are easily measured. (See the pacing chart on page 525 for even-paced splits for track workouts.) The track surface is important. A hard, smooth surface will produce faster times than a soft cinder or dirt track. The fastest surface is the new bouncy synthetic track. The difference may be as much as two seconds for the 440, eight seconds for the mile. Remember this when you run on various track surfaces and compare times. Tracks in poor shape will yield slower times.

If you can't use a track, make up your own speed-workout structure. You can do speed work over measured distances on roads, dirt or wood-chip trails, grassy fields, a shopping center parking lot, park sidewalk, your own back yard. Just measure off the distances you need, and be sure the course is free from obstacles such as potholes or protruding roots. The Atalanta running team and the New York Road Runners classes seldom work out on a track. They run on what they find in New York City.

If you can't run a measured distance, you can run for time. That is, instead of running a three-minute 880 on a track, run hard along a road or path for three minutes and take a recovery jog before starting again. These speed-work variations allow you to do your hard track workouts wherever you go. Remember, the essential thing is the work done. You can even create hills in your flat town by running up a garage ramp, golf course hill, sloped highway grading, or even a flight of stairs.

Running on indoor tracks can cause injury. Beware of them. The tight turns and banked surface create unusual leg stress. Also, you must do 8 to 24 laps to run a mile. Do speed work indoors only as a last resort. Don't run as hard, and do fewer repetitions. Run only the 440–880 distances, and use the outside lanes to minimize the sharp turns. Unless you intend to race indoors—even Pete Schuder cuts indoor sessions for his Columbia trackmen to a minimum—or have access to a good fieldhouse track, avoid indoor speed workouts. Even in the worst weather, it is still usually worthwhile to bundle up properly and get outdoors. Besides, unless they are keying for a cold-weather race, most runners should use the winter to rebuild strength and save the hard track work for the spring and summer. For this reason, Glover refuses to schedule hard indoor track workouts for his Atalanta group in the winter. You can't do hard speed work year-round.

4. Physical and Psychological Limitations

Illness, such as a cold, requires that you run fewer and less intense reps and take more time for recovery. This also holds true if you are nursing a minor injury. Stay away from speed work if the illness or injury becomes more serious.

We also find that performance is affected by the runner's mental state. Anxiety, tension, mental fatigue can require that you take longer recovery periods. Psychological pressures of career, family, or education may cause occasional poor performances. This can be overcome by running with a sympathetic group, or backing off from speed sessions, although sometimes the speed session itself can give runners confidence enough to lift them. Don't take out your stresses on the track. Run a more controlled workout. Runners, like everyone else, have their ups and downs. They just have to learn to take them in stride.

VARIETY

Don't run the same workout every week, week after week. You will soon get bored and stale. Create a variety of workouts by mixing the three types of speed runs with the six basic distances we use—220, 440, 880, mile, short hill, long hill. Keep the distances and speeds fixed throughout each session to keep them simple. Other workouts can be done at varying distances and speeds:

Cut-Downs. Start at a slower than race pace, and increase the pace with each repetition, making the work tougher and tougher.

Pyramids or Ladders. Start with 220, work up to 440, 660, 880—using equal-distance recovery jogs—and then work back down.

Combinations. Alternate 440's and 220's, for example, rather than running only one distance throughout.

Out-and-Back. Run out one minute and back to the starting point, and rest for two to three minutes, then out two minutes and back, out three minutes and back, and so on until you reach five minutes; rest between each out and back. If you are fit, reverse the run and finish by running out one and back one.

GROUPS

To make group running helpful, everyone must stay together at the same pace and make the same effort. For *fartlek* runs, the fastest runners might jog back toward the slower runners and regroup during recovery. The out-and-back and single-file runs are also fun. In the out-and-back, the slower runners, at the turn around, are in the lead, with the faster trying to catch them; at the five-minute out-and-back, the slower runners might actually finish ahead of the faster. This teaches runners the feel of passing and holding off runners. A similar situation on a track or hill can occur when the slower runners start first. This involves the slower runners of the group, and challenges the faster ones. Each runner starts at approximately the lead time needed so that all the runners will finish at about the same time. For single-file runs, line yourselves up single file and start running. Then the last runner sprints to the front and settles into a steady pace until the next runner sprints to the front, and so forth.

For our classes, we break down the groups by ability so they will help each other and not run against others who are much faster. We break them down into groups of 5 km or 10 km ability—since rhythm runs are done at race paces—and each group runs together.

FINAL TIPS

• Don't procrastinate about getting into speed work; do it.

• Finish all your rhythm runs feeling exhilarated and tired, but not exhausted. Power work may leave you feeling rubber-legged, but proud and confident. Strength runs should leave you feeling tired all over, with "a tingle," but not as exhausted as an all-out race.

• Speed work should build up your body, not tear it down. Work hard, but keep control. Ease into the work; follow the principle of adaptation to progressive stress.

• Listen to your body for protests about overstress; obey them, and ease back.

• Drop out immediately if you feel anything unusual happen—a muscle tighten, a sharp pain. Remember the lesson of Guy Gertsch, who thought he had only a sharp cramp in his right thigh at the seven-mile mark of the 1982 Boston Marathon, and collapsed after finishing in 2:47. Doctors set his broken right femur with a steel rod. You can keep going, but you may regret it.

• Train by "going with your strengths." Train specifically for the race you are entering, and don't try to be what you aren't.

• Don't increase both mileage and speed at the same time. Build your mileage and speed carefully. Build your mileage first, and add speed; then cut mileage as you intensify speed.

• Follow the hard-easy method. Always take it easy the day before and after speed workouts.

• Don't jump back into your speed sessions for several days after a short race and several weeks after a marathon.

• Make no sudden changes in surface, shoes, type or intensity of workouts.

• Don't race during training—you'll leave your race on the training runs. Don't compete with others, only yourself.

• Run your sets evenly; don't show off on one and sandbag another.

• In group running, help each other by pushing each other. As the late Jumbo Elliott, track coach of many powerful Villanova University teams, said, "Runners make runners."

• Log every run in your diary, and log your complete workouts: quantity, intensity, rest, weather, shoes, type of track. Then you can more accurately compare workouts and measure progress.

• Generally, the shorter the race, the more speed work you do, the faster it is, and the shorter the distance run.

• Build a positive attitude in your workouts, and carry it into your races and your life. Train to be tougher, wiser, faster.

6. THE SPEED WORKOUT: STRENGTH-TRAINING RUNS

When you analyze why a long-distance runner can run fast for up to several hours, you think of endurance and speed. You should also consider strength a significant factor.

Distance-racing strength is a specific form of muscular strength. It enables distance runners to perform with less effort, yet accomplish the same amount of work. Herbert deVries, an exercise physiologist at the University of Southern California, states that "a maximal level of strength should be developed along with the endurance training program. This allows the muscle group to work at a lower percentage of its all-out capacity, and thus, significantly increase endurance." In other words, as you increase the strength of the muscles used for long-distance running, you will require less effort to run at a particular speed. Your level of endurance increases as a result. The stronger you become, the farther you can run at faster speeds without need for additional oxygen or energy.

Strength-training runs are aerobic-anaerobic runs that are either at the borderline of aerobic and anaerobic work—where breathing becomes labored—or that pass back and forth between the two. Training is intense, and brings improvement in your muscular strength and endurance and pushes you into oxygen debt. These runs combine some of the virtues of continuous aerobic endurance runs and intermittent speed workouts. By improving endurance, speed and strength, they improve your stamina. The term "strength," therefore, refers here not to muscle development with weights, but to the strength of the heart-lung system and the muscular system improved by these runs.

Strength runs cover 4 to 12 miles, and the pace is between 5 km and marathon pace. To minimize injury and fatigue, you run the race distance at slower than race pace, *or* run race pace or faster at distances less than your race distance. The increased strength resulting from these runs will give you these benefits:

- added strength to run faster with less effort;
- the ability to maintain a faster pace for a longer period of time without using additional energy reserves;
- the psychological strength to "hang on" during intense continuous races;
- a stronger ability to overcome hills;
- a resistance to fatigue during races that will help you maintain good running form throughout the race.

Strength training also conditions runners' bodies to transport oxygen more efficiently to their muscle tissues. As you become stronger and more efficient, you rely less on your anaerobic system, and your anaerobic threshold— oxygen debt—will be extended. Your body will also tolerate greater levels of lactic acid, your heart will pump more efficiently, and you will develop a better ability to withstand pain from your running effort (not pain from injury). Your body will recover more quickly from workouts.

Endurance runs done at aerobic levels benefit your heart-lung system. By adding strength-training runs, you increase your muscular strength and endurance. By combining endurance runs with strength runs, you improve your overall fitness, and teach your mind and body to run at or near race pace for long periods.

HOW TO IMPROVE YOUR RACING STRENGTH

You improve your racing strength by systematically over-loading your muscles. This is done by using strength-training runs to progressively increase the intensity and resistance of your workouts.

1. You increase the *intensity* of your workouts by increasing the *speed* of your strength-training runs. The increased speeds force your body to activate more muscle fibers to propel you forward.

2. You increase the *resistance* of your workouts by including more hills in your strength-training runs, and then increasing the elevation of the hills you run. These hills force your muscles to work harder, and this strengthens them.

3. You increase your strength by including weight training as part of your regular program. Some exercise physiologists argue that muscle strength for a specific activity—such as running—is developed best by doing that activity. Others, however, like Clayne Jensen and Garth Fisher, authors of *The Scientific Basis of Athletic Conditioning*, believe that "heavy resistance exercises against external moveable resistance, such as weight training equipment . . . provides the greatest potential for gaining strength, because the resistance can be increased progressively."

We believe that the best way to improve your racing strength is by using five different forms of strength-training runs. These runs work at improving the strength of those muscles *specifically* used for racing. Weight training is an excellent source for *general* strength building used as a supplement to your running. Chapter 26 contains detailed information about using weight training to improve your strength and thus your running.

THE FIVE STRENGTH-TRAINING RUNS

There are five types of strength-training runs that will progressively increase the intensity and resistance of your training workouts. In order of general intensity, easier to harder, they are: modified *fartlek*, rolling hills, fast continuous runs, advanced *fartlek*, tempo runs.

1. *The Modified* Fartlek *Run*

This is a strength run for novice and basic competitors just beginning to include more strenuous training runs in their workout schedules. It is an introduction to speed work for these runners. It is also used by advanced runners returning from injury who are easing into more strenuous runs, and by those runners easing back into more intense workouts after a long layoff from competitive training.

The modified *fartlek* run is generally done on a level or gently rolling course so that only one overload factor (speed) will be manipulated by the runner. If you add hills, you include a second overload factor (resistance), and that is too difficult a challenge at this stage of your development.

The modified *fartlek* run should cover only three to five miles, and last from 30 to 45 minutes. It is done during a five-to-eight-mile medium-endurance run and should be run at the same pace. The only difference is that you now include some short distance runs (100 to 440 yards) that you run at 10 km pace or faster. These are your "speed play" segments. In between, you return to your medium endurance pace. But not too slow. The recovery should be sufficient to eliminate the lactic acid built up during the speed burst. When your heart rate and breathing return to normal, you run another small "speed segment." The workout gradually introduces you to strength-training runs and speed work, and allows your body to adapt to new stresses with little chance of injury.

You may vary the distance or time you run hard within the same workout according to how you feel. The purpose of the modified *fartlek* is to incorporate speed work into your endurance training. It is much less stressful than the typical track workout. *Fartlek* training can also help you work on your form while you run those short, fast spurts.

2. *The Rolling Hills Run*

This strength run introduces resistance work to your training. It is necessary for developing racing strength, and is used by basic, advanced and champion runners.

The rolling hills run includes a fair number of hills that range from a quarter mile to three-quarters of a mile in length. The entire run should cover a distance of four to ten miles, depending on your fitness level. The novice competitor may limit himself or herself to four to six miles at first. The run should last at least 30 minutes, but no longer than 75 minutes. Run a few easy miles before and after the workout.

The run emphasizes the hills. You should approach them in a very positive manner. By "working" or challenging the hills at race pace, you force your muscles to overcome the resistance of the incline, thus increasing your strength. Running downhill, you should work on "falling" instead of resisting the decline. Maintain good hill-running form on uphills and hold a steady brisk conversational pace while running along the flat sections. When you complete this workout, your whole body and soul should tingle.

Rolling hills runs should help you improve your form. The increased resistance and elevation should force you to use good running form to work up and down the hills. The oxygen debt encountered when you challenge the hills will force your body to work under stress. Your body will become more efficient in supplying oxygen and energy sources to your muscles, enabling you to run better.

Make sure that you progressively increase the resistance of the hills you run against. As you become stronger, run steeper hills, and increase the mileage and number of hills included in your rolling hills workout. A frequent diet of hill running will make you a tougher hill runner. You will develop confidence and not be frightened when you run up against one of those killer hills during a race.

3. Fast Continuous Runs

This run stresses speed over a long distance. You want to get the feeling that you are pushing the pace throughout this run. The length and actual speed of the run are secondary to the feel of the run. The fast pace overloads your muscles and cardiovascular system to improve your racing strength. Only runners with the proper preliminary training that has conditioned their bodies to withstand the stress of this workout should try fast continuous runs. It is not recommended for novice competitors. Many runners feel that these are the "bread and butter" of their training schedules, rather than lots of long, slow endurance runs. These runners, however, are very fit and experienced, such as world record holder for the women's marathon (as this book goes to press) Allison Roe, who regularly does both rolling hills runs and fast continuous runs and only does 70 miles a week—compared to the more traditional marathon diet of 100 plus miles a week and plenty of slow, easy endurance runs.

The fast continuous run is done over a level or gently rolling course where you can move along undisturbed at a fast clip. The pace is steady (about half-marathon pace for four to eight miles, marathon pace for eight to ten miles), and you should be able to cover a distance of four to ten miles, depending on your fitness level. Start with the shorter distance. You should complete the entire workout at the same pace. Run a few easy miles before and after the workout.

The key here is the fast, steady pace for the entire distance of the run. If you slow down or lose your concentration, you will diminish the overload (speed) force that you are placing on your muscles.

The fast continuous run improves your cardiorespiratory level of fitness. It makes you mentally a tougher competitor by training you to run faster under pressure and improves your confidence that you can do this. Strength-training runs are progressive: be sure to progressively increase the overloading of your system by increasing the speed of the fast continuous runs as you become stronger. You may also want to lengthen the distance of the run somewhat. You should finish these runs feeling that you have really taxed your body.

4. The Advanced Fartlek *Run*

This workout may be included in all stages of your training. It can be used as an introduction to rhythm and power workouts, or it can be done as an alternative to these types of runs for those who don't like to work out on a track. This difficult workout is not recommended for novice and basic competitors. Basically, this is a transitional workout, which includes some rhythmic running and some power running done intermittently, alternated with endurance running. The workout is very stressful, since it combines both intensity (speed) and resistance (hills) in one workout. It is used only by the advanced and champion competitor. Control the difficulty of the workout to prevent injury. Most runners make the mistake of not taking enough rest between the "speed plays." They become fatigued too early in the workout and begin to force themselves through the run. They may get injured, perhaps straining a muscle or ligament, as they try to "bull" their way through the session.

The advanced *fartlek* run covers varied terrain with some good hills and flat sections. Most *fartlek* sessions are done on trails or golf courses but could be done even in city streets if need be. The distance ranges from four to eight miles, and the entire workout should take 30 minutes to one hour. The runner selects a landmark such as a telephone pole or traffic light and runs hard to it, or chooses to run hard for a set time period such as one minute. The workout is broken into segments of "hard stressful" runs followed by "easy recovery" runs. The hard portion of the run is done at 10 km pace or faster, depending on the length of the segment, which may range from 100 yards to one mile. The recovery portion of the run is done at conversational pace and covers approximately the same distance as the hard run. The faster the bursts, the slower the recovery pace. The distance of the pickups should vary within the workout; for example, 220-rest-880-rest-440-rest, and so forth. The distance may also vary with the terrain, picking up the pace on each hill. The number of pickups per workout varies from 10 to 20; go as you feel. This workout is open to variation. You may vary the length of the hard stressful run as you wish. The workout is done entirely to your "feel" and not structured in any way. This is not a carefree workout, however. It is stressful, placing a large overload on your cardiorespiratory and musculoskeletal systems. The workout is done best alone or in small groups of similar ability. During recovery, faster runners should turn around and jog toward the slower, to regroup. You should run a few easy miles before and after the workout.

Experienced champion runners may benefit from another variation of *fartlek* running. Instead of running hard and then jogging for recovery, they run hard "surges" of one to three minutes off a strong pace and then return to that pace for another four to six minutes before surging again. Basically it is a fast continuous run that includes pickups to simulate racing conditions, where you may have to pick up the pace to pass or move away from another runner. This workout gives you the confidence to pick up your pace in a race even when you already are running hard.

Remember, *fartlek* training means getting tired without feeling tired. It is designed to be intense and different. Allow for variations of speed in an informal but intense run.

5. Tempo Runs

Similar to the fast continuous runs, these are more structured, with the distance and time being measured and recorded accurately. Tempo runs are done at a slightly faster pace than the fast continuous runs. This run is used *only* by advanced and champion competitors preparing for major races. (Beware of turning tempo runs into an all-out race effort.)

The Russians first introduced tempo runs, wanting to simulate race conditions without exposing their runners to the high stress and pressure of actual races. They like the run to teach their runners a feeling for pace, thus the term "tempo."

This run covers a distance of four to six miles at very close to your 10 km pace (90 percent effort). The course should be level, with good footing. Each time you run this workout, you should run the same course and time yourself. As you become more fit, try to improve your time to maintain the overload. This will help increase your racing strength and build your confidence. Run a few easy miles before and after this workout. Be sure to prepare yourself for it, since it is very stressful, and a poor time can be discouraging. Thus, you would taper for a few days going into it.

Safety Note: Be careful when doing the strength-training runs, since they are unstructured and you can't measure accurately how intensely you are training. Ease into these runs.

SUMMARY OF STRENGTH-TRAINING RUNS

STRENGTH-TRAINING RUN	DISTANCE	INTENSITY	RECOVERY PERIOD	HILLS	CATEGORIES OF RUNNERS THAT USE THIS RUN
1. Modified *Fartlek*	3–5 miles	Short bursts at 10 km pace or faster	Yes	None	Novice and Basic
2. Rolling Hills	4–10 miles	Uphills at race pace	Yes	Many	Basic Advanced Champion
3. Fast Continuous Run	4–10 miles	Half-marathon pace for 4–8 miles; Marathon pace for 8–10 miles	No	Few	Advanced Champion
4. Advanced *Fartlek*	4–8 miles	Faster than 10 km race pace	Yes	Several	Advanced Champion
5. Tempo Run	4–6 miles	90% all-out effort for distance run	No	None	Advanced Champion

7. THE SPEED WORKOUT: RHYTHM-TRAINING RUNS

The rhythm workout is pace work with incomplete recovery. It is also called "intervals" because there are rest intervals between work loads. We call it rhythm work because you run at near race pace, and learn to be rhythmic—in tune—with your body. Rhythm runs are faster than endurance runs, but slower than power runs.

The rhythm workout is primarily aerobic and usually run at the top of your training heart-rate range (80–85 percent of maximum heart rate) or the border of aerobic-anaerobic. You do not want to go deep into oxygen debt.

The primary reason for running a rhythm workout is to develop a sense of pace and increase your endurance and speed. Combined with strength work and endurance runs, it allows you to run faster over longer distances, thus improving your race times.

The rhythm speed workout:

• *Develops a sense of pace and rhythm.* Since you accurately time your workouts, you can teach your body to run at a desired pace. This is helpful for those runners who tend to start races too fast or too slow. You learn and then practice the pace that is right for you so you will feel it and run it on race day. The rhythm workout allows you to run at your own selected pace over and over again to get that "feel."

• *Improves speed.* By training at a pace slightly faster than race pace, you progress toward a goal of faster race times.

• *Improves racing form and style.* By training in race-pace form, you will be more efficient, coordinated and relaxed on race day.

• *Builds confidence.* These runs develop your confidence to hold a brisk, steady pace. Since much of rhythm work is done a little faster than race pace, the speed of your race in the early going will feel within your limits. You learn that you have "staying power" and can maintain pace at the end of your race, even when you are tired, by maintaining pace when tired over the last few sets of rhythm runs.

• *Increases endurance.* Improves both your aerobic and muscular endurance.

• *Extends your aerobic-anaerobic borderline.* By training, and racing, at a higher level of aerobic capacity, you are not slowed by oxygen debt and can hold your fast pace longer.

• *Sharpens you for races.*

• *Allows for a flexible workout.* Rhythm workouts are excellent for the novice competitor who needs to ease into speed work, for other runners returning from injury or layoff, and for all runners compensating for bad weather conditions.

• *Measures progress.* When you do *fartlek* runs or endurance runs, you know you are getting fit, but can't prove it. Rhythm workout improvements are measurable: your times improve, your recovery periods are shorter, you do more repetitions at the same pace. Do not do the same workout every week, however, and expect to improve. Use variety: Go back to some of the same workouts every few weeks and compare your times, repetitions, recoveries.

• *Maintains general conditioning.* Moderate rhythm workouts can be used once a week year-round to help you maintain a high level of base fitness even when not building toward a key race.

- *Improves hill running.* They improve your hill-running ability and form as you gain confidence in your handling of hills at race pace.
- *Speeds recovery from races.* Two or three days after a race—a full week after a marathon—very conservative slow-paced rhythm work—low intensity, low quantity, extra rest—will help stretch out your stiff muscles and flush away accumulated waste products. It also helps you psychologically to do something brisk. In our classes on Tuesday evenings following Sunday races, we have our runners move back a group or two in speed, or do fewer repetitions at a slower pace. These workouts must be treated as recovery speed workouts, not training speed workouts.
- *Develops a feel for pack running.* By running in a group, you learn to hang on when you want to drop out, or to hold back and be patient. You learn what it is like to run elbow to elbow in a race with a pack of runners who can "draft" off each other and help each other run a faster pace. In our classes we group runners together by race pace and encourage them to hang together in a tight pack. You should also run some rhythm workouts alone to learn how to judge your own pace.

HOW TO WRITE A RHYTHM WORKOUT

Putting together your own rhythm workout requires planning. You can't merely play with the three variables—quantity, intensity, rest—and hope to come up with the right combinations. Each workout is influenced by many factors, including your training goals, fitness and experience levels, and environmental, psychological and physical limitations. By examining the three variables individually and considering all of these factors you can construct the right rhythm workout for yourself. Before starting:

1. Select the distance of your runs, the number of repetitions you want to do (*quantity*).

2. Determine the amount of rest you will take between each repetition (*rest*).

3. Determine the speed of the repetitions (*intensity*). Speed will depend greatly upon the amount of rest you allow yourself and the distance run. The shorter the recovery period and the greater the distance, the slower the repetitions.

> *Safety Note*: Increase the stress of only one variable at a time.

Selecting Quantity

This covers distance and repetitions. Many reps improve fitness and form. Total mileage (not counting warm-up, cool-down or recovery running) may range from one to two miles for novices to six to eight miles for more experienced runners. In general, you run more reps and longer distances to prepare for longer races and as your fitness level increases. The greater the distances of the reps, the fewer you run.

We use six different distances—from 220 yards to one mile—for our basic workouts. This keeps things simple, and the distances are fixed for the entire workout. As you improve, you may want to vary these. Our six distances are:

1. *220-yard Runs*. Used primarily for short-distance training (5 km and under) to improve speed.

2. *440-yard Runs*. "Quarters" are used for improving form, general aerobic conditioning at slower paces and as a final prep for shorter races at faster paces.

3. *880-yard Runs*. Used at 10 km and under to develop speed and simulate racing conditions. For races longer than 10 km, these runs are used for improving aerobic conditioning, form and pace.

4. *One-mile Runs*. Used mostly for 10 km to marathon training. Excellent for pace judgment and improving aerobic conditioning. Teaches the ability to hold on to a strong pace. A basic workout for marathoners as they build toward the race. More advanced runners may do one-and-a-half-mile and two-mile sessions.

5. *Short Hill Runs (100–220 yards).* Steep enough to challenge, not so steep as to prohibit good rhythm. Excellent for improving form, speed and strength.

6. *Long Hill Runs (440–660 yards).* Not quite as steep as the short hills. Mainly used for psychological purposes. After running a number of these, you begin to feel very confident about running up hills in races. More advanced runners may go as long as a half mile or one mile for these runs.

Determining Rest

Less rest is used for shorter distances, slower speeds, fewer reps. When peaking for a race, you may keep the quantity and intensity the same, but cut back the rest. More rest may be required for novice competitors, or runners coming back from an injury or layoff.

Your recovery time from rhythm runs should be enough to allow your heart rate to return to about 120 beats per minute, or long enough so that you can do the next run at the same pace. You seek *incomplete recovery*: you bring your heart rate up to about 85 percent of maximum and do not let it fall below about 60 percent of maximum. Thus you train aerobically for the entire workout, including the recovery time.

Experienced runners may jog lightly between reps to stay loose; some may walk briskly. Novices should walk. Do not jog on your toes as the track runners do; they do that in order to keep a "bounce" to their ball-heel foot strike. Don't sit down or stand around, either. Keep moving.

The recommended length of rest for the rhythm workout varies from 30 seconds to three minutes. If you require more than the recommended time to recover, you are running the distance too quickly. You should modify your speed. If you recover too quickly, increase the speed of the run. The amount of rest you take controls how fast you can run.

If you are doing a large number of reps at a slow pace you should take as little rest as possible. (Example: 12 × 440 with 30 seconds between each.) If you are training at fast rhythm paces or want to do some longer reps (one mile), you will have to take a longer recovery period. The increased stress of a faster speed or longer distance requires more time for your body to recover.

On hills, rest is determined by how long it takes you to jog down to the bottom. When you reach the top, don't stop. This is a continuous run at intermittent paces. You run up the hill at or near race pace, and down at or near conversation pace. Don't "brake" coming downhill; relax and flow. Run up briskly and flow down easily.

Determining Intensity

Rhythm runs are done near race pace. Running at all-out speed is power work. Rhythm runs give you the feel for your own race pace, and your first run should be at the same speed as your last. They should all be very close in time, just like your splits during a race. You will, therefore, learn to hold back when fresh and keep pushing when tired.

The speed of your rhythm runs will vary from half-mile to marathon pace. Your speed will increase if you want to do work for shorter races or improve your race pace. Your speed will decrease if you run more reps, longer distances, take less rest or are troubled by various limiting factors. We use three speed levels, so you may select the pace you wish based on your goals and fitness level. These speed levels are reference points to guide you in establishing your specific training speeds. Your actual speed may be slightly faster or slower.

1. *Fast Rhythmic Pace.* The speed is faster than race pace for the distance you are training to race. This speed work will help you run smoothly at a faster pace and improve

your time for these races. We use the following fast rhythmic paces for these racing distances:

One mile:	880-yard race pace
5 km:	One-mile race pace
10 km:	5-km race pace
Marathon:	5-km–4-mile race pace

2. *Medium Rhythmic Pace*. The speed is approximately race pace for the distance you are training to race. Choose the pace you can race at now; don't base it on a performance which may have been faster or slower than your present fitness level. Gradually increase that pace toward your goal as your race times improve. Marathon runners use a pace approximately 30 seconds per mile faster than marathon pace so that they'll develop the confidence to go out strong on race day. They do their medium rhythmic pace work at approximately 10 km race pace. We use the following medium rhythmic paces for these racing distances:

One mile:	One-mile race pace
5 km:	5-km race pace
10 km:	10-km race pace
Marathon:	10-km race pace

3. *Slow Rhythmic Pace*. Slow rhythmic runs are generally done at 10 seconds to 30 seconds per mile slower than the medium rhythm pace run. It is slower than race pace, and faster than your daily endurance-run pace. It is used to build aerobic endurance or to ease you into, or back into, speed work. It is also used to help recover from races. Marathon runners do these rhythmic runs at marathon speed, and thus get a feel of marathon pacing. This is a continuous aerobic run—jog, don't walk, for recovery. We use the following slow rhythmic paces for these racing distances:

One mile: 5-km race pace
5 km: 10-mile race pace
10 km: Half-marathon race pace
Marathon: Marathon race pace

Safety Note: When doing slow rhythm work, the tendency is to run the reps too fast. Since a large number of repetitions are used with short recovery, they could quickly lead to fatigue or injury. Slow down! This workout is supposed to be run at a comfortable pace. Don't compete with yourself or others. The challenge for the novice and basic competitor is to hold back on the speed in order to learn marathon pace and complete a comfortable workout; the challenge for the advanced and champion competitor is to do a large quantity of work safely. For reasons of safety, we have severely restricted the quantity for the novice and basic competitor. The advanced and champion competitor will find that this can be a very strong workout if they attempt to do the quantities we suggest on the charts with the minimal rest recommended. For an easier workout when recovering from an injury or easing back into speed work, increase the recovery period and/or decrease the number of repetitions.

Generally, slow rhythmic pace develops endurance, medium rhythmic pace develops strength and a sense of race pace, and fast rhythmic pace develops speed. With three rhythm runs to choose from, you must determine both your short-term racing goals and your long-term seasonal goals. You would not run all your rhythm workouts at marathon pace if you were preparing for the 10 km. But running only 10 km pace will not give you the feel of the marathon. The speed categories are specific to your racing needs.

Your fitness level and running experience will play a very important role in determining the intensity of your workouts. Novices should not do any fast rhythm work. They should train at race pace or slower, which will ease them into the stress of this training.

Controlling Your Rhythmic Pace

The most difficult problem faced by runners just learning to do rhythm workouts is regulating their workout pace. It is one thing to know what pace you should be running and quite another to do several repetitions at that exact pace. Many runners, including experienced racers, begin the workout much faster than the planned pace. You should get into the correct rhythm immediately, so that you don't destroy the purpose of the workout. If you start at too fast a pace, you will have to take too long a recovery or you will run too slow for the remaining repetitions due to fatigue.

If you run the entire workout at a faster pace than planned, consider:

• Cutting back the amount of rest between repetitions.
• Doing more repetitions.
• Increasing your weekly mileage. Some runners naturally do very good speed workouts but not enough distance training, and therefore don't run as well in distance races. We have had runners in our classes doing rhythm workouts meant to break 40 minutes for the 10 km, but who cannot run under 44 minutes for that distance. Check your weekly mileage. Perhaps you aren't getting enough distance work in your training program.

If you cannot run the workout as fast you planned, consider:

• Not doing as many reps. By reducing the number of reps, you may be able to run the remaining ones at a faster pace.
• Giving yourself more rest between reps. Here, 15 to 30 seconds can make a world of difference.
• Adjusting your workouts for the next session. You may have misjudged your fitness level and picked a

pace you are not ready for yet. Or you may be trying to progress too fast with your workouts.

- That you may need more experience at speed work. Perhaps your marathon time indicates that you should be able to run faster times on a track for your workouts than you can handle. You have been able to "bull" your way to fast race times for longer distance thanks to your endurance. More speed work will improve your times at all distances.

HOW TO INCREASE THE SPEED OF YOUR RHYTHM WORKOUTS

As a competitive racer you will want to run your rhythm workouts faster as you become more fit and attempt to improve your race times. Rather than haphazardly trying to increase the speed, we offer a safe two-step method of progressively increasing the speed of your rhythm workouts.

1. Increase the number of repetitions of your workout. You do this by progressively increasing the number of repetitions for each specific distance that you choose to run. You can use the rhythm workout chart as a guideline for choosing how many repetitions to run, beginning with the minimum number recommended and then progressing towards the maximum. In some cases you may feel that you have to do the suggested maximum number before being ready to move on to a faster pace, while in other cases you may feel that after a few weeks of increasing the number of repetitions, you are ready to increase the speed of your workouts without having reached the maximum number suggested. For example, if you are an advanced competitor and run 10 km races at 6:00 pace, you will run your medium rhythm workouts at that pace. Whether you do 220's, 440's, 880's or miles, you will run them at 6:00-per-mile pace. If you choose to run 440's for a workout, use the 10 km training rhythm workout chart on page 506 to set your

pace. It is suggested that you do 12–16 × 440 at 10 km pace (90 seconds). You would begin by doing 12 × 440 at 90 seconds and, over a period of weeks, progressively work towards the maximum of 16 × 440 at 90. If after reaching 14 reps at 90 seconds you feel strong enough and fast enough to increase your pace, move on to step two. Use the same system as you vary your distance runs.

2. Increase the speed of your rhythm runs slightly (usually one to two seconds per 440 yards of your run), at the same time decreasing the number of repetitions you have been doing for each particular distance. Then proceed in the same manner as in step one. For example, if you have completed 14 × 440 in 90 seconds and now feel ready to increase the speed of your rhythm run, you might try to run the 440's at 88-second pace. However, don't attempt to run 14 of them in this initial workout. That would be too difficult for you, might discourage you and possibly cause injury. Begin by doing 12 × 440 in 88 (the minimum on the chart). If you have trouble finishing the workout, you are probably not yet ready to increase the speed of your rhythm runs, and should go back to a 90-second pace and increase the number of repetitions to 16 before attempting to increase your pace.

This two-step approach allows your body enough time to adjust to a specific rhythm before pushing it to faster speeds. If you constantly push yourself to run at faster speeds with every successive workout, you will find that instead of getting faster you will be putting so much strain and pressure on your body that you will end up going slower.

You must increase your speed in steps to allow your body to adapt to the increased work loads. Be patient, for it will take some time to increase your rhythm pace. In the early training stages, progress may be fairly brisk and you may improve your rhythmic pace four to ten seconds per mile in the first month or two. However, as you become better, you will find that it becomes more difficult to increase the speed of your rhythm runs. And it may take four to six months to increase your per mile pace two to four seconds.

Safety Note: Never increase both the number of repetitions and the speed of the rhythm run at the same time. Changing both quantity and speed will only result in placing a great stress on your body and cause you to run a very poor workout or to injure yourself. You must be prepared to run slower times if confronted with adverse weather conditions.

GENERAL GUIDELINES FOR RUNNING RHYTHM WORKOUTS

Keep the following points in mind:

1. The workout is controlled, with no racing between running partners allowed; work together.

2. The rest interval is important for two reasons: a) it keeps you from running too quickly and b) it is essential to the development of your aerobic and anaerobic systems.

3. Concentrate on maintaining a steady pace and don't worry about the speed of your run.

4. Stop the run as soon as the pace falls off sharply. When this happens, it means that you have misjudged your ability to run at a certain pace and a build-up of lactic acid has occurred. Adjust for your next workout.

5. Finish feeling that you have a little left, are not exhausted. The first, middle and last rep should always be at the same pace.

6. Your last hard session should be 10 to 12 days before a key race; if it's much earlier, you lose benefits; if it's later, you don't recover in time.

7. Jog into the start of your runs. Don't start flat out as if you were in a race. This places too much stress on your legs.

8. Develop a rhythm to the repetition and try to stay with it through your workout, even when it becomes difficult toward the end. Stay relaxed throughout the run. If

you begin to press, slow down rather than "bull" your way through. The idea of the workout is to run rhythmically and evenly within your ability.

9. Keep moving during the rest interval by walking or jogging.

CHARTING YOUR PERSONAL RHYTHM WORKOUT

Instead of juggling variables by trial and error, consult the training rhythm workout charts in the appendix. We have developed them based on our work with thousands of runners at all levels. All you have to do is determine your flexible speed workout ranges and head for the track.

Follow these simple steps:

Step One: *Determine Your Fitness Category*. This is for speed work based on the approximate descriptions in Chapter 1. Follow the guidelines on the rhythm workout charts for your category. These are just guidelines. Some experienced runners blessed with natural speed and doing lower mileage may move up a group. Some experienced high-mileage runners who are inexperienced with speed work or are coming off a layoff may move back a group. Older runners may need to move back a group.

Step Two: *Determine the Distance of Your Rhythm Run*. Is it 220, 440, 880, mile, short hill, long hill?

Step Three: *Determine Your Rhythmic Pace*. Is it slow, medium or fast?

Step Four: *Determine the Quantity of Repetitions*. You have a range to choose from on the charts. Start with the lower range; don't go to the higher ranges until ready. You do not have to attempt the highest range. Generally, you work to the highest range before increasing speed, then you reduce the number of reps to the lowest range, and then build back up.

Step Five: *Determine Your Rest*. We use a fixed rest period, but if you need more, decrease the speed of your run. Determine whether you will walk, jog or do a combination of both for your recovery.

The rhythm workout charts are only approximate, like any guidelines. So, too, are the categories of runners we have described. Be flexible with these charts, and you will find they can help you properly set up a good rhythm speed workout.

Here are some sample workouts, one for each category, to show you how:

SAMPLE RHYTHM WORKOUT: NOVICE COMPETITOR

Aiming for a 10 km, just starting speed work
   (Consult the 10 km training rhythm chart on page 506.)
   The workout—medium rhythm workout: 6 × 440, 10 km pace (9-minute miles), 2-minute walk
   Step One. *Fitness category* is novice competitor. You are running at least 20 miles a week and have run a few races. Your best time was 9 minutes per mile for 10 km. You train at about 9:30 per mile. After you have done some modified *fartlek*, you are ready for some conservative rhythm speed work following the novice competitor's chart.
   Step Two. You will begin with the *shorter distances*, then extend to longer distances in future workouts as you become more experienced with speed work. We select here 440 yards.
   Step Three. You will run *medium-paced* runs at 10 km pace to teach you the feel of race pace. This will be two minutes fifteen seconds per 440 at a nine-minute-per-mile pace.
   Step Four. You will do *six reps*. You find this figure on your chart under 440's at medium pace, and pick the lower range under "quantity," since you are a novice at this type of work. This will be enough to give you a feel for pace work.
   Step Five. You will take a *two-minute recovery or rest period* as recommended on the chart. Since you are a novice, your rest will consist of walking.

SAMPLE RHYTHM WORKOUT: BASIC COMPETITOR

Aiming for a 3:30 marathon

(Consult the marathon training rhythm chart on page 507.)

The workout—medium rhythm workout: 4 × 1 mile, 10 km pace (7:30), 3-minute jog

Step One. *Fitness category* is basic competitor. You are running approximately 50–60 miles a week and have a month to go before the marathon. Your best 10 km is about 30 seconds per mile faster than you think you can run for the marathon (7:30 for 10 km, and you hope to average 8:00 for the marathon). You are experienced at speed work and are sharpening for the marathon. Follow the basic competitor's rhythm workout chart.

Step Two. You select *one-mile runs* to help improve your endurance.

Step Three. You will run them at *medium pace*—approximately your 10 km pace of 7:30 per mile.

Step Four. You will do *four reps*. Since you have never done mile speed sessions before, don't try for five.

Step Five. *Rest* will be three minutes of easy jogging to keep loose, or brisk walking, if you prefer.

SAMPLE RHYTHM WORKOUT: ADVANCED COMPETITOR

Aiming for a six-minute pace for 10 km

(Consult the 10 km training rhythm chart on page 506.)

The workout—fast rhythm workout: 8 × 440, 5 km pace (5:50), 1½-minutes walk/jog

Step One. *Fitness category* is advanced competitor. You are running about 60–80 miles per week and have two weeks to go before a big 10 km race. Your best time is 38 minutes. Your goal is to bring that down to a six-minute pace (37:17).

Step Two. You select *440's* to work on your speed.

Step Three. You decide to do them at your present 5 km race pace—*fast rhythmic pace*—to help bring your speed down. For you, this is about 5:50 per mile, close to the pace you plan to go out at for your 10 km, which will be held in cool weather and on a fast course. This is 1:27.5 per 440.

Step Four. You choose to do *eight reps.*

Step Five. *Rest* will be one and a half minutes, which you will do walking until you cool down somewhat from the fast work, and then you will jog a little.

SAMPLE RHYTHM WORKOUT: CHAMPION COMPETITOR

Aiming for sub-six-minute miles for the marathon
(Consult the marathon training rhythm chart on page 507.)

The workout—medium rhythm workout: 10 × 880, 10 km pace (5:30), 1-minute jog

Step One. *Fitness category* is champion competitor. You are running 80–100 miles per week and have run 5:35 per mile for 10 km and 2:42 for the marathon. Three weeks from now you wish to run under six minutes per mile—2:35—for the marathon.

Step Two. You select *880's* to give you a feel for a strong pace, and to increase endurance.

· **Step Three.** You decide that you will run at *medium pace*—a 10 km pace for the shape you are in now. Thus you do 880's at a 5:25-per-mile pace (2:42.5 per 880).

Step Four. You choose to do *ten reps*, since you are in good shape and want a really strong workout.

Step Five. *Rest* will be a one-minute jog—an easy 110. You will run two laps hard, jog a ⅛ lap, then go around again in constant motion.

8. THE SPEED WORKOUT: POWER-TRAINING RUNS

The power workout—called "repeats" because hard effort is repeated—is run at 90 percent effort with complete recovery. Power work combines strength and speed to achieve stamina. Increased power allows you to run faster more comfortably. Power workouts are run anaerobically (above 85 percent of your maximum heart rate). You run in oxygen debt and make friends with the Bear.

Safety Note: Obviously these intense runs should not be done too often. They are excellent for sharpening for races—especially the 10 km and under. They are *not* recommended for the novice competitor.

Power runs:
• *Develop leg strength*—especially the quadriceps—upper-body strength, and knee lift, resulting in increased leg speed, stride length, ankle flexibility and ratio of fast twitch to slow twitch muscle fibers.
• *Improve raw speed.* They develop your "sprinting

speed" by increasing strength and leg speed and improving movement coordination.

• *Condition you for competition.* These workouts, because of their intensity, closely approximate the stress of racing. Repetition of the intense pace improves your mental and physical toughness for racing. Being forced to run through discomfort brings out the competitor in you, and you realize a potential that you didn't know existed until you were pushed hard.

• *Push back your aerobic-anaerobic borderline and improve your ability to run anaerobically.* Like strength and rhythm speed work, the power workout helps train you to run faster without accumulating lactic acid and being forced to slow down. The power workouts push you much further into oxygen debt than other speed workouts, and thus teach you to run more efficiently, and confidently when The Bear does attack you. The shorter the race, the faster the pace, and the more demand there will be for anaerobic conditioning.

• *Improve your racing technique.* By running very fast, you learn better coordination of your body. This improves your racing form and style and helps you develop your "power gear" to shift into when running up short, steep hills at a fast pace and using a finishing kick. Power workouts, by exaggerating proper biomechanical movements, also make you concentrate on driving the arms and lifting the knees. You learn controlled breathing at an intense pace.

• *Provide a psychological boost during training.* Pete Schuder stimulates his Columbia runners during "down" periods of the training schedule by "popping" short, fast runs.

In addition, power workouts are the best speed runs to do in the heat. The short runs don't drive up your body heat, and the long recovery times allow you to drink plenty of fluids. On the other hand, power runs can be risky in the cold: your muscles aren't as loose, and the hard, fast pace may cause them injury. Rhythm runs might be better in the cold.

HOW TO PLAN YOUR POWER WORKOUT

Planning your power workout requires careful consideration beyond the three variables (quantity, intensity, rest). Power workouts are the most dangerous workouts you will run. Since you run at very fast speeds, consider the following factors:

1. *Your Training Goals.* How much speed do you need to attain your goals?

2. *Your Fitness Level and Experience.* Have you been running long enough—or is your fitness level high enough—to consider power workouts?

3. *Your Environment.* Do you have the right facilities for your workouts? Is the weather too cold?

4. *Your Physical and Psychological Makeup.* Can you physically and mentally do these stressful workouts safely?

Taking the three variables and these four factors into consideration, you can construct your own power workout. First, consider the variables.

Quantity. Select the distance of the runs and the number of repetitions you want to do.

Intensity. Determine the speed you want. It should be 90 percent of your all-out effort over your selected distance. (Consult the 90% Effort Guide on page 509 to estimate the pace.)

Rest. Plan for enough rest to allow you to recover completely, so you can run the next repetition hard again. Rest will most often be a walk rather than a jog.

Let's look at these factors in detail, to help you plan your program.

Quantity

This is distance and repetitions. Power workouts require only a few repetitions. You will be using a lot of strength and speed to run fast. This takes energy, and your body will be able to give you only so much during any single workout. If you plan too many repetitions, you will tire and run slower, and not achieve your goal of running fast.

The number of repetitions you run is limited by your fitness level and the distance run. The longer the distance, the fewer the repetitions. The total mileage completed is much less than for rhythm runs.

Total mileage run may range from half a mile for basic competitors (for example, 4 × 220) to three miles for champion runners (3 × 1 mile). We use five different distances for power workouts:

220's. This distance is used sparingly, and only for training for short races. Concentrate on good form, staying relaxed and running fast.

440's. This is the perfect distance for improving your basic speed. It is long enough to keep you from burning out by running too fast, yet short enough to give you a number of reps before becoming too fatigued.

880's. The half mile is a very good distance to use to maintain a fast pace over a longer distance. We use power 880's to prepare for the 5 km and 10 km races.

Miles. These are excellent power runs for the runner who wants to improve speeds over 5 km and up. Fast miles will condition you to feel at ease when running your normal race pace.

Short Hills. These improve your form and style, leg stride and frequency.

Intensity

This is the speed of your power runs. The purpose of the power workout is to run very close to your all-out effort (90 percent) for a specific distance. You have only one thing in mind during all power workouts: *Run fast!*

Your fitness level and running experience will determine the actual time of your power runs, but they will not affect how close to all-out you want to run. Ninety percent effort is the same effort for everyone, but for some it may be a much faster speed than for others. Speed is a relative measure. Power workouts are not controlled pace work, like rhythm workouts, but fast work at 90 percent of your present conditioning. With increased efficiency due to improved form, increased power, and an increased ability to run with oxygen debt, you will run these workouts—and thus your races—faster.

The speed of your runs is also affected by your environment: weather, running surfaces, injury and illness. Since power workouts require strength along with speed, anything that alters that combination determines how fast you can run that workout.

Rest

Since power workouts are intense runs, you must make a *full recovery* after each repetition. The general rule is to take enough rest to enable you to run the next power run as fast as the last. The rest might be a minimum of 4 minutes for shorter distances (220) to 12 to 15 minutes for the mile. If you do the power run properly, you should take a long recovery period.

Most distance runners do not take enough rest during their power workouts. They feel they are slacking off if they rest more than two minutes. But the power workout is successful only if the recovery period between each run is long enough to let you run the next repetition as fast as you ran the previous one.

The rest may be done by walking or jogging. Just make sure that you are loose and relaxed before your next repetition. Rest for hill runs is complete recovery and a slow return downhill to the start. This may mean walking all the way down the hill or walking half way down and jogging the rest of the way.

- Your goal is a good, fast workout. That requires a long rest period. Do not alter this routine.
- Your fitness level and running experience will determine how much rest you need. If you are not very fit, you'll require a lot of rest between power repetitions; fit runners recover faster.

- The environment will also affect your recovery. In cold weather you recover faster than in hot. Running with others will help you recover mentally.
- If you are not feeling well, mentally or physically, you will need more time to recover. Allow for this.

CONTROLLING THE SPEED OF YOUR POWER WORKOUTS

As you introduce power runs into your training, you face two problems. First, determining the speed at which you run a certain distance. What is 90 percent of your all-out effort for the 220 or 440 if you have never run all-out for those distances? (Refer to the 90% Effort Guide on page 509 for guidance.) Second, when you start running at a fast pace you will find it difficult to maintain good running form. You may temporarily lose the coordination between arms and legs, and thus tighten up and lose your rhythm.

To help you, we suggest that you follow these guidelines as you approach your power workout:

Your first power workout should be at a distance you have run previously at a fast rhythmic pace. At first, select longer distances (880 or a mile), as they will be safer.

Your first repetition of the power run should be at a controlled speed. Run your first rep at slightly less than 90 percent effort. Keep yourself under control, and run just fast enough to feel as though you are running hard, but have something in reserve. This is a good rule for *every* power workout you do. Begin slow, let your body adjust.

After your first rep, attempt to complete each additional run at 90 percent effort. You accomplish two things by following this approach. First, you keep the speed of your run just fast enough to complete the workout without running too fast too soon and risking injury. Second, you will take the required amount of rest, since you want to run the next repetition faster than the previous one.

Sample Workout for a 42-Minute 10 km Runner. Goal: you want to do a power workout of repetitive miles. Your workout may be planned in the following manner:

Power workout: 3 × 880, (90% effort–2:55), 6–10 minutes rest.

You begin with a good warm-up to insure that your body is ready for this intense workout. Then you begin the power workout by running the 880 just below 90 percent effort, but still within your capacity (a time of about 3 minutes). After taking a full recovery, which may last from 6 to 10 minutes, you should be ready for your second 880. This 880 is going to be slightly faster than the first one, but still under control. You should be able to run this in the 2:55 to 2:57 range and still have energy left for the last rep. If you have a great deal of trouble making this second goal, it is an indication that you lack speed work and need to do more of this type of training. After taking another full recovery of about 6 to 10 minutes, you should be ready to take on the final 880-yard repetition. Be sure that you feel you can run another 880 at a fast pace before starting. This final power repetition is the one where you concentrate on your best effort. Don't try to blast or overpower the run. If you go out too fast, you will tire and fall short of your goal. Set a strong, even pace (86–87 seconds per quarter); try to break 2:55 for the final 880. If you stay calm and run the workout smoothly, you may surprise yourself.

As you become accustomed to power workouts, try some of the shorter distances to improve your speed. Begin slowly, take plenty of rest between each power repetition, and try to maintain the speed of each successive repetition.

Don't be disappointed if you cannot maintain a fast pace with each successive rep. If you run each power rep at a very fast pace, you will become more and more tired as you continue. Eventually you cannot run any faster. Keep putting out the effort, however, and try to complete the entire workout as best you can.

Here is another example of a power workout. The planned workout is six 440's in 85 seconds with a five-to-eight-minute rest in between. An *actual* workout may go like this:

1. 440 in 88 seconds, 6-minute jog/walk
2. 440 in 85 seconds, 6-minute jog/walk
3. 440 in 84 seconds, 8-minute walk/jog
4. 440 in 85 seconds, 10-minute walk/jog
5. 440 in 86 seconds, 10-minute walk/jog
6. 440 in 87 seconds

HOW TO INCREASE PROGRESSIVELY THE SPEED OF THE POWER WORKOUTS

The speed you run for your power workouts will always be near your all-out effort. Your progress, therefore, will depend on improvements in your basic speed and fast-paced running experience. These improvements will come slowly. Don't let this discourage you, and don't try to rush your development. There are no shortcuts.

The best way to improve your progress with speed training is to develop consistency in your workouts. If you run a mile workout and your times for 3 × 1 mile are 7:10, 7:15, and then 8:15, you are not consistent with your workout. Your goal is to maintain consistent times over the length of your workout. Once you reach that level of consistency, you can then push onward. For example, suppose you plan to run 3 × 1 mile at 7:10 with a 6- to 10-minute rest. You run the first mile in 7:15, holding back slightly, take a six-minute break and run the second mile in 7:10; take an 8–10 minute break, and run the last mile in 7:08. If you can do this, you are ready to increase the intensity of your workouts. You may now want to set a goal of running at a 7:05 pace. Follow this three-step approach:

Step One. Run your first rep at your previous 90 percent effort pace (a 7:10 mile in this example).

Step Two. Run your next rep at your new goal pace (a 7:05 mile in this example).

Step Three. Try to hold this pace for the remaining reps (7:05 in this example). Become consistent at your newer, faster speed. Develop a *consistent* power workout where each of the repetitions is at a similar speed. Going too fast too soon risks high levels of fatigue and discouragement. It could take weeks to rebuild the lost confidence. The entire process may take a few months or more, so be patient. Give your body time to adapt to the faster speeds.

POWER WORKOUT GUIDELINES

Here are the steps you should take during a power workout:
- Do a thorough warm-up.
- Jog into the run. Never run flat out from a standing start.
- Stay relaxed and loose. Tight running restricts your movement and requires extra energy.
- Take the full recovery; walk and jog easily.
- Stretch during your recovery periods and before doing the next rep.
- Do a good cool-down, but don't overstretch tired muscles. Relax and stretch easily after some light jogging.

> *Safety Note*: If you become tight, feel pain, or do not recover in 15 minutes—stop the workout.

CHARTING YOUR PERSONAL POWER WORKOUT

The variables for power workouts must be carefully balanced. The Power Workout Guide on page 508 will help you set up your power workout program. The wide range in quantity and rest allows you to be flexible in your personal program.

Follow these simple steps:

Step One: Determine Your Fitness Category. Based on the descriptions in Chapter 1. However, these are only guidelines. Some runners may move up or back a group. When in doubt, back off; this workout can be dangerous if you are not prepared for it.

Step Two: Determine the Distance of Your Run. (220, 440, 880, mile, short hills.)

Step Three: Determine Your Power Pace. There is only one speed to select: approximately 90 percent of your all-out effort for your chosen distance. Your body will tell you how much of a work load you can handle.

Step Four: Determine the Quantity of Repetitions. Start with the lower range on the Power Workout Guide, and don't go higher until you can handle more reps. You do not have to attempt to reach the highest range.

Step Five: Determine Your Rest. We give you a range. Start with the upper range and work down as you feel completely recovered following your repetitions. You do not have to reach the lower range. Don't be too concerned with these figures. The key is to take enough rest so that you can run hard. If you need more rest than is called for in the upper range, you should adjust the workout.

Here are some sample power workouts, one for each of the three categories that may use this type of intense work, as examples of how you can set up your own workout:

SAMPLE POWER WORKOUT: EXPERIENCED BASIC COMPETITOR

Aiming for a 5 km
  The workout—power: 2 × 880, 90% effort, 6-minute walk

  Step One. *Fitness category* is basic competitor. You are running approximately 30–50 miles per week.

  Step Two. Select *880's* to sharpen your speed for the race.

  Step Three. Your estimated all-out mile time is 7:00. Consult the 90% Effort Guide on page 509 to estimate your 90 percent effort for 880's. In this instance, it would be *3:25.*

  Step Four. Consult the Power Workout Guide on page 508 to see that you should do *two to three reps*, since you feel that two is all you can handle at this speed.

  Step Five. Choose a *six-minute rest*, since previous workouts indicate you can recover in that time, and you walk for your recovery. Take more rest if you need it.

SAMPLE POWER WORKOUT: EXPERIENCED ADVANCED COMPETITOR

Aiming for a fast 10 km

The workout—power: 3 × 1 mile, 90% effort, 10-minute walk and jog

Step One. *Fitness category* is advanced competitor. You are running 60–70 miles a week.

Step Two. Select *one mile runs* to improve your ability to run very hard and stay relaxed for an extended period of time.

Step Three. Your all-out mile time is 5:00. Consult the 90% Effort Guide on page 509 to estimate your *90 percent effort for the mile.* In this instance it would be *5:30.*

Step Four. Consult the Power Workout Guide on page 508 to see that you should do *two to three reps.* You do three.

Step Five. Choose *10 minutes for rest.* This is plenty of time to recover, since your goal is to run some fast miles so that 10 km pace will feel more relaxed.

SAMPLE POWER WORKOUT: EXPERIENCED CHAMPION COMPETITOR

Aiming for a 10 km

The workout—power: 4 × short hills, 90% effort, 7-minute walk.

Step One. *Fitness category* is champion competitor. You are running about 60–80 miles a week.

Step Two. Select *short hills* because the 10 km includes some good hills and you wish to increase your confidence, strength and form for hills, and the late stages of the race. The hill is about 220 yards long and moderately steep.

Step Three. Run at *90 percent effort,* timing the distance only to be able to compare times for each rep for consistency.

Step Four. Do only *four reps* since the hill is fairly steep.

Step Five. *Rest* will be about *seven minutes.* Walk around at the top, catching your breath, and then walk slowly downhill. Take more rest if you need it.

9. THE TRAINING SCHEDULE

The competitive runner must plan not only every workout, but also his or her complete training schedule leading to a specific racing goal. Mileage and speed work must be balanced and planned to come at the right time and in the right amount. Selecting the proper training runs in correct sequence is essential. We use a simple, flexible program to guide you toward your racing goal.

You begin your race two to six months in advance. You follow the principle of foundation training and sharpening to build up to, and then race, a quality performance. Taking shortcuts cheats yourself: you won't be well prepared, and you will probably race poorly and may injure yourself.

First, pick the race or races you want to run, and then train toward this goal. The runner who trains aimlessly or inconsistently won't reach his or her potential. You must gear your training for a specific event or distance.

Your training schedule consists of two important concepts: training *cycles* and training *phases*. The training cycle is the training for and completion of your racing season—the seasonal approach. The key steps you must take along the way to prepare for your race or racing season are called training phases.

YOUR TRAINING CYCLE

This is your running season, when you may run a few races and must design a plan to do that. There are two opposite approaches to competitive training: the one-race season and the year-round season. We recommend an alternative: the long-term or short-term training cycle.

The one-race season covers a long time period, perhaps a year or more, during which every workout is aimed toward one big race. These runners run low-key during the year, make the sacrifice of less significant race results by not racing fully to potential, and reach a very high peak for that one big race. The runner aiming for the Olympic Games, for example, may use this approach. This training philosophy isn't recommended for the average runner, however, because it offers no rewards along the way.

At the other extreme is the runner who trains to race almost every week. Overracing is hard to avoid today since there is a race within jogging distance of almost every runner each weekend. You must restrain your enthusiasm. Unfortunately, the media and race officials often glamorize runners who do ridiculous things like race 20 miles one day and 10 the next or compete the week after a marathon. This runner isn't tough—just stupid. Runners who enter a race week after week "using it as a training run" are cheating—themselves. They always have an excuse for getting beaten or not running a good time, since they ran a race last week or are just getting ready for the one next week. Whatever your reason for wanting to race often on a year-round basis, we do not recommend it unless you take off at least one full month from serious racing and hard training twice a year.

It is possible to compromise between the extremes of the one-race season and the year-round season. One solution is to build to a high fitness level and race one to two times a month or more. With this system you race year round, peaking for certain races. Without built-in rest periods or off-seasons, however, this runner sometimes is forced by injury or burnout to ease back. Many of America's leading road racers follow this system. If you do, use it cautiously and back off occasionally. Remember that runners usually run faster times and have fewer injuries by alternating easy training and racing periods with more intense training and racing periods.

We use two basic types of training cycles for our schedules: short-term (two to four months) and long-term (four to six months). Within that time period, we break down your training cycle into five-part phases. You do four basic things: prepare for battle; battle; lick your wounds and bask in the glory; and prepare again.

The length of your cycle depends on your goals and how long you have before your races. We feel that novice and basic competitors benefit most from following the short-term cycle so that they can enjoy the fun of competing sooner and gain racing experience. Marathon training, however, requires the long-term cycle for all levels of runners. Rushing for this event is risky.

The advanced and champion competitors with more racing experience benefit from both types of schedules. With the short-term cycle, these runners can sharpen and thus race sooner for shorter races: mile, 5 km, 10 km. With the long-term cycle, these runners can improve racing times and continue racing at a high level for a longer period of time (for a series of races at all distances), or go for a quality marathon effort. The longer cycle enables you to build a stronger, more solid base, which lets you train at higher intensities and faster speeds—which equal faster times.

These cycles can also be alternated. You might use the long-term cycle to prepare for a spring marathon and, after rebuilding, use the short-term cycle for a few shorter races in the fall and winter.

The Short-Term Cycle (2–4 Months)

This cycle is most beneficial if you are preparing for races of 10 km or less. The short-term cycle allows you to race well several times a year, since you may use this cycle as many as three or four times in a racing year. Since the build-up period is less demanding, your rest between cycles is shorter, so you can return to racing sooner. It doesn't require as much time to prepare physically and mentally, which makes it more practical for the average runner. Its disadvantages include not enabling you to hold your peak for a long time (three to four weeks, or two to three races) and not giving sufficient preparation for longer races, particularly the marathon.

The Long-Term Cycle (4–6 Months)

This schedule benefits three types of runners. First, this cycle helps those runners who want to run very fast in a single race of 10 km to a half marathon. It also benefits runners—usually high school or college teams—facing a long racing season of four to eight weeks, with several races leading into one or two championship races. Pete Schuder's Columbia University cross-country team uses a six-month cycle for this reason. Third, the cycle helps the long-distance runner, especially the marathoner, prepare adequately for maximum effort in one or two long races. The disadvantages include the long time period for training, having to plan far in advance (which may conflict with other aspects of your life), and the long build-up and long recovery, which may require sacrificing some of your favorite races during the early building period and the rebuilding phase. You can use this system only once or twice a year.

Bob Glover's Atalanta team basically uses this system, since they are primarily a marathon-oriented team and usually aim for two long racing seasons—spring and fall. Usually they will peak in April for a marathon, and then hold the peak—by rebuilding for two to three weeks and then sharpening for two to three weeks—for six to eight weeks for the Avon International Marathon. Then they back off for one to two months before training seriously again for a fall marathon. This system allows them to race

well from March through May, back off for the hot months
of June, July and August, and race well again for Septem-
ber and October. They then back off for the cold months
of November through February. For example, in 1982 they
used the March 6th Avon 20 km, March 21st Brooklyn half
marathon and April 3d Nike Team Challenge 10 km as
sharpening races going into the April 19th Boston Marathon (four runners placed in the top 25). Then they backed
off for a few weeks and sharpened for a few weeks before
winning the June 6th Avon International Marathon in San
Francisco. After this difficult racing season, they kept away
from serious racing and training for two full months.

Using the long-term schedule, you may choose to race
during your off-season but shouldn't expect to, or attempt
to, race as fast. During this time you cannot expect to run
PR's, and you can expect to get beaten by runners you easily defeated when you were "sharp." Don't be concerned
about this. Because some are usually backing off as others
are peaking, the only fair way to judge who is the best runner is to line them all up for the key races when everyone is
prepared for maximum effort. This is why we prefer the
long-term cycle: we want our athletes to do their best when
it counts the most.

YOUR TRAINING PHASES

Both the short-term and long-term training cycles include
five phases.

Phase I: Endurance. Builds your aerobic foundation with
endurance runs.

Phase II: Strengthening. Prepares for more detailed speed
work with strength-training runs.

Phase III: Sharpening. Prepares you for quality races with
rhythm-, power- and strength-training workouts. Also uses
a few hard workouts and races close to your key race to
reach your best "peak" performance.

Phase IV: Tapering. Cuts back on your mileage and speed
work so you enter a race well rested.

Phase V: *Rebuilding*. Regenerates the body for a few weeks after the racing season.

We suggest blending the phases together in a progressive building toward quality racing followed by quality rest. You will also blend together the four types of runs we have discussed: endurance, strength, rhythm and power. Before blending is detailed, we need to examine each phase, discuss its purpose and how to use it.

Phase I: Endurance (Foundation Training)

This is the longest phase, the most important and the easiest to do. The important thing here is putting in plenty of time on your feet and in your training heart-rate range. This initial phase—essential for *every* runner—conditions your cardiorespiratory system and your muscles to run long distances. Your goal is to put in the miles and build to your planned upper limit of mileage. Safely build your foundation. Your starting fitness level is at least 50 to 75 percent of the mileage you intend to build to during this phase.

Long-, medium- and short-distance runs will improve your aerobic system and comprise all, or at least the majority, of the running done during this phase. Gradually increase the length of your long runs throughout this phase until you reach your goal distance.

During this phase you don't race (except for low-key fun races) or do hard speed work. Don't rush this phase. Cheating on endurance and jumping into early speed work results in running some fast early-season race times but causes you to falter in your races during the late season. The stronger your endurance base, the higher you can aim when sharpening for big races. You can look at the endurance work as filling up your reservoir. Whenever you do hard speed work or race, you withdraw from the reservoir. When you do endurance training and slow rhythm training, you are filling the reservoir. Take out too much from the reservoir, and you will run dry.

You should begin blending a small variety of easy speed runs (strength and rhythm runs) into your endurance phase after you feel fit enough to handle this slightly more intense work. Slow rhythm runs, *fartlek* runs and rolling hills are the easiest type of training runs to include in your schedule, since they are the least intense and easiest to control. Including these speed runs in your endurance phase will help stimulate your body and mind so that you will stay motivated and excited about your training.

Build your base before adding harder speed work. The short-term training cycle requires three to six weeks in the endurance phase. The long-term training cycle requires six to twelve weeks in the endurance phase. The longer this phase, the greater your base of endurance.

Phase II: Strengthening

After building your endurance base, you expand your training program to include strength training. The short-term training cycle will take two to four weeks in this strengthening phase. The long-term cycle will take four to six weeks. You maintain your mileage base and make the transition into speed work so that your body is prepared for the faster speed work ahead. You can strengthen your body to handle the added stress of running longer at a faster pace by including the five types of strength runs. You now do endurance runs, plus one or two strength runs per week. Some medium rhythm runs are also considered strength runs, particularly those workouts done on uphills. These may be included for strength runs during this phase.

You should run one or two races in this phase, but will train through them rather than go for an all-out effort. If you race too soon or too often, however, you will overtrain and peak too early in the season, or never reach a peak. Instead of building strength, the excess racing will take away strength. You may also include a supplemental weight-training program to develop overall strength.

Phase III: Sharpening

The sharpening phase is designed to put it all together—endurance, strength and speed—to produce stamina and faster race times. You sharpen for your racing season, perhaps peak for a key race at the end of your cycle. The inclusion of fast rhythmic training runs and power speed workouts will help you improve your speed. Slow and medium rhythmic runs will teach you racing pace, which enables you to carry your speed for the entire length of the race. The short-term training cycle requires that the sharpening phase last one to three weeks, while the long-term phase covers three to four weeks.

This phase combines strength and rhythm runs one to three times a week, and high mileage (but less than in previous phases) with high quality speed work and racing. You use this phase either to keep racing fit for a long time, or to "sharpen" for a single race or a series of two or three races. This is the phase that some runners who compete at a high level year-round attempt to stay at. These runners can reach "mini-peaks." They just lower the mileage for a week or two and increase the intensity of speed work, and are able to race at near peak performance. This system, however, should only be used by the very fit, and even they should take periodic breaks to rebuild. We suggest you sharpen for a few races and then rebuild.

The sharpening phase adds faster speed work aimed at specific race distances or courses, a series of races designed to help you race yourself into top shape for one or two races at the end of your cycle. As you get closer to your race and increase the intensity of your workouts, don't increase mileage. You should decrease it by some 10 to 15 percent; quality is more important than quantity now. Also, as you approach your key race, go after some PR's in a series of two or three shorter races to add confidence and fitness. Space these races to allow for recovery. You should taper for these races more than you did in previous phases; don't train through these races, but go hard. After adequate recovery from each race, you resume your sharpening phase, except when you finish the last race of your season, when you break and move into your rebuilding phase.

Sharpening isn't used by the first-time racer and first-time marathoner. They don't need the stress of speed work on top of the new high-mileage levels. They move from the endurance-base phase directly into the tapering phase. Novice competitors would sharpen with mostly medium (race pace) rhythm runs—they don't do fast rhythm or power runs. Basic competitors may add faster-paced rhythm runs and perhaps a few power runs for shorter races. The advanced and champion runners sharpen with all levels of speed work—medium and fast-paced rhythm runs and power runs. The intensity of these runs varies with the race you are sharpening for. You would sharpen for the mile with rhythm runs at half-mile pace, for the 10 km and marathon with rhythm runs of 5 km and 10 km pace. Guidelines for sharpening for each racing distance are included in the following chapters. The final sessions of your sharpening period should be very specific—on hills if a critical slope approaches you on the race course, on a track or trail if you're going to race there. Try to do some of your runs, if possible, over key points of the course. That helps you "callous" yourself to handle this section of the race when it hits you.

All experienced competitors should sharpen for key races. To us, the term "peaking" means being very "sharp"—achieving a very high level of fitness—at the end of your sharpening phase.

Phase IV: Tapering

This phase involves backing off your mileage and speed work so you are well rested and ready to race. Tapering always follows your sharpening phase (except for the novice racer and novice marathoner, who taper off the endurance phase). If you race during your build-up stage you will probably not taper but just back off a little the day before a race: you maintain mileage to get the full benefit, and "train through" the race. To race well, you need to be well rested. You can't have it all: high mileage, two or three speed sessions, and a good race—all in one week.

How long you taper depends on the distance of the race, your fitness level and what feels best for you. Generally, the longer the race and the less fit or experienced you are, the more you need to taper. If you taper too much, you may lose a little of your racer's edge. If you taper too little, you may not perform well due to fatigue. With experience, you will learn what is best for you. Here are some guidelines:

For the 5 km–10 km. Novice and basic competitors should cut back their mileage for 3 to 7 days prior to the race and continue short or medium endurance runs. Your last hard speed workout should come 10 to 12 days before you race. You may want to take the day off before the race, and run a short distance the day before that, or vice versa.

Advanced and champion competitors should cut their mileage back for 2 to 5 days before the race and run medium and short endurance runs. Your last hard speed work should be 5 to 7 days before you race. You may take a day off one or 2 days before the race, or do easy runs.

For the Marathon. The novice and basic competitor should cut back mileage gradually by 10 to 20 percent per week for the last two or three weeks. The last long run comes two to three weeks before the marathon, the last medium-distance run 4 to 5 days before. Your last hard speed workouts should be 10 to 14 days before the race, and your last moderate speed work should be 5 to 7 days before. During the last week, do short runs, perhaps alternated with days off. Take off the day before or 2 days before, but not both.

Advanced and champion competitors should cut back their mileage by 10 percent two weeks before the marathon, and another 10 percent at the start of marathon week. Your last long run should be 10 to 14 days before, last hard speed workout 10 to 12 days before, and last moderate speed work 4 to 5 days before. The last medium distance run comes 3 to 4 days before the marathon, followed by short easy runs. Take one day off during the last 2 days before the race.

Examples of tapering programs are included in the training schedules within each specific racing chapter. Here are some key points:

- Get plenty of sleep the last week, especially the second and third nights before the race, which are more important than the night before.
- Try to keep off your feet as much as possible in the last few days going into your race.
- Follow the guidelines in Chapter 28 for eating during the last few days before going into the competition.
- Don't take too many days off. You'll feel sluggish. We prefer a day off two days before racing, not the day before.

Many runners feel uncomfortable about cutting back on their training since they worked so hard to get to this point. They're afraid that if they cut back, they are going to lose it all. Tapering is necessary to allow the body to rest and prepare for the big race ahead. If you don't taper, you usually will not respond well in racing situations. Remember—it takes two weeks for the training effect to occur, so any work you do in that time period before a race may help you mentally, but could hurt you physically.

Phase V: Rebuilding

Rebuilding consists of two parts. The rest period required after each race is termed "recovery." The longer rest period required after your racing cycle is completed is termed "rebuilding."

Recovery

The postrace recovery takes anywhere from a few days to several weeks. The less fit you are and the longer the race, the longer the recovery period. Before the race even starts, you should have begun your recovery program. By racing only when you are fit enough for the distance, pacing yourself wisely and going into the race with flexible muscles and a proper diet, you will minimize the tearing down process that is part of racing. Fluids taken during the race will also aid your recovery. Older runners and those nursing injuries will require more time to recover. Runners racing in heat and over hills will too.

Here is a postrace recovery procedure:

• Keep moving when you finish the race. Don't lie down or sit down. After leaving the chute, drink fluids, put on warm-ups, walk. For races shorter than a half marathon, try a little jogging (1–4 miles.)

• As soon as possible, take a long, hot bath. Do some gentle stretching. Drink plenty of fluids and eat carbohydrates after a marathon to replenish lost energy resources.

• Later in the day, go for an easy run, swim, bike ride or walk to aid recovery. Take another bath and do more gentle stretching. Try dancing—believe it or not, it will make an incredible difference the next day. Ask any of the women who danced into the wee hours after the 1981 Avon International Marathon in Ottawa. If you just lie around and don't exercise after a race, your legs will feel like concrete. Force yourself to do the unnatural—exercise when your body doesn't want to.

• Start the next morning with another bath—your third! Do more gentle stretching and take a walk or easy run. You may be better off forgetting about running for a few days after a marathon. Stick to nonweight-bearing exercise such as swimming or biking. The object is to recover by forcing blood into the legs to remove waste products, so why abuse the body by compelling it to run on blistered feet and tired legs? After races shorter than a marathon, or after a marathon if you feel up to it, do some light jogging the next day.

• Get plenty of sleep for several days after your big race, and do lots of gentle stretching anywhere and any time you can.

• Beware of a "false high" you may get a few days after a big race. Hold back on your training.

• Gradually increase your mileage back to your normal comfortable level. Recovery is your priority for two to three days after a 5 km, up to a week after a 10 km–half marathon, and for two weeks or more after the marathon. By the third week after the marathon, you may be able to run your normal mileage. Don't rush it. You can usually return to normal mileage within three to five days after a 5 km, three to seven days after a 10 km–half marathon, and three to five weeks after a marathon. Take it easy.

• Experienced runners find that *easy* speed work (slow rhythm) a few days after a race of half-marathon or shorter distance helps them recover faster.

The recovery from races of half marathon or less comes, it seems, almost naturally. You listen to your body and ease back into the running and speed work. But recovery from a marathon or longer takes a long time and deserves as much planning as your premarathon schedule. Besides recovering from muscle soreness, you need time to restore your body chemistry to its normal balance. This takes a longer time than you can feel the need for, so you must force yourself to hold back.

Race Spacing

How long should you wait before racing again? Our advice is:

• Never race 5 km races more than two or three weekends in a row (one or two for novice and basic competitors).

• Never race 10 km races more than two weekends in a row. Novice and basic competitors should skip at least a week.

• For races of 15 km to a half marathon, skip at least two weeks before racing that distance again. Novice and basic competitors should wait at least three weeks.

- For marathons, wait at least four to eight weeks. Novice and basic competitors should wait two to six months before marathoning again.

Here are flexible guidelines for determining when you can race again at any distance after completing a race:

RACE DISTANCE	MINIMUM WEEKS OF TRAINING BEFORE RACING AGAIN FOR NOVICE AND BASIC COMPETITORS	MINIMUM WEEKS OF TRAINING BEFORE RACING AGAIN FOR ADVANCED AND CHAMPION COMPETITORS
5 km	1–2 weeks	1 week
10 km	2–3 weeks	1–2 weeks
Half marathon	3–4 weeks	2–3 weeks
Marathon	6–8 weeks	4–6 weeks

Rebuilding

After your racing season or peak race, you need a break in your training schedule. This marks the end of your seasonal cycle. You need time off to relax and to allow your mind and body to recover from the intense training and racing season. Sometimes after running your big race, you get "the blues" syndrome, when you don't feel like running any more because of the effort to train and race. Your long-sought-after goal has been achieved. The rebuilding phase then becomes a necessary vehicle to get you going again.

Rebuilding from the hard training discipline may include some easy running or one of the aerobic alternatives discussed in Chapter 26. This stage should consist of easy runs, and should lead into Phase I (Endurance) when your training cycle begins again. Your mileage base should be cut back, but not by more than 25 to 50 percent of your maximum mileage base. If you cut by more, you will need to take much longer to build your base for the next cycle.

For the short-term cycle, we suggest that your rebuilding phase take *at least* three to four weeks. For the long-term cycle, we believe *at least* four to eight weeks are needed. *Our basic rule: all runners should take at least two breaks from hard training and racing each year; each break should last a month or more.*

The following charts summarize how the five phases fit into the short-term and long-term training cycles. First-time racers and marathoners skip Phases II and III since they need to concentrate on building their endurance base.

THE SHORT-TERM (2–4 MONTH) TRAINING CYCLE— FIVE-PHASE TRAINING SCHEDULE (FOR LESS THAN MARATHON DISTANCE/SHORT SEASON)

PHASE	EXPERIENCED COMPETITOR (WEEKS)	NOVICE RACER (WEEKS)
I. Endurance	3–6	6–12
II. Strengthening	2–4	x
III. Sharpening	1–3	x
IV. Tapering	1–2	1
V. Rebuilding	3–4	3–4

Note: The two-to-four-month (8–16-week) cycle goes from the beginning of Phase I to the completion of your hard race or races. Then you enter the rebuilding phase (V), after which you may wish to start over again with Phase I or just maintain a good level of fitness and not race again for a while.

THE LONG-TERM (4–6 MONTH) TRAINING CYCLE— FIVE-PHASE TRAINING SCHEDULE (LONG RACING SEASON OR MARATHON BUILD-UP)

PHASE	EXPERIENCED COMPETITOR (WEEKS)	NOVICE MARATHONER (WEEKS)
I. Endurance	6–12	16–24
II. Strengthening	4–6	x
III. Sharpening	3–4	x
IV. Tapering	1–3	2
V. Rebuilding	4–8	4–8

Note: The four-to-six-month (16–24-week) cycle goes from the beginning of Phase I to the completion of your long racing season or marathon. Then you enter the rebuilding phase (V), after which you may wish to start over again with Phase I or just maintain a good level of fitness and not race again for a while.

BLENDING THE PHASES OF YOUR TRAINING SCHEDULE

You can choose to incorporate the five phases into your training schedule in two ways: The Single-Phase Build-up Method and the Blending Phase Method.

The Single-Phase Build-up Method

This is the system favored by some elite runners. We do not recommend it for the average runner. With this method you concentrate on finishing one complete phase at a time before "stepping up" to the next phase. For example, you would begin your training cycle by doing as much foundation training—the endurance phase—as suggested in our charts or longer. During this phase you do only endurance runs. Then you proceed with the strengthening phase. Here you would concentrate on doing only strength-training runs—mostly hills—alternated with endurance runs for recovery. After completing this phase, you would move into the sharpening phase, which includes doing several rhythm and power workouts. From there, you taper for the race. We do not recommend this method for the average runner, since suddenly changing from one phase to another promotes injury. For the elite runner, however, it does allow for a thorough build-up for a key race and is normally done over a long-term training cycle.

The Blending Method

This is our preferred method. You begin with endurance training, introducing easy speed runs (an occasional strength run or slow rhythm run) to allow your body to adapt gradually to harder workouts. You emphasize the endurance runs as the major part of training during this phase, as you continue to increase your mileage base to a peak level.

When you become more fit, stronger and slightly faster,

you blend in more difficult strength and medium rhythm runs as you move into the strengthening phase. During this phase, your weekly mileage base will level off and you begin to concentrate on making improvements in your strength and speed by increasing the intensity and quantity of speed work.

The blending process continues during the strengthening phase as you begin to introduce faster speed workouts. Initially you may increase the speed of your *fartlek* runs so that your "bursts" or "pickups" become faster than race pace, and then include one or two fast rhythm workouts to further blend in speed before moving on to the sharpening phase.

During the sharpening phase, you blend in all types of speed runs—strength, medium rhythm, fast rhythm and power—done at high intensity in a final effort to "peak" for your key race. Still, most of your runs are endurance runs, used for recovery and maintaining your aerobic fitness level, although you will want to cut back on the weekly mileage levels slightly.

Blending lets you adapt to progressive stress. It allows your mind and body gradually to grow accustomed to more intense training. Blending allows you to continue building your endurance, strength and speed throughout your training cycle. This system adds variety to your program, since you aren't running the same type of workout every week. Finally, blending makes you better prepared to "gear up" for races because you can modify your training program faster.

Using these guidelines, plan your short- or long-term schedule, and stick with it. The next chapter will teach you how to write that schedule.

10. HOW TO WRITE YOUR OWN TRAINING SCHEDULE

We can't list a detailed training schedule for each and every runner who reads this book—and we shouldn't. You have to plan and write your own schedule, because only you know which goals you want to pursue, what your training needs are, and how much training you can tolerate. We have included model training programs for each category of runner at the end of each specific racing distance chapter. These models were developed from the guidelines below. Your schedule must remain flexible enough, however, so that when warning signs of fatigue or injury appear, you can back off. That would be the action a personal coach would take. You can't just follow blindly either a training schedule you put together months ago or the model programs we have developed for you.

By now you should have acquired a sound understanding of how to use the various types of runs and why they are used with the five phases that make up your training cycle. Now it is your turn to do the writing. Whether you decide to use a short-term or a long-term training cycle for a 5 km race or a marathon, you can begin putting together your own training schedule following a six-step approach.

THE SIX STEPS TO WRITE YOUR OWN TRAINING SCHEDULE

Step One: Determine Your Fitness Category

In order to develop the best training program to fit your needs, you must first decide which of the four fitness categories you will use as your flexible guide for determining how much mileage you will run and the specific speed work you will do. Refer to Chapter 1.

Step Two: Select Your Races and Time Goals

Choose the particular race or set of races for which you wish to train. Your choice should be far enough in the future to fit into your short-term or long-term training cycle. If you decide to train for the marathon, be sure that this race is four to six months away so that you will have time to follow the long-term cycle. Consider doing one or two early-season races to ease you back into racing and to measure your fitness. Choose two or three races to help you sharpen for the final, key race of your training cycle. These races should be spaced far enough apart to allow time for recovery and to increase the intensity of your speed work. Your selection of the "big race" should be made carefully. Some may choose a national, regional or local championship. Others may favor a "celebrity race" that attracts big-name runners. Many choose the fastest course around and usually in the cooler months of the year so that they can aim for a very fast time. The race should be important enough to you that you will want to "sharpen" for this particular event.

Mark the date of your selected race or set of races on your training calendar and plan your training schedule so that you gradually build toward these dates. Using our Three-Goal System (Chapter 19), set race time goals to help you establish your training goals. *Note*: Although you aim for your best time at the end of the cycle, factors such as bad weather, injury, hills may interfere. You may run your best race earlier, during your sharpening phase, if conditions are most favorable at this time. The model schedules at the end of each racing distance chapter include examples of race distances and which week to run them. These are only guidelines. Pick the date and distance of your build-up races according to your needs and the racing distances available.

Step Three: Determine Your Training Cycle and Phases

Using the previous chapter as a guide, determine the length of the training cycle—short-term or long-term—that you will follow and how much time you will need to spend with each training phase: endurance, strengthening, sharpening and tapering.

Step Four: Determine Your Weekly Mileage and Long-Run Goals

Using the guidelines in Chapter 3, determine your weekly mileage and long-run goals for your entire cycle. Make sure you can tolerate this level of mileage. If it is a big increase, you may need a longer period of time to build up to this new level. Take that into consideration when selecting the length and date of your races. Gradually increase the weekly mileage over the entire endurance phase until you reach your desired level. This mileage base is maintained throughout the strength phase and then is cut back when more intense sharpening work is included in the training schedule. Cut back your mileage and speed work for a few days going into and after your build-up races. The mileage is cut back further as you taper the last one to two weeks before your key race. The length of your long runs also gradually increases as you become more fit.

Step Five: Plan Your Individual Workouts

Use the following Guide for Scheduling Your Training Runs to decide when to schedule the 30 basic types of training runs. When scheduling far in advance, you must

GUIDE FOR SCHEDULING YOUR TRAINING RUNS: 30 WORKOUTS TO CHOOSE FROM IN WRITING YOUR INDIVIDUAL TRAINING SCHEDULE

	WHEN USED	WHY USED	CATEGORIES OF RUNNERS
ENDURANCE RUNS:	Year-round, 4–7 times per week	Build aerobic endurance, foundation for speed work and racing	All
1. Short	Year-round, 1–3 times per week	Easy days, recovering and tapering	All
2. Medium	Year-round, 3–5 times per week	Major source of foundation mileage	All
3. Long	Mainly in endurance and strength phases. Especially important when marathon training. Approximately 1–3 times per month	Build aerobic endurance and mental toughness	All
STRENGTH RUNS:	In preparation for racing season—used in all phases, but emphasized in strengthening phase; 1–2 times per week	Build muscular strength and speed	All
4. Modified *fartlek*	Used in all phases; 1–3 times per month	Introduction to speed work, for a moderate strength run	Novice and Basic
5. Rolling hills run	Late in endurance phase, throughout strength phase. Used for training for all distances, especially when training for a hilly race; about every other week	Build general strength, confidence over hills	Experienced Basic, all Advanced and Champion
6. Fast continuous runs	Strength and sharpening phases, especially for 10 km–marathon training, twice a month or less	Build ability to hold a fast pace, used as pace work for marathon training	Experienced Basic, all Advanced and Champion

155

GUIDE FOR SCHEDULING YOUR TRAINING RUNS
(Continued)

	WHEN USED	WHY USED	CATEGORIES OF RUNNERS
7. Advanced *fartlek*	Used during all phases and for all distances. Particularly important for cross-country training; about once a week	Improve ability to switch gears, running form, confidence on hills	All Advanced and Champion
8. Tempo	Late in strength phase and early in sharpening phase. Mainly used for one mile–10 km; 1 or 2 times during entire training season	Simulate racing conditions	Experienced Advanced and Champion
SLOW RHYTHM RUNS: (Slower than race pace)	Endurance and early strength phases; sharpening and tapering phases for marathon training; for recovery from races; once per week	Build aerobic endurance; transition into speed work; to teach race pace for marathon training	All
9. 220's	All phases for one mile–5 km; once or twice during season	Introduction to faster rhythm workouts	All
10. 440's	All phases for all distances, especially one mile–5 km; used a few times during season	General aerobic conditioning; teach race pace for novice and basic marathoners	All
11. 880's	All phases for all distances, especially 10 km–marathon; used a few times during season	General aerobic conditioning; teach race pace for all marathoners	All
12. Miles	All phases for all distances, especially 10 km–marathon; used a few times during season	General aerobic conditioning; teach race pace for all marathoners	All
13. Short hills	Late endurance phase, early strengthening; for all distances; 1 or 2 times per season	Introduction to hill training, to teach proper form	All

MEDIUM RHYTHM RUNS: (Race pace)			
14. 220's	Late endurance, strengthening, sharpening and tapering phases; 1–2 times per week	Develop racing pace, build strength and speed	All
15. 440's	Late endurance, strengthening and sharpening phases; for mile–5 km; 2 or 3 times per season	Introduction to race pace work, improve ability to recover quickly	All
16. 880's	Late endurance, strengthening, sharpening and tapering phases; for all distances, especially 5 km–10 km; several times per season	Develop sense of race pace, improve racing form	All
17. Miles	Same as 440's; particularly good as last hard workout 10–12 days prior to a key 5 km–4-mile race	Same as 440's	All
18. Short hills	Late endurance, strengthening, sharpening and tapering phases; for all distances, especially 10 km–marathon; particularly good as last hard workout 10–12 days prior to a key 10 km–marathon race; several times per season.	Simulate racing conditions, build confidence, teach ability to hold pace when tired	All
19. Long hills	Strengthening, sharpening phases; for all distances, especially when building for races on hills; several times per season	Improve ability to hold race pace and form on hills, build strength, speed and confidence	All
	Strengthening, early sharpening phases; used for specific training for hilly courses, especially 10 km–marathon	Simulate race conditions over hills, build confidence	All

GUIDE FOR SCHEDULING YOUR TRAINING RUNS
(Continued)

	WHEN USED	WHY USED	CATEGORIES OF RUNNERS
FAST RHYTHM RUNS: (faster than race pace)	Late strength, sharpening and tapering phases; when peaking for key races; several times per season for 10 km and under, few times for race training above 10 km	Improve speed, race pace, and form; transition into power workouts	Experienced Basic, all Advanced and Champion
20. 220's	Primarily used in sharpening phase; mostly for mile–5 km; 1 or 2 times per season	Introduction to fast rhythm work	Experienced Basic, all Advanced and Champion
21. 440's	Late strength, sharpening and tapering phases; all distances, especially mile–10 km; few times per season	Make race pace seem more comfortable, improve speed	Experienced Basic, all Advanced and Champion
22. 880's	Same as 440's	Same as 440's	Experienced Basic, all Advanced and Champion
23. Miles	Late strength, sharpening phases; mostly for 10 km–marathon; 1 or 2 times per season	Build strength, teach ability to hold space and form under stress	All Advanced and Champion
24. Short hills	Sharpening phase; mostly for mile–10 km; 1 or 2 times per season	Build strength and speed; improve form for fast paces	Experienced Advanced and Champion
25. Long hills	Late strength phase; mostly for 10 km–marathon; no more than once per season	Build confidence	Experienced Advanced and Champion

POWER RUNS: (90% of all-out effort)		
	Use cautiously in late strength and sharpening phases; when peaking for key races; used few times	Build speed and confidence; improve ability to run in oxygen debt
26. 220's	Sharpening phase; mostly mile–5 km	Improve leg speed	Experienced Basic; all Advanced and Champion
27. 440's	Late strength and sharpening phases; mostly mile–10 km	Improve race pace	Experienced Advanced and Champion
28. 880's	Late strength and sharpening phases; mostly mile–10 km	Same as 440's, good introduction to power workouts	Experienced Basic, all Advanced and Champion
29. Miles	Late strength and sharpening phases; mostly 5 km–marathon	Simulate racing conditions, build confidence	Experienced Basic, all Advanced and Champion
30. Short hills	Late strength phase; mostly mile–5 km	Improve ability to power up hills in races	Experienced Basic, all Advanced and Champion Experienced Champion

be flexible and realize that it is impossible to run the exact workout and mileage each day of the week as you had planned. But by writing down a plan, you will be motivated to stay reasonably close to your predetermined schedule. Analyze the schedule periodically and make modifications as necessary for such factors as injury, illness and bad weather. It is important that you have faith in your carefully planned schedule and stick to it as closely as possible. Estimate the specific mileage you wish to run each day, balancing long runs, races, speed work and easy days. Determine the general type of speed work you need to accomplish each week. Use the rhythm and power guides in the appendix to establish the quantity and intensity of these runs. Determine the exact number of repetitions and specific speed of each run a few days before your workout so that you can make adjustments according to how your training has been progressing.

Step Six: Plan Your Rebuilding Phase

Rebuilding is recovering from the entire cycle. Although this three-to-eight-week period following your key race may seem to be anticlimactic, it is essential. Plan this phase in advance, and don't cut it short by rushing back into hard training.

We do not include examples of rebuilding in our model training schedules in the following chapters, since the training should consist entirely of short and medium endurance runs. Following is an example of a four-week rebuilding phase:

WEEK #	MON.	TUE.	WED.	THU.
1	Short Endurance	Off	Short Endurance	Short Endurance
2	Off	Short Endurance	Medium Endurance	Short Endurance
3	Off	Short Endurance	Medium Endurance	Short Endurance
4	Off	Short Endurance	Medium Endurance	Short Endurance

The purpose of the rebuilding phase is to rest and regenerate after a hard training cycle and gradually build up to a conservative level (about 50–75 percent of your peak base) of mileage. The example below shows a runner rebuilding to a level of 30–35 miles a week—about 60–70 percent of his or her peak mileage of 50 miles per week. There should be no long runs, speed workouts or races included in the schedule during this phase. At the end of this rebuilding phase this runner can continue to maintain basic fitness by running 30–40 miles a week of endurance runs only, or may choose to start a new training cycle by building the mileage back up and adding some easy speed work and long runs during the endurance phase.

WRITE YOUR SCHEDULE

Use the blank training schedule on page 163 to write your individual training program. (Step numbers are keyed on the schedule.)

1. *Write in your fitness category* where indicated.

2. *Write in the races* you wish to run building to a key race (in this example races are indicated for weeks 5, 9 and 12). List race time goals and record actual race times on the Goal Setting/Race Selection Sheet on page 164.

3. *Write in the number of weeks of your training cycle.* This schedule is for 12 weeks—a short-term cycle. For a long-term cycle you may use an 18-week schedule. *Write in how many weeks you will spend in each phase.* In this example: endurance—4 weeks; strengthening—4 weeks; sharpening—3 weeks, tapering—1 week.

FRI.	SAT.	SUN.	TOTAL
Short Endurance	Off	Short Endurance	20 miles
Medium Endurance	Short Endurance	Medium Endurance	30
Medium Endurance	Short Endurance	Medium Endurance	30
Medium Endurance	Medium Endurance	Medium Endurance	35

4. *Write in your goals for weekly mileage* from the beginning of your cycle through your last race. *Write in your goals for long runs* and when you plan to run them. In this example, we have included 4 long runs—weeks 2, 4, 6 and 8).

5. *Write in the specific type of run* (consult the Guide for Scheduling Training Runs) *and your daily mileage for the entire cycle.* You have listed your races and your long runs; the next step is to write in your speed workouts. Then balance the hard days—races, long runs and speed workouts—by writing in the easy days—short and medium endurance runs and off days. In this example, we have demonstrated how to write in each of the three major types of speed runs—strength, rhythm and power—as well as an endurance run. When recording a speed run, list both the distance of the speed run and the total mileage for the day, which includes your warm-up and cool-down. (Example for week 9: 10 × 440 is 2½ miles of running, and with warm-up and cool-down, the total mileage for the workout is 6 miles.) Fill in all of the speed days first, then the endurance days to complete your schedule.

6. *Write your rebuilding schedule.*

SAMPLE TRAINING SCHEDULE

Fitness Category: ①

PHASE/WEEK		MONDAY	TUESDAY	WEDNESDAY	THURSDAY	FRIDAY	SATURDAY	SUNDAY	TOTAL MILEAGE
Endurance	1			⑤ Short Endurance ④					30 ④ →
	2							④ Long Endurance ⑩	34 ④
	3								36 ④
	4							④ Long Endurance ⑩	38 ④
Strengthening	5			⑤ Strength ⑥ Rolling Hills ④				② Race	38 ④
	6								42 ④
	7								40 ④
	8							④ Long Endurance ⑩	40 ④
Sharpening	9		⑤ Medium ⑥ Rhythm 12 x 440					② Race ⑩	37 ④
	10								35 ④
	11		⑤ Power ⑥ 4 x 440						30 ④
Tapering	12							② Final Race	20 + Race ④

Note: For this sample schedule weeks 13—16 would be the rebuilding phase.

GOAL SETTING/RACE SELECTION FOR A RACING SEASON

PREDICTION

DISTANCE	ACCEPTABLE GOAL	CHALLENGING GOAL	ULTIMATE GOAL
5 km	23:00	22:30	22:00
10 km	47:00	46:00	45:00

ACTUAL

RACE DISTANCE	DATE	ACTUAL TIME
5 km	9/8	22:40
10 km	10/16	46:05
10 km	11/16	45:30

Part II
SPECIFIC
TRAINING

11. YOUR FIRST RACE

Why race?

• It gives your running life a goal, a focus. You circle the race date on your running calendar and train for that day. This helps you get "over the hump" that some runners face who are having trouble moving through dull periods of their training.

• You make friends. Races give you the opportunity to meet other runners. It is often a large social gathering, a party in running shorts. You may meet potential running partners, or even runners who become close friends. You can exchange training tips and experiences. Also, training for a race gives you a great topic of conversation with other runners.

• You can test yourself. Racing gives you a method of measuring your progress toward some specific goal. Finishing a race is a great achievement: you have set a goal and accomplished it; you may also get satisfaction from doing something physical, especially if you have not been successful in athletics in the past. At this early racing level, your competition is entirely against the "old you." Racing lets you discover the new you.

• You aim toward running a marathon. Your first race—

which is *not* the marathon—is a stepping stone along the path toward running the "ultimate challenge." You must start with shorter races.

Some runners don't want to race. They dislike the competition. They run for the pleasure of it. Nina Kuscsik, the first women's division winner of the Boston Marathon, doesn't think of racing as competition but as running with other people "to show off what you can do."

The era of the "fun run" and the "fun racer" is upon us. Now more runners enter races to achieve higher personal goals and to meet friends and see some new countryside. In tougher competitive races, there are a few top-level runners, and a mass of back-of-the-packers to keep even the slowest runner company. The first and foremost goal for all of them is the finish line.

SELECTING YOUR FIRST RACE

Pick a race. The distance should be long enough to challenge you but short enough to be completed without pain. We recommend a distance between two miles and 10 km (6.2 miles). Choose a local race; traveling to an event adds to your excitement and stress. Pick either a low-key "fun run" or a big mass-participation event filled with fellow runners of every level of training. Keep away from races with killer hills, and don't race on a hot day. In other words, minimize your obstacles. Women may prefer women-only races.

TRAINING FOR YOUR FIRST RACE

If you are now running for 20–30 minutes at a time, three to five times a week or more, you are ready to train for your first race. Do not concern yourself yet with speed work or the various phases of training used by more experienced runners. You should concentrate on building up your endurance base to the point where you can run and finish a race comfortably, tapering off as you approach that race date.

You need a minimum amount of mileage and long runs to be able to race and reach the finish line with reasonable comfort. Our basic guidelines are: your weekly mileage should be at least two or three times the distance of the race, and you should be running this mileage six to eight weeks prior to the race itself. You should also complete three longer runs, covering at least two-thirds of the race distance, prior to the week before the race. Never try to cram mileage in during the last few weeks before a race. Build gradually. For example, if you plan to run a four-mile race, you should be running at least 8 to 12 miles a week, with long runs of at least 3 or 4 miles. For a 10 km (6.2 miles), you should be running 12 to 18 miles a week, with minimum long runs in the 4-to-6-mile range.

Remember the hard-easy system. Alternate your three types of conversational endurance runs—long, short, medium. Run up and down a few hills if the race route includes them. A few days before your first race, take it easy. No amount of additional training now will help you.

Use the following charts as models for your first race. We prefer that you race 5 km–4 miles before your first 10 km, but many runners race first at the 10 km distance since it is a more popular and frequently run race.

EIGHT-WEEK TRAINING PROGRAM FOR YOUR FIRST RACE (5 km–4 MILES)

WEEK	MON.	TUES.	WED.	THURS.	FRI.	SAT.	SUN.	TOTAL MILEAGE
1	Off	2	2	2	Off	2	Off	8
2	Off	2	2	2	Off	2	2	10
3	Off	2	2	2	Off	2	2	10
4	Off	2	3	2	Off	2	3	12
5	Off	2	3	2	Off	2	3	12
6	Off	2	3	2	Off	2	3	12
7	Off	2	3	2	Off	2	3	12
8	Off	2	2	2	Off	2	Race (5 km–4 miles)	8 + race

EIGHT-WEEK TRAINING PROGRAM FOR YOUR FIRST RACE (10 km)

WEEK	MON.	TUES.	WED.	THURS.	FRI.	SAT.	SUN.	TOTAL MILEAGE
1	Off	2	3	3	Off	2	4	14
2	Off	2	3	3	Off	2	4	14
3	Off	3	3	3	Off	2	5	16
4	Off	3	4	3	Off	3	5	18
5	Off	3	4	4	Off	3	4	18
6	Off	3	4	3	Off	3	5	18
7	Off	3	4	3	Off	2	4	16
8	Off	4	2	2	Off	2	Race (10 km)	10 + race

TIPS FOR YOUR FIRST RACE

Goal

Finish. Experience your first race, don't race it. Your first race should be slightly longer or slightly faster than your usual jog. *Run* your first race. Later you can *race*.

Shoes

Wear your faithful, well-cushioned, well-broken-in training shoes. You don't need a fancy new pair just for the race.

Organize Yourself

Get enough sleep the night before your first race. Pack, and check, all your needed "goodies." Arrive early and warm up properly. This may include a little light jogging along the first 100–200 yards of the race course.

Don't Overdress or Underdress

Beginner racers usually wear too much clothing. You should start feeling slightly underdressed. Your body will heat up during the race, and even clothing that was comfortable for training runs may now feel too heavy. If the weather is cool, try dressing in layers. You can remove a hat, gloves, even a sweatshirt. Tuck them into your shorts or hand them to a friend along the road. Don't discard clothing unless the day is truly warm; a drop in temperature, a sudden wind, rain or snow, and you'll want it all back. Take layers off progressively until you find the right level. In the heat, cover your body with light, loose, reflective clothing.

Eating

On race day, don't eat or drink anything out of the ordinary. This is not the time to experiment. (Save that for your training days.) Do not eat within several hours of the race. Carbohydrate loading is only for experienced racers and long racing distances.

Put on Your Number

Put your number on long before the race starts, to get the feel of it. Some are on stiff paper that may jab your chest or stomach. Adjust it now, not during the race. Remember, you are only doing a training run with a number on. Relax.

Fear Not

Afraid of finishing last? That's unlikely if you are well prepared and follow these guidelines. Some runners will start too fast and struggle in last, or attempt to run the distance without proper mileage "in the bank" beforehand.

Gain confidence by planning your race strategy in advance; break the course into small sections, and know where key landmarks and hills are located. Run from mile marker to mile marker. Be confident in knowing you have prepared well and properly. Everyone is nervous before a race, even elite runners.

Starting Pace

Stand toward the back so you won't get caught in the opening sprint. Begin slowly, and if you feel good after a while, pick up your pace toward the end. Another approach is to start slowly and let as many runners get ahead of you as possible. (If you start too fast, they'll pass you later anyway.) Then, as you feel good toward the end of the race, pick up your pace and pass some of them; you're the tortoise passing the hares who went out too fast. This gives you confidence and the excitement of passing runner after runner over the last mile or two of the race.

Drink

Pour the fluids into you and over you. In warm weather, drink fluids even for a two-mile run. You should be used to drinking from your training runs.

Walk

Nowhere on the race application does it say you can't walk. Take walk breaks, especially on those tough hills, but keep moving. Never stop, unless you are hurt, and run the whole way if you can. But if your pulse soars, or you can't "catch" your breath and run at conversation pace, or your legs tire, take brisk walk breaks. Cheat: since you should drink water at the stations and pour it on yourself, walk with your cup of water as you slowly drink it. Everyone will think you are only walking so you can drink! Avoid walking across the finish line; take your walk break earlier, and jog across smiling.

Run with a Partner

Run your first race with a friend, to help each other along. Make a promise not to race each other but to finish together, no matter what. If an experienced runner volunteers to run with you, make him or her promise to go at your pace.

Don't Be Competitive

You aren't out there to beat people. Your goal is to finish. Don't race against anyone who passes you or whom you pass—you'll lose your sense of an even pace. Chat with the runners around you, wave to your fans, laugh, have fun. This is a fun race for you, not a serious race as it is for those up ahead. Try to run the race as slowly as you can—that way you'll be sure to set a personal record (PR) in your next race.

No Finishing Sprint

Don't be a hot dog and finish the race with a face-twisting, arm-whirling mad sprint. It's stupid and dangerous. Finish with good form; pick up the pace a little. Be in control.

Warm-Up and Cool-Down

Stretch thoroughly both before and after your race, just as you do for your workouts. Don't sit down right away after finishing. Walk around and then stretch.

Smile

Remember to smile as you cross the finish line. Look at the clock for your time. Congratulations! You are now an experienced racer!

Analyze the Results

Now that you have won *your* race, think it over. What went well? What problems did you have, and why? What worked and what didn't in terms of equipment, starting pace, water, finish and so forth? Do you need more work on hills? Did you drink enough fluids? Use the experience as background to help you prepare and run your next race. Reevaluate your training program, and select a new racing goal. Make it either farther or faster, but not both—not yet. Don't race too soon or too often.

You may choose to improve your time for that distance race or to increase your race distance. You may want to move from four miles to the popular 10 km (6.2 miles), and later to 10 miles, the half marathon and then the marathon. Take these races, as you take your training, step by step. However, you don't have to keep racing longer and longer distances, and if you aren't properly prepared for them, you shouldn't.

Recover

After the race, take it easy the next few days with less and slower running. Even though you will not be racing hard, you will still be under a lot of stress from the excitement and exertion of your first race. Recover carefully.

Don't be in a hurry to make the transition from beginner runner to a more serious racer. The "too much too soon" syndrome will leave you injured or frustrated or both. It can take from three to five years to progress safely from jogger to veteran marathon runner. The following schedule is a guideline to help you progress from your first race to faster racing times. You are now on the mileage and racing treadmill. It, and you, keep going. You constantly set new goals, and you surprise yourself when you see how far you've come. In this instance, do look back. You'll be pleased. Remember, you can level off any time. You can back down a step or more. You can progress at a slower pace. From our experience, we feel that this progression will take you safely to whatever level you seek.

THE RACER'S PROGRESSION—FROM BEGINNER RUNNER TO SERIOUS COMPETITOR

PHASE I: STARTING OUT

1. Beginner runner—build to 30 minutes | 3 mo.
2. Intermediate runner—build to and maintain 15–20 miles a week | 3–6 mo.
3. Beginner racer—build to *run* first race (5 km–10 km)—an experience | 3 mo.

9 mo.–1 yr. *85*

PHASE II: RACING FEVER/MARATHON FEVER

4. Novice competitor—more exposure to races at distances up to half marathon—learn to *race* and improve times | 6 mo.–1 yr.
5. Novice marathoner—build up to *run* a marathon—an experience | 6 mo.

1–1½ yr. *86*

PHASE III: GETTING BETTER

6. Basic competitor—train to improve race times 5 km–half marathon | 6 mo.–1 yr.
7. Veteran marathoner—train to *race* a marathon | 6 mo.

1–1½ yr. *87*

PHASE IV: GETTING SERIOUS

8. Basic competitor, advanced competitor and champion competitor—train to improve times for 5 km–half marathon in order to have the speed to improve times for the longer distances. The cycle now repeats itself if you choose to race both long and short. Improvements in speed and short race times will help improve longer race times. Improvements in endurance and stamina from marathon training will also help you to improve your times for shorter races.

12. YOUR FIRST MARATHON

"Marathon mania" has swept not only the USA but the world as the symbol and the glamour event of the road-racing boom. The standard marathon event of 26.2 miles (42.195 kilometers) is run through the streets of almost every major city in the United States, and the world. It has become a vacation attraction offered by travel agents in such exciting spots as San Francisco, Honolulu, New York, London, Rome, Berlin, Paris, Montreal, Madrid, Stockholm, Rio de Janeiro, Athens, and even Peking and Moscow. What a way to see a city—by running a marathon through its streets!

The marathon is the longest and most difficult race for most runners. It symbolizes the peak of physical and mental performance. Once you finish a marathon, you are a real runner. According to Richard Traum, "Anyone who honestly takes the time to train can finish a marathon. You don't have to be much of an athlete, just patient and disciplined. You have to put in the time." Traum has completed four marathons with an artificial leg. Linda Down, a cerebral palsy victim, completed the 1982 New York Marathon in eleven hours on crutches. And you're never too old to run your first marathon. Eighty-year-old Ruth Rothfarb made her marathon debut at the 1981 Avon International Marathon in Ottawa, becoming the oldest female (so far) to complete the distance. The youthful octogenarian then danced into the wee hours of the morning to celebrate.

PICKING YOUR FIRST MARATHON

Don't choose a hot one, a hilly one, or a race that won't include a lot of novices like you. If possible, choose one near your home. Your only goal in this first race is to finish.

TRAINING FOR YOUR FIRST MARATHON

Before training for your first marathon, you must have one or, preferably, two years of running logged in your diary and must have run several races of varying lengths. If you have been running 20 miles a week for the last several months, you may be ready to begin your build-up to the marathon.

You need a minimum amount of mileage and long runs to reach the marathon finish line in comfort. The key here is balance. You don't need speed work or the training phases mentioned earlier. Your only phases will be to build up your endurance base so you can finish the race and to taper your training before the race. Balance the right amount of weekly mileage, the right amount and frequency of long runs. You must be willing to put in the time and not take shortcuts. Also, you must avoid the temptation to overtrain. If you train too little, you won't make it to the finish line. If you train too much, you won't make it to the starting line. The percentage of marathon starters who cross the finish line is much higher than the percentage of runners who start marathon training and make it to the starting line. Follow our minimum and maximum training guidelines for surviving both marathon training and the marathon itself.

Mileage

Move gradually from a base of 20–30 miles a week to 40–50 miles a week, and hold there for *at least* eight weeks before tapering for the marathon. We prefer 50 to 55 miles a week, but no more than 60 miles a week unless you are an experienced racer in the advanced or champion competitor category. Taper your miles for at least two weeks going into the marathon.

Long Runs

From a base of long runs of between 6 and 10 miles run *each* week, build gradually to *at least* two or three runs of 16 to 18 miles within the eight weeks before your marathon. This is a minimum. We prefer three or four runs of 18 to 20 miles each during those eight weeks, but no longer than 20 miles or three-and-a-half hours, whichever comes first. Then no long runs beyond 15 miles for the two weeks before the marathon, or beyond eight miles one week before the race.

The First-Time Marathon Four-Month Training Schedule (from a 25-mile-a-week base)

Thousands of runners have completed their first marathons following the three basic schedules we use. The following four-month training program is our minimum schedule for those runners training for their first marathon.

THE FIRST-TIME MARATHON FOUR-MONTH TRAINING SCHEDULE (FROM A 25-MILE-A-WEEK BASE)

WEEK	MONDAY	TUESDAY	WEDNESDAY	THURSDAY	FRIDAY	SATURDAY	SUNDAY	TOTAL MILEAGE
1	Off	4	4	4	4	3	6	25
2	Off	4	5	4	4	3	8	28
3	Off	4	5	4	5	2	10	30
4	Off	4	6	4	5	4	10	33
5	Off	4	6	5	6	4	12	37
6	Off	4	6	4	5	4	14	37
7	Off	4	6	4	6	4	16	40
8	Off	4	10	4	6	4	12	40
9	Off	4	8	4	4	2	18	40
10	Off	6	8	4	6	4	14	42
11	Off	4	8	4	6	3	20	45
12	Off	4	10	4	8	5	14	45
13	Off	4	10	4	6	3	18	45
14	Off	4	6	6	6	4	14	40
15	Off	4	8	5	4	10	4	35
16 (Race Week)	Off	4	6	4	Off	2	Race Day Marathon	16 + Race

Note: When you race you may need to adjust your daily and weekly mileage downward. Do not attempt to combine long runs and races on the same day or weekend.

The First-Time Marathon Six-Month Training Schedule (from a 20-mile-a-week base)

Ideally, you should plan six months ahead of your marathon. This obviously allows you more time to prepare for the race, and also gives you a deeper endurance base as well as flexibility in case of lost training time due to illness, injury or travel. A busy schedule mandates a long-term plan.

The program on page 181 takes exactly half a year—26 weeks of preparation: one week for every mile of the marathon. It is basically the same as the four-month plan, but is our preferred training schedule and builds to a base of 50 miles per week.

The First-Time Marathon Three-Month Training Schedule (from a 40-mile-a-week base)

This will work—and not be a disaster—*only* if you have a solid base of endurance: *at least* one or two months at 35 to 40 miles a week. This foundation will allow you to build for the marathon within three months. *This is not a shortcut for the novice competitor.* It is often used for your second marathon after following our longer schedule for your first marathon.

From our base of 40 miles a week, start with Week 15* of the 26-week schedule on the following page and count down toward the marathon.

THE FIRST-TIME MARATHON SIX-MONTH TRAINING SCHEDULE (FROM A 20-MILE-A-WEEK BASE)

WEEK	MONDAY	TUESDAY	WEDNESDAY	THURSDAY	FRIDAY	SATURDAY	SUNDAY	TOTAL MILEAGE
1	Off	3	4	3	4	2	4	20
2	Off	3	4	3	4	3	5	22
3	Off	4	4	3	4	3	6	24
4	Off	4	5	3	4	3	7	26
5	Off	4	5	3	5	3	8	28
6	Off	4	6	3	5	4	8	30
7	Off	4	6	3	5	4	10	32
8	Off	4	6	4	6	4	10	34
9	Off	4	6	4	6	4	12	36
10	Off	4	8	4	6	4	12	38
11	Off	5	8	5	6	4	12	40
12	Off	5	8	5	6	4	12	40
13	Off	5	7	5	5	3	15	40
14	Off	5	8	5	6	4	12	40
*15	Off	5	8	5	5	5	15	42
16	Off	5	5	10	5	5	12	42
17	Off	6	8	6	6	4	15	45
18	Off	6	6	10	6	5	12	45
19	Off	6	8	6	6	4	18	48
20	Off	6	6	12	6	6	12	48
21	Off	6	8	6	6	4	20	50
22	Off	6	6	12	8	6	12	50
23	Off	6	8	6	8	Off	20	45
24	Off	4	4	8	4	5	15	40
25	Off	5	5	12	Off	5	8	35
26	Off	4	6	4	Off	2	Race Day Marathon	16 + Race

Note: When you race you may need to adjust your daily and weekly mileage downward. Do not attempt to combine long runs and races on the same day or weekend.

TIPS FOR YOUR FIRST MARATHON

Training

• Check with your *physician* before beginning the stressful training for a marathon.

• Find a *partner* or two who are training for the same marathon; run together, and if possible, run the marathon together.

• Train for two to four weeks in the same trusty *shoes* you'll run the marathon in. *Not* racing flats. If you travel to the race by plane, do not check your shoes, but carry them on board with you. Shoes that are well broken in are the marathoner's most cherished possession.

• Determine your *schedule*, and plan each day to marathon day.

• *Progress gradually* in both mileage and long runs. Long runs build confidence; don't neglect them. Also, one run a day is plenty; no two-a-days yet.

• Take *one day off* a week, sometimes two. If you feel tired or get injured, take another day off, or more.

• *Adjust your training* for lost days. You can gradually make up lost time. Be sure to return slowly, however. "Listen to your body," and avoid injury. If your schedule fatigues you or you become injured, back off. You must push through to a small degree, but if you continue to run through fatigue or injury you will do more harm than good. *Return slowly* and gradually take shortcuts to get back into your schedule. You might repeat the week you were out or take two to four weeks to catch up. Don't panic. A long-term schedule will allow you to miss even a few weeks and still make it to the finish line. You may decide to just stay two weeks behind the schedule—this will be adequate. If you miss a month or more, however, seriously consider skipping this marathon.

• *Stretch* before and after each workout.

• *Respect the heat.* Slow down in hot weather. Cut back your mileage or long run if the heat becomes a burden. Drink lots of fluids, try to run in the morning or evening.

• *Respect the cold.* Wear layers and vent excess heat while you run. Don't toss away gloves or hat too soon. A change in wind direction will make you regret it. Tuck them in your shorts, tie your Windbreaker around your waist.

• *Respect the changes in your life*, such as family, work, diet, a new companion or baby, falling in or out of love. Be flexible in your training—but also be consistent.

• *Respect the long run*. It is very important, but requires several days from which to recover.

• Practice *drinking fluids* on your long runs, to find the fluid best for you (we recommend water), and see how your stomach likes it.

• *Practice walking* during your long runs to get the feel of starting again. You don't need to run the whole 26.2 miles on race day.

• *"Train, don't strain."*

• *Keep a detailed diary*, recording every aspect of your training, including diet, shoes, clothing, weather and time of day, unusual stresses, and so forth.

• *Race occasionally.* This is a good way to prevent yourself from starting too fast on race day and blowing all your training. A few races—increasing the distance from 10 km to the half marathon or 30 km—will give you confidence and a long run. Race at least once a month in the last three months prior to your marathon.

• Get more *sleep* as your mileage increases, and *eat moderately, reducing excess weight* without following any crash diet which will be an added stress.

• *Tapering is very important.* Last-minute training will do harm, not good. We actually know of a runner who, three days before his first marathon, ran 26.2 miles indoors on a track to see if he could cover the distance. He could—three days early; but not on race day.

Prerace

• *Eat* carbohydrates during the last three to four days before, but *don't deplete. Don't stuff yourself* with unfamiliar foods before long runs and races.

• Get to the race early with your *equipment and number* (if you've already picked it up).

• *Don't overdress or underdress*. Peel during the race. Hint: it is better to start out a little cool than just right or too hot.

• Apply Vaseline or foot powder to your feet to *prevent blisters*. You should try this for your training runs. Apply Vaseline around your *crotch and inner thighs* to minimize chafing. Cover your *nipples* with Vaseline or a Band-Aid to prevent rubbing. In cold wind, Vaseline on your *face* will protect your skin.

• *Avoid the premarathon hoopla*. Don't spend hours on your feet walking around to prerace clinics, exhibits, and so forth. Don't get caught up in all the excitement and drain away energy.

• Two days or the day before, *go for a short, easy jog*. Take the other day off.

• Don't avoid *sex* the day or night before the marathon. You'll be more relaxed and sleep better. Do avoid staying up all night looking for it.

• *Wake up* at least three hours before starting time if the marathon starts in the morning. If you insist on eating, eat light and at least three hours before the race.

• *Stay off your feet* as much as possible before the race.

• *Warm up*, stretch, walk, jog across the starting line and out a few hundred yards to get the"feel" of the course. Use the *toilet* one last time.

• *Drink* fluids 10–15 minutes prior to the start.

• Your *goal*: finishing in comfort. A 12-minute-a-mile jog is a five-hour marathon. The first-time marathoner often runs between four and five hours; many finish slower than that. But remember—the slower you finish, the easier it will be to improve your time.

• *Fear not*. You won't finish last, and someone will still be at the finish line when you get there. The Honolulu Marathon prides itself on the fact that the last-place finisher comes in over eight hours.

The Race

• *Drink* plenty of fluids. On a hot day, drink *water* and pour it over yourself.

• Slow down your starting *pace* on a *hot day* by as much as one minute a mile.

• *Start* at the back of the pack. Run very *slowly*, well within your ability and training. (30 seconds to a minute slower than your normal 10-mile training pace).

• Concentrate on maintaining *good form*. Use a short, economical stride, bringing the knees up just enough so you can keep your legs moving. Use the heel-ball footstrike and shuffle stride.

• If you are *injured* (limping, in pain) or feeling *ill*—perhaps from the heat—walk. If the symptoms remain or increase, go to an aid station. *Leave the race.* You are not a hero for continuing, but a fool. People have pulled muscles, broken bones, and died during marathons. Be sensible.

• *Walk* during the race if you feel tired or if you cramp. In the heat, your legs may feel like cement pillars after 15 miles. Just keep moving briskly; alternate running and walking if need be, but don't sit down no matter how strong the urge.

• No one ever said it was going to be easy. You have to have *fortitude*. If you have trained properly and do not feel ill or are not hampered by an injury, then you should finish as long as you can handle it mentally. Dig down deep for extra strength and keep going. Friends and spectators offer encouragement. This is why you can go those extra six miles beyond your 20-mile training run—you have the support of all the runners around you and all the spectators along the course. If you can, find a group to run with during the race to help each other along through periods of weakness. Everyone feels like quitting many times. You are not alone. Keep moving, take it one step at a time, one mile marker at a time, and *smile* when you cross the finish line. You're a marathoner!

Postrace

• *Stretch and walk* after you finish. *Do not sit down.* Drink fluids continuously. Follow our guidelines for eating and drinking after racing.

• Take a *hot bath* as soon as you can, or take a whirlpool

or easy swim. *Walk. Stretch* gently. Repeat the following morning.

• Treat all *blisters* and other *ailments* promptly and properly.

• *Return* gradually to *running.* Don't train or race hard for *at least* four to eight weeks. *Recover, rebuild.*

• *Analyze your results.* Your first comment will be "Never again!" Within a few hours you will probably be saying to your nonmarathon friends, "If I had only. . . ." You will now understand that with a few longer runs, a month or two more of endurance training, some speed work here and there, and an extra helping of spaghetti, you might have lowered your time by 15 minutes. (Okay, so you lie a little.)

• During this recovery period, create *a new marathon training schedule* following our guidelines in Chapter 14.

• *Plan well, train intelligently, race wisely.*

SOME CONCLUDING WORDS

You don't ever have to run a marathon. Don't ever let anyone push you into something you don't want to do. The lure of this popular event creates a lot of peer pressure. Desire is the only emotion that will get you through your training and to the finish line. Some runners never race; some love the 10 km races or the half marathons. Find your desire and follow it.

Also, if you've entered the marathon but your training is not up to the minimum, don't go. Instead, start training for the next marathon. Treat the marathon with respect. Better to postpone than to fail.

Finally, don't take racing, or marathon running, too seriously. Rumor has it that there is life after running. There is even life after—or without—marathoning. But there is also nothing like that feeling when you cross the finish line of your first marathon. Head up, legs tired but still churning, arms pumping, you hug the runner in front of you in the chute. You congratulate each other. You smile, you laugh, you cry. And—damn!—you know you are *good*!

13. THE 10 KM– HALF MARATHON

The most popular and frequently run distance race in America is not the marathon. The marathon attracts more publicity, but each year more runners compete at the 10 km distance. The Pepsi Challenge 10 km series alone consists of more than 150 races across America. The 10 km is raced on the track (where it is the longest standard Olympic distance) and on the roads. It is a race long enough to attract big fields, but unlike the marathon, it can be raced frequently after short recovery periods. It doesn't require as much mileage or time commitment as the marathon and is much less stressful.

Many runners specialize at this distance. They may lack the raw speed to excell at 5 km or lack endurance and the ability to handle the high mileage needed for quality marathons. Some runners are psychologically better suited for the 10 km than the marathon: they can maintain concentration and confidence for 10 km but are too impatient to hold back and run an even marathon pace. Your personality may dictate that you stick to the 10 km range. This is our recommended upper limit for racing among teenage runners; heavier but not overweight runners often can't excel beyond this distance.

The 10 km is a good challenge of endurance for the novice competitor, and it is used for "speed workouts" by marathon specialists. In fact, we believe that the secret to running faster marathons is to train like a 10 km runner and improve times over this distance before concentrating on your next marathon effort. Most runners should train to race the 10 km and then add specific training modifications when gearing up for shorter or longer events. The 10 km combines speed with endurance; that is, the speed of the 5 km with the endurance of the marathon. The average runner can safely enjoy the full range of road racing if he concentrates most of the time on the 10 km. For this reason, our 10 km training program appears first here, and is the core of our training philosophy.

This 10 km training program is designed for all four fitness categories and uses the six-step approach outlined in Chapter 10. With minor adjustments, the 10 km runner can compete successfully at distances of 15 km, 10 mile, and half marathon. To train for these distances, increase the weekly mileage and long runs by at least 10 percent.

STEP ONE: DETERMINE YOUR FITNESS CATEGORY

STEP TWO: SELECT YOUR RACES AND TIME GOALS

Plan your build-up races strategically. Choose time barriers to break for your key races. Common 10 km time barriers include 60:00; 50:00 (8:00 mile); 46:30 (7:30 mile); 43:00 (7:00 mile); 40:00; 37:00 (6:00 mile); 35:00; 31:00 (5:00 mile); and 30:00.

STEP THREE: DETERMINE YOUR TRAINING CYCLE AND THE LENGTH OF YOUR PHASES

Most competitors find the 12-week, short-term cycle to be sufficient for the 10 km. Determine the length of your training phases by deciding on which areas you need to concentrate the most. If you have a solid endurance and strength background but have done little speed training, you may need to spend more time on the sharpening phase. If you have not spent enough time on endurance and strength, you may need to concentrate on developing a solid base of endurance and strength, and spend less time sharpening with speed work. To be successful at the 10 km distance, you will need to develop a well-balanced training program incorporating endurance, strength and speed.

Here is a guide to selecting your phases for 10 km training:

DESCRIPTION	NOVICE	BASIC	ADVANCED	CHAMPION
Length of build-up	12 weeks	12	12	12
Endurance phase	5 weeks	4	4	4
Strengthening phase	4 weeks	4	4	4
Sharpening phase	2 weeks	3	3	3
Tapering phase	1 week	1	1	1
Rebuilding phase	4–6 weeks	3–6	3–4	3–4
Number of races in cycle	3–4	3–4	3–5	3–5

STEP FOUR: DETERMINE YOUR WEEKLY MILEAGE AND LONG-RUN GOALS

Since you will be adding speed workouts to your schedule, your body must be strong enough to handle this extra work load. Training for the 10 km requires that you have a good mileage base. Long runs, often neglected by the 10 km runner, need to be included during the endurance and strength phases. In most cases, don't include long runs during the sharpening and tapering phase of your schedule. They make you feel flat and slow and take away energy that will be needed to handle the more intense speed work.

Follow the *flexible* weekly mileage goals listed in the chart on page 191 to adjust for the amount of *time* spent training and your age and running experience. The mileage ranges reflect an *approximately* equal effort for all levels and all ages of runners. The recommended mileage figures should be averaged for at least six weeks prior to tapering for the 10 km.

Endurance Training Pace for the 10 km. Most 10 km competitors should run medium endurance runs at *approximately* 1½ minutes per mile *slower* than their *present* 10 km race pace. They may run slightly faster than these guidelines suggest for short endurance runs and slightly slower for long endurance runs.

Note: As you become more fit, your training pace naturally becomes faster. Slow your training pace to adjust for heat, cold, hills, fatigue, major increases in mileage and other factors. Pace will also be slower when recovering and rebuilding from races than during your strengthening and sharpening phases.

STEP FIVE: PLAN YOUR INDIVIDUAL WORKOUTS (*See model schedules at the end of this chapter*)

Novice Competitor

(This runner has experienced one or more 10 km races and now wishes to improve his or her time by adding speed work.)

Endurance Phase (5 weeks): 1 speed workout per week after 2–3 weeks of endurance runs only; 1–2 long runs during phase; 1–2 low-key races at 5 km–5 mile distances. The primary concern for this runner should be to build a solid base of mileage. As you become more fit, it becomes important to begin gradually to blend in some speed work along with your endurance training. In our model we introduce speed training with a modified *fartlek* run during the third week of endurance training. This workout gives you the feel of running faster without being too demand-

WEEKLY MILEAGE GOALS FOR 10 KM TRAINING

	AGE 18–40	AGE 40–50	AGE 50–60	AGE 60+	MILEAGE OF LONG RUNS	LONG RUNS PER MONTH
NOVICE:						
Men and Women	20–30	20–30	20–30	20–30	6–10	1–2
BASIC:						
Men and Women	30–55	30–45	30–40	25–35	8–12	1–2
ADVANCED:						
Men	50–75	45–65	50–60	40–50	10–18	2–3
Women	45–65	40–60	35–55	35–45	10–18	2–3
CHAMPION:						
Men	70–90	60–80	50–70	40–60	15–20	2–3
Women	60–80	50–70	40–60	30–50	15–20	2–3

ing. If you were to jump directly into a track workout after doing only endurance runs on the road, you might overtax your body. The next step is then to gradually blend slow rhythm runs into your training program during the last 1–2 weeks of the endurance phase. Start with the minimum number of repetitions listed on the rhythm guide chart in the appendix for the distance that you select. Your schedule should also include a race early in the season to give you both an idea of what shape you are in and more experience at racing. A 5 km or 4 mile race would serve this purpose but should not be an all-out effort, since you are not yet strong enough to race a 10 km.

Strengthening Phase (4 weeks): 1 speed workout per week; 2 long runs during phase; 1–2 races up to 10 km. Continue to blend in modified *fartlek* runs, slightly increasing the speed of the spurts and cutting back on the rest to improve your strength. Introduce medium rhythm runs (10 km pace) to simulate race pace conditions, increase speed and build confidence that you can handle such a pace for your race. During this time maintain your mileage level. If the training becomes too difficult for you to keep your mileage up, you must back off from the speed training, doing less and at a slower intensity. If you feel very strong and can handle the increased work load, introduce slow rhythm hill repetitions to help you with your hill running and to help you develop the ability to sustain your effort in the latter stages of your 10 km race. Your first 10 km race should be run during this phase, after you have completed a number of medium rhythm runs. This race should not be an all-out effort, but you should attempt to test yourself. Don't be surprised if you attain a PR.

Sharpening Phase (2 weeks): 1–2 speed workouts per week; no long runs, usually no races this close to the final race of the season. During the sharpening phase you may wish to introduce a second weekly speed workout to further improve your speed for the upcoming race. Maintain your weekly mileage at previous levels so that the 10 km doesn't seem too long for you. A solid rhythm workout at

10 km pace done 8–10 days prior to your final 10 km race will help you feel confident about running at the right pace and being able to race well.

Tapering Phase (1 week): no long runs; one race—10 km. The last speed workout should take place five to six days prior to the 10 km and should be a conservative workout. We suggest a modified *fartlek* run, using the pickups to give you one last feel of race pace. The last week of training should be low-key and relaxed. The short and medium endurance runs need to be easy, and two days off are recommended so that your body will be well rested for a good race-day effort.

Basic Competitor

Endurance Phase (4 weeks): 1 speed workout per week after 2 weeks of endurance runs; 2–3 long runs and 0–1 race during phase. Build a solid mileage base with endurance and slow rhythm runs. The initial slow rhythm workout should be included no later than the third week. They are introduced at this time to prepare you for the more intense strength training you will want to pursue during the next phase. You may substitute a modified *fartlek* workout during Week 3, if you have had little experience with speed training.

Strengthening Phase (4 weeks): 1–2 speed workouts per week; 1–2 long runs and 1–2 races at less than 10 km distance during phase. Build strength by initially increasing the intensity of your rhythm workouts to 10 km race pace (medium rhythm runs) and including rolling hills strength runs. As you become stronger and have adjusted to the work load, include a second speed workout per week (when not racing on the weekend) to increase your work load further. The 5 km race during the first week of strength training is used to estimate your fitness level, give you racing experience, and serve as a hard workout. Do not alter your training for this race. Maintain your base mileage throughout this phase.

Sharpening Phase (3 weeks): 1–2 speed workouts per

week; no long runs; 1–2 races. Use the 10 km race as a measure of your training and a guide to preparing for your final big race. It may be run during the first or second week of this phase. Fast rhythm workouts should be used to increase your speed, enabling you to race faster. Reduce your weekly mileage and work load as you increase the intensity of your speed runs.

Tapering Phase (1 week): 1 speed workout; no long runs; 1 race—10 km. Your final speed workout is done five to six days prior to your key race and should be run at race pace but at a reduced number of repetitions. This is not the time to test yourself to see if you are ready for a good race; if you do, you may leave your race on the practice track. Reduce your mileage for the week as you take proper rest for the race.

Advanced Competitor

Endurance Phase (4 weeks): 1–2 speed workouts per week; 2–3 long runs and 1 race during phase. Blend in low-key speed workouts in the early stages of your endurance phase to quicken the rhythm of your training runs and to improve your form and style. Select longer distances (880's and miles) to improve your aerobic fitness level as well. Strength runs (rolling hills and advanced *fartlek*) serve as an excellent introduction to the strength phase. A 10 km race early in the season is necessary to prepare you mentally and physically for the more important races near the end of your training cycle.

Strengthening Phase (4 weeks): 1–2 speed workouts per week; 1–2 long runs and 1–2 races during phase. Include advanced strength runs, medium-paced rhythm runs (880's, miles, short and long hills) and if possible, a race at a longer distance than 10 km. In our model we used a 10 mile race for overdistance work. Speed work should be included twice a week, except for the week following a race, to include enough resistance work to build strength. During the final week of this phase introduce a fast-paced rhythm workout to prepare your body for the sharpening phase.

Sharpening Phase (3 weeks): 1–2 speed workouts; no long runs; 1 race during phase. Improve your racing speed during this phase by increasing the speed of your medium rhythm runs toward goal race pace and using fast rhythm and power runs. Reduce weekly mileage. A 10 km race will prepare you for your final 10 km. This race should be a strong effort and must be analyzed carefully so that you can make minor changes in your workouts prior to your key race. Four or five one-mile rhythm runs at race pace 9–12 days prior to your 10 km can be used as a final hard workout.

Tapering Phase (1 week): 1 speed workout; no long runs; 1 race—10 km. One final rhythm workout four or five days prior to the race run at 10 km pace and at a reduced number of repetitions will prepare you for your race without tiring you out. Reduce mileage to rest for your key race.

Champion Competitor

Endurance Phase (4 weeks): 1–2 speed workouts; 2–3 long runs and 1 race during phase. A combination of slow rhythm and strength runs each week will help you maintain a good sense of rhythm while building a solid base of mileage. An early season race at a longer distance (15 km–half marathon) is used to test your endurance. You shouldn't expect a PR for this overdistance race. Run a strong, controlled race.

Strengthening Phase (4 weeks): 2 speed workouts per week; 1–2 long runs and 1–2 races during phase. Include two or three speed workouts (all types of medium rhythm runs, including hills, and advanced strength runs) per week to build strength and speed. A race during this phase should be included, and run fairly hard to test your mental toughness and strength. All of your speed workouts during this phase are geared towards improving your ability to maintain a fast pace over long distances.

Sharpening Phase (3 weeks): 1–2 speed workouts; no long runs; 1 race during phase. Fast, intense speed workouts are necessary at this time to help you improve your 10 km race pace. Increase the speed of your medium rhythm runs toward goal race pace, and add fast rhythm runs, advanced *fartlek*, and one or two power runs to help improve your speed and prepare you mentally for competition. Decrease your mileage. Race a hard 10 km during this phase to record a good performance and practice your racing strategy. A workout of five or six one-mile medium rhythm runs 9–12 days prior to the race is recommended as a final hard workout at race pace.

Tapering Phase (1 week): 1 speed workout; no long runs; 1 race—10 km. One final speed workout four or five days prior to your key race at 10 km pace is used to give you a psychological lift. The distance you run is short (440 yards) and the number of repetitions is kept low so that you do not overtrain during this final stage of your preparation. Reduce mileage to rest for your key race.

STEP SIX: PLAN YOUR REBUILDING PHASE

12-WEEK 10 KM BUILD-UP SCHEDULES

The model training schedules on pages 197–200 should be used to help you write your own program. The exact mileage you will run, distance and dates of your build-up races, and the days of your different types of runs will vary with your individual needs, age, sex and other factors that influence your running. Use these models as a guide to create a specific training program that can help you reach your racing goals. Understand the concepts behind these schedules, don't just follow them blindly. We have not included an example of the rebuilding phase. Follow the model in Chapter 10 to write your rebuilding program.

to beach
Beach to Booknot
Brookhurst
.5 .5 .5
2 miles 2 miles

NOVICE COMPETITOR'S 12-WEEK 10KM BUILD-UP SCHEDULE

PHASE	WEEK	MONDAY	TUESDAY	WEDNESDAY	THURSDAY	FRIDAY	SATURDAY	SUNDAY	TOTAL MILEAGE
ENDURANCE	1	Off (1)	Medium endurance (4)	Medium endurance (4)	Medium endurance (4)	Off (1)	Short endurance (2)	Medium endurance (4)	18
	2	Off (1)	Medium endurance (4)	Medium endurance (5)	Medium endurance (4)	Off (1)	Short endurance (2)	Medium endurance (5)	20
	3	Off (1)	Strength Modified fartlek 3 (4)	Short endurance (4)	Medium endurance (4)	Off (1)	Short endurance (3)	Long endurance (6)	20
	4	Off (1)	Slow rhythm 6 x 440 (4)	Short endurance (4)	Medium endurance (5)	Short endurance (2)	Short endurance (3)	Medium endurance (5)	22
	5	Short endurance (2)	Slow rhythm 4 x 880 (4)	Medium endurance (4)	Medium endurance (4)	Short endurance (3)	Off (—)	Race 5 Km (5)	22
STRENGTHENING	6	Short endurance (2)	Off (—)	Medium endurance (5)	Strength Modified fartlek 3 (5)	Short endurance (3)	Short endurance (3)	Long endurance (8)	25
	7	Off (1)	Medium endurance (5)	Medium endurance (4)	Medium rhythm 5 x Short hills (4)	Short endurance (4)	Medium endurance (2)	Medium endurance (6)	25
	8	Short endurance (3)	Medium rhythm 4 x 880 (4)	Short endurance (3)	Medium endurance (5)	Short endurance (3)	Off (—)	Race 10 Km (7)	25
	9	Short endurance (2)	Off (—)	Medium endurance (4)	Short endurance (3)	Strength Modified fartlek 3 (5)	Short endurance (3)	Long endurance (8)	25
SHARPENING	10	Off (1)	Strength Modified fartlek 3 (5)	Short endurance (3)	Medium endurance (5)	Medium rhythm 6 x Short hills (4)	Short endurance (3)	Medium endurance (5)	25
	11	Off (1)	Medium rhythm 6 x 880 (5)	Short endurance (3)	Medium endurance (4)	Short endurance (3)	Medium endurance (4)	Medium endurance (4)	23
TAPERING	12	Off (1)	Strength Modified fartlek 3 (5)	Short endurance (3)	Medium endurance (4)	Short endurance (3)	Off (3)	Race 10 Km (—)	15 + race

BASIC COMPETITOR'S 12-WEEK 10KM BUILD-UP SCHEDULE

PHASE	WEEK	MONDAY	TUESDAY	WEDNESDAY	THURSDAY	FRIDAY	SATURDAY	SUNDAY	TOTAL MILEAGE
ENDURANCE	1	– Off	5 Medium endurance	4 Short endurance	6 Medium endurance	5 Medium endurance	4 Short endurance	6 Medium endurance	30
ENDURANCE	2	– Off	5 Medium endurance	4 Short endurance	6 Medium endurance	5 Medium endurance	4 Short endurance	10 Long endurance	34
ENDURANCE	3	– Off	6 Slow rhythm 10 x 440	4 Short endurance	8 Medium endurance	6 Medium endurance	4 Short endurance	8 Medium endurance	36
ENDURANCE	4	– Off	6 Slow rhythm 6 x 880	5 Short endurance	6 Medium endurance	6 Medium endurance	5 Short endurance	10 Long endurance	38
STRENGTHENING	5	6 Medium endurance	6 Medium rhythm 8 x 440	6 Medium endurance	6 Medium endurance	8 Medium endurance	6 Off	8 Race 5 Km	40
STRENGTHENING	6	4 Short endurance	– Off	6 Medium endurance	6 Medium endurance	8 Strength Rolling hills 4	6 Medium endurance	12 Long endurance	40
STRENGTHENING	7	– Off	8 Medium endurance	5 Short endurance	6 Medium rhythm 6 x 880	6 Short endurance	8 Strength Modified fartlek 4	8 Medium endurance	40
STRENGTHENING	8	2 Short endurance	6 Medium rhythm 4 x 1 mile	4 Short endurance	8 Medium endurance	8 Strength Modified fartlek 4	6 Short endurance	10 Long endurance	40
SHARPENING	9	5 Short endurance	4 Medium rhythm 8 x Short hills	5 Medium endurance	8 Medium endurance	6 Medium endurance	5 Off	8 Race 10 Km	35
SHARPENING	10	4 Short endurance	– Off	6 Medium endurance	6 Medium endurance	5 Short endurance	6 Fast rhythm 8 x 440	8 Medium endurance	35
SHARPENING	11	– Off	6 Strength Modified fartlek 4	4 Short endurance	5 Fast rhythm 5 x 880	5 Medium endurance	4 Short endurance	6 Medium endurance	30
TAPERING	12	2 Short endurance	6 Medium rhythm 6 x 880	4 Short endurance	4 Short endurance	4 Short endurance	– Off	– Race 10 Km	20 + race

198

ADVANCED COMPETITOR'S 12-WEEK 10KM BUILD-UP SCHEDULE

PHASE/WEEK		MONDAY	TUESDAY	WEDNESDAY	THURSDAY	FRIDAY	SATURDAY	SUNDAY	TOTAL MILEAGE
ENDURANCE	1	6 Medium endurance	5 Slow rhythm 12 x 440	6 Medium endurance	6 Medium endurance	6 Medium endurance	4 Short endurance	12 Long endurance	45
	2	8 Medium endurance	6 Slow rhythm 8 x 880	6 Medium endurance	8 Medium endurance	8 Medium endurance	4 Short endurance	10 Medium endurance	50
	3	8 Medium endurance	8 Slow rhythm 5 x 1 mile	6 Medium endurance	8 Strength Advanced fartlek 5	8 Medium endurance	6 Short endurance	10 Race 10 Km	50
	4	4 Short endurance	6 Medium endurance	8 Medium endurance	8 Medium endurance	8 Strength Rolling hills 6	8 Short endurance	15 Long endurance	55
STRENGTHENING	5	8 Medium endurance	8 Medium rhythm 12 x Short hills	8 Medium endurance	8 Medium endurance	8 Medium rhythm 8 x 880	8 Medium endurance	12 Medium endurance	60
	6	8 Medium endurance	8 Medium rhythm 4 x 1 mile	8 Medium endurance	10 Strength Advanced fartlek 6	10 Medium endurance	4 Short endurance	14 Race 10 miles	60
	7	4 Short endurance	8 Medium endurance	8 Medium endurance	8 Medium endurance	8 Medium endurance	10 Strength Advanced fartlek 8	12 Medium endurance	60
	8	8 Medium endurance	6 Fast rhythm 10 x 440	8 Medium endurance	8 Medium endurance	8 Medium rhythm 14 x Short hills	7 Medium endurance	15 Long endurance	60
SHARPENING	9	8 Short endurance	6 Fast rhythm 3 x 1 mile	8 Medium endurance	8 Medium endurance	6 Medium endurance	4 Short endurance	10 Race 10 Km	50
	10	4 Short endurance	8 Medium endurance	8 Medium endurance	8 Medium endurance	6 Medium endurance	6 Fast rhythm 8 x 880	10 Medium endurance	50
	11	8 Medium endurance	4 Fast rhythm 8 x Short hills	4 Short endurance	6 Medium endurance	8 Medium rhythm 5 x 1 mile	6 Short endurance	10 Medium endurance	50
TAPERING	12	6 Medium endurance	6 Fast rhythm 10 x 440	8 Medium endurance	6 Short endurance	4 Short endurance	— Off	— Race 10 Km	30 + race

199

CHAMPION COMPETITOR'S 12-WEEK 10KM BUILD-UP SCHEDULE

PHASE/WEEK		MONDAY	TUESDAY	WEDNESDAY	THURSDAY	FRIDAY	SATURDAY	SUNDAY	TOTAL MILEAGE
ENDURANCE	1	8 Medium endurance	8 Slow rhythm 10 x 880	8 Short endurance	6 Medium endurance	10 Medium endurance	5 Short endurance	15 Long endurance	60
	2	8 Medium endurance	7 Slow rhythm 16 x 440	7 Medium endurance	8 Medium endurance	10 Medium endurance	6 Short endurance	18 Long endurance	65
	3	10 Medium endurance	8 Strength Rolling hills 5	8 Medium endurance	10 Slow rhythm 6 x 1 mile	10 Medium endurance	4 Short endurance	16 Race 15 Km	68
	4	6 Medium endurance	10 Medium endurance	10 Medium endurance	10 Strength Advanced fartlek 6	8 Medium endurance	6 Short endurance	20 Long endurance	70
STRENGTHENING	5	10 Medium endurance	6 Medium endurance	14 Medium endurance	14 Strength Advanced fartlek 8	10 Medium endurance	9 Strength Rolling hills 7	14 Medium endurance	75
	6	11 Medium endurance	8 Medium rhythm 14 x Short hills	14 Medium endurance	10 Medium rhythm 5 x 1 mile	12 Medium endurance	8 Short endurance	12 Race 5 Km	75
	7	10 Medium endurance	12 Medium endurance	8 Medium rhythm 12 x 440	10 Medium endurance	8 Medium rhythm x 1 mile	7 Short endurance	20 Long endurance	75
	8	11 Medium endurance	10 Medium endurance	14 Medium endurance	8 Fast rhythm 4 x 1 mile	12 Medium endurance	6 Medium rhythm 16 x Short hills	14 Medium endurance	75
SHARPENING	9	14 Medium endurance	6 Power 4 x 880	12 Medium endurance	12 Medium endurance	8 Medium endurance	6 Short endurance	10 Race 10 Km	64
	10	10 Medium endurance	8 Medium endurance	10 Medium endurance	10 Medium endurance	12 Medium endurance	8 Fast rhythm 8 x 880	8 Medium endurance	64
	11	12 Medium endurance	6 Fast rhythm 10 x Short hills	10 Medium endurance	8 Medium endurance	8 Medium rhythm 6–7 x 1 mile	8 Short endurance	10 Medium endurance	64
TAPERING	12	6 Medium endurance	6 Fast rhythm 12 x 440	6 Medium endurance	8 Medium endurance	6 Short endurance	4 Short endurance	– Race 10 Km	36 + race

14. THE MARATHON

Since Frank Shorter's triumphant win in the 1972 Olympics, the marathon has grown to become the glamour event of road running. The key to marathon running is planning and completing a training program that will prepare both your body and your mind for the 26-mile 385-yard distance. To attempt a marathon without proper training is to risk failure or serious injury. Yet we all hear of marathon runners who just "jump into a marathon" on the spur of the moment. Both of us have done this—with painful and lingering consequences. That's why we both can say with determination that running a marathon on a whim—or considering six to eight weeks of training adequate preparation—can be very risky. Don't get caught up in the popularity of this exciting distance event. Train. Prepare. And then enjoy.

Take the time to plan a long-term training program of about four to six months, and then follow that schedule as closely as possible before running your marathon. This is necessary for all levels of competitors. Every runner must give this race the respect and training it deserves. You can't expect to train properly for and race more than two or three marathons per year; and only one or two for novice competitors.

This marathon training program is for all four fitness categories and uses the six-step approach outlined in Chapter 10.

STEP ONE: DETERMINE YOUR FITNESS CATEGORY

STEP TWO: SELECT YOUR RACES AND TIME GOALS

Plan your build-up races strategically. Choose time barriers to break for both your key build-up races (10 km–half marathon) and for your marathon. Common marathon time barriers include: 4:00; 3:55 (9:00 mile); 3:45; 3:30 (8:00 mile); 3:15 (7:30 mile); 3:03 (7:00 mile); 3:00; 2:50 (6:30 mile); 2:40; 2:37 (6:00 mile); 2:30; 2:24 (5:30 mile); 2:20.

The four-to-six-month build-up is a long time to hold your interest. Intermediate goals, shorter races along the way, will keep you motivated and help you evaluate your progress. By establishing and meeting these secondary goals, you will also salvage your racing season and your training if injury, bad weather or other factors beyond your control spoil your marathon or cause you to miss it completely. Be careful not to overrace—it will interfere with your ability to maintain the necessary high mileage. Many marathoners, especially inexperienced ones, don't race often enough going into a marathon and thus are out of touch with what a race feels like. Compete at least once a month, but no more than twice a month (about every three to four weeks) in your last three months of training.

Use races early in your program for fun and to build strength. "Train through" these events without tapering. Select a few races in your last month or two (10 km–30 km) and go for a good time, perhaps even a PR. You will be in very good shape, and recording good performances will give you the incentive to continue training for the marathon. Experienced marathoners may also be able to hold their peak and run a second marathon six to eight weeks after the first. Take three weeks' rest before returning to speed work after the first marathon. After the second marathon, take one to two months off from serious training.

STEP THREE: DETERMINE YOUR TRAINING CYCLE AND THE LENGTH OF YOUR PHASES

We recommend a long-term training cycle: a four-month (16-week) build-up with the endurance, strengthening and sharpening phases followed by a two-week taper, and then at least four weeks of rebuilding after the marathon. The entire cycle should last at least five-and-a-half months. If you already have a solid base of endurance and are already near your peak mileage goal, you may be able to use a three-month build-up. Start by gradually easing into the strengthening phase.

Novice and basic competitors are concerned mostly with the endurance and strengthening phases. They will spend little time (one to two weeks) in the sharpening phase, which primarily consists of reducing mileage and a final short race. If these runners haven't done much base training, more time should be spent on the endurance phase. If you have been running for several years and have a fairly solid foundation of endurance training, you may want to move to the strengthening phase sooner.

Advanced competitors will spend more time in the strengthening phase and less in the endurance phase. The stronger you are, the better you will be at pushing your body through the depletion stages late in the marathon. The sharpening phase is fairly short (three weeks) and includes a final hard race of 10 km–half marathon.

The champion competitor's training program should emphasize the individual talents of the runner. This means that you may choose a long strengthening phase at high mileage if you are a naturally strong runner, or a long sharpening phase at less mileage if you are gifted with good speed. You should work to improve your weaknesses, but concentrate on your attributes. For most champion marathoners, a three-to-four-week sharpening phase will be used to improve basic speed.

For all runners, to be successful at the marathon distance, you must first build the endurance and strength to go the distance at your normal training pace or slightly faster. Then you must work on speed to enable you to race at a pace which may be more than a minute per mile faster than your training pace. If your weakness is not being able to go the distance comfortably, work more on your long runs and the endurance and strengthening phases. If you can easily go the distance but have trouble pushing a fast pace, you need to emphasize the strengthening and sharpening phases to build speed over distance and train more like a 10 km runner. By using an 18-week build-up, you should have plenty of time to work on each of the key training phases.

Here is a guide to selecting your phases for marathon training:

DESCRIPTION	NOVICE	BASIC	ADVANCED	CHAMPION
Length of build-up	18 weeks	18	18	18
Endurance phase	10	8	6	6
Strengthening phase	4	6	7	6
Sharpening phase	2	2	3	4
Tapering phase	2	2	2	2
Rebuilding phase	4–8	4–8	4–6	3–6
Number of races in cycle	4–5	4–5	5–6	5–7

STEP FOUR: DETERMINE YOUR WEEKLY MILEAGE AND LONG-RUN GOALS

All runners need to be careful not to increase mileage too fast. Follow the general guidelines for increasing and managing mileage and long runs in Chapter 3. Be sure to "plateau" occasionally as you build. Level off at a consistent mileage base at the end of the endurance phase and maintain it throughout the strengthening phase. As you increase the intensity of your speed work, cut back your mileage and cut back more in the tapering phase—over a two-to-three-week period.

The novice and basic competitor need enough mileage to allow them to run through the Wall, but not so much that they will become overly fatigued or injured. Too much can be as bad as too little.

The advanced and champion runner will have to be very careful about balancing hard days and easy days when doing high mileage. This runner needs enough mileage to allow him or her not to be worried about reaching a "collapse point." They should not fear the Wall itself, but rather the inability to push a fast pace. They must have both high mileage and quality speed work. This is a very demanding schedule, but trying to run as fast as you can for 26.2 miles is a very demanding task.

This is probably the only event you will race for which you haven't completed training runs longer than the race distance. Consistent high weekly mileage and regular long runs are necessary to train your body and mind to rise to this severe challenge. No matter how fast you are or what your experience level, without a solid base of mileage prior to your build-up and throughout your training cycle, you are a potential victim of the Wall.

Long runs are essential for the marathon because they teach you to burn off fat reserves after glycogen has been depleted and give you the mental confidence that you can go the distance. Gradually increase the length of your long runs as you get in better shape, until you are on your feet close to the time you will be racing (but not beyond three-and-a-half hours).

Follow the *flexible* weekly mileage goals on page 206 to adjust for the amount of *time* spent training and your age and running experience. The mileage ranges reflect an *approximately* equal effort for all levels and all ages of runners. The recommended mileage figures should be averaged for at least 8 weeks prior to tapering for the marathon.

WEEKLY MILEAGE GOALS FOR MARATHON TRAINING

	AGE 18–40	AGE 40–50	AGE 50–60	AGE 60+	MILEAGE OF LONG RUNS	LONG RUNS PER MONTH
NOVICE:						
Men	50–55	45–55	40–50	40–50	16–20	1–2
Women	45–50	45–50	40–50	40–50	16–20	1–2
BASIC:						
Men	55–65	50–60	45–55	45–50	18–20	2
Women	50–60	45–55	45–50	40–50	18–20	2
ADVANCED:						
Men	65–85	60–80	55–65	50–60	18–20	2–3
Women	55–75	55–65	50–60	45–55	18–20	2–3
CHAMPION:						
Men	80–100	70–90	60–80	50–60	20–23	3
Women	70–90	60–80	50–70	45–55	20–23	3

Endurance Training Pace for Marathoners

The advanced and champion competitors race marathons at faster than their endurance training pace. *Most* novice and basic competitors run marathons at slower than their endurance training pace. Therefore:

A. The advanced and champion competitors do marathon training endurance runs at *approximately* one minute per mile *slower* than their *present* marathon race pace for their medium endurance runs. They may run slightly faster for short endurance runs and slightly slower for long endurance runs.

B. The novice and basic competitors run at *approximately* 1–1½ minutes per mile *slower* than their *present* 10 km race pace for their short and medium endurance runs when marathon training. Their long runs may be up to 2 minutes per mile slower than 10 km race pace.

Note: As you become more fit, your training pace naturally becomes faster. Slow your training pace to adjust for heat, cold, hills, fatigue, major increases in mileage and other factors. Pace will also be slower when recovering and rebuilding from races than during your strengthening and sharpening phases.

STEP FIVE: PLAN YOUR INDIVIDUAL WORKOUTS (*See model schedules at the end of this chapter*)

General Guidelines for Developing the Marathon Training Schedule

Pre-endurance Phase. Before beginning your marathon build-up, it is essential that you have already been running for several weeks at a mileage base that is within 15–20 miles per week of your peak mileage goal. This running can be done entirely at an easy conversational pace. Additionally, you should do a few long runs of 8–10 miles if you're a novice or basic competitor, and 10–12 miles if you're an advanced or champion competitor, before starting the endurance phase. Without this pre-endurance-phase work, you will not be able to handle the build-up of mileage and long runs safely.

Endurance Phase. During this phase, all marathoners gradually build up to their target weekly mileage and long runs. Run a few fun races at 5 km–10 km to maintain enthusiasm for racing. Don't be concerned with your time. Gradually blend in speed workouts: late in this phase for novice competitors, in the middle of the phase for more advanced marathoners. Highly experienced marathoners who already have a good base of fitness may be able to cut the endurance phase short by 4–6 weeks—thus they will only need a 12–14-week build-up because they have already done much of the work for the endurance phase. For example, the Atalanta marathoners coming off the 1982 Avon International Marathon in June took it easy for a month and then started a 12-week build-up for the New York Marathon in October. They were already strong from their previous build-up phase, and thus didn't require an 18-week build-up. Be careful, however, not to take short-cuts here. Most runners are not experienced enough to carry their conditioning over from one cycle to another, and should spend more time between cycles rebuilding and then use a longer build-up going into the marathon.

Strengthening Phase. Maintain your peak level of mileage and long runs. Gradually add more speed work to your schedule, especially short and long hills rhythm runs, fast continuous runs, advanced *fartlek*, and one-mile medium-pace rhythm runs (at 30 seconds per mile faster than your present marathon pace—or approximately your present 10 km race pace). As you get stronger, increase the quantity and intensity of those runs without lowering your mileage. The marathoner does more repetitions and longer distances for speed work than the 10 km runner. Run two or three races during this phase of 10–20 miles to improve your ability to hold a strong pace over long distances. Ten-kilometer races are too short to teach this. Use fast, continuous runs and your early races to run near your marathon goal pace. This teaches you to run relaxed and with good form at marathon pace. Don't run these races all-out. After several more weeks of high mileage, speed work, and racing, you may be surprised to find that you can run a marathon at the same pace that you ran for an earlier race of 10–20 miles, and possibly faster. Races here should be progressive—gradually improve your relative times. Train through the races, but taper near the end of this phase and run a hard race, going for a good performance. Race about once every three weeks during this phase and the following sharpening phase.

Sharpening Phase. Reduce mileage by at least 5–10 miles as you increase the intensity of your speed work. The marathoner usually doesn't do power workouts. This runner sharpens by increasing the quantity and intensity of long medium-pace rhythm runs and fast continuous runs, and by adding fast rhythm runs. One or two hard races of 10 km to half marathon are used to help you sharpen and predict your marathon time, and thus your starting pace. For example, Atalanta's marathoners used the Avon half marathon three weeks before the 1982 New York Marathon to go for PR's and sharpen physically and mentally for the marathon. Good performances at this point after months of hard work greatly increase your confidence. Taper for the races and go for a good time. Don't try to fit everything—a long run, race and speed work—into your weekly schedule during this phase or the previous one. It is better during the sharpening phase to skip a long run than to cut back too much on your speed work and racing.

Tapering Phase. Reduce your mileage by about 10 percent each week for the two-week phase. The last long run for novice and basic competitors is approximately three weeks before the marathon, two weeks for advanced and champion competitors. The last hard workout (long medium rhythm runs) should be 10–12 days before the marathon. Any speed work after that should be brisk, not hard, and with plenty of recovery. Run several times during the last 1–2 weeks at the time of day of the marathon start. We prefer that you take a day off on marathon week two days before the race, not the day before. Tension is usually high the day before and a *short* run will relax you. If possible, jog over the last 2–3 miles of the course to the finish and visualize yourself recording a good time. None of your training in the last 10 days will significantly improve your marathon performance, and it could hinder it. Taper! If you are nursing an injury, back off—perhaps even take several days off, or swim or bike. Many runners develop all kinds of aches and pains as they taper, and anxiety increases as the race approaches. Most often these problems are psychological and will disappear when the race begins.

Rebuilding Phase. Don't rush back into training. Adequate recovery is even more important after the marathon than after shorter races. You should then rebuild slowly before starting to train for another racing season. It will take less experienced runners longer than more advanced runners to get back into normal training. All runners should take a month or more off from serious training after running a hard marathon. A marathon run over a hilly course (downhills tear you down more than uphills) or on a hot day requires a longer recovery period, and consequently a longer rebuilding phase. An injury suffered or aggravated during the marathon will also require a long recovery period before training is resumed. Respect this race. Even if you feel great, you are vulnerable to injury and illness for several weeks after you cross the finish line. Recover. Rebuild.

Novice Competitor

(This runner has experienced at least one marathon, and now wishes to train seriously and improve his or her time.)

Endurance Phase (10 weeks): 1 speed workout per week after 4–6 weeks of endurance runs; 4–5 long runs during phase; 1–2 low-key races. Speed work, which we don't use for the first-time marathoners, is introduced here late in the phase with controlled modified *fartlek* and slow rhythm runs. The pace of these runs is *anticipated* marathon race pace. Short races are used for fun and experience; a half marathon is used late in the phase to develop knowledge of pacing over a long distance in preparation for the marathon.

Strengthening Phase (4 weeks): 1 speed workout per week; 2 long runs during phase; 1 race at end of phase. The longer rhythm runs and continued use of modified *fartlek* are used to build strength and confidence for the marathon. Slow rhythm workouts should be used occasionally to teach you the feel for marathon race pace. Run a serious race at the end of this phase to give yourself a positive lift.

Sharpening Phase (2 weeks): 1 speed workout per week; 1 long run 3 weeks prior to the marathon; no racing prior to marathon. Since this runner is more concerned with building endurance and strength, extend the training program used in the strength phase, but cut back the mileage and do medium rhythm workouts to improve speed and put a little zip into training.

Tapering Phase (2 weeks): 1 speed workout per week; no long runs; 1 race—marathon. A final easy speed workout at marathon race pace is used 5–6 days before the race to give you a feel for your starting pace, and help keep you from starting too fast.

Basic Competitor

Endurance Phase (8 weeks): 1 speed workout per week after 3–4 weeks of endurance runs; 4–5 long runs per phase; 1–2 low-key races. Introduce strength workouts and slow rhythm runs during this phase to add some zip to your endurance training. Modified *fartlek* and longer slow rhythm runs at *anticipated* marathon pace are most suitable at this time, since they are fairly easy workouts and will not disrupt your efforts to build your mileage base.

Strengthening Phase (6 weeks): 1 speed workout per week; 2–3 long runs and 2–3 races during phase. Gradually increase the quantity and intensity of your speed runs during this phase as your mileage levels off. This will insure that you continue to improve your strength, speed and confidence. During the latter part of phase, increase the speed of rhythm workouts to 10 km pace (medium rhythm). A race near the end of this phase should be a serious attempt to record a good time.

Sharpening Phase (3 weeks): 1 speed workout per week; 1 long run 3–4 weeks prior to marathon; 1 race at all-out effort during phase. Include some hard, fast workouts to improve your speed and build confidence in your ability to run fast.

Tapering Phase (2 weeks): 1 speed workout per week; no long runs; final race. A speed workout at marathon race pace is used 8–10 days before the race to give you the feeling of your starting marathon race pace. Your last speed workout (modified *fartlek*) done 5–6 days prior to the race is done at medium effort, on roads similar to marathon surface to familiarize yourself with marathon conditions.

Advanced Competitor

Endurance Phase (6 weeks): 1–2 speed workouts per week; 3–4 long runs and 1 low-key race during phase. Most advanced competitors already have a good mileage base and can therefore spend more time on strength and speed training. Include some strength and slow rhythm runs early in the endurance phase to develop your rhythmic flow and feel for marathon pace. Any races run during this phase are trained through, with no special preparation necessary, since they are used to build confidence.

Strengthening Phase (7 weeks): 2 speed workouts per week; 3–4 long runs and 2–3 races during phase. Include two speed workouts per week whenever you are not coming off a race. Carefully increase speed of rhythm runs to 10 km pace during the phase to improve your speed. Blend in strength-training runs to build strength and confidence throughout the phase. Increase the quantity and intensity

of workouts at a rate where you are able to maint
present mileage levels. Include a number of hill w
in both strength runs and rhythm runs. Do not do more
than one track workout per week. The longer distance race
run near the end of the phase should be run seriously, so
decrease your work load that week to be properly rested
for this big effort.

Sharpening Phase (3 weeks): 2 speed workouts per week;
1–2 long runs, the last two weeks prior to marathon; 1
race. One or two fast rhythm workouts (5 km pace) at the
longer distances may be included to help you increase
speed and build confidence. Continue using strength runs
that include hills, since this type of workout helps improve
your form and leg speed and builds confidence for the big
races approaching. The 10 km race (or a race of similar
length) is taken seriously, and you must decrease your
work load to get enough rest to make a good run of it.

Tapering Phase (2 weeks): 2 speed workouts per week; no
long runs; one race—marathon. Reduce both mileage and
the intensity of speed work. The last hard workout is a one-
mile, medium rhythm workout done 10–12 days before the
marathon. The pace you average per mile for this workout
is approximately 30 seconds per mile faster than your marathon race pace. Use both this workout and your recent all-
out half marathon and 10 km race times to help determine
your marathon goal time and your starting pace. (See
Chapter 19 for guidelines for predicting race times.) Use
the advanced *fartlek* workout as your final speed workout in
a controlled manner as a preparation for your big race.

Champion Competitor

Endurance Phase (6 weeks): 1–2 speed workouts per week;
4–5 long runs and 1–2 races during the phase. Begin
strength speed runs by third week to regain rhythmic flow
and racing form. The slow rhythm workouts late in this
phase are usually done at *anticipated* marathon race pace.
Include some low-key hill training late in the phase to

blend in strength work. Any races run during this phase will be low-key with no time taken off from training.

Strengthening Phase (6 weeks): 2 speed workouts per week; 3–4 long runs and 2–3 races at 10 km or longer during phase. Long rhythm workouts (880–mile) at 10 km pace and hard strength runs are emphasized during this phase. "Load up" on the number of repetitions as you gain strength to become mentally tougher for the long haul of the marathon distance. A race at the end of the strength phase (10 miles and up) should be an honest-effort race with a go for a PR.

Sharpening Phase (4 weeks): 2 speed workouts per week; 2 long runs during phase; one race at half marathon or under. Reduce your mileage and the number of repetitions while increasing the intensity of the workouts to emphasize a final speed build-up for fast races at the end of your training cycle. Race for a PR during this phase.

Tapering Phase (2 weeks): 2 speed workouts per week; no long runs; 1 race—marathon. Further reduce mileage and decrease the intensity of workouts while slightly increasing the number of repetitions as a final confidence builder for the marathon. The last hard workout is a one-mile, medium rhythm workout done 10–12 days before the marathon. The pace you average per mile for this workout is approximately 30 seconds per mile faster than your marathon starting race pace. Use both this workout and your recent all-out half marathon and 10 km race times to help determine your marathon goal time and your starting pace. (See Chapter 19 for guidelines for predicting race times.) Use the advanced *fartlek* workout five days prior to the race in a controlled manner as a final preparation for your big race.

STEP SIX: PLAN YOUR REBUILDING PHASE

18-WEEK MARATHON BUILD-UP SCHEDULES

The model training schedules on pages 216–23 should be used to help you write your own program. The exact mileage you will run, distance and dates of your build-up races, and the days you will do your different types of runs will vary with your individual needs, age, sex, and other factors that influence your running. Use these models as a guide to create a specific training program that can help you reach your racing goals. Understand the concepts behind these schedules, don't just follow them blindly. We have not included an example of the rebuilding phase. Follow the model in Chapter 10 to write your rebuilding program.

THE NOVICE COMPETITOR'S 18-WEEK MARATHON BUILD-UP SCHEDULE

PHASE / WEEK	MONDAY	TUESDAY	WEDNESDAY	THURSDAY	FRIDAY	SATURDAY	SUNDAY	TOTAL MILEAGE
1	Off	Medium endurance 6	Medium endurance 6	Medium endurance 5	Short endurance 4	Medium endurance 6	Medium endurance 8	35
2	Off	Medium endurance 5	Medium endurance 5	Medium endurance 5	Medium endurance 5	Short endurance 3	Long endurance 12	35
3	Off	Short endurance 4	Medium endurance 8	Medium endurance 6	Medium endurance 6	Short endurance 2	Long endurance 14	40
4	Off	Medium endurance 5	Medium endurance 6	Medium endurance 6	Medium endurance 6	Short endurance 4	Race 5 Km 8	35
5	Short endurance 4	Off	Medium endurance 6	Medium endurance 6	Medium endurance 6	Medium endurance 8	Medium endurance 10	40
6	Off	Medium endurance 6	Medium endurance 7	Strength Modified fartlek 6	Medium endurance 7	Short endurance 3	Long endurance 16	45
7	Off	Medium endurance 6	Medium endurance 8	Medium endurance 6	Medium endurance 6	Short endurance 4	Race 10 K 10	40
8	Short endurance 4	Off	Medium endurance 6	Strength Modified fartlek 8	Medium endurance 6	Short endurance 3	Long endurance 18	45
9	Off	Medium endurance 6	Slow rhythm 6 x 880 7	Medium rhythm 8	Medium endurance 6	Short endurance 4	Race ½ Marathon 14	45
10	Short endurance 4	Off	Medium endurance 8	Medium endurance 8	Strength Modified fartlek 7	Medium endurance 8	Medium endurance 10	45
11	Off	Medium endurance 8	Medium endurance 6	Medium rhythm 5 x Short hills 6	Medium endurance 6	Short endurance 4	Long endurance 20	50
12	Off	Medium endurance 8	Slow rhythm 5 x 1 mile 8	Medium endurance 9	Medium endurance 8	Short endurance 5	Race 10 miles 12	50

Phase (left margin): ENDURANCE / STRENGTH-ENING

216

THE NOVICE COMPETITOR'S 18-WEEK MARATHON BUILD-UP SCHEDULE (Cont'd.)

PHASE/WEEK		MONDAY	TUESDAY	WEDNESDAY	THURSDAY	FRIDAY	SATURDAY	SUNDAY	TOTAL MILEAGE
STRENGTH-ENING	13	4 Short endurance	— Off	8 Medium endurance	10 Medium endurance	8 Strength Modified fartlek	8 Medium endurance	12 Medium endurance	50
	14	8 Medium endurance	8 Medium rhythm 6 x 880	5 Medium endurance	8 Medium endurance	6 Medium endurance	— Off	10 Race 10 K	45
SHARPEN-ING	15	4 Short endurance	— Off	8 Medium endurance	5 Medium rhythm 6 x Short hills	8 Medium endurance	— Off	20 Long endurance	45
	16	4 Short endurance	4 Short endurance	8 Medium endurance	6 Medium endurance	5 Medium rhythm 3 x 1 mile	6 Medium endurance	12 Medium endurance	45
TAPERING	17	— Off	8 Medium endurance	6 Medium endurance	6 Slow rhythm 8 x 880	4 Short endurance	6 Medium endurance	10 Medium endurance	40
	18	— Off	6 Slow rhythm 10 x 440	4 Short endurance	4 Short endurance	— Off	2 Short endurance	26.2 Race Marathon	16 + race

217

THE BASIC COMPETITOR'S 18-WEEK MARATHON BUILD-UP SCHEDULE

PHASE/WEEK		MONDAY	TUESDAY	WEDNESDAY	THURSDAY	FRIDAY	SATURDAY	SUNDAY	TOTAL MILEAGE
ENDURANCE	1	Off	— Medium endurance	6 Medium endurance	7 Medium endurance	5 Short endurance	6 Medium endurance	10 Medium endurance	40
	2	Off	— Medium endurance	7 Medium endurance	6 Medium endurance	7 Medium endurance	4 Short endurance	15 Long endurance	45
	3	4 Short endurance	8 Medium endurance	8 Medium endurance	5 Short endurance	7 Medium endurance	8 Medium endurance	10 Medium endurance	50
	4	Off	— Medium endurance	8 Medium endurance	6 Strength Modified fartlek	4 Medium endurance	4 Short endurance	18 Long endurance	50
	5	4 Short endurance	8 Medium endurance	8 Medium endurance	6 Medium endurance	6 Medium endurance	4 Short endurance	10 Race 10 Km	50
	6	4 Short endurance	— Off	8 Medium endurance	8 Strength Modified fartlek	6 Medium endurance	6 Short endurance	20 Long endurance	50
	7	5 Short endurance	10 Medium endurance	8 Medium endurance	5 Slow rhythm 6 x 880	6 Medium endurance	8 Medium endurance	10 Medium endurance	55
	8	5 Short endurance	6 Medium endurance	6 Medium endurance	5 Strength Modified fartlek	8 Medium endurance	8 Short endurance	18 Long endurance	55
STRENGTHENING	9	5 Short endurance	5 Medium endurance	7 Slow rhythm 5 x 1 mile	8 Medium endurance	8 Medium endurance	5 Short endurance	14 Race 1/2 marathon	55
	10	4 Short endurance	5 Short endurance	10 Medium endurance	10 Medium endurance	8 Strength Modified fartlek	8 Medium endurance	10 Medium endurance	55
	11	6 Medium endurance	6 Medium rhythm 4 x Long hill	5 Medium endurance	8 Medium endurance	5 Medium endurance	4 Long endurance	20 Long endurance	55
	12	5 Short endurance	5 Medium endurance	8 Medium rhythm 5 x 880	6 Medium endurance	10 Medium endurance	7 Short endurance	4 Race 10 miles	50

THE BASIC COMPETITOR'S 18-WEEK MARATHON BUILD-UP SCHEDULE (Cont'd.)

PHASE/WEEK		MONDAY	TUESDAY	WEDNESDAY	THURSDAY	FRIDAY	SATURDAY	SUNDAY	TOTAL MILEAGE
STRENGTH-ENING	13	5 Short endurance	5 Short endurance	10 Medium endurance	8 Slow rhythm 5 x 1 mile	8 Medium endurance	4 Short endurance	15 Long endurance	55
STRENGTH-ENING	14	5 Short endurance	6 Medium rhythm 10 x Short hills	8 Medium endurance	8 Medium endurance	6 Medium endurance	4 Short endurance	8 Race 10 K	45
SHARP-ENING	15	4 Short endurance	6 Medium endurance	6 Medium endurance	6 Medium rhythm 6 x 880	6 Medium endurance	4 Short endurance	20 Long endurance	52
SHARP-ENING	16	4 Short endurance	7 Medium endurance	6 Medium endurance	6 Medium rhythm 5 x Long hills	7 Medium endurance	6 Medium endurance	14 Medium endurance	50
TAPERING	17	4 Short endurance	6 Medium endurance	5 Medium endurance	8 Slow rhythm 6 x 1 mile	8 Medium endurance	6 Medium endurance	10 Medium endurance	45
TAPERING	18	4 Short endurance	4 Strength Modified fartlek	4 Short endurance	4 Short endurance	— Off	3 Short endurance	26.2 Race Marathon	20 + race

THE ADVANCED COMPETITOR'S 18-WEEK MARATHON BUILD-UP SCHEDULE

PHASE/WEEK		MONDAY	TUESDAY	WEDNESDAY	THURSDAY	FRIDAY	SATURDAY	SUNDAY	TOTAL MILEAGE
ENDURANCE	1	8 Medium endurance	8 Medium endurance	6 Medium endurance	6 Medium endurance	7 Medium endurance	5 Short endurance	15 Long endurance	55
	2	6 Short endurance	6 Medium endurance	8 Medium endurance	10 Medium endurance	8 Medium endurance	8 Medium endurance	10 Medium endurance	60
	3	8 Medium endurance	8 Strength Advanced fartlek	8 / 6 Short endurance	6 Medium endurance	10 Medium endurance	5 Short endurance	18 Long endurance	65
	4	8 Medium endurance	8 Medium endurance	10 / 6 Strength Advanced fartlek	10 Medium endurance	10 Medium endurance	8 Medium endurance	11 Race 10 K	65
	5	7 Medium endurance	8 Medium endurance	8 Medium endurance	8 Slow rhythm 8 x 880	8 Medium endurance	6 Short endurance	18 Long endurance	65
STRENGTHENING	6	10 Medium endurance	10 Strength Advanced fartlek	12 Medium endurance	10 Medium endurance	8 Medium rhythm 12 x Short hills	8 Medium endurance	12 Medium endurance	70
	7	10 Medium endurance	10 Medium rhythm 8 x 880	10 Medium endurance	10 / 6 Strength Advanced fartlek	10 Medium endurance	6 Short endurance	14 Race 10 miles	70
	8	6 Short endurance	6 Medium endurance	10 Medium endurance	10 Medium rhythm 12 x 440	8 Medium endurance	6 Short endurance	20 Long endurance	70
	9	8 Medium endurance	8 Medium rhythm 4 x 1 mile	12 Medium endurance	10 / 6 Strength Advanced fartlek	10 Medium endurance	6 Short endurance	16 Race 20 K	70
	10	6 Short endurance	8 Medium endurance	10 Medium endurance	10 Strength Fast continuous run	7 Strength Rolling hills	6 Short endurance	20 Long endurance	70
	11	10 Medium endurance	10 Medium rhythm 5 x 1 mile	8 Medium endurance	10 Medium endurance	10 Medium endurance	6 Short endurance	18 Long endurance	70
	12	10 Medium endurance	10 Medium rhythm 10 x 880 mile	8 Medium endurance	10 Medium endurance	8 Medium endurance	6 Short endurance	15 Race ½ marathon	65

THE ADVANCED COMPETITOR'S 18-WEEK MARATHON BUILD-UP SCHEDULE (Cont'd.)

PHASE/WEEK		MONDAY	TUESDAY	WEDNESDAY	THURSDAY	FRIDAY	SATURDAY	SUNDAY	TOTAL MILEAGE
SHARPENING	13	6 Short endurance	8 Medium endurance	10 Medium endurance	9 Slow rhythm 10 x 880	12 Medium endurance	10 Medium endurance	15 Medium endurance	70
	14	8 Medium endurance	8 Medium rhythm 5–6 x 1 mile	8 Medium endurance	8 Medium endurance	8 Medium rhythm 8 x Long hills	5 Short endurance	20 Long endurance	65
	15	8 Medium endurance	6 Fast rhythm 6 x 880	8 Medium endurance	8 Medium endurance	6 Medium endurance	4 Short endurance	10 Race 10 K	50
	16	5 Short endurance	7 Medium endurance	8 Medium endurance	8 Medium endurance	8 Strength Rolling hills	4 Short endurance	20 Long endurance	60
TAPERING	17	6 Short endurance	7 Medium rhythm 5–6 x 1 mile	8 Medium endurance	8 Medium endurance	10 Strength Advanced fartlek	4 Short endurance	12 Medium endurance	55
	18	5 Short endurance	5 Strength Advanced fartlek	6 Medium endurance	4 Short endurance	— Off	3 Short endurance	26.2 Race Marathon	23 + race

THE CHAMPION COMPETITOR'S 18-WEEK MARATHON BUILD-UP SCHEDULE

PHASE	WEEK	MONDAY	TUESDAY	WEDNESDAY	THURSDAY	FRIDAY	SATURDAY	SUNDAY	TOTAL MILEAGE
ENDURANCE	1	8 Medium endurance	8 Medium endurance	10 Medium endurance	8 Medium endurance	10 Medium endurance	8 Medium endurance	18 Long endurance	70
ENDURANCE	2	10 Medium endurance	10 Medium endurance	12 Medium endurance	10 Medium endurance	12 Medium endurance	9 Medium endurance	12 Medium endurance	75
ENDURANCE	3	12 Medium endurance	12 Strength Advanced fartlek	10 Medium endurance	8 Medium endurance	12 Medium endurance	6 Short endurance	20 Long endurance	80
ENDURANCE	4	10 Medium endurance	10 Medium endurance	14 Strength Rolling hills	12 Medium endurance	14 Medium endurance	10 Medium endurance	10 Race 10 Km	80
ENDURANCE	5	10 Medium endurance	10 Medium endurance	12 Slow rhythm 6 x 1 mile	12 Medium endurance	10 Strength Advanced fartlek	6 Short endurance	20 Long endurance	80
ENDURANCE	6	10 Medium endurance	10 Medium rhythm 15 x Short hills	10 Medium endurance	14 Medium endurance	14 Strength Advanced fartlek	7 Short endurance	20 Long endurance	85
STRENGTHENING	7	10 Medium endurance	10 Medium rhythm 8 x 880	14 Medium endurance	12 Strength Fast continuous run	14 Medium endurance	9 Medium endurance	16 Race 10 miles	85
STRENGTHENING	8	8 Medium endurance	8 Medium endurance	14 Medium endurance	12 Strength Advanced fartlek	12 Medium endurance	6 Short endurance	22 Long endurance	82
STRENGTHENING	9	10 Medium endurance	10 Medium rhythm 5 x 1 mile	14 Medium endurance	12 Strength Advanced fartlek	12 Medium endurance	10 Medium endurance	17 Race 20 Km	85
STRENGTHENING	10	8 Medium endurance	12 Medium endurance	12 Medium endurance	12 Strength Rolling hills	12 Medium endurance	9 Medium endurance	20 Long endurance	85
STRENGTHENING	11	10 Medium endurance	10 Medium rhythm 6 x 1 mile	12 Medium endurance	12 Strength Fast continuous run	12 Medium endurance	7 Medium endurance	22 Long endurance	85
STRENGTHENING	12	10 Medium endurance	10 Medium rhythm 10 x 880	12 Medium endurance	11 Medium endurance	8 Medium endurance	6 Short endurance	18 Race ½ marathon	75

THE CHAMPION COMPETITOR'S 18-WEEK MARATHON BUILD-UP SCHEDULE (Cont'd.)

PHASE/WEEK		MONDAY	TUESDAY	WEDNESDAY	THURSDAY	FRIDAY	SATURDAY	SUNDAY	TOTAL MILEAGE
SHARPENING	13	6 Short endurance	10 Medium endurance	14 Medium endurance	10 Slow rhythm 12 x 880	14 Medium endurance	12 Strength Advanced fartlek	14 Medium endurance	80
	14	10 Medium endurance	10 Medium rhythm 6-8 x 1 mile	9 Medium endurance	12 Medium endurance	12 Strength Fast continuous run	7 Short endurance	20 Long endurance	80
	15	10 Medium endurance	8 Fast rhythm 6 x 880	12 Medium endurance	12 Medium endurance	8 Medium endurance	4 Short endurance	12 Race 10 Km	66
	16	6 Short endurance	12 Medium endurance	12 Medium endurance	10 Medium endurance	10 Strength Advanced fartlek	5 Short endurance	20 Long endurance	75
TAPERING	17	8 Medium endurance	10 Medium rhythm 6-8 x 1 mile	10 Medium endurance	8 Medium endurance	6 Strength Rolling hills	10 Medium endurance	14 Medium endurance	70
	18	5 Short endurance	6 Strength Advanced fartlek	8 Medium endurance	5 Short endurance	— Off	4 Short endurance	26.2 Race Marathon	30 + Marathon

TIPS FOR MARATHON RACING AND TRAINING

Basic Guidelines

Follow the basic guidelines for marathon training and racing which apply to experienced marathoners. Don't get cocky and forget the basics just because you are a veteran of the marathon.

Weight

Your body weight is extremely important. Every extra pound you carry beyond our recommended guidelines (see Chapter 30) will slow you down much more dramatically in the marathon than for shorter distances.

Racing Shoes

Lightweight, experienced marathoners may choose to use racing flats. They make the runners "feel" lighter and allow them to flow more easily at a fast pace. A few ounces of weight saved here may be helpful to the runner trying to race at a very fast pace. However, this runner isn't out on the course as long as the average marathoner and thus doesn't absorb as much pounding. For this reason, training shoes should be used by novice and basic marathoners and by all heavy runners. These runners do not benefit by sacrificing shock absorption for a few less ounces of shoe weight. Hilly marathon courses are safer to race in training shoes; foot or leg injuries may require that you use the shoe that gives you the most protection. Much of the difference between training and racing shoes is psychological. When Bob Glover ran a 2:37 marathon effort in the 1978 Carolina Marathon, a PR at the time by several minutes, he raced in training shoes. Somehow he had misplaced one of his racing shoes and didn't discover the error until race morning; so he was forced to race in his trusty training shoes. His worries about being slowed down by a heavier shoe disappeared when the gun went off and he had to concentrate on his race. He didn't remember until the next day that he had run a strong race without benefit of racing shoes. In fact, his legs and back ached less in the final stages due to the extra cushioning. We recommend lightweight racing shoes for a fast featherweight; lightweight training shoes for the average marathoner; and regular training shoes with excellent cushioning for novice and basic competitors and heavy runners. Use the shoes you will race in for several speed workouts and a few races as you sharpen for the marathon. Also, make sure that the shoes are not too tight, especially in the toe box. Unlike in shorter races, your feet will swell significantly during the marathon and you will need room in the shoes for them to expand. You can test this by doing a long run in these shoes. Be careful not to get your feet, shoes and socks soaked during a race—your shoes get heavy and your feet will slip around in them. Direct people to spray water over your head, not on your feet.

Eating and Drinking

Experienced marathoners may choose to deplete and carbohydrate load. We prefer that you not deplete, but carbohydrate load for your final three days. Go with what works best for you. Follow the guidelines for eating and drinking before, during and after the marathon in Chapters 28 and 29. A safe combination of eating, drinking and racing is much more crucial in the marathon than in shorter races.

Race Pacing

Plan your pace according to the guidelines developed in Chapters 19 and 20. You should train to be comfortable at this pace and then go out at it with confidence. Stick with it. Don't panic and decide it is too fast or too slow. If you run the race more than two to three minutes faster for the first half than for the second half, you went out too fast and may have made your final time slower. Of course, heat and hills may cause everyone to slow for the second half of the race. If you run the race more than two to three minutes faster for the second half than for the first half, you should have started faster, and may have been able to run a faster time. Starting too fast in a short race brings out the Bear. Starting too fast in a marathon brings out the Bear, and the Wall follows shortly. It is much more devastating to start too fast in the marathon than in shorter races. Use a pack of runners around you to help you flow with a good pace, or follow a runner you know will run an even pace at about your goal pace. Then move up when you feel good. Don't make a move to pick up your pace too early. Relax to at least the halfway point before deciding that you can go for a faster time. It is easy early in the race to think you can go faster, but it is another story over the last five or six miles when you are battling depletion and heavy legs.

Race Planning

Plan for your marathon, train for it, and then go for it with confidence. Don't chicken out at the last minute because you think you need one more long run or some other extra training, and decide to wait a few weeks for another marathon. Don't start the race with the attitude that you will drop out early if you don't feel good. You must go into it believing that you will finish, and finish well. However, it is sometimes wise to pick a backup race a week or two later in case a sudden snowstorm or heat wave makes running a strong marathon impossible. Don't waste a marathon on an extremely bad day. A marathon effort will tear you down physically and mentally. You can't just go out the next week or two after completing a poor marathon—or even if you dropped out en route—and jump into another one for a second chance.

Form

Over the 26.2-mile distance, inefficient racing form will cost you much more time than in a shorter race. Refer to our guidelines in Chapters 21–23. Keep the arms moving in the late stages of the race, and the legs will keep moving.

The Wall

The Wall is greatly played up by the media, which likes to dramatize the pain of the marathon. If you train with sufficient mileage and long runs, pace yourself wisely and have a positive attitude, you will not have problems with the Wall. It is much more of a psychological barrier than a physical one for the well-trained runner.

Persevere

More than in any other race distance (except perhaps the ultramarathon) you will feel like quitting time and again. You must talk yourself out of these "bad patches." Keep moving and concentrate on your form and pace. Pick up the pace or alter your form slightly for a few seconds to give yourself a mental lift. Or concentrate on reeling in a runner ahead of you. You must be patient in the early stages and aggressive in the late stages. Think about all that training time and all those hard workouts that would be wasted if you let up just because you were uncomfortable. Many runners miss their goal time because they are unable to keep pushing through short lapses of self-doubt. They lose confidence, slow down, and fall behind their pace schedule. Relax, and believe in yourself. Have faith in your training program. Work hard to get the most out of your body so that after the race is over you won't feel that you have cheated yourself by giving in to temporary discomfort.

On the other hand, if injury forces you to alter your form seriously, or if you experience real pain due to injury or extreme discomfort due to heat, back off. Drop out if necessary. If you continue, you risk not only losing several weeks of training, but your health. If you are struggling with the early pace which you have set for yourself, honestly evaluate your situation. If you are certain that you are physically unable to keep the pace, slow down and readjust your goal for this race. Overcome adversity, but don't try to be a hero and finish no matter what. Don't feel that you are a failure if you make an intelligent decision to drop out. Prove yourself in the next marathon on your schedule.

Postmarathon Depression

You put in a lot of time and effort, making many sacrifices along the way, to attempt to race a good marathon. But the marathon is a risky event. If you have a bad day, catch a stitch, develop bad blisters, have problems with your shoes, have an old injury act up, or trip and bang your knee, all your preparation can go down the drain. This is why we encourage you to go for good times for a few shorter races in the last weeks prior to the race. You will have something to show for all your training if the marathon race ends up being a disappointment.

Even if you ran a good race, you may feel depressed for the next few weeks. Just as in postpartum depression, your "baby" has reached the finish line and your long-sought-after goal, around which your life revolved for months, has been achieved, leaving you feeling empty. Take some time off from serious running and enjoy activities that you had to give up because you were spending most of your non-working time running. Maintain minimal mileage levels, however, by doing a few easy runs per week. Then when you feel the urge to train again, set new racing goals and write a new training schedule. We recommend that you now train for shorter races.

15. THE 5 KM–4-MILE RACE

The 5 km racing distance is becoming increasingly popular. It is raced regularly on the track at high school and college meets, and internationally at all levels. Many road races are held at both the 5 km and 4-mile distance. Nearly 15,000 men and women, representing hundreds of companies, annually run the 3.5-mile Manufacturers Hanover Corporate Challenge in New York City. The training guidelines in this chapter pertain to the 5 km range—3.1 miles to 4 miles.

We recommend this distance for your first race because it is long enough to challenge the novice but short enough so that you can complete it without having to do much more mileage than you are used to. Milers often race this distance as a transition to road racing; 10 km and marathon runners use it as a break from longer races and to improve speed. It doesn't require a long recovery period, thus it can be raced frequently.

This racing distance should not be taken lightly. A hard 5 km will test your ability to hold a fast pace over distance. The event requires good basic speed with a solid background of endurance training. Although it is often used for overdistance racing for track runners and underdistance racing for long-distance runners, many athletes specialize in the 5 km. We feel that all competitors should race more often at this distance.

This 5 km training program is designed for all four fitness categories and uses the six-step approach:

STEP ONE: DETERMINE YOUR FITNESS CATEGORY

STEP TWO: SELECT YOUR RACES AND TIME GOALS

Plan your build-up races strategically. Choose time barriers to break for your key races. Common 5 km time barriers include: 25:00 (8:00 mile); 23:00 (7:30 mile); 21:30 (7:00 mile); 20:00 (6:30 mile); 19:00; 18:30 (6:00 mile); 18:00; 17:00 (5:30 mile); 16:00; 15:30 (5:00 mile).

STEP THREE: DETERMINE YOUR TRAINING CYCLE AND THE LENGTH OF YOUR PHASES

Most 5 km racing goals can be achieved by using a 12-week, short-term training cycle. As long as you have a good foundation of endurance training, you will not need to add too much additional time to get yourself in shape for the 5 km. The key is to have the endurance and strength to support the faster speed training of the sharpening phase which is necessary for success at this distance.

Here is a guide to selecting the length of your training phases:

DESCRIPTION	NOVICE	BASIC	ADVANCED	CHAMPION
Length of build-up	12 weeks	12	12	12
Endurance phase	5	4	3	3
Strengthening phase	4	4	4	4
Sharpening phase	2	3	4	4
Tapering phase	1	1	1	1
Rebuilding phase	3–4	3–4	3–4	3–4
Number of races in cycle	3–4	3–4	3–5	3–5

STEP FOUR: DETERMINE YOUR WEEKLY MILEAGE AND LONG-RUN GOALS

The mileage base for the 5 km falls somewhere between that for a miler and that for the 10 km runner. If you are primarily a 10 km runner and are using the 5 km for developing more speed and strength, you may want to lower your mileage somewhat (but no more than 10 percent off your weekly 10 km rate). If you are a miler using the 5 km to develop greater endurance and strength, you may want to increase your mileage slightly (about 10 percent) to broaden your foundation base. For those who consider themselves 5 km specialists, follow the guidelines below.

Your needs and goals determine the length of your long runs. If you anticipate running longer races along with the 5 km, you will want to include some longer runs in your training. If you wish to concentrate on the 5 km, however, you will need to minimize the length of your long runs. Longer runs take away from your ability to handle intense speed work.

Follow these *flexible* weekly mileage goals in training for the 5 km. The recommended mileage figures should be averaged for at least six weeks prior to tapering for the final race. Runners age 50+ should use the lower end of the recommended mileage range.

FITNESS CATEGORY	WEEKLY MILEAGE	MILEAGE OF LONG RUN	LONG RUNS PER MONTH
Novice competitor	15–25	5–8	1–2
Basic competitor	25–40	8–10	1–2
Advanced competitor	30–50	8–12	1–2
Champion competitor	40–70	12–16	1–2

Endurance Training Pace for the 5 km

Most 5 km competitors should run medium endurance runs at *approximately* 1½ to 2 minutes per mile *slower* than their *present* 5 km race pace. They may run slightly faster for short endurance runs and slightly slower for long endurance runs.

Note: As you become more fit, your training pace naturally becomes faster. Slow your training pace to adjust for heat, cold, hills, fatigue, major increases in mileage and other factors. Pace will also be slower when recovering and rebuilding from races than during your strengthening and sharpening phases.

STEP FIVE: PLAN YOUR INDIVIDUAL WORKOUTS (*See model schedules at the end of this chapter*)

Note that 5 km competitors follow the same basic training philosophy as described for 10 km competitors. Special training adjustments for the 5 km are specified.

Novice Competitor

This runner has run one or more 5 km races and now wishes to improve his or her time by adding speed work.

Endurance phase (5 weeks): 1 speed workout per week after 2 weeks of endurance runs; 1–2 long run and 1–2 races during phase. The 5 km runner does the slow rhythm runs at 10 mile race pace which allows the body to adjust to the faster pace of the 5 km race after doing only easy endurance training. A 5 km race is used at the end of this phase to gain racing experience. Do not attempt to run this race all-out. Build your weekly mileage to peak level during this phase.

Strengthening Phase (4 weeks): 1–2 speed workouts per week; 1–2 long runs and 1–2 races during phase. Introduce speed workouts at 5 km pace during this phase as you build strength and speed. A second speed workout each week is included if you are able to maintain your mileage base without becoming too tired. Any races during this phase are serious attempts at recording good performances.

Sharpening Phase (2 weeks): 1–2 speed workouts; no long runs; 0–1 race. This runner sharpens for the 5 km by doing several rhythm workouts at race pace. The middle distances (440–880) are most useful. Maintain your weekly mileage base. The 4 × 880 workout nine days prior to the race will give you a good indication as to the pace you will be able to handle.

Tapering Phase (1 week): 1 speed workout; no long runs; 1 race—5 km. The final speed workout (modified *fartlek*) is done 5–6 days prior to the 5 km. Run this workout in a very controlled manner, simulating the race. Include several days off and short, easy days in the last week to insure that you are well rested for the big race.

Basic Competitor

Endurance Phase (4 weeks): 1–2 speed workouts per week after 2 weeks of endurance training; 1–2 long run and 0–1 race during phase. Include slow rhythm runs at 10 mile race pace and some strength runs to allow your body gradually to adjust to faster speeds than your normal endurance runs. Increase your weekly mileage base to your peak level.

Strengthening Phase (4 weeks): 1–2 speed workouts per week; 1–2 long runs and 1–2 races during phase. Build to two speed workouts per week to develop the necessary strength and speed for this short, intense race. Near the end of this phase, as your body becomes stronger, include longer 5 km pace rhythm runs (880–mile) to help simulate racing conditions. Maintain your peak weekly mileage level. Include a 5 km race at less than all-out effort to gain experience.

Sharpening Phase (3 weeks): 1–2 speed workouts per week; no long runs; 1–2 races. Use this phase to improve your racing speed by slightly increasing the intensity of your medium rhythm runs toward goal race pace and by adding faster paced rhythm runs (one-mile pace). Include modified *fartlek* to simulate racing conditions. Use the bursts to "change gears" and pick up your pace. Decrease your weekly mileage as you increase the intensity of your workouts. One to two 5 km races are used in the phase to test you at this distance. Aim for good performances.

Tapering Phase (1 week): 1 speed workout; no long runs; one race—5 km. The last race pace rhythm workout is done 5–6 days prior to the 5 km and at a low number of repetitions to insure that you do not overtrain. For the rest of the week, take it easy and prepare mentally for the big race.

Advanced Competitor

Endurance Phase (3 weeks): 1–2 speed workouts per week; 1–2 long runs per phase and no races. This phase is used to build your weekly base mileage to its peak level and improve your rhythmic "flow" by including slow rhythm runs and some strength runs.

Strengthening Phase (4 weeks): 2–3 speed workouts per week; 0–1 long run and 1–2 races during phase. Build strength by increasing the number of speed workouts per week while maintaining your weekly mileage base. Increase your speed by using medium rhythm runs. This will prepare you for more intense speed work and will help you maintain your race pace for the entire 5 km distance. Include a longer race (10 km–15 km) as overdistance work. This should not be an all-out effort.

Sharpening Phase (4 weeks): 2–3 speed workouts per week; no long runs; 1–2 races during phase. Increase the intensity of your medium rhythm runs slightly toward goal race pace and add fast rhythm runs (one-mile pace) and power runs. Two to three of these hard workouts are used per week to increase speed. Decrease your mileage to compensate for the intensity of the work. The 5 km race during this phase should be a serious effort and you should work at being competitive and running relaxed using good form at this fast pace.

Tapering Phase (1 week): 1 speed workout; no long runs; one race—5 km. Do one last race pace speed workout at a reduced number of repetitions to prepare for the big race. Reduce weekly mileage and take plenty of rest.

Champion Competitor

(This runner follows a very similar schedule as that of the advanced competitor, except that more mileage is run and the quantity and intensity of the speed work is more difficult.)

Endurance Phase (3 weeks): 2 speed workouts per week; 1–2 long runs. See Advanced Competitor.

Strengthening Phase (4 weeks): 2–3 speed workouts per week; 0–1 long runs; 1–2 races. See Advanced Competitor.

Sharpening Phase (4 weeks): 2–3 speed workouts per week; no long runs; 1–2 races. See Advanced Competitor.

Tapering Phase (1 week): 1 speed workout; no long runs; one race—5 km. See Advanced Competitor.

STEP SIX: PLAN YOUR REBUILDING PHASE

12-WEEK 5 KM BUILD-UP SCHEDULE

The model training schedules on pages 236–39 should be used to help you write your own program. The exact mileage you will run, distance and dates of your build-up races, and the days you will do your different types of runs will vary with your individual needs, age, sex, and other factors that influence your running. Use these models as a guide to create a specific training program that can help you reach your racing goals. Understand the concepts behind these schedules, don't just follow them blindly. We have not included an example of the rebuilding phase. Follow the model in Chapter 10 to write your rebuilding program.

NOVICE COMPETITOR'S 12-WEEK 5KM BUILD-UP SCHEDULE

PHASE	WEEK	MONDAY	TUESDAY	WEDNESDAY	THURSDAY	FRIDAY	SATURDAY	SUNDAY	TOTAL MILEAGE
ENDURANCE	1	— Off	3 Medium endurance	3 Medium endurance	3 Medium endurance	— Off	2 Short endurance	4 Medium endurance	15
ENDURANCE	2	— Off	3 Medium endurance	3 Medium endurance	3 Medium endurance	— Off	2 Short endurance	4 Medium endurance	15
ENDURANCE	3	— Off	4 Strength Modified fartlek 3	2 Short endurance	3 Medium endurance	— Off	2 Short endurance	4 Medium endurance	15
ENDURANCE	4	— Off	3 Slow rhythm 8 x 220	3 Medium endurance	4 Medium endurance	— Off	2 Short endurance	6 Long endurance	18
ENDURANCE	5	— Off	4 Strength Modified fartlek 3	3 Medium endurance	3 Medium endurance	3 Short endurance	— Off	5 Race 5 Km	18
STRENGTHENING	6	2 Short endurance	2 Short endurance	4 Medium endurance	5 Medium rhythm 4 x 440	— Off	3 Short endurance	4 Medium endurance	20
STRENGTHENING	7	— Off	3 Slow rhythm 5 x Short hills	3 Short endurance	— Off	5 Strength Modified fartlek 3	3 Short endurance	6 Long endurance	20
STRENGTHENING	8	— Off	4 Medium rhythm 3 x 880	4 Short endurance	— Off	5 Strength Modified fartlek 3	3 Short endurance	5 Medium endurance	20
STRENGTHENING	9	— Off	4 Medium rhythm 5 x 440	4 Medium endurance	4 Medium endurance	3 Short endurance	— Off	5 Race 5 Km	20
SHARPEN-ING	10	2 Short endurance	3 Short endurance	4 Medium endurance	4 Medium rhythm 4 x 880	— Off	2 Short endurance	5 Medium endurance	20
SHARPEN-ING	11	— Off	4 Medium rhythm 6 x 440	3 Short endurance	— Off	4 Medium rhythm 4 x 880	3 Short endurance	4 Medium endurance	18
TAPER-ING	12	— Off	5 Strength Modified fartlek 3	3 Short endurance	2 Short endurance	2 Short endurance	— Off	— Race 5 Km	12 + race

236

BASIC COMPETITOR'S 12-WEEK 5 KM BUILD-UP SCHEDULE

PHASE / WEEK		MONDAY	TUESDAY	WEDNESDAY	THURSDAY	FRIDAY	SATURDAY	SUNDAY	TOTAL MILEAGE
ENDURANCE	1	Off [—]	Medium endurance [4]	Short endurance [3]	Medium endurance [5]	Medium endurance [5]	Short endurance [3]	Medium endurance [5]	25
	2	Off [—]	Medium endurance [4]	Short endurance [3]	Medium endurance [5]	Medium endurance [5]	Short endurance [3]	Medium endurance [5]	25
	3	Off [—]	Slow rhythm 10 x 220 [3]	Short endurance [3]	Medium endurance [4]	Medium endurance [4]	Short endurance [3]	Long endurance [8]	25
	4	Off [—]	Slow rhythm 4 x 880 [4]	Short endurance [3]	Medium endurance [4]	Strength Modified fartlek 3 [5]	Medium endurance [5]	Medium endurance [6]	27
STRENGTHENING	5	Short endurance [3]	Medium rhythm 6 x 440 [5]	Medium endurance [5]	Medium endurance [6]	Medium endurance [6]	Off [—]	Race 5 Km [5]	30
	6	Short endurance [2]	Medium endurance [4]	Medium endurance [4]	Medium endurance [4]	Strength Modified fartlek 4 [6]	Off [—]	Long endurance [10]	30
	7	Off [—]	Slow rhythm 8 x Short hills [5]	Medium endurance [5]	Medium endurance [5]	Strength Modified fartlek 4 [6]	Short endurance [3]	Medium endurance [6]	30
	8	Off [—]	Medium rhythm 2 x 1 mile [3]	Medium endurance [5]	Medium endurance [5]	Strength Rolling hills 4 [6]	Short endurance [3]	Long endurance [8]	30
SHARPENING	9	Off [—]	Fast rhythm 3 x 880 [5]	Medium endurance [5]	Medium endurance [5]	Short endurance [4]	Off [—]	Race 5 Km [6]	25
	10	Short endurance [3]	Off [—]	Medium endurance [5]	Medium endurance [4]	Medium rhythm 7 x 440 [4]	Short endurance [3]	Medium endurance [6]	25
	11	Off [—]	Fast rhythm 3 x 880 [4]	Short endurance [3]	Medium endurance [6]	Strength Modified fartlek 4 [6]	Off [—]	Medium endurance [6]	25
TAPERING	12	Off [—]	Medium rhythm 8 x 440 [4]	Short endurance [3]	Medium endurance [4]	Medium endurance [4]	Off [—]	Race 5 Km [5]	15 + race

ADVANCED COMPETITOR'S 12-WEEK 5KM BUILD-UP SCHEDULE

PHASE	WEEK	MONDAY	TUESDAY	WEDNESDAY	THURSDAY	FRIDAY	SATURDAY	SUNDAY	TOTAL MILEAGE
ENDURANCE	1	Medium endurance 5	Slow rhythm 10 x 440 5	Medium endurance 5	Medium endurance 5	Medium endurance 6	Short endurance 4	Long endurance 10	40
ENDURANCE	2	Medium endurance 6	Slow rhythm 6 x 880 5	Medium endurance 5	Medium endurance 6	Slow rhythm 10 x Short hills 6	Medium endurance 5	Medium endurance 7	40
ENDURANCE	3	Medium endurance 6	Slow rhythm 4 x 1 mile 6	Short endurance 4	Strength Advanced fartlek 4	Medium endurance 7	Short endurance 4	Long endurance 12	45
STRENGTHENING	4	Medium endurance 6	Medium rhythm 6 x 880 6	Short endurance 5	Medium endurance 8	Strength Rolling hills 5 8	Medium endurance 7	Medium endurance 8	48
STRENGTHENING	5	Medium endurance 8	Medium rhythm 3 x 1 mile 8	Medium endurance 7	Strength Advanced fartlek 4	Medium endurance 8	Short endurance 5	Race 10 Km 8	48
STRENGTHENING	6	Short endurance 5	Medium endurance 8	Medium endurance 8	Strength Advanced fartlek 4	Medium endurance 8	Medium rhythm 3 x 1 mile 6	Medium endurance 7	48
STRENGTHENING	7	Medium endurance 8	Strength Advanced fartlek 6	Short endurance 8	Strength Advanced fartlek 4	Medium endurance 7	Strength Fast 4 continuous run 7	Medium endurance 7	48
SHARPENING	8	Medium endurance 8	Fast rhythm 6 x 440 8	Short endurance 6	Strength Advanced fartlek 4	Medium endurance 6	Medium rhythm 7 x 880 6	Medium endurance 8	45
SHARPENING	9	Short endurance 6	Power 2 x 1 mile 5	Medium endurance 5	Medium endurance 6	Medium rhythm 12 x 440 6	Medium endurance 8	Medium endurance 8	45
SHARPENING	10	Medium endurance 8	Medium rhythm 4 x 1 mile 6	Short endurance 5	Strength Advanced fartlek 4	Medium endurance 8	Short endurance 5	Race 5 Km 7	45
SHARPENING	11	Short endurance 4	Medium endurance 6	Medium endurance 6	Medium endurance 6	Fast rhythm 4 x 880 6	Short endurance 4	Medium endurance 8	38
TAPERING	12	Medium endurance 6	Medium rhythm 7 x 880 4	Short endurance 4	Medium endurance 5	Medium endurance 5	Off —	Race 5 Km	24 + race

238

CHAMPION COMPETITOR'S 12-WEEK 5 KM BUILD-UP SCHEDULE

PHASE/WEEK	MONDAY	TUESDAY	WEDNESDAY	THURSDAY	FRIDAY	SATURDAY	SUNDAY	TOTAL MILEAGE
ENDURANCE 1	10 Medium endurance	6 Slow rhythm 12 x 440	8 Medium endurance	8 Medium endurance	8 Strength Advanced fartlek 4	8 Medium endurance	12 Long endurance	60
2	10 Medium endurance	8 Slow rhythm 5 x 1 mile	8 Medium endurance	10 Medium endurance	6 Slow rhythm 12 x Short hills	6 Medium endurance	10 Medium endurance	60
3	10 Medium endurance	6 Slow rhythm 8 x 880	8 Medium endurance	8 Strength Rolling hills 6	10 Medium endurance	8 Medium endurance	15 Long endurance	65
STRENGTHENING 4	10 Medium endurance	7 Medium rhythm 4 x 1 mile	8 Medium endurance	10 Medium endurance	8 Strength Advanced fartlek 6	10 Medium endurance	12 Medium endurance	65
5	10 Medium endurance	10 Medium rhythm 10 x Short hills	8 Medium endurance	9 Strength Fast 5 continuous run	10 Medium endurance	6 Short endurance	12 Race 10 Km	65
6	6 Short endurance	8 Medium endurance	10 Medium endurance	10 Strength Advanced fartlek 6	10 Medium endurance	9 Medium rhythm 14 x 440	12 Medium endurance	65
7	10 Medium endurance	9 Medium rhythm 4 x 1 mile	10 Medium endurance	8 Fast rhythm 4 x 880	8 Medium endurance	8 Strength Advanced fartlek 5	12 Medium endurance	65
SHARPENING 8	10 Medium endurance	8 Strength Tempo run 4	8 Medium endurance	10 Medium rhythm 12 x 440	10 Medium endurance	6 Short endurance	8 Race 5 Km	60
9	6 Short endurance	10 Medium endurance	8 Medium endurance	8 Strength Advanced fartlek 5	8 Medium endurance	8 Fast rhythm 4 x 880	12 Medium endurance	60
10	10 Medium endurance	6 Power 3 x 1 mile	6 Short endurance	6 Strength Advanced fartlek 5	6 Medium endurance	6 Short endurance	8 Race 5 Km	50
11	6 Short endurance	8 Medium endurance	8 Medium endurance	8 Medium rhythm 4–5 x 1 mile	6 Short endurance	6 Fast rhythm 12 x 220	8 Medium endurance	50
TAPERING 12	8 Medium endurance	8 Medium rhythm 8 x 880	4 Short endurance	6 Medium endurance	6 Medium endurance	6 Off	— Race 5 Km	30 + race

16. THE MILE

This event is the focus of most track meets and the basic measure of all runners: you train at a 7:30-per-mile pace and race at a 6:30-per-mile-pace. The Wanamaker Mile in the Millrose Games, in New York's Madison Square Garden, is the classic event of the classic meet of the indoor season, and 19,000 spectators stand to cheer its participants. The excitement of the mile has been with us for decades, even before Roger Bannister broke the elusive four-minute barrier in 1954. The excitement returned to the headlines in 1981 when Great Britain's Sebastian Coe and Steve Ovett ran world-outdoor-record miles, and the first world class mile race down a city street saw elite runners sprinting down New York City's Fifth Avenue before thousands of spectators and millions of television viewers.

High school and college runners see the mile as the prestige event for them, and the mile is catching on with adults who run the distance on a track or in the increasingly popular road mile runs. The mile requires different training and racing methods than are used for the longer road races. Your training schedule should efficiently combine speed, strength and endurance runs. You will have to keep constantly alert to how your body reacts to the stressful training of the mile. It is very important that you remain flexible in your program and make adjustments when necessary.

Whether you are experimenting with the distance for the first time or have experience in competing at this event, you must keep the following points in mind:

• *Speed Work.* The key to running the mile is power: that means improving both your speed and your strength. Speed work for the mile is much faster than for other distances. Medium rhythm pace is your one-mile pace, slow rhythm runs are done at 5 km pace, and fast rhythm runs are done at half-mile pace. You will run speed work for up to 50 percent of the time when training for the mile, compared to 5 to 15 percent for the 10 km–marathon. You will race and train much more anaerobically. You won't hit the Wall in the mile, but you will carry the Bear.

Speed workouts will help your energy system become more efficient and help you handle the oxygen debt incurred when running the mile. Fast rhythm runs will force you to become accustomed to running fast while accumulating lactic acid. Power repetitions teach you to run in oxygen debt while maintaining good form and style. Refer to the One-Mile Training Rhythm Workout Guide on page 504 and the Power Workout Guide on page 508 for help in designing your speed workouts.

• *Muscular Strength.* Along with increasing your speed, you will need to increase your muscular strength. Your muscles will have to propel you forward in what feels like a sprint. Strength-training runs are included in the miler's regular training routine, as well as weight training for the legs, upper body and abdominals. You will become stronger overall and, as a result, faster. Power speed work and fast rhythm workouts on the track and hills should be included following a build-up of strength-training runs.

• *Form.* The same running form that you use for your long-distance runs will not help you in the mile. In fact, it may slow you down. You will need to learn the ball-heel footstrike and the power stride.

• *Warm-up.* Due to the intensity of this event from the very start of the race, it is important that you properly warm up and cool down following the guidelines in Chapter 27.

• *Flexibility.* Due to changed running form and the increased stress from additional speed training, you will place more strain on your Achilles tendon, lower leg muscles and major joints. It is very important that you incorporate into your training an extensive program of flexibility exercises for the hamstrings, Achilles tendons, ankles, lower back, knees and hip flexors.

• *Recovery.* You will need more rest than usual after hard speed work and races. You are using different muscles and a different energy supply system. Use your easy days wisely following the hard days. For the highly experienced miler in the early stages of training, hard workouts two days in a row are sometimes used to teach the body to respond to the high intensity of work demanded by the mile. The third day should be easy.

• *Racing Shoes.* Inexperienced milers should wear racing flats, not spikes. Experienced milers should race in spikes only after breaking them in gradually during workouts.

• *Training on the Track.* You should do one or two speed workouts a week on the track to get the feel for its surface and turns, but don't do your endurance runs there. Track running will help you get a feel for racing, and when your laps are timed, you will develop a sense of rhythm and pace for the mile. Speed workouts can also be done on trails, hills and grass fields for variety.

• *Build-up Races.* Most milers like to race the mile frequently during their training cycle. Some runners even race every weekend. Generally, you should race the mile at least two or three times during your training phase if you are an inexperienced miler, and four to seven times if you are an experienced miler. Racing the mile will teach you a great deal about pace, strategy and your individual strengths and weaknesses. The more you race, the more you will learn and the faster you will be able to race for the final mile run of your training cycle. If you can't find a track meet to race a mile in, you may need to just do it by yourself as a time trial. If possible, recruit others to run with and to time you and cheer you on.

CATEGORIES OF MILERS

We have replaced our four fitness categories for road racing with two broad categories for the mile. For the most part, the basic and some advanced competitors would fit into our inexperienced miler category. The novice competitor isn't fit or experienced enough at racing to run the mile all-out. Most champion competitors and many advanced competitors, along with the majority of high school and college track runners, would fit into the experienced miler category.

The Inexperienced Miler

This category includes the following runners:

A. The young runner (age 12–15) who is experimenting with the mile for the first time or is in his or her first few years of running. We recommend that this runner limit his mileage to 15–20 miles a week and work on developing leg speed and good racing form. Young runners will have many years ahead of them in which to build endurance with higher mileage. They should also be careful not to overrace.

B. Women who have not run the mile competitively before or have not run faster than a 6:00 mile. Women should be able to run under 50:00 for 10 km before attempting to train for the mile.

C. Men who have not run the mile competitively or have not run faster than a 5:00 mile. Men should be able to run under 45:00 for 10 km before attempting to train for the mile.

We have included speed restrictions here because training for the mile is very intense work. The inexperienced miler does not have the speed or strength to follow the more difficult training program for the experienced miler. Before racing the mile, you should have run a few shorter races of 5 km–4 miles.

The Experienced Miler

This category includes the following runners:

A. The high school runner who has a good training background, and if a boy, can run faster than a 5:00 mile; if a girl, faster than a 6:00 mile. *Note*: Many high school track programs require the runner to race more frequently than we suggest. To adjust, substitute your scheduled races for speed-workout days on our schedule and reduce your weekly mileage. Generally, high school milers do not run more than 40–50 miles a week.

B. Women road runners who have competed regularly at 5 km–10 km and can run faster than a 6:00 mile. This runner should be able to break 42:00 for 10 km.

C. Men road runners who have competed regularly at 5 km–10 km and can run faster than a 5:00 mile. This runner should be able to break 37:00 for 10 km.

D. Track-oriented men and women who train to race under 5:00 and 6:00 respectively for the mile.

The following training program is designed for our two categories of milers and uses the six-step approach outlined in Chapter 10.

STEP ONE: DETERMINE
YOUR FITNESS CATEGORY

Use either the inexperienced or experienced miler's program. Your decision should be based primarily on how well your body can handle the much more intense work necessary to run the mile competitively.

STEP TWO: SELECT YOUR RACES AND TIME GOALS

You should run at least two one-mile competitions during your training cycle. Use the first one to get the feel of the race, familiarize yourself with the speed of the event, and the different type of fatigue, strategy, etc. Then use the second mile race to improve your time. You should also pick time barriers to break as you compete. Common barriers to break include (pace per 440-yard lap is noted after each barrier): 7:00 (1:45), 6:30 (1:37), 6:00 (90 seconds), 5:30 (82.5 seconds), 5:00 (75 seconds), 4:40 (70 seconds), 4:30 (67.5 seconds) and 4:20 (65 seconds).

It will take time to reach your goals, perhaps over a number of racing seasons. You may progress rapidly and then stall out for a while. As you become stronger, faster and more experienced at racing shorter distances, you will eventually reach your realistic goals. Don't rush. Speed must be carefully developed, or you will become an ex-miler.

STEP THREE: DETERMINE YOUR TRAINING CYCLE AND THE LENGTH OF YOUR PHASES

We use a shortened, 8-week schedule for the inexperienced miler. This is the minimal amount of training needed to improve significantly for this event. Much more time spent doing this intense training is liable to cause you either to lose interest or become injured. The experienced miler should follow a 12-week short-term training cycle to allow for a sufficient build-up of endurance, strength and speed. All milers should have a good background of mileage before starting the endurance phase.

Here is a guide to selecting your phases for mile training:

DESCRIPTION	INEXPERIENCED MILER	EXPERIENCED MILER
Length of build-up	8 weeks	12
Endurance phase	2	3
Strengthening phase	3	4
Sharpening phase	2	4
Tapering phase	1	1
Rebuilding phase	3–4	3–6
Number of races in cycle	2–3	4–8

STEP FOUR: DETERMINE YOUR WEEKLY MILEAGE AND LONG-RUN GOALS

The mile requires less of a mileage base than do longer
distance events, but training for it requires a balance between easy endurance runs and intense speed work. The
miler doesn't need to do long runs for as long a distance as
the road racer. In fact, long runs may do more harm than
good. During your training for the mile, long runs may
make you feel heavy and sluggish, throw off your rhythm
for the race, and take time away from specific mile training.
Training pace for all endurance runs will be similar to that
of the 5 km runner (see page 230).

Follow these mileage guidelines when training for the
mile:

FITNESS CATEGORY	WEEKLY MILEAGE	MILEAGE OF LONG RUNS
Inexperienced miler	20–40	6–10
Experienced miler	40–60	8–14

STEP FIVE: PLAN YOUR INDIVIDUAL WORKOUTS (*See model schedules at the end of this chapter*)

Inexperienced Miler

Endurance Phase (2 weeks): 2 speed workouts per week; 0–1 long run; no races. Before starting this phase, it is necessary that you already have put in at least a solid month of endurance training. A short endurance phase is used as a transition to the much faster paced runs used to train for the mile. Introduce speed work with modified *fartlek* and rolling hills. Slow rhythm runs are added, but these are now done at 5 km pace. Listen to your body for signs that this harder introductory speed work is too much for you at this point.

Strengthening Phase (3 weeks): 2 speed workouts per week; 0–1 long run and 1–2 races during phase. During this phase you will begin to work harder at your two speed sessions each week. Do plenty of work on hills to add strength along with a 5 km road race. Toward the end of this phase, introduce a race-pace rhythm run based on your present predicted speed for the mile. Races of 3 km–5 km are used to improve strength.

Sharpening Phase (2 weeks): 2–3 speed workouts per week; no long runs; 1–2 races per phase. Add fast rhythm workouts to improve speed. These are done at your predicted speed for the 880, so be very careful not to overstrain and pull a muscle at what will probably feel like an all-out sprint for you. Reduce your weekly mileage. Race a mile during this phase to become familiar with the event.

Tapering Phase (1 week): 1–2 speed workouts; no long runs; 1 race—1 mile. Reduce mileage, don't overtrain. One rhythm workout at the pace at which you feel you can race the mile is used early in the week to give you a final feel for race pace. Use a minimal number of repetitions so as not to take strength away from your final all-out effort for the mile.

Experienced Miler

This runner spends most of his or her time improving strength and speed.

Endurance Phase (3 weeks): 2 speed workouts per week; 0–1 long run and 0–1 race during phase. Make the transition into faster work by including several strength runs and then slow rhythm runs at 5 km race pace. Include a 5 km or similar-distance race (3 km, 2 or 4 mile) to develop strength, endurance and the ability to maintain a fast pace over longer distances.

Strengthening Phase (4 weeks): 2–3 speed workouts per week; 0–1 long run; 1–2 races during phase. Gradually begin to do three hard sessions per week, introducing rhythm runs at your present one-mile race pace and finally fast-paced runs at your estimated 880 pace. Include one or two one-mile races during this phase to gain racing experience and test your fitness level. Don't expect to race fast times in these early races. If you wish to continue working on strength building, run a 5 km race instead of a mile.

Sharpening Phase (4 weeks): 2–3 speed workouts per week; no long runs; 2–3 races during phase. You should concentrate on these key areas: increasing your leg speed with short, fast rhythm runs using proper running form; increasing the power drive in your legs with hard, explosive power workouts on a track or hills; and improving your ability to run with the Bear on your back. Include at least two one-mile races in this phase to bring down your time.

Tapering Phase (1 week): 2 speed workouts; no long runs; 1 race–one mile. It is very important that you not overtrain here after spending so much effort building up for your final mile race. It is better to do too little mileage and speed work in the last week than too much.

STEP SIX: PLAN YOUR REBUILDING PHASE

THE MILE BUILD-UP SCHEDULE

The model training schedules on pages 249–50 should be used to help you write your own program. The exact mile-

THE INEXPERIENCED MILER'S 8-WEEK BUILD-UP SCHEDULE
MEN: 5 MIN MILE TO 6:30 MILE
WOMEN: 6 MIN MILE TO 7:30 MILE

PHASE / WEEK		MONDAY	TUESDAY	WEDNESDAY	THURSDAY	FRIDAY	SATURDAY	SUNDAY	TOTAL MILEAGE
ENDURANCE	1	Off (—)	Strength Modified fartlek (5)	Short endurance (4)	Medium endurance (6)	Strength Modified fartlek (5)	Short endurance (3)	Medium endurance (6)	30
ENDURANCE	2	Off (—)	Strength Rolling hills (5)	Medium endurance (6)	Strength Modified fartlek (5)	Short endurance (4)	Medium endurance (5)	Medium endurance (5)	30
ENDURANCE	3	Off (—)	Slow rhythm 10 x 220 (4)	Short endurance (5)	Medium endurance (6)	Strength Rolling hills (5)	Short endurance (4)	Medium endurance (6)	30
STRENGTHENING	4	Slow rhythm 8 x 440 (5)	Short endurance (5)	Slow rhythm 4 x 880 (5)	Short endurance (5)	Strength Rolling hills (7)	Off (—)	Race 5 Km (4)	30
STRENGTHENING	5	Short endurance (4)	Off (—)	Medium endurance (6)	Slow rhythm 3 x 1 mile (5)	Short endurance (4)	Medium endurance (6)	Medium rhythm 6 x 440 (5)	30
SHARPENING	6	Short endurance (4)	Fast rhythm 3 x 880 (5)	Short endurance (4)	Fast rhythm 4 x 440 (4)	Short endurance (4)	Strength Modified fartlek (5)	Short endurance (4)	30
SHARPENING	7	Medium endurance (6)	Fast rhythm 8 x 220 (5)	Short endurance (4)	Medium rhythm 8 x 440 (5)	Short endurance (4)	Off (—)	Race Mile (3)	27
TAPERING	8	Short endurance (4)	Short endurance (4)	Medium rhythm 3 x 880 (5)	Short endurance (4)	Short endurance (4)	Off (—)	Race Mile (3)	21 + race

249

THE EXPERIENCED MILER'S 12-WEEK BUILDUP SCHEDULE
MEN: SUB 5 MIN MILE
WOMEN: SUB 6 MIN MILE

PHASE / WEEK	MONDAY	TUESDAY	WEDNESDAY	THURSDAY	FRIDAY	SATURDAY	SUNDAY	TOTAL MILEAGE
ENDURANCE — 1	Medium endurance (7)	Strength Advanced fartlek (7)	Short endurance (5)	Medium endurance (7)	Strength Rolling hills 5 (7)	Short endurance (5)	Medium endurance (7)	45
ENDURANCE — 2	Medium endurance (8)	Strength Advanced fartlek (7)	Short endurance (5)	Strength Fast 6 continuous run (9)	Medium endurance (7)	Short endurance (4)	Race 5Km (5)	45
ENDURANCE — 3	Short endurance (5)	Medium endurance (8)	Medium endurance (10)	Slow rhythm 12 x 440 (6)	Short endurance (5)	Slow rhythm 8 x Short hills (6)	Medium endurance (10)	50
STRENGTHENING — 4	Slow rhythm 8 x 880 (7)	Medium endurance (6)	Medium endurance (6)	Strength Advanced fartlek (8)	Short endurance (6)	Medium endurance (7)	Medium endurance (10)	50
STRENGTHENING — 5	Slow rhythm 12 x Short hills (8)	Medium endurance (8)	Medium endurance (8)	Slow rhythm 4 x 1 mile (8)	Medium endurance (7)	Slow rhythm 12 x 440 (6)	Race 1 mile (5)	50
STRENGTHENING — 6	Short endurance (5)	Medium rhythm 8 x 440 (6)	Medium rhythm 5 x 880 (6)	Strength Advanced fartlek (10)	Medium endurance (9)	Slow rhythm 4 x 1 mile (6)	Medium endurance (8)	50
STRENGTHENING — 7	Medium endurance (8)	Medium endurance (10)	Medium endurance (6)	Medium endurance (6)	Medium rhythm 10 x 440 (6)	Medium endurance (6)	Fast rhythm 10 x 220 (8)	50
SHARPENING — 8	Medium endurance (8)	Medium rhythm 10 x 440 (8)	Short endurance (6)	Fast rhythm 12 x 220 (7)	Short endurance (5)	Medium rhythm 5 x 880 (6)	Short endurance (5)	45
SHARPENING — 9	Medium endurance (8)	Power 3 x 880 (8)	Medium endurance (6)	Medium rhythm 10 x 440 (8)	Medium endurance (6)	Short endurance (5)	Race 1 mile (4)	45
SHARPENING — 10	Short endurance (6)	Strength Advanced fartlek (6)	Medium endurance (8)	Fast rhythm 6 x 440 (8)	Medium endurance (8)	Power 3 x 880 (5)	Medium endurance (7)	45
SHARPENING — 11	Medium endurance (8)	Fast rhythm 12 x 220 (8)	Medium endurance (6)	Medium rhythm 10 x 440 (6)	Short endurance (5)	Short endurance (5)	Race 1 mile (4)	40
TAPERING — 12	Short endurance (5)	Medium rhythm 3 x 880 (5)	Short endurance (5)	Strength Advanced fartlek (5) / 3	Short endurance (5)	Off	Race 1 mile	24 + race

age you will run, distance and dates of your build-up races, and the days you will do your different types of runs will vary with your individual needs, age, sex and other factors that influence your running. Use these models as a guide to create a specific training program that can help you reach your racing goals. Understand the concepts behind these schedules, don't just follow them blindly. We have not included an example of the rebuilding phase. Follow the model in Chapter 10 to write your rebuilding program.

Pace Progression

As you begin your training cycle for the mile, your fast, medium and slow rhythm workouts will be slower in each area than at the end of your last mile racing season. Obviously, you were in better shape then. Now, you want to increase the speed of your rhythm runs progressively toward your race goal pace so that your body adjusts to the increased intensity without breaking down. If you find that at the start of your speed program you are having a hard time running slow rhythm workouts at your 5 km pace, or that it takes two days to recover from the workout, you are not fit enough to handle this intensity. You should either slow down the pace of your runs or increase the number of weeks that you do endurance training.

STRATEGIC TIPS FOR
THE INEXPERIENCED MILER

Starting

Racing the mile may be a new experience for you. First of all, there will probably be only a few other competitors at the starting line. Usually no more than ten can safely compete. Secondly, everyone runs very fast when the starting gun goes off. There is no shuffling along waiting for a place to open, no time to check your watch or say hello to a friend. You are off and flying, or else. It is important, therefore, that you follow these instructions for the start of the mile:

• Make sure you are ready to run when the starter calls you to the line. You should be finished warming up and ready to go.

• The starter usually gives two commands: "Take your marks," and firing the gun. Be ready to go when the starter tells you to take your mark. Often the starter will fire the gun immediately after the command.

• Make sure that the runners on either side of you give you enough room to run freely. If they squeeze you in, use your elbows to move them away.

Establishing Your Race Pace

Invariably, you will go out faster than your anticipated race pace. Don't panic. Get control of yourself quickly, relax, and settle into your own race pace as soon as possible. This is essential if you are a first-time racer. Try to get your breathing under control and rhythmic. Panic breathing will cause you to stay tight and continue running fast until exhausted. By concentrating on getting your breathing under control, you will also start to settle into your race pace.

Listen for Your Splits

Most mile races are run on a 440-yard or 400-meter track. You will have to go around the track four times to complete the mile. Each time you complete one lap you should hear a time called for that lap. These are your splits (the mile is split into 4 × 440). Before running your mile race, you should determine your 440 splits. This will enable you to run as even a pace as possible. For example, if you want to run a 6:00 mile, your 440 splits will be 0:90, 3:00, 4:30 and then your final time.

Race Tactics

The inexperienced miler should concentrate only on running an evenly paced race. Leave the tactics of racing against others to the more experienced runners. Get into your pace, stay relaxed, run rhythmically. Don't get caught trying to run with people faster than you. Run *your* race.

STRATEGIC TIPS FOR THE EXPERIENCED MILER

- Start quickly to get into a good position, and then settle into your pace.
- Make no big moves early in the race. These include sprints to discourage opposition or catch another runner.
- Know your natural strengths and use them in the race. If you have good natural speed, wait until the last possible moment to use it. If you are a very strong runner, use your long, extended kick over the final 440 to 660 yards.
- Concentrate on competing rather than on running a certain time. You will run better when battling the competition.
- Don't get "boxed in"—stuck behind slower runners without being able to pass. Run slightly off the right shoulder of the runner in front of you so you can easily pass if this runner slows down.
- Pump your arms when you need to pick up your speed.
- Stay forward on your feet to maintain good rhythm and forward drive, especially when you want to "kick."

Safety Note: Due to the intensity of this event from the very start of the race, it is important that you do the proper warm-up and cool-down routines, following the guidelines in Chapter 27.

17. CROSS-COUNTRY

Bounding down a wooded trail, I suddenly careen to the left, then to the right, and climb a short, steep, rocky hill. I mount the crest, burst down the other side, uncontrollably flowing along meandering paths as birds and other animals scurry away. As I pick up the pace and roller-coaster along, I fantasize that I am pulling away from my competition and powering out of the woods to cross the finish line in an open field.

—BOB GLOVER

No other type of running offers such variety of terrain, scenery and emotional experiences as cross-country. As every experienced "harrier" knows, cross-country racing is a love-hate relationship. It is a scenic, serene and rewarding experience only *after* the race is over. The race itself is a gut-wrenching ordeal that demands careful preparation and promises no "runner's high." To the untrained, a 10 km cross-country race over a tough, hilly course would be as devastating as a marathon on the roads.

Cross-country runners must prepare for this unique test of their stamina and competitive spirit. Most cross-country courses—usually in parks or golf courses—include numerous hills and valleys, sharp turns, narrow paths, and difficult footing that will quickly make you forget the idyllic setting and force you to respond to the challenge ahead.

The tempo is also very different from road races. In cross-country racing, you will have difficulty settling into a steady pace or rhythm. Throughout the entire race you will be changing speeds as you attempt to negotiate turns, uphills, downhills. Thus the advanced *fartlek* becomes an essential training run. Courses in New York City's Van Cortlandt Park and Philadelphia's Fairmount Park contain hills with such appropriate names as "Cemetery Hill" and "Parachute Hill." In Europe, plowed fields, haystacks and water jumps are added to the courses to make them more challenging. When Pete Schuder and his Columbia team traveled to England to compete against Oxford, the course included a quagmire of mud a foot deep, the usual impossible hills, and a wide brook. The times for the 5.5 mile course were slow, shoes and uniforms a mess, but the runners had a great time competing against each other and Mother Nature.

If you are still eager, don't make the mistake of jumping into any cross-country race. Your road-running training will be of little use here. You must train specifically for the cross-country event to run the course successfully.

CATEGORIES OF CROSS-COUNTRY RUNNERS: INEXPERIENCED AND EXPERIENCED

As with the mile, we have replaced our four fitness categories for road racing with two broad categories for cross-country. For the most part, the basic and some advanced competitors would fit into our inexperienced category. The novice competitor, like many basic competitors, is not fit or experienced enough to race over difficult terrain. Most champion and many advanced competitors, along with the majority of high school and college runners, would fit into the experienced category.

The Inexperienced Cross-Country Runner

This category includes the following runners:

A. Young runners (age 12–15) who are new to the sport of cross-country or who are in their first few years of running. We recommend that these runners limit their mileage to 20–25 miles per week and race only at distances of one-and-a-half miles or less. These runners will need to modify our model eight-week schedule by lowering the mileage totals.

B. Men and women road racers who are running cross-country for the first time, or who have previously run the event but only wish to dabble with it. Men should be able to run 45:00 or better and women 50:00 or better for a 10 km on the roads before attempting to compete at this event. These runners should limit their cross-country races to 5 km and use the 10 km Rhythm Workout Guide on page 506 when doing rhythm runs—not the 5 km chart.

The Experienced Cross-Country Runner

This category includes the following runners:

A. The high school runner who has a solid background of distance training and is able to run 40–50 miles per week, including hard speed work. This runner is able to run the 5 km on the road or track under 19:00 if a boy and under 22:00 if a girl. Since most high school cross-country courses are between 2½ miles and 5 km, this runner should follow the training schedule we have developed at the end of this chapter for that distance and use the 5 km Rhythm Workout Guide on page 505 as a guide to setting speed workouts.

Note: Many high school programs require the runner to race more frequently than we suggest. To adjust, substitute your scheduled races for speed-workout days on our schedule and reduce your weekly mileage.

B. Women who have experienced racing cross-country and who are able to run 42:00 or faster for 10 km on the roads. Most women's cross-country races are contested at distances from 3 km to 5 km. Use the training schedule and rhythm guide as explained above for the high school runner if you're going to train for this distance, and the 10 km cross-country schedule and rhythm guide if you're going to race 5 miles to 10 km.

C. Men who are experienced at running cross-country and who are able to run faster than 37:00 for 10 km on the road. Most open and college cross-country races are contested at distances ranging from 5 miles to 10 km. Use the 10 km cross-country schedule and follow the 10 km rhythm charts.

The following training program is designed for our two categories of cross-country runners and uses the six-step approach outlined in Chapter 10.

STEP ONE: DETERMINE YOUR FITNESS CATEGORY

Use either the inexperienced or experienced program. Your decision should be based primarily on how well your body can handle the much more intense work necessary to manage the hilly terrain and other challenges which cross-country offers.

STEP TWO: SELECT YOUR RACES AND TIME GOALS

Select only a few races to run during your training cycle. These races are very taxing and require time to recover properly. You must really get mentally "up" for this event, and you can't do that every week. Ideally, space your races, running only one every two to three weeks. It is very difficult to set a time goal for a particular cross-country course, since all courses are different and usually you are more concerned with beating your competitors and the course itself than the clock. A 38:40 10 km cross-country time on one course may be excellent because the course is very hilly, while the same time on a flat course may be slow. As an alternative to reaching for certain time barriers, you may choose to better your time over the same course or to defeat other runners of similar experience in your age group.

STEP THREE: DETERMINE YOUR TRAINING CYCLE AND THE LENGTH OF YOUR PHASES

All runners should have a good background of aerobic training before beginning the endurance phase. The inexperienced cross-country runner should limit his or her training to a short-term, 8-week cycle. This minimum period will allow you to improve at this event without overtaxing your body. The experienced cross-country runner must devote a minimum of 12 weeks (short-term cycle) to train properly for top performances. The strength phase for both categories of runners is very important because of the strength required to race up and down hills. At least 3–5 weeks of strength training, including advanced *fartlek*, rolling hills runs and specific hill training, are needed. The inexperienced runner doesn't need to spend as much time sharpening for the race since he or she is more concerned with running a strong race to the finish than running at fast speeds. The experienced runner will spend much more time on sharpening, especially if the course is short (3–5 km) or flat and fast.

Here is a guide to selecting your phases for cross-country training:

DESCRIPTION	INEXPERIENCED COMPETITOR	EXPERIENCED COMPETITOR
Length of build-up	8 weeks	12
Endurance phase	3	4
Strengthening phase	3	5
Sharpening phase	1	2
Tapering phase	1	1
Rebuilding phase	3–4	3–6
Number of races during cycle	2–3	4–5

STEP FOUR: DETERMINE YOUR WEEKLY MILEAGE AND LONG-RUN GOALS

Your weekly mileage goals are determined by several factors:

1. *Your training phase.* When you include difficult strength-training runs in your schedule, your mileage may

drop a little since the runs you do for cross-country are harder than the normal strength workouts you would do for a road race. You may have to give your body more time to recover from the stress.

2. *Cross-country races.* For the inexperienced runner, cross-country racing is more difficult than road racing, so you will need longer rest periods with reduced mileage after each race. Also, all runners will need more mileage if training for a 10 km than if training for a 5 km.

3. *The weather.* Cross-country training begins in the heat of summer and ends in the snows of winter. Weather will be a major factor in your mileage and running. Cross-country is a fall sport. Use the long, hot summer for endurance training to build a solid foundation before starting your training cycle.

You should decide what level of mileage you can handle best and benefit from the most. Continue including long runs in your training schedule as though preparing for distance races on the road. These runs will toughen you for the terrain of cross-country. Training pace for all endurance runs would be similar to that of 10 km and 5 km (see pages 190 and 231).

Follow these mileage guidelines when training for cross-country:

FITNESS CATEGORY	WEEKLY MILEAGE	MILEAGE OF LONG RUNS
Inexperienced competitor (5 km)	30–50	10–15
Inexperienced competitor (1½ miles)	20–25	4–6
Experienced competitor (10 km)	60–100	15–20
Experienced competitor (5 km)	40–60	8–12

STEP FIVE: PLAN YOUR INDIVIDUAL WORKOUTS (*See model schedules at the end of this chapter*)

Inexperienced Competitor

Endurance Phase (3 weeks): 1–2 speed workouts per week; 2–3 long runs and 1 race during phase. The three-week endurance phase is primarily used to maintain a high level of aerobic fitness and to prepare the body for the more intense strength work necessary for cross-country. Include modified *fartlek* and rolling hills runs to simulate race conditions. Increase mileage to your peak level.

Strengthening Phase (3 weeks): 1–2 speed workouts per week; 1–2 long runs and 1–2 races during phase. Use this phase to improve your ability to handle hills. Hill training will benefit you greatly even if your races are mainly over flat courses. Do several of your strength and rhythm runs over cross-country trails rather than on the road or track to familiarize yourself with running cross-country. Your first race should be more of an experience than a competitive race. Keep it low key so that you will want to come back for more.

Sharpening Phase (1 week): 2 speed workouts; no long runs; no races. This one-week phase consists of reducing your mileage and doing race-pace rhythm workouts or faster, variable speed runs such as rolling hills and advanced *fartlek*.

Tapering Phase (1 week): 1 speed workout; no long runs; 1 race—5 km cross-country. Your last speed workout should be 5–6 days prior to your key race and be low key. Be sure to be well rested for your contest against nature. Remember the lessons learned from the previous races.

Experienced Competitor

Endurance Phase (4 weeks): 2 speed workouts per week; 2–3 long runs and 1 race during phase. A successful cross-country racing season is dependent on building a solid base of mileage *prior* to starting the 12-week build-up schedule. Pete Schuder's Columbia University cross-country team that won the Ivy League Championship in 1979 stayed on the roads from early June until the end of August, and gradually increased each runner's base mileage from about 60–65 miles per week to 80–85 miles. Most of the mileage was run at a comfortable conversational pace and a few road races were used to maintain interest. When the team members returned to campus in late August, they began specific cross-country training following a 12-week build-up schedule. The 4-week endurance phase should be used to maintain your aerobic base and also to blend in slow rhythm workouts and strength runs which allow your body to adapt to the rigors of cross-country training. A race during this phase is used to gain experience in the unique challenges of cross-country racing.

Strengthening Phase (5 weeks): 2 speed workouts per week; 2–3 long runs and 1–2 races during phase. Include several hill workouts and advanced *fartlek* runs in this phase. Rhythm hill workouts in particular will improve your leg strength, increase your ability to drive up hills, and improve your racing form. *Fartlek* best imitates cross-country racing conditions. If possible, run some of these workouts on the course you plan to race, or a similar course. *Fartlek*, like cross-country racing, demands that you keep changing your speed and form as you go through the course. Other specific workouts can include runs of one to two miles over the most difficult portion of the course. Repeat this run three to five times during this workout, depending on the shape you are in. Also, you may choose to run a time trial at 80 to 90 percent effort over the entire course, or parts of it, to get a good feel for the course under racing conditions.

You should run at least one cross-country race during this phase to test yourself both physically and mentally. Run the race at less than all-out effort, but be competitive against your opponents and the course. Reduce mileage coming off this race to ensure proper recovery. Cross-country races demand more recovery time.

Sharpening Phase (2 weeks): 2 speed workouts per week; no long runs; 1 race. Include faster-than-race-pace workouts to:

1. Improve your racing speed.
2. Make it easier for you to start out faster than race pace in order to get a good position in a crowded field.
3. Make it easier for you to pick up the pace to pass runners quickly on narrow paths.

Include workouts that are very specific to your races:

1. Hilly courses would require some final short drills over hills.

2. Flat, fast courses or shorter race distances than 10 km require that you include longer, race-pace rhythm runs to help you maintain a steady pace.

3. Run the first 880 yards of your race course at the pace you will start at to give you a feeling of jumping out in good position for the race.

4. Finish some of your workouts by briskly covering the last 880 yards of the course at race pace. This will help you get your mind and body accustomed to finishing strongly.

Include a cross-country race during this phase, which you should run at all-out effort. Concentrate on staying calm, for any tightness will cause you to lose your ability to run efficiently. Don't allow the course to defeat you by trying to overpower it. Use this race as your final learning experience prior to your big meet. Reduce weekly mileage to accommodate intense training.

Tapering Phase (1 week): 1 speed workout; no long runs; 1 race. Allow your mind and body to relax. Reduce your mileage and complete your last race-pace workout early in the week at a reduced work load.

STEP SIX: PLAN YOUR REBUILDING PHASE

CROSS-COUNTRY BUILD-UP SCHEDULES

The model training schedules for cross-country on pages 263–65 should be used to help you write your own program. The exact mileage you will run, distance and dates of your build-up races, and the days you will do your different types of runs will vary with your individual needs, age, sex and other factors that influence your running. Use these models as a guide to create a specific training program that can help you reach your racing goals. Understand the concepts behind these schedules, don't just follow them blindly. We have not included an example of the rebuilding phase. Follow the model in Chapter 10 to write your rebuilding program.

THE INEXPERIENCED CROSS-COUNTRY COMPETITOR'S 8-WEEK BUILD-UP (5KM)

PHASE	WEEK	MONDAY	TUESDAY	WEDNESDAY	THURSDAY	FRIDAY	SATURDAY	SUNDAY	TOTAL MILEAGE
ENDURANCE	1	— Off	7 Medium endurance	6 Medium endurance	6 Medium endurance	7 Medium endurance	4 Short endurance	10 Long endurance	40
ENDURANCE	2	— Off	6 Slow rhythm 6 x 880	5 Short endurance	8 Medium endurance	8/5 Strength Modified fartlek	6 Medium endurance	7 Medium endurance	40
ENDURANCE	3	5 Short endurance	7 Medium rhythm 4 x 1 mile	7 Medium endurance	7 Medium endurance	7/5 Strength Rolling hills	— Off	12 Long endurance	45
STRENGTHENING	4	7 Medium endurance	8/4 Strength Advanced fartlek	7 Medium endurance	8 Medium endurance	8 Medium endurance	— Off	7 Race X–C—5Km	45
STRENGTHENING	5	5 Short endurance	— Off	8 Medium endurance	7 Medium endurance	6 Medium rhythm 4 x Long hills	7 Medium endurance	12 Long endurance	45
STRENGTHENING	6	— Off	8/4 Strength Rolling hills	7 Medium endurance	7 Medium endurance	8/5 Strength Advanced fartlek	5 Short endurance	10 Medium endurance	45
SHARPENING	7	— Off	7 Medium rhythm 4 x 1 mile	6 Medium endurance	6 Medium endurance	8/5 Strength Rolling hills	5 Short endurance	8 Medium endurance	40
TAPERING	8	6 Short endurance	4 Medium rhythm 6 x 880	4 Short endurance	6 Medium endurance	5 Medium endurance	— Off	5 Race X–C—5Km	25 + race

Use the 10Km training rhythm guide when doing rhythm speed workouts.

THE EXPERIENCED CROSS-COUNTRY COMPETITOR'S 12-WEEK BUILD-UP SCHEDULE FOR 2½ MILES TO 5KM

PHASE	WEEK	MONDAY	TUESDAY	WEDNESDAY	THURSDAY	FRIDAY	SATURDAY	SUNDAY	TOTAL MILEAGE
ENDURANCE	1	Medium endurance 6	Medium endurance 6	Medium endurance 6	Medium endurance 6	Medium endurance 6	Short endurance 5	Long endurance 10	45
ENDURANCE	2	Medium endurance 6	Slow rhythm 8 x 880 — 6	Short endurance 6	Medium endurance 5	Strength Advanced fartlek 8 / 4	Medium endurance 7	Medium endurance 7	45
ENDURANCE	3	Medium endurance 6	Slow rhythm 5 x 1 mile — 7	Short endurance 4	Medium endurance 4	Strength Rolling hills 6 / 4	Short endurance 4	Long endurance 12	45
ENDURANCE	4	Short endurance 4	Medium rhythm 7 x 880 — 7	Medium endurance 7	Strength Advanced fartlek 7 / 4	Short endurance 7	Race Cross country 5Km — 6	Short endurance 5	40
STRENGTHENING	5	Medium endurance 6	Medium endurance 6	Medium endurance 6	Slow rhythm 10 x Short hills — 5	Medium endurance 6	Short endurance 4	Long endurance 12	45
STRENGTHENING	6	Short endurance 4	Medium rhythm 6 x Long hills — 8	Medium endurance 6	Medium endurance 6	Strength Advanced fartlek 7 / 4	Short endurance 5	Medium endurance 8	45
STRENGTHENING	7	Medium endurance 7	Medium rhythm 4 x 1 mile — 6	Short endurance 4	Medium endurance 4	Medium rhythm 6 x 880 — 6	Medium endurance 7	Medium endurance 8	45
STRENGTHENING	8	Strength Rolling hills 6 / 4	Medium endurance 6	Strength Advanced fartlek 7 / 4	Medium endurance 6	Short endurance 8	Race Cross country 5Km — 5	Short endurance 4	40
STRENGTHENING	9	Medium endurance 7	Medium endurance 7	Medium endurance 8	Strength Advanced fartlek 6 / 4	Medium endurance 6	Fast rhythm 4 x 880 — 4	Short endurance 4	40
SHARPENING	10	Medium endurance 6	Fast rhythm 8 x 440 — 6	Medium endurance 6	Medium endurance 6	Short endurance 6	Race Cross country 5Km — 4	Short endurance 4	35
SHARPENING	11	Medium endurance 6	Medium endurance 6	Short endurance 4	Strength Advanced fartlek 4 / 4	Short endurance 6	Medium rhythm 4-5 x 1 mile — 6	Short endurance 4	35
TAPERING	12	Medium endurance 6	Strength Advanced fartlek 5 / 3	Medium endurance 6	Short endurance 4	Off	Race Cross country 5Km —	Short endurance 4	25 + race

Use the 5 K training rhythm guide when doing rhythm speed workouts.

Note: This schedule builds to Saturday races when most high schools compete.

THE EXPERIENCED CROSS-COUNTRY COMPETITOR'S 12-WEEK BUILD-UP SCHEDULE FOR 5 MILES TO 10KM

PHASE	WEEK	MONDAY	TUESDAY	WEDNESDAY	THURSDAY	FRIDAY	SATURDAY	SUNDAY	TOTAL MILEAGE
ENDURANCE	1	10 Medium endurance	10 Medium endurance	6 Short endurance	10 Medium endurance	12 Medium endurance	6 Short endurance	16 Long endurance	70
ENDURANCE	2	12 Medium endurance	12 Slow rhythm 8 x 880	6 Short endurance	12 Medium endurance	10 Strength Rolling hills 6	12 Medium endurance	12 Medium endurance	70
ENDURANCE	3	12 Medium endurance	12 Slow rhythm 6 x 1 mile	6 Short endurance	12 Medium endurance	10 Strength Advanced fartlek 6	6 Short endurance	16 Long endurance	70
ENDURANCE	4	10 Medium endurance	9 Medium rhythm 8 x 880	8 Medium endurance	10 Strength Rolling hills	10 Medium endurance	8 Medium endurance	10 Race Cross-country 10Km	65
STRENGTHENING	5	5 Short endurance	10 Medium endurance	10 Medium endurance	12 Medium endurance	8 Medium rhythm 14 x Short hills	6 Short endurance	16 Long endurance	65
STRENGTHENING	6	10 Medium endurance	10 Strength Advanced fartlek 6	6 Short endurance	12 Medium endurance	10 Medium rhythm 7 x Long hills	6 Short endurance	16 Long endurance	70
STRENGTHENING	7	10 Medium endurance	10 Medium rhythm 5 x 1 mile	6 Short endurance	12 Medium endurance	10 Strength Rolling hills	10 Medium endurance	12 Medium endurance	70
STRENGTHENING	8	10 Medium endurance	10 Medium endurance	6 Short endurance	8 Strength Advanced fartlek 6	8 Medium endurance 6	6 Short endurance	10 Race Cross-country 10Km	60
STRENGTHENING	9	5 Short endurance	8 Medium endurance	10 Medium endurance	10 Strength Fast continuous run 6	10 Medium endurance	7 Fast rhythm 6 x 880	10 Medium endurance	60
SHARPENING	10	10 Medium endurance	7 Medium rhythm 14 x Short hills	8 Medium endurance	10 Strength Advanced fartlek 6	6 Short endurance	4 Short endurance	10 Race Cross-country 10Km	55
SHARPENING	11	5 Short endurance	8 Medium endurance	10 Medium endurance	10 Medium rhythm 8 x 880	6 Short endurance	8 Fast rhythm 3 x 1 mile	10 Medium endurance	55
TAPERING	12	8 Medium endurance	6 Strength Advanced fartlek 4	8 Medium endurance	8 Medium endurance	6 Short endurance	Off	10 Race Cross-country 10Km	36 + race

Use the 10Km training guide when doing rhythm speed workouts.

RACING TIPS FOR THE CROSS-COUNTRY RUNNER

You will have to react quickly during your cross-country races. Here are some points to look out for in the race:

The Course

Arrive early. Walk or jog key sections of the course, even if you think you know it. You may have overlooked or forgotten some obstacles, or new ones may have been put in just for this race. Check landmarks and direction arrows so you will know where you have to go and how far you have to run. Pick out a point in the course where you want to start your finishing drive.

Clothing

Cross-country is often run in cool weather. Be careful: you may be cool at the start and heat up during the race. A turtleneck shirt under your racing jersey, and perhaps a hat and mittens, should get you through all but the worst conditions. Be sure to bring a dry set of clothes, and change into them immediately after finishing. Don't stand around. If you race in early season, you can encounter heat too. Be sure to drink fluids before the race. But there are no water stations along the course, so back off a little if you begin to feel dizzy or nauseated.

Shoes

Do not wear spikes, even if the course is grass or dirt, unless you have had a great deal of experience running in them. Most good shoe companies have racing "flats" for cross-country that hold the ground and won't snag on roots or rocks.

Starting

Courses are narrow, so watch for flying elbows and legs at the start that might knock you off stride. Novice runners should be alert to the fact that cross-country starts are faster than road races. Do not go out too fast!

Your first three-quarters of a mile to one-and-a-half miles will be faster than your anticipated race pace, even if you go out cautiously. Your breathing will be labored, since your effort to get position will be great. Don't panic! Force yourself to relax and control your breathing. If you continue to take short, shallow breaths, you will go into oxygen debt very quickly and will slow down as you continue the race.

Relax

The most difficult, yet important, part of running a cross-country race is to stay relaxed and just flow along the course. Imagine yourself being swept along a fast-moving stream. If it feels as if you are going against the current, you are not running relaxed.

Pacing

The changing terrain will give you problems. Be prepared to shift gears constantly as you run up and down hills. Try to keep the effort of the run constant, even though your actual speed varies greatly.

Be aggressive, but also be smart as you run. Accept the challenge of the hills, and run them as best you can without trying to "blast" up them. Relax and flow downhill.

Passing

Don't be timid about passing people in the race. Sometimes the only way to get by on the narrow path is to put on a burst. Do it! Yell "track," and you'll get a peephole to bang through.

Strategy

As you wind around the wooded trails, keep contact with others so you don't get lost or have to slow down. Run with teammates or friends in the early going. When Pete Schuder's Columbia Lions won the Ivy League Championships, the top seven went out in a pack and gave each other encouragement along the course. Also, don't stay too close behind a runner, or you won't see roots, rocks, ruts and other obstacles.

Persevere

You will surely believe that your lungs and thighs are burning, that you are dying or lost or sick. The race is short, remember, and everyone else is suffering with you.

Cross-country is a different kind of sport. You don't just chug along, chatting with the pack. You must conquer not only your competition, but also Mother Nature's obstacles and your protesting body. Cross-country, as we said at the beginning, is best appreciated when it's over. Try a run along the woods one day for a break. Watch a high school or college race one fall weekend. More and more running clubs are sponsoring cross-country races for the average competitor like you. For example, the national Road Runners Club age-group championships are held each November in New York City's Van Cortlandt Park, and hundreds of runners of all ability levels from age 2 to age 70 show up to enjoy the run, the scenery and the experience.

18. BEYOND THE MARATHON— THE ULTRA

For some runners, the 10 km or a half marathon is the upper limit. For most, the marathon offers the ultimate challenge. A chosen few, however, enter the world of the ultramarathon.

Ultras are any distance beyond 26.2 miles, most commonly 50 km (31.1 miles), 100 km (62.2 miles), 50 and 100 miles. The 50 km is considered a long marathon and the transition run between the marathon and an ultramarathon. For others, like Tom Osler, one of America's most experienced ultramarathoners, "The shortest ultramarathon worthy of the name is the 50-miler."

Ultras may be run on a road or a track. They may include challenges like seeing how many miles the runners can cover in 24 or 48 hours, or even six days. Ultras may be raced or run alone across country.

Who runs ultras? Anyone who can run a marathon comfortably can run an ultramarathon uncomfortably. You only need psychological strength and patience; this race requires discipline over long periods of time. There are two types of ultramarathon runners. One finishes the marathon feeling that he or she could have run longer. They are curious: Can I meet the challenge of the ultra? They

want to test themselves, to see if they can complete an ultramarathon run, and then return, hopefully satisfied, to
the shorter distances. Other runners, like Marcy Schwam,
run the ultramarathon and get hooked. They run it again
and again, by choice, varying their distances and improving
their times. Marcy, for example, went from the 50 km to
being the first woman to complete the six-day race. She set
several American and world records: 24 hours, 48 hours,
and six days on the track among them. Like Marcy
Schwam, the ultramarathon runner aims to break barriers—the six-hour barrier for 50 miles, for example. Ultra
runners drop back to run with the rest of us on occasion,
but the ultra is their race, their challenge.

Ultramarathons, then, are survived or raced. The 100
km in Biel, Switzerland, started in 1959, attracts thousands
of runners. In Europe such events are called "hike and
walk," and so they are. In the U.S., the John F. Kennedy
50-Mile-Run in Maryland is a rugged hike and walk along
mountainous trails that attracts hundreds of entries. In
South Africa, the 54-mile Comrades Marathon is a serious
race attracting more than 4,000 runners. All of these races,
like the shorter distances, are composed of front-runners
out to win, and the back of the pack running to finish.

TIPS FOR YOUR FIRST ULTRAMARATHON

Don't consider running an ultramarathon until you have
run two 26.2-mile marathons and can complete the marathon in reasonable comfort. In fact, Ted Corbitt, the wily
veteran ultramarathoner, advises that a "Baby 50"—the 50
km—be run before a 50-miler is attempted.

Pick a Distance of 50 Miles or Less

Train like a marathoner. If you are adequately trained—
60–70 miles a week with long runs of 20 miles—you don't
need any other special conditioning to survive an ultra of

50 km or 50 miles. You don't need more mileage or longer runs now. You'll wear yourself out or get injured. Later, when you are ready to race an ultra, you will want to increase your mileage with longer runs.

Run the Ultra Slowly, but Not Too Slowly

This means slower than your marathon pace and even slower than your training pace. But running too slowly may be unnatural and cause you to tire or become injured.

Take Breaks

Your only goal now is to finish the ultramarathon so you can brag about it. In Bob Glover's first 50 km, he ran all the way; it is just five miles beyond the marathon. But for his first 50-miler—400 laps around an unshaded track on a hot day—he had to resort to all sorts of tricks to survive. One of them was the planned break. Take walk breaks early to conserve energy for later, rather than running as fast as you can praying that you can stagger to the finish line. Glover walked a quarter mile after running each five miles. Those who didn't passed him early, but he breezed by them later in the run when they were walking—not by choice. The tortoise always beats the hare in the ultra. Glover even changed his clothes during the breaks, including his shoes, and went to the bathroom, drank fluids and ate a small container of baby food. Break your own ultra into small segments of about five miles each. Take short breaks after each one; it's great relief. Most ultramarathons are run around loops, which makes taking breaks easy.

Don't Stop Moving During Your Breaks

If you sit down for a long time, you'll tighten up. Keep progressing toward the finish line. Waste as little energy as possible going in any other direction.

Bring Your Own Support System

Friends can help you with food and drink, counting laps (you won't be accurate at this after a while), handling your equipment, and encouraging you to keep going. They should also recognize when you should stop, and drag you off the course if need be.

Drop Out

If you get injured and start favoring your injury, stop running. You'll make the injury far worse. But if you are merely tired and want to quit, don't. You probably feel better than many of the other runners.

Keep One Goal Firmly in Mind: Finish

Just as with your first race and your first marathon, the goal of your first ultra is to finish the run. You experience your first ultra, you don't race it.

Concentrate on Each Five-Mile Segment

Run the ultra in five-mile segments at first, and later in one-mile sections. Thinking too far ahead may destroy you mentally. Start with the attitude that you are going for a fun run. When you pass the marathon distance, you are an ultramarathoner and should think only about keeping moving; you can walk if you want. Be calm, don't panic. You will run in and out of "bad patches." Take the race after 26.2 miles one mile at a time. Remember: the ultra requires extreme patience and mental toughness. In its late stages, the ultra is simply mind over body.

Drink Plenty of Fluids

Pour into you water and drinks with sugar and electrolytes. You'll need to replace lost energy sources and minerals.

Eat Little and Conservatively

While eating isn't necessary, if you do eat, be sure it's something that agrees with you. French fries are out. So is pizza. Glover found that baby food digested easily. But it sure tasted bad after baking in a 90-degree sun.

RACING ULTRAS

Jim Shapiro is one of those runners who accepted the challenge beyond the popular marathon and became a serious ultramarathoner, even running across the United States. He described his running mates in his book, *On the Road: The Marathon*: "The real solo artists, the crazies of the sport, all belong to that select and unnoticed fraternity known as ultramarathoners. They are the mammoth distance specialists, inspired lunatics who yearn to achieve mind-breaking feats like running non-stop through Death Valley or across the United States or around Hawaii or to dash through the 50-odd miles of a classic race, like the London-to-Brighton run, in times of 6 hours or less. They are the gnawers, the mental bulldogs whose motivation for clamping shut on the almost-impossible can sometimes try the understanding of family and friends. They do not stay home much when they are in training. Some of them might be gone all day on a 40-mile training run. They might call from another city to tell you proudly what county they are in before they catch a train back. They plead to be let out of cars long before there are road signs announcing the destination. 'I'll meet you later,' they announce confidently. And they usually do. For in spite of their all-too-frequent aches and sprains, they are ridiculously healthy most of the time."

TIPS FOR RUNNING FASTER ULTRAS

Many of the tips useful to first-time marathoners are also of benefit to first-time ultramarathoners.

Mileage

Start training with a base of 60 to 70 miles a week, and gradually increase to 80 or 100. You won't improve your fitness level much beyond 100 miles a week. Many veteran ultramarathoners, in fact, get by with only 50 to 70 miles a week; they've already got plenty of "miles in the bank," plus a few ultra runs. Most top ultramarathon runners, however, put in high mileage. The key is the accumulation of mileage over a long period of time, combined with long training runs and the experience of surviving ultramarathons.

The Ultra Long Run

As you build mileage for your ultramarathon, also increase the length of your long runs. This conditions you mentally as well as physically. You learn to keep going when you think you can't, and your legs learn to carry your body for long distances. Your body also learns to use fat rather than glycogen as a primary fuel.

Do an exceptionally long run once every three weeks, or twice every four weeks, as you approach your race. This might be 30 to 50 miles; or, run only for time, say four to ten hours. Take many fluid and walk breaks; just complete the distance to get a feel for it. Don't exhaust yourself. You should be able to return to your normal training runs within a few days. Any run beyond 26 miles is specific training for your ultramarathon.

Two suggestions: First, run these long runs point-to-point. (For instance, from one town to another.) That will give you a strong desire to finish. Bring along someone in a car with all your training "goodies" and to get you home. Second, run loops of about five miles, and stop after each loop to drink and walk.

Train Progressively

Most of your training runs should be at a slow, conversational pace, but some speed work, such as one-mile rhythm runs and short races, will help to build strength. Even the marathon may be speed work for the true ultra runner. Faster running serves as a change of pace, but build slowly on a base of endurance and confidence with consistent mileage and ultra runs. While ultramarathoners will benefit somewhat from speed work and shorter races, 90 to 95 percent of their training should be done just to accumulate time on their feet.

Taper and Rebuild

Follow the marathon tapering program. Rebuild carefully according to your experience and fitness level.

Prepare Mentally

You will experience discomfort—no doubt about it. Restrain your emotions during the early part of the race; don't allow yourself to get too "psyched up." Look at the ultra start as a fun-filled training run with friends. In shorter races you get all charged up and run out with the leaders. But in the ultra, the early leaders seldom even finish. Hold yourself back physically and emotionally. Use your mental energy later, when your physical energy has run dry. Run the race at your pace.

Select a Good Handler

Behind every good ultramarathoner is a great handler. He or she is essential. Make sure that your handler is dependable and knows you well enough to judge when to push you and when to get you to stop.

Run Straight Lines

By running all the way to the inside of a loop course, or by cutting tangents on curves (if allowed), you will save many minutes over the course of an ultramarathon. At the end, the minutes will feel like hours.

Change Your Pace

Periodically change your footstrike, stride and pace. You will run heel-ball with mostly short, economical strides. Put in a few bursts at a quicker pace, especially if the course is flat and without hills for variety. Use different muscles, and let some of those that are getting tired take a break. For the most part, run an even pace, starting a few seconds a mile faster than your goal pace. Some top ultra runners prefer to start slow for the first five to ten miles and then pick it up. A few top runners, like Marcy Schwam, start fast and hold on.

How Does It Feel?

The first 20 miles are like any other training run. You should hit the marathon mark in comfort. If you've trained properly, you'll burn stored fuel (glycogen) for the first 30 to 35 miles. Then, no matter how fit you are, you'll be running on mental strength. You will have exhausted your glycogen reserves; you may be dehydrated and suffering from mineral imbalances. Your legs will be tired, your back stiff, your stomach upset, your feet hurting and probably full of blisters. You may wish that the Bear and the Wall were around—old friends, those—instead of what Glover calls "the Death Grip."

From 30 to 40 miles during his 50-mile race, Glover thought he was going to die. It was awful. He mentally wrote his will and obituary. By 40 miles, however, he felt somewhat better, perhaps because his body was supplying energy with slow-burning fat. At 45 miles, he suddenly felt "high" as he realized he was going to finish the race. He couldn't slow down, and ran his fastest five-mile split of the day. In the ultra, you too may run through various moods or even experience hallucinations. The best explanation of how a champion ultramarathoner conquers physical fatigue with mental desire to win is in John Chodes's book *Corbitt*, in which Ted Corbitt explains his thoughts during ultramarathon races, and even mind-breakers like the 24-

hour track race. Read it before your ultra, or even your
next marathon.

YOUR TRAINING PROGRAM

Here is a typical seven-day training schedule for the serious ultramarathoner recommended by Marcy Schwam and
Stu Mittleman, national class ultramarathoners. Aside from
the ultra long run, it is very similar in mileage distribution
to Marcy's marathon training schedule, which would include a second speed-work day. This is the program that
she followed to break the women's 50-mile world record.

MONDAY	TUESDAY	WEDNESDAY	THURSDAY
easy 4–6	easy 5, AM easy 5–8, PM	15–20	10–15*

FRIDAY	SATURDAY	SUNDAY	TOTAL WEEKLY MILEAGE
10–15	easy 5–10	20–50	90–100

*(Include 4–6 × 1 mile at 30 seconds per mile faster than marathon pace,
3 minute rest.)

The ultramarathoner has extended the previous limits of
our physical boundaries. The marathon has become a com-
monplace run—the challenge now lies beyond. Thousands
of runners are exploring their limits by running longer ultramarathons, or entering the increasingly popular off-
shoot of the ultra, the triathlon. This is an endurance event
consisting of long runs, swimming and biking in sequence
during one tough day.

Like the marathon, when you complete the ultramarathon you will come to know more about your special inner
self—a part of our humanness we are just coming to know.

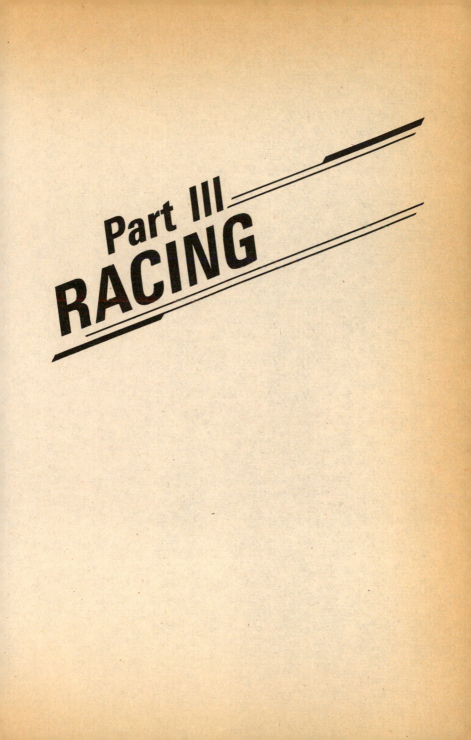

Part III
RACING

19. GOAL SETTING AND RACE-TIME PREDICTION

Competitive runners have three goals: finishing, running a good time (perhaps a PR) and placing high among their peers, or even winning. For the first-time racer and marathoner, the goal is finishing. Perhaps later you'll set a goal to finish in the top 50 percent of the field, and still later, as you improve, to finish among the top 25 percent. Eventually, you may set a goal to place in your age division, or even win a race.

For most competitive runners, the goal isn't finishing or winning, but improving their times. In effect, they race against themselves every time. This is a wonderful contest that can go on for years and lead you, year after year, to better racing times. Goals challenge you one step at a time: for example, finishing a marathon, breaking four hours, then a few years later, breaking three-and-a-half hours.

Your progress will come quickly at first and then slowly, in amounts that will still be satisfying. You may reach plateaus, or even regress slightly, before moving ahead again. Goals must be challenging but realistic. You need to set both short-term goals—steps up the ladder—and long-term goals. Long-term goals may be for a year from now, or four years from now. They give you general direction—

like moving up from novice to basic competitor. We believe the most important goal you set is the one for a year from now. This goal should change as you improve. It should always be a year away—a tantalizing objective, out of reach, guiding you in the direction of improvement. By keeping your goal a year away, you won't be in a rush to try too much too soon.

Short-term goals are both the goals of your racing season and the immediate goal of your next race. We suggest three levels of short-term goals to guide our runners, and we call it the Three-Goal System:

Goal 1: The Acceptable Goal. This is a pre-selected minimum race time. It takes into account factors of weather, training, personal health, and so forth—as should each of our goals. It represents reasonable progress. Usually this goal time would be to improve the previous PR by a few seconds.

Goal 2: The Challenging Goal. This goal represents a significant improvement in your race time. It is a challenging, realistic goal that requires you to put out a strong effort; it is also a goal you can reach. It would be a solid new PR.

Goal 3: The Ultimate Goal. This is your dream time. If everything goes right, maybe you can hit this very demanding goal. Usually you take six months to a year to reach this goal. But "popping" one of these fast times helps you enter a much higher level of competition.

Going into the 1981 Boston Marathon, Marilyn Hulak's greatest dream was to break the three-hour barrier. This was a realistic goal since her previous best, six months prior, was 3:11. But her training was going very well, and she kept racing faster and faster times. She amazed everyone by running a 1:20 half marathon six weeks prior to Boston, which her coach, Bob Glover, figured predicted a sub-2:50 marathon time. After the race, he confided to her: "Marilyn, you are way ahead of schedule; you can be a national class runner a year from now if you want it bad enough." He was being conservative; she was already almost there, but even so she was shocked by his statement. She trained very hard for the next few weeks to sharpen for the big race.

They set three goals for her for the Boston Marathon. Her acceptable goal had to be adjusted, due to her progress, from just improving her time to breaking three hours. That was her biggest barrier—anything else would be gravy. The challenging goal would be low 2:50's, a possible time after her half-marathon result. The ideal, ultimate goal would be to improve upon her half-marathon quality effort and break the national class standard of 2:50. She was advised not to tell anyone of her secret goals— others might think she was crazy, and it would put too much pressure on her. She stated that her goal was just to try to break three hours. She approached the race with enthusiasm and confidence. Without the benefit of a goal-setting plan and race-time prediction she would only have aimed for a three-hour marathon and probably finished with a lot left over. Instead, she started at a pace that would allow her to break 2:50 and held on to become the first New York finisher with a national class time of 2:45:57. "Where did Hulak come from?" New Yorkers asked. They didn't know that she had carefully followed a secret plan.

But jumping over all those steps between 3:11 and 2:45 made it difficult for her to improve. So her goals had to be altered: first, to run consistent times at this level; then, to accept smaller improvements after her dramatic leap. The next year she ran three more marathons between 2:46 and 2:48—all in hot weather—leading into the 1982 Boston Marathon. Her goals there were: acceptable—2:45, challenging—2:43, ultimate—2:39. A 35:17 10 km time, a PR by nearly two minutes, three weeks before Boston, confirmed that she was in better shape than the year before. She set out at a 2:42 pace, hitting exactly 1:21 at the half-marathon mark. However, it was a hot day and along with everyone else she slowed, finishing in 2:47:24. She was disappointed and felt that she wasn't improving, but rather getting worse. After analyzing the results with her coach, however, she realized that she really had run a much better race than the year before even though she ran a minute-and-a-half slower. First, she placed 16th—higher than the year before—in a very strong field. Second, almost all runners ran at least five minutes slower than their PR or goal time because of the heat. So we figured she'd been successful after all. She placed in the Top 20 in her fourth straight "Triple Crown" event of women's marathoning (Boston, New York, Avon) and ran the cooler-day equivalent of a 2:42. Faster times and success don't always go hand in hand.

With the three-goal system, you are always a winner. Prerace goals and postrace analysis must take into consideration many factors. The acceptable goal, in some cases, may be just to finish within a few minutes of your previous best time rather than make a strong improvement. The factors that should influence your goal setting include:

Your Purpose

If you are just rounding into shape in the endurance or strengthening phase, you may not be able, or want, to race well. You may prefer to use the race as a hard strength run without tapering. You adjust your goals and are not concerned about time. Or you may decide to use the race for pace work for a longer race later. A half marathon, for example, may be run strongly at comfortable marathon pace rather than all-out. In this case, your goal will be to hold an even marathon pace throughout the race.

Your Fitness Level

Maybe you are tired, overtrained, and need to take it easy during the race. Or you haven't put in the training you planned and need to adjust your goals downward.

You're Coming Back

After an injury, illness, or layoff from competition, you will need to adjust your goal times. Atalanta's Angella Hearn ran a 2:53 in the 1981 New York Marathon. She then aimed for a 2:45 in her native London Marathon, but injury forced her to do most of her training in a swimming pool. Her goals were adjusted downward—acceptable: sub-3:00; challenging: 2:52 (a PR); ultimate: sub-2:50. She ran the London Marathon in 2:50:05.

Your Age

Slowly we grow older, and the times come harder. You may have to set new goals. Alicia Moore, however, began dramatically lowering her times after her 50th birthday. At the age of 52, she won her age division for the 1982 Boston Bonne Bell 10 km race and she set the American record for her age group for the 30 km race. She had a late start as a runner and benefited from hard speed work with the New York Road Runners and Atalanta groups. Eventually, all of us have to give in and adjust our time goals downward with age. But we get new goals as we enter new age divisions, and thus can start all over again by setting new PR's for our new age group.

Your Weight

If you've added a few pounds since your last race, you may have to subtract some time for the extra baggage.

Your Environment

Heat and cold, snow, rain, ice, wind—all of Mother Nature—may slow you down. You should adjust your race goals. On the other hand, consider a tailing wind when you analyze race results. Heat slows every runner at one time or another: if you expect to run a 40-minute 10 km and the temperature is 80°F, chances are you will run at least a minute or two slower. Start with a pace appropriate to your revised goal, and consider in your postrace analysis the factors you encountered—especially the weather.

The Course

Hills, poor footing or turns may make you adjust your race goals. You may run faster on a flat course than on your normal hilly one and should adjust your goal pace accordingly. If you race over the same course again, you can more accurately set racing goals.

Your Head

If you are "psyched up" for a race and know you are really fit, you may "go for it" and start off at a pace aimed for your ultimate goal time. On the other hand, stress, poor training or fatigue may undermine your confidence, and you probably should take the pressure off and aim for a conservative goal.

The Crowd

If the start of the race is packed and you cannot start as fast as you wish, take this into consideration. Time how long it takes to get going at your intended pace after reaching the starting line, and give yourself two goal times—from where the gun went off and from where you got rolling. Crowded races also make it difficult to pass, or get fluids at water stations. Some runners also run slower times in small races where they run alone without benefit of other racers pushing them.

Look around you at the start. You know who usually finishes just ahead of or just behind you. Start off pacing yourself off the runners you want to catch up to and beat. Don't be intimidated and assume they're bound to beat you just because they always have in the past. After the race, if your time was off, see what your competitors did. If everyone ran, say, three minutes slower than normal due to heat and hills, you can better gauge how to evaluate your performance relative to your goals. Spectators also make a difference. If you need a crowd to pick you up, a

marathon in the country with only the cows watching may
result in slower times. In summary, consider the impact of
crowds on your performance and goals, both in the race
and along its course.

PREDICTING RACE TIMES

Consider all of the above factors. Be fair to yourself. To set
your own goals, disregard super race times which are ques-
tionable measures of performance due to special circum-
stances: strong tail wind, downhill course, or the possibility
of a short course.

Knowing in advance what your finishing time *should* be—
approximately—and therefore what your starting pace
should be, is a great advantage. Without such a goal, you
won't know how and when to push yourself or even what
pace to start with. We have developed a system that helps
predict what times our runners are capable of racing over
given distances. We determine what they should run for a
specific distance based on their times for other races and in
workouts, and then adjust the goal times upward or downward based upon the influencing factors above. With experience at measuring the factors that influence your race
times, and a feel for what you are capable of doing, you can
use this system to predict accurately your racing times.
While neither this nor any other system is foolproof, most
of the time we are correct within a few seconds of our predictions.

Different runners and coaches have different systems.
German track expert Toni Nett based his time-prediction
rules on statistical data. His formula, developed over two
decades ago, for predicting the results of 10 km time from
the 5 km time was: 10 km time equals two times your 5 km
time plus one minute. Going the other way, Nett said: 5 km
time equals your 10 km time minus one minute and divided by two. (For example, if you run 16 minutes for the 5
km, your 10 km time would be 33 minutes.)

Manfred Steffny, former German Olympic marathon

runner and coach of Christa Vahlensieck when she was the women's world record holder for the marathon, devised a theory for predicting marathon times based on 10 km times he had collected. Steffny's theory was originally published in the March 1975 issue of *Spiridon Magazine* and later in his book *Marathoning*. His theory goes like this: *A ratio of approximately 1:5 exists between 10 km times and marathon times. Starting with a 10 km time of 30:00 equaling a marathon of 2:20:00, add or subtract 5 minutes for every change of 1 minute in the 10 km time.* For example, 31:00 for the 10 km would be 2:25:00 for the marathon. This formula compares well with computerized time comparisons detailed in *Computerized Running Training Programs* by James B. Gardner and J. Gerry Purdy and those developed by the National Running Data Center.

After analyzing many race times for 10-mile and half marathon distances, we predict that approximately every 30-second difference in the 10 km time is a difference of 50 seconds for 10 miles and 1 minute 15 seconds for the half marathon. These predictions are listed in the Race-Time Comparison and Predictor Chart on page 510. They teach a basic lesson. There is a relationship between your pace per mile for all distances. These relationships are consistent for all levels of runners; we all slow down at about the same rate over longer distances. Here's another interesting relationship: an increase or decrease in performance for the following times is equal:

    5 km—15 seconds
    10 km—30 seconds
    10 miles—50 seconds
    half marathon—1 minute 15 seconds
    marathon—2 minutes 30 seconds

Theoretically, if you improve your time by 30 seconds for the 10 km, for example, you should be able to race the other distances faster as well, and by the times noted. Thus, if the marathon runner does speed work aimed at improving his or her 5 km and 10 km times, with added speed and specific marathon training, he or she can also improve marathon times.

HOW TO USE THE RACE PREDICTION SYSTEM

Using the chart to predict your times, you can do the following:

- Set your three goals more efficiently.
- Establish a starting pace based on your time prediction for every race you enter.
- Analyze your race results and compare them to race times at various distances to determine your best performances, and perhaps your best events.

Goals

Assume you have run a 10 km in 42:00, and that in two weeks you will run a half marathon and four weeks later an important marathon. You should set goals for both races based on your 10 km time. Consult the Race-Time Comparison and Predictor Chart on page 510 and note that 42:00 for the 10 km is equivalent to 1:35:00 for the half marathon and to 3:20:00 for the marathon. You can use these times, assuming conditions are similar for all three races, to set realistic goals. For example:

1. Acceptable Goal: a present PR for these distances
   half marathon: 1:40:00
   marathon: 3:35:00

2. Challenging Goal: as predicted from the chart
   half marathon: 1:35:00
   marathon: 3:20:00

3. Ultimate Goal: faster than predicted
   half marathon: 1:32:00
   marathon: 3:15:00

By hitting your challenging goals for your sharpening races, you may have conditioned yourself physically and mentally to take a good shot at your ultimate race-goal time for your final peak race.

Establishing Pace

Before you run, you must know the pace you will start out with. Dare yourself with your ultimate goal pace; test yourself with your challenging goal pace; or be conservative and start at your acceptable goal pace. Consult the Pacing Charts on pages 512–23 to find the pace per mile that you must average for the race distance. For example, to run 1:35:00 for the half marathon, the goal pace from the chart would be 7:15 per mile. To achieve 1:35:00 for the half marathon—a challenging goal—start no faster than a 7:05 pace and no slower than a 7:10 pace. The key is to start a few seconds per mile faster than your goal pace based on your race-time prediction.

Analyze Your Results

After you have finished the race, analyze your time and compare it to your best performance at other distances. Perhaps you ran a 1:35:00 half marathon and then ran a strong 3:15:00 marathon. Comparing race times, you can see that your marathon time is much better than the 10 km and half-marathon times. You have moved up a notch in your competitive running. Now use this time as a gauge by which to seek improvement at other distances. Record in your diary your race time, pace per mile (from the Pacing Charts on pages 512–23), and perhaps your equivalent times for other distances, and use this information to set your goals for the next racing cycle. If you see a trend emerging—better relative times for either the shorter, longer or middle distances—you may determine that these are your best events, or that you need more specific training for the events that you are behind on.

Predicting Times from Your Speed Workouts

These rough guidelines, based on our team workouts, can help you determine how your training is going and what times you might expect. They are especially useful ten days to two weeks prior to your race as a good final sharpening workout to help determine your fitness level.

• Take your times for six to eight 5 km-paced 880 rhythm runs, with a two- to three-minute rest. The average pace per mile is near (within ten seconds per mile) your potential pace for a race of 5 km.

• The average pace for one-mile medium pace rhythm runs (10 km), with a three-minute rest, is near the potential race pace for 10 km and approximately 30 seconds per mile faster than the potential marathon time. The novice and basic competitors run four to six repetitions, while the advanced and champion competitors run six to eight repetitions.

All time comparisons and predictions, here and anywhere else, are obviously estimated. Use them to set *flexible* goals; adjust those goals for the various influencing factors. The accuracy of your predictions increases when the race distance you are predicting from is close to the race distance you are setting a goal for—for example, predicting a half-marathon time from a 10-mile time. Predicting marathon times from 5 km or even 10 km times, or vice versa, is more difficult. The comparisons assume that you will do the required specific training for each distance (more mileage for the marathon, more speed work for the 5 km, and so forth). Some runners lack speed but have plenty of endurance, while others can run fast but not over long distances. Women, who have less muscle power than men, often find they run faster for the marathon than for the 5 km or 10 km. Time comparisons are most accurate when based on your performance in a series of races peaking for a big race. This system will guide you to faster times as you confidently measure progress.

20. MENTAL PREPARATION FOR RACING

Mental preparation is perhaps the most neglected factor in racing. Many runners set racing goals and prepare themselves physically to meet them. They reach the starting line in superb condition, but something happens before they finish. These runners don't reach their athletic potential because they only train themselves physically and don't prepare mentally. At the 1981 U.S. Olympic Training Center in Colorado, sports psychologist Dr. Jerry Lynch asked a dozen elite marathon runners what percentage of a runner's success is due to each of the following: (a) natural ability; (b) diligent training; (c) positive mental attitude; (d) good coaching. The answer: "An overwhelming majority of the athletes said that the greatest percentage of a runner's success is due to *positive mental attitude*." Obviously, in addition to developing a carefully planned training schedule, you must also have a positive mental attitude about yourself and your running. You should work to develop a high degree of personal motivation, confidence, and a relaxed attitude as part of your mental preparation for running.

MOTIVATION

Set clear, reachable motivating goals for yourself: winning an award, achieving a time, beating a competitor. Goals give you the focus and willpower to do all the arduous training necessary to prepare physically for the race. Effective goal setting is an essential technique for establishing a positive mental attitude. Our Three-Goal System and race time prediction method, discussed in the previous chapter, are important factors in your mental preparation for racing.

Another motivating force is your support system. Knowing that your family, friends and coach (and even your competitors) will be at the finish line should help push you through hard workouts and races. The group feeling developed in a team race will also spur you to greater efforts. Your coach's role in laying out time and place goals, establishing strategy, and assuring that you are indeed ready for a great performance also helps. If you don't have a coach, use this book to help prepare yourself physically and mentally.

Third, by achieving short-term goals—training distances and times, faster races and recognition—you will be motivated to continue training in order to reach even higher goals. The key is to set and attain short-term goals that reinforce your physical training and spur you toward your long-term race goal. Your support group should congratulate you on your achievements—and if they don't know about them, tell them so you can receive their accolades. It is important that others know about your success, no matter what your racing-skill level.

CONFIDENCE

To win—whatever "winning" means to you—it is essential to develop a winning attitude and a positive self-image. You must believe in yourself. Dr. Lynch notes in *The Runner*: "Creating a better self-image will enable you to release and utilize the talents and abilities you already possess. Once you have developed an accurate profile, your goals will be realistic and attainable because they will be in concert with that profile. The attainment of goals spells success, and success increases self-confidence. Greater confidence broadens the chances for further success and opens the door to optimal performance." Picture yourself as an athlete, set realistic but challenging goals, and confidently "go for it." Although you can't do it every time, it is possible to talk yourself into a superior performance if you have the proper training along with a little luck on race day.

You also must learn to want to be successful. As Flip Darr, former U.S. World Games swim coach, said: "It takes a hungry person to be a champion. Although true champions don't let it show, they are on ego trips. The ego satisfaction they get from winning makes the necessary hours of effort worthwhile." All of us are champions to various degrees, and all of us have egos that demand satisfaction. Learn how to satisfy your ego and accept achievement. Don't put yourself down. Build yourself up, physically and mentally. When another runner says, "Nice race," reply, "Thanks. I worked hard for it." You did; don't reject a compliment. Be quietly confident before the race, show reserved pride after the race.

You can condition yourself to be psychologically stronger on race day just as you condition your body to be physically stronger. Long training runs and consistently high mileage build confidence. Increasingly faster times during speed workouts and build-up races also contribute to your physical and mental confidence. If you're an experienced runner, an ultrahard workout "callouses" you and puts you on the starting line believing in yourself. Learning to relax and concentrate will also improve your performance.

RELAXATION

Methods of relaxation include transcendental meditation, yoga, and hypnosis. The process of learning to control tension in specific muscles by tensing and then releasing tension from one muscle group at a time was pioneered in 1920 by Dr. Edmund Jacobson, author of *Progressive Relaxation*. Other good sources of relaxation programs helpful to runners are *The Relaxation Response*, by Herbert Benson, and *Relax and Win*, by former San Jose State track coach Bud Winter. The relaxation routine we recommend in Chapter 27 can be used before and after each workout and race. You must enter competition mentally psyched up for a strong effort, yet relaxed.

Relaxation involves physical and mental skills. To avoid tensing up, you must learn, according to Winter, to work at less than 100 percent effort. You learn to let the muscles not directly involved with running—such as the muscles in the face, neck and shoulders—relax. During the stress of racing, the ability to relax and maintain proper form and style results in less energy lost, increased confidence and faster times. If tension hits you in a race, breathe deeply three or four times as you do in your relaxation routine, and think positive.

You can also use relaxation exercises to get rid of mental tensions so that you can free up the mind for positive visualization of your racing—both before and during the event. We suggest belly-breathing exercises combined with shoulder shrugs for five to ten minutes, once or twice a day during the days leading into a big race, to help you prepare for visualization. Then five or six deep breaths, or sighs, should leave you feeling relaxed enough to visualize clearly your upcoming race. You may want to sit quietly while doing this, and you may want to continue the deep breathing for several minutes. The idea here is to get into a deeply relaxed state. Too many runners experience stress before hard workouts or races (this routine can also help you with your training runs). They become anxious about their opponents, or the distance, or the Wall or the Bear. "Such anxiety," says Dr. Lynch, "interferes with the fluidity of the muscle function. When the muscles begin to tighten and become less fluid, the mind begins to send messages to quit. The thought of stopping in a race in-

creases anxiety, creating a vicious cycle. Relaxation and visualization techniques can decrease anxiety, allow you to
burn less energy because you're not in a state of stress, and
thus improve your coordination and increase your endurance. Relaxation also has the effect of clearing the mind
and enhancing your concentration, perhaps the most important ingredient in athletic excellence.''

VISUALIZATION

One of the best mental preparations involves "imagery rehearsal," or visualizing yourself performing well. Several
professional athletic teams, including the Dallas Cowboys,
have used this technique. The process is simply one of
learning to relax and then seeing yourself doing what you
want to do and doing it well.

Visualization trains the athlete to experience mentally
the event as if he or she were living it. Dr. Thomas Tutko,
author of *Sports Psyching: Playing Your Best Game All of the
Time*, tells athletes to "relive" their best performances
over and over until they actually can achieve them almost
automatically. "It's like putting a tape into your brain, as
you would with a computer." You control the imagery; you
should actually imagine your muscles in action as you rehearse your race.

The technique works because it follows the psychological principle that the closer one comes to simulating an actual situation, the greater one's chances of developing the
skill to perform it. By imagining yourself successfully running, you will actually improve your form and racing
speed. By training the subconscious mind to perform the
way we want, it will "tell" our conscious mind to perform
in that manner. Obviously you can't just dream about a fast
time and then do it, but it can be achieved more readily
when it has first been "practiced" in your mind.

Visualization begins with a positive self-image and goal
setting. Write your goal on a piece of paper and tape it to
your wall, or take a digital clock and set it for your race

time—2:59 for a sub-three-hour marathon, for example—
then unplug it and place it in a prominent place so you can
see it often. Seeing it often, your mind accepts it as a realistic goal. You then begin to imagine yourself crossing the
finish line in that time, making the time seem even more
possible. Think about it often, including during your training runs and in the race itself.

The next step is to achieve a state of deep relaxation as
described above. Then focus on your goal. Lynch suggests
that you mentally rehearse the entire race: " 'See' the
crowd, 'hear' the noise, 'smell' the air, 'feel' your body relax; imagine every aspect of the run by incorporating every
sense." Visualize yourself starting your race full of energy,
conquering the hills, running with good form, outracing
your competitors, reaching mileage markers at your goal
times, and finishing ahead of your competitors within your
time goal. Repeat the whole mental process several times
before your key race. You become a movie director and
run the movie of your race through your mind.

Visualization can be practiced at quiet times during the
days leading into your race, and before your training runs.
Some runners continue "visualizing" into their runs and
races by "seeing" themselves running up an approaching
hill, or finishing the workout or race strongly. Time for visualization varies from at least 30 seconds to three or four
minutes. Avoid too much mental rehearsing the night before the race. It may leave you emotionally drained. Instead, you may wish to do the relaxation exercises before
going to sleep. On race day, go through your event visually
one more time as a final tune-up, and then relax. In order
to hold your mental concentration, avoid discussions with
others in the final moments. Reflect on your visualizations,
as well as on some of your tough training sessions when
you hit "bad patches" in the race.

Dr. Tutko noted that "the main purpose is to help the
athlete achieve his or her maximum potential, no matter
what their ability might be. You can be in charge of mental
factors, rather than having them be in charge of you."

Whether, you follow these visualization techniques consci-entiously, or merely occasionally daydream about your race, you can see yourself as a confident, successful run-ner. But remember that you must have a solid training pro-gram to back up your visualization. It is not enough just to dream about running fast without putting in the hard train-ing.

THE PRERACE CHECKLIST

To free you to focus on your positive mental attitude and imagery, be sure to eliminate prerace details from your concern. Make a check list of what must be done before the race, and do them. Here are a dozen tips:

• Enter the race early. Don't train for it and then find that you missed the entry deadline.

• Plan your prerace tapering and eating routine day by day. Also plan your race-day fluid intake. Remember to drink fluids 10 to 15 minutes before the start.

• Pack your running shoes first. Then work your way from your feet up your body to your head. Pack one item at a time the night before leaving for the race. Include extras of everything, especially shoes, and pack for the weather. Remember toilet paper, Vaseline, Band-Aids, extra pins, soap, towel, lock, and a dry set of postrace clothes. Never check your bag of racing gear with an airline or other ser-vice.

• Arrive at the race two hours before the start. Plan all travel arrangements with this in mind. If possible, arrive one or two days before the race. Stick with your regular time schedule if the race is in another time zone, unless you can arrive much earlier than a day or two before the race. A good rule of thumb is to allow one day of acclimati-zation for every hour time change; therefore, if you live in New York and run the London Marathon, you should ar-rive in London five to six days before the race to adjust to the change. If you are traveling from New York to Califor-nia, for example, and will arrive only two days before a race, plan to eat, sleep and run according to your New York time zone. Use the most comfortable means of travel you can arrange and afford. Driving for several hours should be avoided if possible. If not, break it up with walking, stretching and running breaks. Don't travel more than one to two hours in the morning on a race day—it's too hectic. It is better to arrive the night before and stay over, starting the day relaxed.

• If possible, check in and pick up your number a few days before the race. If not, get your number at least an hour before race time. Pin it on your running shirt right away so you don't lose it. Also, double check the time and location of the start.

• A good night's sleep is most important *two* nights before the race. Follow your normal routine, and go to bed early. Also, follow your normal training diet.

• Check out the course by car or bike. Jog parts of it, especially the start and finish, to get a feel of it. Memorize landmarks, and visualize yourself running strong and passing them. Often a less confident runner will get "psyched out" by touring a marathon course since it seems so long. But the confident runner has the advantage of knowing where the hills, turns, etc., will hit him or her on race day and will not be surprised by them.

• On race day, get up three hours before the start. Have someone awaken you as a backup to your alarm. Remember—if you insist on eating, do it at least three hours before the race, and eat light.

• Get the weather report, and adjust your clothing to it.

• At the starting point, turn in your sweats early. If it's cool, wear an old throwaway outfit or a clean plastic bag to keep warm.

• Make a final bowel movement and empty your bladder well before the start of the race. Don't be modest. Your comfort is at stake, and the bushes may be your only choice.

• Take all safety precautions and apply all skin protection—Vaseline, suntan lotion, etc.—well before the start.

Then stretch and use the "imagery rehearsal" technique. Start gearing up for battle. Get psyched for a strong effort.

DEALING WITH PRERACE ANXIETY

Your prerace planning should include learning how to deal with prerace anxiety. According to sports psychologist Dr. Robert N. Singer in *The Physician and Sportsmedicine* magazine: "Any meaningful event is bound to produce heightened arousal (perhaps too much), anxiety, and tension within athletes. Emotions that get out of control are a problem for many athletes, regardless of their sport.

"Obviously, thought processes and elevated emotions need to be quieted. Many coaches make the mistake of trying to stimulate athletes just before competition. Although some may need to be stimulated, many others may need to be more relaxed to attain an optimal arousal state. An optimal arousal state exists for each person for each event. Athletes must train themselves to be in this state, just as they train to develop the mechanical skills necessary to succeed in an event."

You need to learn to reach the emotional state that will give you the best results. Getting "psyched up" for a shorter race may help you get off to a good, confident start, but such a tactic could backfire in the marathon, where you need to start off slower and reserve your emotional energy for late in the race when your physical resources run low.

The competitive runner on race day must be prepared to manage thoughts of the physical and mental stress he or she will face during the actual race. Self-imposed stress is necessary in practice to help the athlete cope with this pressure. According to Singer, "Athletes must take practice seriously and believe that a practice run . . . is the real thing. They should develop the necessary attitudes and emotions to be psychologically prepared to compete. It is difficult to be a good contest competitor without being a good practice competitor." Relaxation exercises and visualization of your race on race morning will also help you conquer prerace nerves.

Athletes who run superior workouts and race well in low-key races but then perform poorly in big races must analyze the reason for "choking." They may be victims of the fear of failing—letting down their coach, family or friends—or the fear of success. The runners should discuss their fears with others, if possible with a well-trained sports psychologist. For these athletes, Dr. Singer recommends that they develop a positive attitude on race day and over the days leading into the race by mentally visualizing and reliving their successes in practice and in other races.

STRATEGY

Prerace strategy and the proper execution of your game plan is a very important part of racing success. Mistakes here can be just as devastating as a poorly planned training schedule. There are three ways you can run a race: against yourself (for a PR), against the course (for time), and against your competitors (for place). Your race strategy will reflect that choice, plus the course, weather and the fitness level of you and your competitors.

Here are five basic variations for pacing when running against yourself or time:

• Start slowly, gradually pick it up, finish fast. This is best for novices and those runners returning to racing after a layoff. It challenges you only minimally, however.

• Start slowly, pick it up to a strong pace, and hold that pace to the end. You open at slower than goal pace, then after a few miles increase your pace to 10 to 15 seconds per mile faster than goal pace, and continue to the finish—although you may slow the pace somewhat as you tire.

• Start fast and hold on. This method may bring failure to the inexperienced runner. Those who start this way often find themselves running the second half of the race, and particularly the last few miles, at a much slower pace. If you start too fast, you could very well blow the race and finish in a much slower time, and much more uncomfortably, than if you had paced yourself more wisely. Sometimes by "building a cushion," you can dare yourself to hang tough and finish with a good time. Usually, however, the result is that as your pace slips away so does your confidence, particularly if many runners pass you. Then you begin to fall apart mentally as well as physically, resulting in an even worse time, often in dropping out.

• Start fast, relax in the middle but keep pushing, and pick it up at the end. This is a good method for many top runners.

• Pace yourself evenly for time or effort. This, together with the previous method, is usually the preferred one. Pick your starting pace using the guidelines in the previous chapter, based on your goals and race-time prediction. Success in racing is most often achieved using near-even pacing (for even pacing guidelines, refer to the Pacing Charts on pages 512–23).

There are two keys to near-even-paced racing:

1. Start slightly faster than goal pace (within five to ten seconds per mile). This is less than all-out race effort. You must be patient, actually holding yourself back so that you will be stronger at the end. Learn the patience of holding back and the feel of race pace in your rhythm-training runs. By starting out slightly faster than your goal pace, you leave a little room for error in case you are slowed later by a big hill or a head wind. You may find that you can keep the pace up and really "pop" a good time.

2. When you begin to tire, the effort necessary just to hold the pace will increase. Then you begin to think of the last few rhythm runs in your workout where you strive to maintain pace by increasing effort slightly and concentrating on holding racing form.

Usually you will succeed if you start slightly ahead of goal pace, begin to run at goal pace or slightly slower as

effort increases later in the race, and hold on to the end
where you can put together a final drive to the finish. Even
pacing means being close to the ideal, steady pace all the
way rather than actually running the same pace per mile
every step of the way. You should be flexible, but consistent with your pace.

Hills and wind will tend to throw you off pace. Run up
hills and into the wind at the same effort as race pace,
which means you'll slow down your speed somewhat. You
can make up some time by using the downhills and tail
wind: don't let up and coast, apply steady effort.

Adjust your pace according to the time "splits" along
the course and according to your body's signals. When you
adjust your pace according to the times given at various
mileage markers, keep in mind the hills of the course and
the direction of the wind. These factors may increase or
decrease your actual speed pace. Memorize or write down
and carry your split-goal times (to be under seven-minute
pace at each mile marker, for example), so you can easily
adjust at each reference point. If you find yourself slightly
off pace, you can easily adjust. If you are much too slow,
you'll need to compromise your time goal. If you are way
ahead, you should gradually slow down until you reach a
more sensible pace. You may feel great at this point, but
you risk falling apart a few miles down the road. Split times
and mile markers are occasionally inaccurate. Wear your
own watch to check splits. Racing experience and pace
work on a track will help protect you against inaccurate
mile markers. Eventually you will automatically flow into
the proper pace but you must concentrate on keeping it
going or you will unconsciously slow down and lose valuable time. With experience you will learn to "red line," to
run at the edge of your physical and mental limits. With experience at racing and with race-pace workouts, you will
learn to feel what pace is right for you by monitoring your
breathing. You will know that you can pick it up or should
slow it down, despite what the watch says. Don't let the

watch cause you undue pressure and make you run too fast or too slow. Don't become dependent on a watch. It is used as an aid, not a crutch.

Here are four basic tactics for racing against competitors:

• Pace yourself to run your best time and hope that will be good enough to outdistance your rivals.

• Burst out and lead from the start. This can be dangerous. Your opponents know where you are and can pick you off. You can also burn out. It is a tremendous psychological burden to know you are being followed. This strategy works only if you are fit enough to hold the lead to the end. You may be able to get enough of a lead to discourage your opponents and steal a victory. Unless you are sure you can break away, however, don't lead.

• Follow and work off the energy of your opponents, and move away from them in mid-race. You can gradually increase the pace until your opponent "breaks," or use a series of surges—short, quick accelerations—to push into the lead and hold it. If someone bursts on you, slowly move back to him or her; don't respond immediately. Decide in advance—while studying the race course—where you will make a strategic move; at the crest of a hill runners are vulnerable, or you can use your downhill skills to open a lead. Most races are won or lost with such tactics, but they are very dangerous for the nonelite runners, since they require superb conditioning.

• Outkick your opponent at the end. If you have superior speed, hang back in contact with your opponents and then outsprint them at the end. This takes careful timing. You can sprint out too soon, run out of gas, and be passed again. Respond to kickers by moving with them and then, if possible, outkicking them from behind. These methods may result in a win, but could also cause you to run slower. Sometimes you must choose to go for either time or place.

Strategy and confidence building start long before you reach the starting line. But a good strategy, planned ahead of time, will give you an extra mental edge. The following strategy tips may help you defeat your competitors, whether you are fighting for the win or to beat a "friendly" rival back in the pack:

• Don't worry about other runners before the race. Concentrate on your image and your goals. Don't look at flashy uniforms or fancy shoes, or listen to bragging or complaining. Beware of competitors trying to "psyche you out." Focus on yourself.

• Your strategy will differ with each race distance. In a 5 km race, if you don't hold close contact with your opponents from the start, you cannot make up the distance. You must go out and run with them from the opening gun. In marathons, you can follow far enough behind to see them, relax, set your pace, and have plenty of time to catch up.

• Look around at the start and during the race. Pick some runners who are better than you to pace off, and then try to reel them in as the race progresses. Early in the race, don't be as concerned with your place as with staying within striking distance of your opponents. During the race, get aggressive, and set small goals of passing each runner as you go along.

• Analyze the course and the weather. Make sure you know where all the hills come and *exactly* where the finish line is. With a downhill course and a tail wind, you can start faster and will get some help over the last few miles. Conversely, you'll need to save energy if the course is hilly near the end and the wind against you. Many of the runners on the course tour bus for the 1982 Avon International Marathon in San Francisco got psyched out because the bus took several hours to cover the route (making the course seem very long), and the hills began to look even worse than they were as the moans on the bus increased. By riding the course himself along with some of his Atalantans, Bob Glover was able to determine that a change of strategy was needed: throw away the time goals and race against the other runners instead. Starting paces were adjusted by ten seconds and the runners were advised to aim to place in the top 30 in order to win a medal and help the team score, and completely forget about running a fast time. Knowing this decision, team members no longer feared the course, and they had a big advantage over other runners who didn't rise to the challenge of the hills and those who didn't go over the course first, and stubbornly went ahead with their previous race-time goals.

• Work together. On the hilly Avon course, Atalantans Sharon Barbano, Marilyn Hulak, Maddy Harmeling and Marcy Schwam worked together, sharing the pace through the hills for most of the race. The result was that they placed in the top 31 runners in a world class field and led the team to its fourth straight Avon International Championship and the 1982 National Athletics Congress Championship. They won despite the fact that on paper several teams were stronger. But over the hills of San Francisco, they were mentally superior and thus physically superior to 20 other clubs.

• Use the runners around you. You can use them to hold or push your pace, break the wind, or help you up hills. Take turns sharing the pace so everyone gets a fair ride. If the group's pace slows, make a move toward the next group. If it's too fast, back off and look for runners coming up.

• Never panic. If your opponent passes you, watch him or her closely for signs of fatigue. Switch gears easily and glide back into contention gradually. Stay relaxed.

• During the race, concentrate on pace, your opponents, and flowing rhythmically with good style and form. Some mind-wandering is inevitable, but the key is to recover quickly and get back into your concentrated effort, or you will lose precious seconds. Look straight ahead. You are not sight-seeing if you are going for a good time. You don't have the energy to waste waving to your fans. Thank them for their support after the race. Think of yourself as strong but relaxed.

Some runners "disassociate"—they enter a trance state by repeating a mantra over and over, relive part of their lives, or stare at another runner's back or ear—in order to avoid the pains of racing. Although a few top runners have success with this method, most attempt to "associate" with the pain and discomfort of the race, which tell them how hard they can push themselves. Sports psychologist William P. Morgan conducted a study which showed that top marathon runners constantly monitor body signals of respiration, temperature, heaviness of the legs, etc. They keep thinking "stay loose," "keep the pace up," "form together." The average runner may find that by disassociating while running up a troublesome hill, for example, he can conquer it, but he should return to monitoring his body's signals. The runner who associates can better preserve fuel and avoid injury. Interestingly, Morgan found that top runners don't "hit the wall." They feel only minor discomfort since they read their bodies, adjust pace and avoid trouble.

• Run the first half of the race, especially the marathon, controlled. Hold back your emotions until the last stages of the race, when the going gets tough. Become more aggressive gradually. When you feel bad, remember that runners around you feel worse.

• Be alert at all times. If an opponent tries to surge, be mentally prepared to go with him or her. If you think they are going too fast, ease back and later slowly reel them in. Make a big move only toward the end, unless you know you are fit enough to pull it off earlier.

• Listen to and watch your opponents. If they are breathing hard, or their form is getting sloppy, take advantage of this "bad patch" and move ahead.

• A good time to pass an opponent is when he or she is taking water. But remember: you've got to drink too. You should practice getting your fluids in quickly so you can take advantage of an opponent's temporary pause.

• Don't try to run away from your competitors by sprinting uphill during the middle of the race. If you are a good hill runner, you will increase your lead over the distance. Try to stay close to the others so they will "pull" you over the hills. When running uphills, pick landmarks along the way as short-term goals to make it easier. Make your moves at the crest, when many runners let up momentarily, or on the downhills, where many runners coast.

• Get aggressive when the going gets tough. Flash back to previous races where you ran tough, or to the hard training runs leading into this race. This will boost your commitment to keep pushing. Sometimes directing anger at your competitor or picking up the pace will overcome fatigue. Change your form for a few strides when you feel tired. Slowing down is the easiest thing to do, but it will defeat you psychologically.

• Use strategy that best fits your mental and physical strengths, and consider those of your opponent. Atalanta's Marilyn Hulak won a 25 km race in Central Park and a trip to the Rome Marathon with some daring strategy. She started out very fast and opened a large lead over her rival, who had greater speed and usually beat her. With the physical strength of 100-mile training weeks and the mental goal of going to Rome, Marilyn caught her opponent by surprise and held on for victory. She then placed second in Rome.

Don't let your opponents get such a big lead that you can't make it up. On the other hand, don't go out very fast with them and risk blowing up. It is better to go out faster than normal to keep within striking distance but still be reasonably comfortable. Don't wait until it is too late to track down an opponent from behind. Make a move to get near him or her with at least two miles to go, and then concentrate on closing ground.

• Develop a strong finishing kick. Most road races are won by staying with or slightly behind the leaders and then making a strong move toward the end. (Where that "end" point is differs, of course, from a 5 km to a marathon.) If you have a strong finishing kick, try to keep the pace slow and wait until the last minute to make your move. Otherwise, gamble early. If you can't break a faster opponent early with surges or a hard early race, start your final kick at least a quarter mile or half mile from the finish and try to wear him or her down.

Let's detail some techniques about your finishing kick. This is as much a mental as a physical weapon. Your kick demands more than pure speed or strength at the end of the race. It also requires positive thinking, concentration and the conviction that you can "turn it on" and win. Your ability to finish fast gives you the psychological edge of knowing that you have another "gear" you can use.

The kick demands leg strength at the end of a race. You will improve that strength by aerobic endurance runs, with weight training and speed work, and by running an evenly paced race. Most competitive runners have enough strength at the end of a race but cannot find the gear to sprint because they lack leg speed.

You can develop a finishing kick by spending some time on it during your training. There are six parts to making a finishing kick: speed, strength, racing form, concentration, positive thinking and practice. Concentration and positive thinking, as we've said, give you the confidence that you have the strength and speed to win with a finishing kick. If you believe you have it, you do.

Practice pulls all these elements together. There are several ways that your training runs can be adjusted to help develop your finishing kick. First, incorporate fast "pick-ups" into some of your distance runs to simulate the finishing kick. Do some fast rhythm or power 220's or 440's as you visualize the race finish. If possible, practice your kick over the finish line of the course. Also, you may run the final rhythm repetition at a faster pace than the rest of your workout to simulate kicking late in a race. When doing this, be sure that you are prepared for the added stress. Ease into this training. Do this type of training late in the season, after your strength and speed have developed.

During a race, start your kick early (880 yards to one mile out) if you're not blessed with natural speed. Otherwise, start your kick later (220–440 yards). It isn't the fastest runner who wins, but the runner who with brain and brawn reaches the finish line first. Don't ever give up. You can pick up precious seconds or places by concentrating on your finishing drive all the way *through* the finish line. *Please*: Don't be a runner who sprints only the last few yards to the cheers of the undiscriminating crowd. By now, every serious runner knows the difference between the hot stuff and the hot dog. If you've got that much left, you should have run faster sooner.

There are general, overall strategies to consider, too.

Starting. Your general strategy should be to line up with those you are competing against and be ready to get out and stay with them. Then settle into your pace.

Passing. Pass decisively so your opponent knows you are feeling strong and lets you go. Then ease back into your pace. Don't waste energy by passing the same runner back and forth. Usually, passing really means going past runners who are slowing down because they started too fast.

Breaking up the race. Divide the course into segments and visualize yourself reaching each of them in sequence. Run each race segment to segment in your mind many times before actually racing the route. Then, during the race, set short-term goals of reaching each segment rather than starting and focusing only on the finish line.

ANALYSIS

Analyze the entire race the day after you run it, and make notes in your diary about your performance. Learn from your successes and mistakes.

- Was my prerace mental preparation adequate?
- Did I execute my race strategy properly?
- Was my pacing effective?
- Were my start and finish good?
- Did I concentrate during the race on pace, form, breathing, etc.?
- Was I in control?
- Did I run the time I had planned? Why or why not?
- How can I improve next time?

The best runners are not always the ones who will win. You can defeat runners who are physiologically superior if you are mentally superior. At the top level of competition, it is mental preparation and mental toughness that separates the winners from the losers. For all levels of runners, the ability of the mind to get the most out of the body is the difference between a good performance and a great one. The mind, not the body, is therefore the most important single factor in racing success.

Part IV
TECHNIQUE

21. RUNNING FORM

The most ignored ingredient in successful racing is *technique*. This is the art of blending form and style to produce a more efficient, faster runner. *Running form* refers to the biomechanics of running. (Biomechanics is the biology of motion, the study of the mechanisms of movement.) Running form, according to Dr. Peter Cavanagh, professor of biomechanics at Pennsylvania State University, "involves the most economical use of physiological resources with the least risk of injury." *Running style* is how you look and feel when you run.

Various studies have demonstrated that some runners are much more efficient than others. This means that in most cases, improving a runner's form will improve his or her running results. Some runners have form quirks that apparently offset musculoskeletal asymmetrics naturally and shouldn't be changed. Bill Rodgers, for example, flails his right arm to compensate for a short left leg; still, no one is going to change his form for better results.

You should run naturally, as long as that is biomechanically sound. Former University of Oregon and U.S. Olympic coach Bill Bowerman wrote in *Runner's World*: "Every human being is built on the same basic set of biomechanical functions: muscles working in concert with each other, muscles moving and augmenting bone structures, joints connecting rigid bones to allow them to support the body in differing planes. Every runner, therefore, starts with the same machine. No two bodies, however, have the same interaction of parts. Some are more efficient than others. Working with a runner's basic running form as dictated by the biomechanical structure, certain modifications can be made that merely make what nature gave the runner function more efficiently."

The four basic biomechanical principles of running are:

1. footstrike
2. forward stride
3. body angle
4. arm drive

These general principles apply to everyone, but no one form works for every runner. The main thing is to have the best biomechanical form and still run with a relaxed, flowing, rhythmic style.

Long, slow distance training can cause the competitive runner to lose touch with proper racing form. When the runner needs to go faster in races, he or she finds it difficult to master that skill. To be comfortable with a racing form, you must practice it regularly. It is a skill that you will learn, and then sharpen consistently—or lose. Practice your running form both at race pace and faster.

In a race, poor form leads to fatigue. And fatigue will lead to poor form. Thus you must keep working on your form. By concentrating on its main aspects—without trying to run perfectly—and running in a relaxed style, you will be more efficient, and thus a more productive racer.

If you are new at racing and speed workouts, a concerted effort at making improvements in your running form may result in dramatic improvements in your racing performances. We have seen novice competitors improve their 10 km times by two to five minutes after spending up to ten weeks working on form in our classes with the New

York Road Runners Club and North Jersey Masters Track Club. As you become a more experienced competitor, continued emphasis on proper running mechanics will enable you to move up in the pack.

FOOTSTRIKE

One of the greatest controversies in running concerns how your feet should hit the ground: footstrike. Coaches, elite runners, sports doctors, exercise physiologists, and even the authors of this book disagree on what method is best. Here is the range of opinion:

• Gabe Mirkin, M.D.: "Always land on your heels. That way, you will not strain your calves and Achilles tendons. . . . Running on your toes will eventually wear you out and slow you down."

• Bill Squires, who coached Bill Rodgers and Alberto Salazar: "Be conscious of the error of landing on the heels. Make first contact on the ball of the foot."

• Arthur Lydiard, coach of several New Zealand Olympic champions: "Don't run on your toes. This works calf muscles unnaturally, which is uncomfortable and tiring over long distances. It is most economical and natural to come down with a nearly flat foot, with the heel hitting first and a slight roll in from the outside edge of the foot. There are many good runners who run on their toes, but I contend they would run better still, in distance work, with a nearly flat footfall."

• Bill Bowerman, who has coached heel-ball, flat-footed, and ball-heel footstrikers: "Serious runners will want to experiment. The main reason for learning the ball-to-heel footstrike, for those who have sufficient coordination to master it, is to develop a strong sprint stride to use at the finish of the race. It is not advisable for continuous use over long distances since it is tiring and increases risk of injury."

What do the elite runners do? Bill Rodgers, Grete Waitz and Allison Roe—all winners of the New York Marathon—run ball-heel. Former marathon world record holder Derek

Clayton runs heel-ball. Most track coaches promote ball-heel footstrike in order to achieve maximum speed. Generally, doctors and fitness experts prefer the heel-ball method, which minimizes injury. Pete Schuder spent most of his life running ball-heel; he had to use this method as a national class quarter-miler. As a track coach, he mostly trained runners in distances under 10 km—events that require more speed. Bob Glover, on the other hand, spent most of his life running heel-ball as a marathoner. As a fitness teacher, he promotes heel-ball for safety reasons. But as Glover got much faster as a runner, he started naturally running more ball-heel in races and then in training runs. He still uses heel-ball when he isn't in top shape, but learned from Pete how to perfect ball-heel form to help improve his race times. In turn, Pete learned from Bob that the average runner cannot handle the stress of the ball-heel footstrike. Our combined experiences form the position taken in this chapter.

Clearly, there is a lot of confusion about footstrike, including the terms. We use these five in this book:

1. Heel Strike

Not recommended. Avoid this extreme of the heel-ball method. You should not make initial contact with the ground by jamming your heel into it and then slapping your forefoot down hard. It puts a tremendous stress on your body and may cause injury.

When we tell you to land on your heels, we mean that you gently land on the heel and then allow the forefoot to come down quietly as the body rolls over the foot and pushes off the ball. The difference is in impact: proper heel impact must be gentle, heel-ball.

2. Toe Strike

Not recommended. Avoid this extreme of the ball-heel method. Landing high on your toes should be restricted to the ballet dancer and the sprinter. With this method, you may quickly develop injuries of the shin, ankle, calf or forefoot. Some elite runners may appear to run on their toes. But they are actually landing ball-heel-ball: hitting just behind the ball of their foot, touching down gently on the heel, and pushing off the ball.

3. Flat-Foot Strike

In the flat-foot strike, the entire sole meets the ground at one time, but as lightly as possible. Knee lift is quick and the entire action similar to riding a bike. Some runners are more comfortable landing flat-footed or on the outside of the entire foot instead of on the heel. This is all right as long as you are comfortable. However, we find it hard to believe that anyone can run fast using the flat-foot strike. Runners who think they are may be using a subtle variation of ball-heel or heel-ball: hitting almost flat-footed, landing near the heel and easing to the ball, or hitting low on the ball and easing lightly to the heel. Since this is a minor modification of the heel-ball or ball-heel footstrike, we don't use the flat-foot strike as an option.

4. Heel-Ball Strike

Recommended for beginners, for injury prevention, for heavier runners, for a slower pace. This method is used with the shuffle stride.

This technique involves touching gently on the outside of the heel, rolling inward lightly to the ball of the foot with your knee slightly bent to absorb shock, and lifting off from the big toe. Done properly, this is more of a shock-absorbing light flick than a bone-jarring crash. The slight rocking motion between heel contact and push-off insures proper cushioning and effective forward propulsion. The result is a hitting and springing motion which is less jarring and increases acceleration. Your toes should be pointing as straight forward as possible.

5. Ball-Heel Strike

Recommended for highly conditioned light runners who
want speed and can safely coordinate the method to help
them train for and maximize their running speeds. This
method is used with the power stride.

According to Pete Schuder, the heel-ball footstrike does
not allow you to increase the length of your stride, and
thus gain speed. In fact, he says, due to the position of
your body as your heel hits the ground, you must keep
your stride very short in order to keep your balance. As
your heel first hits the ground, your center of gravity is located behind the support leg, forcing you to pull your body
forward. If you attempt to increase your stride by reaching
out with your lead leg, you will find it hard to pull your
body forward without losing your balance. Your hamstrings are not strong enough to do this. To propel yourself forward with the heel-ball method, Pete says, you must
use a short shuffling action in which your legs only slightly
reach out in front of you. The pulling action of the legs
forces you into a "squat" from which you cannot lengthen
your stride. To run faster with the heel-ball method, you
would have to increase the number of steps you take per
second: your stride frequency.

The ball-heel method, Pete argues, allows you to increase both your stride length and your stride frequency.
This advanced method of footstrike enables you to place
your center of gravity over your support leg. Your foot is
now in perfect position to drive your body forward with a
strong pushing action. The length of your stride is now dependent on how hard you push forward and not how far
you reach ahead of your body.

Your footstrike with the ball-heel method touches the
ground behind the ball of the foot, on the outside edge,
and as the foot rolls inward, the knee bends slightly to absorb shock. The heel gently touches the ground so that the
entire sole of the shoe makes contact. Then you roll up to
the ball of the foot for lift off, pushing off the big toe. You

should concentrate on "popping" off the ground with a light flick rather than pounding into the ground. If you use this footstrike method correctly, you may wear out your running shoes on the balls of the feet as quickly as on the heels.

Should you change your running footstrike? There are more than a dozen points to consider:

Fitness and Experience. Beginning runners, racers and marathoners should run heel-ball. With experience and improved fitness, you may want to change to the ball-heel method. Novices do not have the strength in the lower leg and ankle to safely master the ball-heel technique. Many experienced competitive runners will train most of the time using heel-ball footstrike and use ball-heel strike in races, although perhaps not for the marathon distance, and in speed workouts.

Injury. Even an experienced ball-heel runner may be forced to train heel-ball when suffering from such injuries as Achilles tendonitis, shin splints or back injury. This would lessen stress on impact and the pull on the Achilles and calf. Runners prone to stress fractures or injury in the Achilles tendon, ankle or calf will want to run heel-ball, which is the safest running footstrike. (Injuries from heel-ball strike usually come from hitting too hard on the heel or overstriding.)

Speed of Runs. Don't use ball-heel until you are able to run at a quick pace (about a 6:00–7:00 mile). At that pace you can run with a lighter footstrike. It is difficult to run a 6:00-per-mile pace on your heels. Generally, the faster you run in training or racing, the more likely you are to use the ball-heel method. Jogging ball-heel at a slow pace places a stress on the lower leg.

Mileage. If you are running 60 miles a week using the ball-heel method and gradually increase to 80–90 miles, you may find that the additional pounding on your legs is fatiguing and is making you vulnerable to injury. You may want to train heel-ball. This often occurs naturally. Conversely, if you cut back your mileage and mostly run heel-ball except in races, you may feel bouncier and quicker and switch to ball-heel more often in training. Most runners, except the very top competitors, run more heel-ball in training to give them more cushioning.

Distance of the Race. You are likely to run ball-heel during shorter races when you'll be going faster. A middle-of-the-pack and up runner in a 10 km will do better with ball-heel if comfortable. You must be very fit to stay up on the balls of your feet for long races.

Coach, Doctor, Running Idol. Coaches tend to treat all runners the same. Beware of the coach who wants you to change your footstrike. Make sure it is right for you. If you get injured and your doctor tells you to run heel-ball for safety, you may be concerned about returning to ball-heel. You should do so only after your injury mends, and return gradually. The elite runner often weighs very little and is very light on his or her feet. Don't try to copy your running idol—what works for him or her may not work for you.

Weight. You increase the force of impact on your body by three pounds for every pound you are overweight. The heavy runner, therefore, must emphasize shock absorption. Run heel-ball.

Foot Type. A runner with a high arch and dropped forefoot may be more comfortable running ball-heel.

Surface. Running on ice or snow may require a flat foot or heel-ball strike to achieve a firmer grip.

Terrain. Run uphill ball-heel and run downhill as you do on the flats. You may lessen shock by running ball-heel downhills.

Age. It may be too late, after years of running, to change styles without injury. It is safer to use heel-ball. The best time to learn ball-heel is when you are young and being taught the proper mechanics of distance running and sprinting.

Habit. Most men learn to play pivot sports on the balls of their feet: soccer, football, basketball. When they start running, they often start that way, too. It is safer to start heel-ball, however, and then return to ball-heel when ready.

Comfort. Three major factors to consider are the safest way, the fastest way, the easiest way. Experiment, but don't change unless it feels right for you. We don't have all the answers to what is best for the runner. Your body will give you clues.

Switching to the Ball-Heel Method

Most runners start with the heel-ball method. Then, as they reach a faster level, they may want to switch to ball-heel. How should you do this?

First, allow your body to adjust to the new method. Give your legs time to get used to the new position of your feet. Remember: changing footstrike is almost like starting to run all over again. If you start too quickly, and try to do too much too soon, you may become very sore or injured. Be sure to stretch and strengthen your muscles, especially your Achilles tendon and calf.

Start by jogging a little with your foot hitting behind the ball of the foot. Do this before and after your usual work-

SUMMARY OF WHO LANDS WHERE

	HEEL-BALL	BALL-HEEL
Novice runners and racers, most marathoners	X	
Heavy runners	X	
Runners with lower-leg injuries	X	
Training and/or racing at 6–7 min. per mile or faster	X	X
Training and/or racing at 7-min. pace or slower	X	
Most middle-of-pack and back runners	X	
Most elite runners		X
Most runners between middle and elite	X	X
Most track racers		X
Finishing kick		X
Uphill		X
Downhill	X	X

outs. Just get the feel of landing behind the ball. Pete Schuder helps runners by having them imagine they are jumping rope. When you do this, you should land right behind the ball of the foot. Slowly introduce the ball-heel footstrike into a light training session, preferably a 220-yard slow rhythm speed session or an uphill workout. Periodically during your training runs and races, concentrate on using the new method. Finally, after many workouts, use the footstrike throughout a short race. Be patient. You are learning a new skill which may take several months to master.

FORWARD STRIDE

The second biomechanical principle of running is forward stride.

Stride length is the distance between successive ground contacts of the right and left feet, heel to toe as measured in distance covered on the ground. *Stride frequency* is the total number of right- and left-foot ground contacts per minute. *Running speed* can be defined as the product of the length and frequency of stride. Therefore, there are only three ways to increase your speed:

1. Increase the length of your stride.
2. Increase the frequency of your stride.
3. Increase the length and frequency of your stride.

Each runner finds a stride that works best for him or her at a given pace and then makes adjustments by "switching gears" to increase speed.

There are two basic types of runners: the shuffler and the power runner.

The Shuffler

This runner runs very low to the ground with little vertical lift. He or she skims the surface with short, rapid strides, little knee lift or back kick. As a heel-ball runner, this runner moves along in a very efficient manner with few extraneous motions. The heel-ball action allows the runner to increase his or her frequency of stride and thus increase speed with little difficulty. But this runner's center of gravity is slightly behind the support leg, pulling the body forward and making it difficult to increase stride length. If this runner reaches out too far in front to increase stride length, he or she will overstride. This may cause imbalance, inefficiency or even injury. This runner can generate more speed only by increasing the frequency of his or her stride, not its length.

Distance runners who spend many hours on the roads learn to run with as little effort as possible. Their bodies take short, shuffling steps to conserve energy. Derek Clayton wrote in *Runner's World*: "When I started training for the marathon, my form changed naturally. Running 20 miles a day shortened my stride length. It also eliminated the tendency to lift my knees. Gradually, my power stride evolved into one of economy . . . I developed a very natural leg action I call 'the Clayton shuffle.' Through miles and miles of training, I honed my leg action to such a degree that I barely lifted my legs off the ground. It was economical and easy on the body. But it 'happened.' It grew slowly through many hours of training." Alberto Salazar, who broke Clayton's world record with a 2:08:13 in the 1981 New York Marathon, also changed his stride over the years into his own "shuffle stride." Amby Burfoot, the 1968 winner of the Boston Marathon, is another notorious shuffler.

Obviously the shuffle stride is widely used, and over the long distance its efficiency may be preferred over the speed of the power stride.

The Power Runner

This runner uses the ball-heel footstrike, runs with a slight forward lean, "pops" off the ground, and has more knee lift and a longer stride.

To run fast using this method, you must lift your knees and open your stride. Proper knee lift requires that you bring your knees forward ("lead with the knees") and high enough so that your legs can follow through and extend themselves to the longest possible length without strain, and allowing them to drop naturally in front of you. If you keep your knees low, or throw your forefoot out in front of you, you will prevent yourself from getting that full, natural stride. Instead, you will take short, choppy steps. If you raise your knees too high, your body will lean too far back, and you will bounce up and down as you run and lose your forward drive.

A marathon runner, of course, will not run that distance with high knee action. It is important to maintain knee lift relative to the speed being run. To hold form, strong quadriceps are needed; they may be strengthened by running hills and by weight training.

For the ball-heel runner, Newton's Third Law of Motion—for every action there is an equal and opposite reaction—becomes the key ingredient in attempting to make improvements in speed. Your ability to run faster is dependent not only on stride frequency, as is the case for the shuffler, but also on how well you are able to push off with the support leg. By keeping your center of gravity (hips) in front of your support leg, you are able to push hard into the ground with the support leg. This force into the ground is countered with an equal and opposite force that propels your body forward. The greater the drive into the ground, the greater the thrust forward.

The power stride increases the ground distance covered with each stride without forcing you to reach out to do so. This happens not because the foot hits further out by reaching, but because you are covering more ground in the air due to increased power at push-off. You increase force, thus ground distance. Many runners are confused by this, and reach out and thus overstride. In baseball, for example, base runners are taught to run through first base, not jump towards it, since running through is faster.

If you are going at a relatively slow pace, the drive into the ground is minimal, resulting in a fairly small stride length. However, if you wanted to increase your speed quickly, you would begin to push your body forward by powerfully driving off your support leg. Your stride opens, resulting in your being able to cover a greater distance in a similar period of time.

The most important point to remember in increasing your stride length using the ball-heel footstrike is to keep your hips in the proper position. If you allow yourself to sit back too far, so that your center of gravity is behind the support leg, you will be forced to *pull* your body forward, thus cutting down your stride.

After you make initial contact with the ground just behind the ball of your foot, it is important to allow your entire foot to then touch the ground. *Do not* try to stay up on the ball of your foot. Total contact with the ground gives you a larger surface area with which to generate a counter force in pushing you forward. Allowing all of your foot to make contact with the ground also allows your hips to move ahead of the support leg prior to push-off. You should also have your support leg bent slightly at the knee so that your hips can come directly over the lead leg.

The ball-heel runner increases speed by increasing the frequency of the stride and the length of the stride. The heel-ball runner, as we've described, increases his or her speed by increasing the frequency of the stride. But this runner can only minimally increase stride length without overstriding.

The power stride is used by most track runners, elite runners, and runners powering uphill or finishing with a kick. Only the very fit use this stride for marathons. The power stride may produce more speed, but it is less efficient over long distances than the shuffle stride. Many runners train with a slight shuffle stride and race marathons with that stride; they usually race shorter distances with the power stride.

Stride Length

Stride length depends on running speed and the incline of the road. Running faster, as we've discussed above, involves increasing the length of your stride. Stride length obviously shortens during uphills and lengthens on downhills.

At any given pace, everyone has a stride length that is best for him or her; usually it is the most comfortable. It is determined by your body through time, by trial and error, but stride may change with increased (lengthened) or decreased (shortened) flexibility, increases in mileage (shortened), increases in power-type speed workouts (lengthened). Stride length must not be copied from any other runner nor imposed by coaches. There is no one optimal stride length for all runners.

Overstriding causes braking and extra shock. It is better to understride than overstride. Studies show that the average runner overstrides, while Dr. Peter Cavanagh and others at Pennsylvania State University have discovered that elite runners have shorter strides than slower runners.

Stride Frequency

Running faster also involves increasing the frequency of your stride. Dr. Cavanagh's studies also show that the stride frequency of elite runners was nine steps per minute faster than that of the average runner. Quicker strides, therefore, are better.

Don't try to change your stride if it is best for you. You can improve speed by learning to "switch gears" and move into the power stride when you need it. For some, this will be the finishing kick; for others, shorter races; and for the gifted few, the full marathon.

BODY ANGLE

Too many runners worry about how they should run: erect, bent over or whatever. The best advice is to relax. Allow your body to move as freely and with as little rigidity as possible.

Bill Bowerman emphasizes that an erect, but not stiff, posture is the most essential element in a smooth and efficient running form. He notes: "The best postural position for a distance runner is an upright one. You should be able to drop a plumbline from ear level and it would fall straight down through the line of the shoulder, the line of the hip and then onto the ground." This suggests that the runner runs perfectly erect. Leaning too far forward from the waist forces the muscles to work to maintain balance, causing potential injury to the lower leg muscles and back. Leaning backwards has a braking effect and places a severe burden on the back and legs. The heel-ball runner using the shuffle stride runs nearly erect, but relaxed.

Body angle is important for the ball-heel runner. According to Brooks Johnson, the 1984 Women's Olympic track coach and Pete Schuder's coach when Pete was an AAU All-American, "We must place the body in a position of jeopardy; we must lean forward, or otherwise upset our equilibrium. Simply stated, running is a series of falls and recoveries." The important point to emphasize is that the runner normally runs relatively upright. While running quickly with the ball-heel footstrike you should employ a very slight forward lean, which allows for a more fluid stride.

Three areas are important to your running posture:

Hips

Keep your hips relaxed, forward and up; pull in your "caboose" and bring the pelvis forward slightly. This allows your legs to push your body forward, since your center of gravity is in front of you, and it also enables your legs to rotate unrestricted through their entire range of motion. If you allow your hips to drop down and back, however, you will become a "squat" runner, which is a very inefficient way to move quickly.

Upper Torso

Keep your upper body up and out in front of you in an unrestricted and relaxed manner. The back should be as straight as is comfortable. The shoulders should "hang" in a relaxed manner. Don't pull your shoulders so far back that you pinch your shoulder blades together and build up tension. Just keep the shoulders relaxed, and even allow them to curve a little. Your chest should feel flat, never thrust out at military "attention." If your upper torso leans too far forward, bending at the waist, you will force your hips too far back and drastically cut down on the length of your stride.

Head

Your head will help keep you erect. If you bring your head too far forward, you will start to lean forward, bending at the waist. Don't look at your feet; keep your eyes straight ahead. Bring your head too far back, and you will force your body to be too erect, or worse, you'll lean backwards. Tilting your head to one side or the other will also throw off the efficiency of your movement. The head weighs about ten pounds (more for our thick-headed friends), so keep it centered on your shoulders in a natural, relaxed position.

A few more points about your running posture: Good posture is essential to good body mechanics. It results from good muscle tone, which gives you the ability to keep your body at a proper running posture, especially late in a race when you're tired.

ARM ACTION

In running, your arms are in some ways as important as your legs. They are not just along for the ride. If you use your arms properly, they will make your legs go faster by propelling your body forward. You will also maintain good rhythm and balance and conserve energy.

Position

Your arms should hang loosely from the shoulders. If you carry them too high, the result will be a shortened stride, shoulder twisting, muscle fatigue and tension in your shoulders and upper back. Arms carried too low contribute to forward lean or a side-to-side and bouncing motion. Too little forward or backward arm swing will result in a lack of proper forward drive, lift and balance. Either flopping your arms or rigidly holding them in position contributes to inefficiency of motion.

Carry your arms between your waistline and chest. On the upswing, your hand should come close to your body at about your pectoral muscles. On the downswing, your hand should lightly graze the side seam of your running shorts. The arms naturally swing in front of your torso, but your hands should never cross the midline of your chest. Arms moving across the body cause side-to-side motion and a shortened stride. Keeping your elbows unlocked and slightly away from your body will help maintain proper arm motion. Every runner will vary slightly in arm position. The main objective is to carry your arms in a relaxed and efficient manner.

Motion

Arms balance the runner. Their motion helps propel you forward. Your arms should move in a vertical plane from front to rear, and should synchronize with the opposite leg. The arms act as a lever and balance for the leg drive and should move in the same plane as the leg. As the left leg pushes into the ground, your right arm is driven down at the same instant, adding to the driving force. When the right leg drives into the ground, your left arm propels downward. The faster the beat, the quicker the arms move.

You might want to practice arm and leg synchronization before a mirror, perhaps to the beat of music. First try your arm swing, and then synchronize it with an easy lifting of your legs, moving from heel to toe and back while standing in place. Get the feel of arms and legs in rhythm with each other.

Forearm and Elbow

When you swing your arms, concentrate on moving them from the elbow down, driving from the forearm. *This is the most important ingredient in proper arm drive.* Many runners swing from the shoulder, locking their arms at the elbow. This is a slow and inefficient method that requires a great deal of energy to move the large muscles of the shoulder and the length of the entire arm. When driving your arms hard in a race or workout, you should end up feeling a little stiff the next day in the forearms, not in the shoulders.

Imagine that you are cross-country skiing, and pushing yourself along the trail with your poles. The motion is very similar to running, and the movement is from the forearm down, which makes your elbow open and close with each swing. Do not lead with the elbow, but with the hands, wrists and then forearms. Keep your elbows unlocked, and swing your arms from them as though on hinges.

Try swinging your arms first from the shoulders—the wrong way—and then from the elbow. Grab your upper right arm just above the elbow with your left hand. Do not allow the elbow to move backward as you raise the arm up and then drive it down, using the elbow as a hinge. See how much easier it is to swing the arms from the elbow? This is because the radius of your swing is very short, compared with swinging from your shoulders, and also you get more driving action downward, which propels you forward. Don't lock your elbow; this common error makes the shoulders sway and dip and will not allow you to drive downward with the arm. The elbows should be "open" and should bend and straighten a little with each arm swing. They should neither point away from the body nor be tucked in close to it.

The Hands

Proper hand position is essential to correct arm drive. Percy Cerutty, the famous Australian coach, emphasized that "all natural running begins in the person's fingers and is transferred to the legs and feet." Your hands should be held loosely, so that your thumb and forefinger or middle finger just touch, "cupping." The thumbnail faces up. Fists clenched or fingers held stiffly create tension; hands hanging loosely cause the arms to flail. Both create an inefficient running motion.

The Wrists

The wrists should be relaxed and loose. At the top of the swing, cock your wrist slightly upward. At the bottom, flick your wrist as if lightly snapping a whip, turning your palm somewhat down and in. The snapping allows you to stay loose and rhythmic.

Arm Drive

For slower running, hold your arms in a comfortable, relaxed position and keep their action to a minimum. When you want to go faster, your arms should swing from the chest just past your hips. There should be a pulling action, as in swimming, or a snapping motion, as in snapping a whip, on the downward swing. Dr. Cavanagh's research indicates that proper arm motion "increases running speed by providing small amounts of 'lift' and 'drive.'" Arm action reduces the amount of force needed to lift the body from the ground, and also aids in propelling the body forward. Without using their arms at all, Dr. Cavanagh found, runners needed four percent more oxygen to run at the same speed than when using their arms. You can test the theory by running uphill first with your arms at your side, then using your arms properly.

Keep your arms and shoulders relaxed and strong. The success of your arm drive will be enhanced by improving your upper body strength. The use of weight training, and hand weights, will help.

TOTAL FORM

By driving the arms, maintaining proper body angle, and utilizing the proper footstrike and forward-stride techniques—all together—you will have arrived at near-perfect form, for you. Form must be practiced as a unit, not just piece by piece. The proper form for running along at training pace is best practiced by training regularly with comfortable form and periodically checking out your form body part by body part. Proper form for racing needs to be practiced in speed workouts. Rhythm-training runs help you adjust to the biomechanics of race pace. Power-training runs exaggerate your form and thus force you to concentrate on it more, making it easier to learn and remember.

We have found with our classes and teams that the best way to teach proper form is to do runs up a short, steep hill. The hill should be approximately 100 yards long and steep enough to challenge you, but not ridiculously steep. After proper warm-up, and followed by proper cool-down, you should run repetitions up the hill at 10 km race pace, concentrating on the following:

1. *Footstrike.* Keep up on the ball of the foot and "pop" off the road.
2. *Forward Drive.* Push off the back foot, lift the knee (lead with the knees) and drive up and forward.
3. *Body Angle.* Lean slightly into the hill, push the hips forward and up. Keep the head up.
4. *Arm Action.* Drive the arms downward in a vertical plane from the elbow in short, quick strokes, keep the shoulders down and relaxed, don't lock the elbows.

The steepness of the hill forces you to use better form in order to get up it. If you were to practice your form on the flat at first, you would tend to stay down on your heels, stay erect and not drive forward with your arms. Later, after a few hill sessions, you should practice your total form by doing pickups of 100 yards on the road or track.

For your first attempt at hill training, four to six hills (four for novice competitors, up to six for veterans who have never done speed work) at a medium effort, with a jog back to the start, will be enough. Since it helps to run with others, get a group together if possible to help each other along. As you go up the hill, try to keep an even-paced rhythmic flow to your run. If you really run hard up the hill, you may never get through the workout. Remember, the major purpose of this workout is to emphasize proper running form. The secondary benefit is that you will get a good workout from this exercise, but don't let that take precedence. Work on form, even if it means having to slow down to do it.

After you have concluded this drill, do an easy recovery jog on the flat, every once in a while concentrating on push-off, knee lift and arm swing. By doing this type of workout about once every two or three weeks for a few months, you will find that you have made dramatic improvements in your form. But you can't quit then—form doesn't come to you automatically, but it leaves you quickly. Periodically return to doing workouts on the track and hills that emphasize keeping your good form together.

To go faster using proper form, remember the four "drives":

1. *Drive off* the back foot.
2. *Drive up* with the knee.
3. *Drive forward* with the hips.
4. *Drive down* with the arms.

22. RUNNING WITH STYLE

You can spot your running friends way off in the distance. Some shuffle, some flow, some rock and some roll. Runners have individual styles: their running "signatures." Many experts in the field say that little should be done to change your style of running (how you look and feel when you run). We shouldn't fool with Mother Nature. Others feel that improvements can be made.

Some runners have tried to attain the perfect style and failed—but not necessarily as racers. Australian Derek Clayton wrote in *Runner's World*: "I don't think I have a particularly pretty style. If I had my choice, I would rather look like Frank Shorter. Frank's movements are so effortless that he makes it look like running doesn't hurt. He is light on his feet, has fluid arm movements, and seems effortless in his breathing. To me, Frank Shorter looks the way a runner should.

"I made an unsuccessful effort to alter my style. I would consciously try to keep my head from rocking and run so that my shoulders didn't sway. I felt like a tin soldier, and probably looked like one as well.

"By running the 'right' way, I had suddenly lost interest in running. It became extremely painful for me to have to think of what I was doing every step. My aim in life was to become a world-record holder. If it meant looking bad to get it, then so be it. I realized that you can't copy someone else's style. With imitation, you risk injury and, more important, you can kill the joy of running."

For the most part, you are born with a certain style that changes as you do. As youngsters we seemed to have a natural tendency to run with a very rhythmic and fluid style. As we grow older, many of us lose strength and flexibility as we cut back in physical activity. When the adult returns to exercise, he or she often lacks knowledge of proper running form and style.

The best we can do for you is to help you clean up bad habits. Running doesn't have to look right, but it should feel right. What is right for Frank Shorter or Derek Clayton may not be right for you.

When done properly, your style will flow as a complete, unconscious action. We believe that you can make improvements in your style and form. But we encourage you to work at correcting the most common errors rather than trying to emulate "the perfect style." At first, trying to make improvements in your running style may seem very difficult. But if you are patient, you may very well find that you will begin to look and feel more relaxed and efficient as a runner.

Ideally, to improve your style you should have a coach or knowledgeable runner watch you run. If no one is available to help you, check your style by catching your reflection in mirrors or store windows. Analyze the following four points of running style in detail.

1. RHYTHMIC FLOW

Running should be a graceful and elegant form of locomotion. Developing a rhythmic flow to your running style means learning to run to an "inner beat." If you ever learned to type or took piano lessons, you may remember how difficult it was to establish a cadence or rhythm. Typing and music teachers use metronomes to help their students learn the rhythm of finger movement. Runners need to learn a rhythmic style of running. Most of us find it occasionally, but too often it is a one-run, momentary thing, and hard to recapture. Since you cannot take a metronome with you when you run, here are some skills that will help you understand running rhythm and make it part of every run:

• During your training runs, try visualizing yourself as a very well-coordinated athlete. Concentrate for a few moments on emulating that gifted runner. This may also be done during a quiet moment *before* you run.

• Do short repetitive runs of 100–220 yards, and concentrate on running smoothly and being relaxed. Work at keeping everything in step. This is best done with a group of runners who run at your level and stride: attempt to keep in step with one another for the entire distance, like marching in a band. Or do the same on a slight downhill course of similar distance. A downhill slope of a few degrees will help you learn to flow.

• Play a fast song on your stereo, and run in place. Keep step to the beat. Count as you run—1-2-3-4/1-2-3-4—keeping the count steady and in step with the leg stride. Breathe out every time you count 4 to help keep a cadence.

2. LIGHT FEET

Heavy-footed running may indicate problems in your running form. If you hear yourself making hard, slapping noises with your feet as you run, think seriously about making some changes. "Grinders," as these heavy-footed runners are affectionately known, usually do not survive the rigors of distance running. They suffer painful foot, leg and hip injuries and are frustrated because they can't increase their speed.

Running "light," on the other hand, is the style of the runner who floats along the roads making scarcely any sound. This is easier to visualize than attain. But many of the drills used to develop running rhythm can also be employed here, since light, gentle running is rhythmic, too. Some other drills that will help you run light:

• Jump rope at double beat. Make yourself jump twice per rotation. Jumping quickly forces you to be light on your feet. When you first try this, jump only a short time. You will be using muscles in your legs and ligaments in your joints that you haven't used before. Two to five minutes of rope jumping per day is sufficient; you aren't a springtime schoolgirl in the play yard. One runner we know started jumping rope when at the Laundromat waiting for his weekly wash. After 30 minutes of rope jumping, his clothes were clean, but he could hardly walk. He had to take two days off from running to recover. Moral: Don't do things in extremes, especially new things. Begin slowly, build slowly. Another hint: Try rope jumping without the rope. You won't trip as often. (If you're tripping over imaginary ropes, see your doctor immediately!)

• Run noiselessly. While out on a run, concentrate on not making any noise. See how close you can get to your friends before they hear you coming. Just focusing on this will help you run more gently and easily.

3. RELAXATION

Many runners find that their running style is restricted by tightness and the inability to relax. You hear coaches yell this all the time: "Relax! Relax!" But it's easier said than done. In fact, when someone is told to relax, the opposite usually occurs: He or she tenses up. A more positive phrase might be "hang loose," and that's what we really mean.

Here are some points to remember to help you run more relaxed:

• Let your chin hang loosely. Too often we see runners who grit their teeth from the start of the race to the finish. Keep your mouth slightly open and loosen your jaw. This will keep the muscles in your neck and shoulders relaxed.

Occasionally let the head roll from side to side and then return, shrug the shoulders and let them drop, or drop your arms loosely at your side to promote relaxation.

• Check yourself every once in a while as you run. Make sure your shoulders haven't risen to your ears, causing your arms to rise and become ineffective. Check your hands and make sure the fingers are still cupped and not held tightly together. Squeezed hands cause your arms to tighten and restrict your free-flowing movement.

• Check your wrists to be sure they are loose. Do they flick at the bottom of the swing as they should, thus helping you keep a steady beat to your rhythm?

• Check your breathing.

4. BREATHING

If listened to carefully, this one sound will tell you a great deal about yourself. Quick, shallow breaths may indicate nervousness; we've known runners who actually hyperventilated at races. "Panic breathing" can cause your entire body to tense up. Other runners start too fast, and never "catch" their breaths during the run. Make a determined effort to slow down your breathing by taking deeper breaths which are regular and rhythmic. Breathing, then, is part of your running rhythm and style.

Pete Schuder suggests that to establish a cadence, a runner should breathe out every second right step for part of the run. Force the breath out and then slowly breathe it in. Other runners count their breaths, which is also a form of distraction during a particularly difficult long run.

Regular rhythmic breathing is no different on the run than while you are at rest. The rate remains about the same, while breathing volume uniformly rises. Make your breathing your metronome; use it to measure the pace of your runs.

Some runners enjoy breathing in time to their footstrike, while others feel this is a nuisance. There are two basic suggestions here. Breathing should be relaxed, and should follow the principles of "belly breathing." Most of us breathe backwards: we suck in the stomach as we take a breath. With proper abdominal breathing, the belly expands as you breathe in, flattens as you breathe out. The expansion of your abdomen means that your diaphragm is fully lowered and your lungs are inflated to the maximum, allowing more efficient intake of oxygen. Improper breathing can also cause the dreaded side stitch.

As Bob Glover said in *The Runner's Handbook*, there are three R's to running: run tall, run relaxed, run naturally. These will contribute to your running style.

23. RACING TECHNIQUE

Form and style during a training run differ greatly from form and style during a race. In racing, you must concentrate on your technique to maximize your potential. Efficient racing technique will shave seconds, even minutes, off your time and give you an edge over your competitors who are breathing out of control, carrying their arms too high, or barely lifting their feet.

Race technique involves the ability to maintain good form and style throughout an evenly paced race and to be able to shift gears, making necessary alterations in form. The competitive runner must be prepared for six variations in his or her race:

1. Starting
2. In the Race
3. Passing
4. Uphills
5. Downhills
6. The Finish

1. STARTING

In crowded races, you may just be shuffling along at the start. Run cautiously with your hands up in front of you to ward off other runners and help maintain balance. Flow into a steady running rhythm as soon as possible. The serious competitor may wish to get out front quickly and establish his or her position in the field. This start requires some adjustments:

• Swing your arms as soon as you begin to run. This will help you generate some speed for the first 50 to 100 yards. Bring your knees up and run briskly with "quick feet," but do not sprint. Do not overstride. Keep in control. Your breathing will be faster; don't let it get out of control. Often, runners panic breathe because they start too quickly. If your breathing is too fast, slow it down and get it in rhythm with your running.

• Stay loose and relaxed. Don't run tight. As soon as you can, get into your race pace and establish a good rhythm. Make that rhythm as comfortable as possible, yet push your physical limits.

The secret of a good start is to move quickly into your flow—the pace your body is trained for—as soon as you stake your position in the crowd.

2. IN THE RACE

After you have settled into your race pace, concentrate on your style and form. This should now be your greatest concern—even more than the runners around you. Don't leave your technique lessons on the training road—use your knowledge to fight off bad habits and the fatigue that tries to ruin your form. Check yourself periodically throughout the race. Better yet, have your coach or a friend meet you at various spots along the way to check your form and yell any corrections at you. Hearing the words called out to you will help you keep a good racing technique. Here is what your coach or friend should look for, and yell:

• "Don't overstride!" Don't grind or squat. Keep your hips forward.
• "Lead with the knees! Get your knees up!"

- "Run tall and easy!" Think relaxed.
- "Stay up on your feet!" If you are trying to maximize your speed by using the ball-heel footstrike, concentrate on staying "forward and up" throughout the race. It is easy to lose concentration and fall back on your heels to a heel-ball footstrike.
- "Push off your back foot!"
- "Use your arms!" Swing from your forearms. Don't lock your elbows. Drive down, not across your body.
- "Keep your hands and wrists loose!"
- "Rhythm breathe!"
- "Flow!" Keep a nice rhythm.

3. PASSING

You will have to change your running form in order to pass a competitior in a race. You will have to increase the speed of your run and use as little energy doing so as possible. Hard, forceful surges may be costly and bring on fatigue and slower times. Proper passing technique will get you by your opposition with enough left for a strong finish. Passing requires that you concentrate on the following:

- Increase your arm swing. Pump your arms faster and your legs will go faster.
- Increase the power drive with your support leg.
- Lift your knees. This will help you run faster.
- Return to race pace. Having passed your opponent, settle back into your race pace by slowing down your arm swing, decreasing the power drive and decreasing your knee lift. Allow yourself to relax and develop your racing rhythm by concentrating on doing rhythmic breathing.

Passing a runner requires that you stay relaxed and use little extra energy. This is particularly important early in a race, where an all-out effort to pass someone will spell disaster for you later. Do not floor your accelerator and blast past your competition. Use your fuel cautiously; accelerate gradually and smoothly.

4. UPHILL

When you round the bend and see the Big Hill, don't wince. Prepare! Learn to shift gears—both mental and physical—and use proper technique to propel yourself up that hill. Attack the hill before it attacks you, by changing your form; too many runners go uphill out of control without using their arms and foot drive. Hill-running techniques can improve your racing times dramatically.

Runners combat hills three ways: in daily training runs, in hill-training speed sessions, and in races. Each is approached slightly differently. In hill speed training, you run uphill to improve overall form, strength and speed. You might practice an exaggerated knee and arm drive and drive up the hill ball-heel. You wouldn't use this exaggerated motion in a race unless you were sprinting up a final hill or trying to power away from a competitor on a hill as a surge strategy.

For most hills, you should try to maintain, as nearly as possible, the rhythm and form you use on the flats. A few changes are necessary, however, to compensate for the incline and increased resistance.

Running hills in daily running and at normal race pace involves trying to get up the hill with a fluid, economical technique. In your daily training, run up hills fairly quickly and practice proper technique (see below). Surprisingly, it is easier to run uphill quickly with good form than slowly in poor form. Technique differs slightly for different hills and in different racing conditions. Basically there are three methods, or "gears," for running uphill:

Gear 1: Training Pace and Evenly Paced Racing

Keep a steady stride throughout the climb. First, increase your knee lift. If you don't, the angle of the hill will cut down the length of your stride and you won't be able to get your feet up and out in front of you. It's like climbing stairs: you want to pick up your feet more.

• Increase your cadence slightly, but don't overstride. Tighten your stride for economy. By maintaining a normal or slightly shorter stride, you will keep your center of gravity over or slightly in front of the drive leg. Consequently, your force is directed up and forward, which is the precise direction you want to go. In a race, you will be maintaining normal stride length due to the added push-off and knee lift but will feel as if you are shortening your stride.

• Increase your arm swing slightly. By driving the arms a little bit more, you will overcome the pull of gravity. But don't exaggerate the arm drive. Uncontrolled, jerky motion will slow you. The arms should move as described previously, bending at the elbows with a smooth rhythm that matches the frequency of your stride. Don't reach out in front of you; keep your elbows slightly away from your body, hands relaxed.

• Push harder off your back foot. The faster you wish to run, the harder you push. Do not try to bounce up the hill; drive up the hill.

• Lean into the hill slightly. This increased lean will help you keep your center of gravity forward; you lean forward slightly just to maintain an upright position relative to the pull of gravity. The steeper the hill, the greater your lean. Keep your hips slightly forward, chest forward, back straight, chin up and eyes ahead. If you look down near your feet, your hips will fall back, destroying your erect, efficient posture.

One other trick here: Focus your eyes on an object 10 to 15 yards ahead and watch it pass, and then focus on another object. Psychologically, you can also pull yourself uphill with your eyes.

• Don't tense up. Don't bring up your arms to fight the hill, and don't tighten your neck, hands, forearms, shoulders. This tension diverts energy from the real struggle of racing uphill and may cause fatigue and a slower time. Run relaxed.

• Maintain an even, steady rhythm. Races are won by runners who get up the hills with the minimum loss of energy. Attack the hills with finesse, not muscle, by steadily moving uphill with good form and reasonably controlled breathing.

Gear 2: Steep- or Long-Hill "Downshift"

If you face a steep or long hill, the first thing to do is cut back your stride. Just as you downshift your car when going up steep or long hills, so too you downshift in running. To do this you must:

• Cut down the length of your stride and increase your stride frequency.
• Swing your arms faster and keep the swing short and controlled.
• Reduce the amount of drive off your back foot; since you are going slower, you will not need to drive forward as hard.
• Lift your knees slightly so that your stride isn't too short and choppy.
• Continue to lean into the hill with your hips.
• Don't panic! Stay relaxed.

Bob Glover once raced up the highest peak in the eastern United States, Mount Washington, in New Hampshire. The run was an eight-miler—with only one hill. Glover started off in 90-degree heat using Gear 1, and after two miles shifted to Gear 2. Soon he thought he was in his death gear. His right foot fell asleep due to pressure from the angle of the hill, and he started to walk. Later he tried Gear 2 again, but was soon passed by several veterans twice his age—and they were walking! Lesson: when climbing steep and long hills, you may get to the top faster by alternating running and walking. When walking, bend over at the waist and drive with your arms. Whatever you do, don't stop.

Gear 3: "Power Shifting"—For Hill Training and for Your Win

You only use this gear in a race when you know you have the power to use it and still finish. Most runners don't want to challenge a hill, and so they hold back, waiting to make their moves on the downhill and flats. You may be able to move away from your competitors if you can power uphill.

As you power uphill, keep the following in mind:

• Drive your arms faster. Make your arm stroke short, deliberate and quick, with the movements beginning at your chest and ending at the top of your hip. Keep your arms close to your body. Don't allow them to swing out in front of you or way behind you. Don't raise your arms and try to "box" your way to the top.

• Lean your body forward. Lean from your hips, not from your waist.

• Lift your knees. Make the effort to get your knees up so you can maintain good stride. If you try to run up a hill keeping your knees low, you will lose power.

• Power hard off your back foot. Your efforts will be unrewarded unless you push off your back foot with power.

• Don't overstride, it will cause you to lose power and thus run slower.

• Keep relaxed. Impossible to relax while hammering up a steep hill? Not so: belly breathe; keep your shoulders, neck and jaw from tensing up. Let your legs do the power work assisted by your arms. You'll recover your breath at the top.

5. DOWNHILL

Downhill technique is ignored by most coaches—and most books. Uphill technique is more glamorous. But once you've passed 'em going up, don't let 'em pass you going down. Most runners think downhill running is easy: take off the brakes, and roll. It is essential to let gravity do much of the work, but you must master the technique of

TECHNIQUE FOR UPHILLS

	ARMS	BODY ANGLE	KNEES	FOOTSTRIKE	STRIDE
Gear 1 Medium speed	Slight increase in swing	Slight forward lean; hips forward	Increase lift	Ball-heel, push off back foot	Maintain stride and slightly increase frequency, maintain actual stride length
Gear 2 Steep-hill downshift	Quicken drive, short strokes	Forward lean, hips forward	Increase lift	Ball-heel, reduce drive off back foot	Shorten stride, greatly increase stride frequency
Gear 3 Power up	Drive hard, with intense, short swing	Forward lean, hips forward	Greatly increase lift	Ball-heel, push hard off back foot	Slightly increase stride length, increase frequency, don't overstride

letting yourself go while running in a controlled manner. This takes practice.

In an attempt to get down a hill as quickly as possible, some runners flail their arms and legs all over the place; they may get injured or lose their rhythm and speed. Others fight the downhill and lean back, shorten their stride, dig in their heels, and raise their arms to "brake" them.

You should develop a feel for downhill running. Some runners compare it to "throwing" themselves downhill; others feel like a mountain stream flowing smoothly with the hill. You can actually improve your race times more by perfecting your downhill technique than by perfecting your uphill technique. The speed with which you run downhill is regulated by the lean of your body and the length of your stride. With these two regulators, you can use three gears to run downhill:

Gear 1: Maintaining a Steady Race or Training Pace

As you start downhill, try to keep your form as close as possible to that used on the flats. Allow gravity to do most of the work for you.

Forward Lean. Keep your body perpendicular to the ground, back straight (don't bend at the waist), and your hips pushed forward over your lead leg. Your forward momentum will keep you from falling on your face. The angle of your lean helps determine how fast you go downhill. To maintain a steady pace, hold the angle of your body so that the center of gravity is over your lead leg. If you lean too far forward, you will pick up speed; leaning back will cause you to slow.

Stride. Maintain your stride length by bringing your knees up. As you lean forward going downhill, you will have to lift your knees higher to maintain your stride length. You can help control the speed of your run by where you place your lead leg. On a steep descent, you will want to shorten the length of your stride slightly to hold back your speed. On a gradual decline, you may have to push off your back foot to keep a steady forward speed.

Arm Swing. Keep your arm swing under control. Unlike running uphill, downhill running uses the arms mostly to maintain balance and rhythm. There is no need to swing the arms hard; gravity is powering you downhill. Don't swing your arms wildly, windmilling all over the place as you go downhill; this causes you to lose balance and rhythm. Keep your elbows slightly away from the side of your body. Get your arms in rhythm with your legs.

Footstrike. Use the same footstrike that you use on the flats. However, Dr. Steve Subotnik suggests: "Concentrate on landing on the ball of the foot. If you're landing on your heels, you're overstriding. This is important because the foot and leg absorb shock much better when you land on the ball of the foot under a bent knee, than when you land on the heel in an almost straight-knee position." The ball-heel form absorbs shock and helps you hold forward motion as you run. But it may be uncomfortable. If you strike behind the ball of the foot, concentrate on lifting your feet quickly, hitting lightly and pushing off against the slant of the running surface. If you are more comfortable running heel-ball, concentrate on hitting the heel very gently and quickly rolling your foot forward so you don't jam your heel into the ground. Most important, do not bounce on your toes or overstride by landing hard on your heels.

Relax. Keep your arms, shoulders, neck and chin relaxed. Practice will help alleviate tension. But as Dr. Subotnik warns: "I tell runners to master this downhill technique, then to avoid it whenever possible. That is, even if you are a great downhill runner, you should do as little of it as you can. No one can tolerate a lot of hard downhill running and no one should try."

Gear 2: Downshifting for Very Steep or Long Hills

Sometimes you may want to slow down as you run downhill. Some races feature "super hills" down which it would be dangerous for you to "fly like an eagle." To help you slow down without losing form or putting on your brakes, here are some suggestion for downshifting:

The Forward Lean. Although difficult to do, try to lean forward slightly, allowing your hips to ride directly over your support leg. The natural tendency, especially on steep hills, will be to lean backwards.

Reduce the Length of Your Stride. A shorter stride will slow down your speed. As you decrease the length of your stride, you will increase its frequency. Be sure to bend your knee slightly as you land to allow for greater shock absorption and to keep your center of gravity over the lead leg. Don't jam your heel into the ground.

Use Your Arms for Balance and Rhythm. To keep your balance, bring your elbows farther away from the sides of your body. This will help you stabilize yourself.

Relax. Allow your body to move freely but keep it under control. Tension will create fatigue and soreness, so relax.

Gear 3: Power Shifting and Increasing Your Speed

Good downhill runners gain a huge advantage when they can increase the speed of their descent without using much energy. Running fast downhill without losing balance or rhythm requires concentration on keeping a controlled yet free-flowing movement. You can significantly increase your downhill speed by using the following techniques:

Increase Your Forward Lean. As noted above, the more you lean forward as you run downhill, the faster you will have to run to maintain your balance. The result is that your stride frequency increases. Initiate your forward lean with your hips, not your upper body. If you bend forward at the waist, you will force your center of gravity behind your support leg, which will cause you to slam your heel into the ground as you plant your lead leg.

Increase the Length of Your Stride. Do not attempt to lengthen your stride by reaching farther out in front of you. Reaching out will cause you to overstride, which

DOWNHILL TECHNIQUE

	ARMS	BODY ANGLE	KNEES	FOOTSTRIKE	STRIDE
Gear 1 Medium speed	Normal to slightly faster swing, elbows slightly away from body	Forward, keep perpendicular to surface	Increase lift	Ball-heel or heel-ball	Normal stride length, maintain stride frequency
Gear 2 Steep-hill downshift	Same	Same	Increase lift	Same	Shorten stride length, increase frequency
Gear 3 Faster speed powershift	Same, faster swing	Same, increase lean	Increase lift	Ball-heel	Increase stride length and frequency

makes you land hard on your heels and actually brakes your forward progress. Increase your stride length by increasing push-off and knee lift.

Swing Your Arms Vigorously and Keep Your Balance. As you increase your leg speed, increase your arm swing to keep a smooth and flowing rhythm. Control your arm swing by moving the arms up and down rather than flailing them side to side or way out in front of you. Keep your elbows away from the side of your body.

Rhythm Breathe. Since you are running downhill at a fast pace, your breathing rate may increase or even become labored. Concentrate on maintaining rhythmic breathing; continue breathing deeply and avoid shallow panic breathing.

Relax. Learn to "let go" and allow your body to "fall" downhill. Just as in skiing, you are less likely to fall and get injured and will have more control if you learn to push fear out of your mind, relax and let yourself go.

6. THE FINISH

In the ideal race, you will have run at an even pace and left a little strength for a strong finish. More likely, you will be just holding on or tailing off. Although this may seem to be an inappropriate time to be concerned with running form, proper technique will help you finish strong and cut seconds from your time.

For years, Pete Schuder thought he was helping his long distance runners by yelling at them near the end of their races, "C'mon, move faster! Gut it out to the finish!" It wasn't until Pete tried a hard marathon himself that he realized that the most annoying thing that can happen to runners is to have someone yell at them to run faster near the finish line. Trying to gut it out may make runners tense up. Instead, someone should yell, "Stay loose, keep your arms moving, knees up." The emphasis should be on a relaxed rhythm and efficient technique; otherwise, you may finish with head rolling, arms and shoulders high, shortened stride or "survival shuffle." Finish with finesse, not brute force.

Holding On—Maintenance Finish

When you've extended yourself beyond your limits, worked hard to run fast, you don't want to lose it all. How do you hold on until the end?

- Maintain your form as well as possible. Keep your arm swings in a vertical plane from the elbow forward. Don't lean backward. Keep leading with the knee, and concentrate on proper stride.
- Keep your breathing rhythmic. This will help you maintain your rhythmic flow.
- Don't panic. Stay relaxed, keep your confidence up. Believe you'll finish, and you will.

Tailing Off—Survival Technique

There are times when you miscalculate your pace or are undertrained. You find yourself coming up short near the finish. You may have met the Bear, or in a longer race, you may hit the Wall.

Finishing with the Bear on Your Back (Oxygen Debt). You may feel stiff and heavy and unable to make your muscles move. You should follow the same techniques as mentioned above in Holding On, but shorten your arm drive, cut down your stride, and thus use less energy to move yourself forward. Stay rhythmic, don't panic, shuffle on in.

Finishing Through the Wall (Glycogen Depletion). Inadequate energy supplies may cause you to develop leg cramps. Your body will want to quit. You don't feel winded; you just cannot make your legs go. You feel like going to sleep. You have hit the Wall. This usually happens—if it does—at around 20 miles. Jack Shepherd, however, used the survival technique for the last 11 miles of the 1978 New York Marathon. If you hit the Wall, follow the guidelines for

Finishing with the Bear on Your Back and run as easily as possible. Take the course in small segments. One woman we know ran the New York Marathon from water station to water station. Shepherd ran from one block to the next. Walk when you want to, and stretch your leg muscles to get rid of cramps. If you walk, pick the spot ahead of you where you'll start running again, and do it. Run slowly and keep going. Even well-conditioned runners sometimes find themselves struggling to the finish line. National class marathoner Marty Cooksey crawled across the line on her hands and knees after her legs gave out at the 1978 New York Marathon. We won't teach you the techniques of a finishing crawl. But if you feel that bad, consider walking in or dropping out. We know of another woman who pushed herself too hard in New York and collapsed a quarter-mile from the finish with a broken leg. The desire to finish, obviously, must be tempered with common sense.

Finishing Kick

This may be a gradual shifting of gears and build-up of speed over the final mile, or a sudden acceleration during the last 50–100 yards following a build-up of speed over the final quarter mile.

The trick is to move into a new pace, switch gears and put new form and reinvigorated muscles to work. You will usually have a finishing kick, even when you feel exhausted. The key is to find and push that special button, shift gears, and finish strong. Here's how you should see yourself:

- Vigorously increase your arm drive to initiate the kick and carry it through to the finish. Remember: the faster you swing your arms, the faster you move your legs.
- Increase your power drive off the support leg to lengthen your stride. The stride will become snappier and longer. In the kick, you want to increase both stride length and frequency.

- Greatly increase knee lift to allow proper follow-through of your lead leg.
- Move farther up on the ball in your ball-heel strike. Push off over the big toe. Your heel should come off the ground more quickly in the recovery stage. Hit the ground less with a push and more with a "pop." Feel that you are "popping" your feet and knees up from the road or track.
- Run tall; look 20–30 yards ahead and then at the finish line through to the end. Lift from the hips.

Stay relaxed, and maintain a rhythmic cadence to your breathing so you can continue your finishing kick all the way to the finish line. Think of the form you have used in speed workouts. Continue the drive through the line; don't let up just as you approach it.

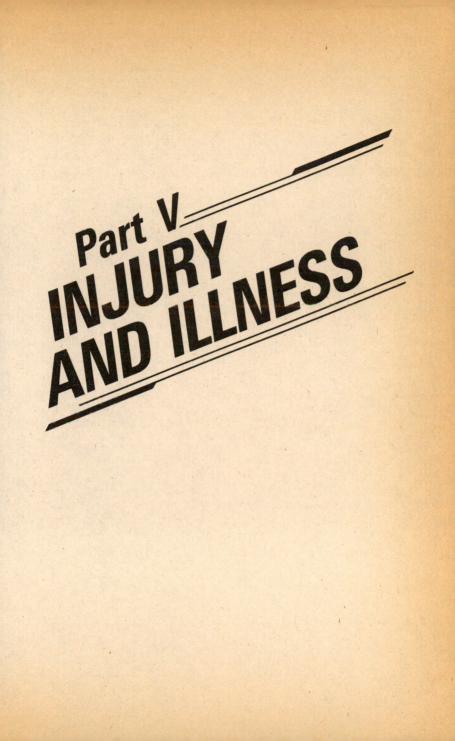

Part V
INJURY AND ILLNESS

24. TWENTY-FOUR CAUSES OF INJURY AND ILLNESS

Competitive running contributes little to health and fitness. In truth, it tears you down more than it builds you up. But competitive runners are running for sport, not fitness. Like other athletes, they must learn to accept the inevitability of injury and illness; they must also try to minimize their effect on their ability to perform.

It is safe to say that every year of competitive running will find you injured or ill at least a few times. Your best and safest response is to be conservative—hold back, and return to running cautiously. For the competitive runner, there is a fine line between overtraining and undertraining. Too much training may lead to injury or illness, too little may lead to underachievement. You will determine these outer limits for yourself and strive for the injury-free competitive area between. Often this is what makes the difference between winning and losing at all levels of competition. Many runners get into great shape only to become injured or ill and never make it to the starting line. The runner who loses training time again and again will be in worse shape than the conservative and consistent runner. An important part of competitive training is learning to prevent injuries and illness and knowing how and when to return to running.

"Diseases of excellence," as Dr. George Sheehan calls running injuries, are a part of the sport. The runner must accept this fact. You must be constantly aware of the warning signs and prepare to analyze the causes of these problems. They are seldom a result of accident, although most often they seem to "just happen" for no reason at all.

The causes of injury and illness seem to fall into one of three areas: training errors, inherited physical weaknesses, and environmental influences. Rather than dealing in detail with the treatment of specific injuries, which many running books have already covered, we will explain the causes of injury and illness and how training may be affected. (For detailed treatment of injuries and illnesses, con-

---

QUESTIONS TO ASK WHEN INJURED OR ILL

These are some of the questions we ask runners who become sick or injured. The goal is to discover the reason or reasons you developed your problem. Often more than one factor is involved. The basic question is: What have you done differently in your running or your daily routine that may have caused the injury or illness? Use the following checklist to help you determine the cause of your problem or, better yet, to help prevent a problem from occurring:

1. Are your feet or legs structurally weak? (Your doctor may have to answer this for you.)
2. Do you have good flexibility?
3. Do you warm up and cool down properly for all runs?
4. Do you overstretch?
5. Are your opposing muscles weak? (Abdominals, quadriceps, etc.)
6. Do you have any previous injuries that might make you vulnerable?
7. Did you return from an injury or illness too quickly?
8. Is your running form proper?

sult *The Runner's Handbook* or *The Runner's Repair Manual* by Dr. Murray Weisenfeld, a New York City podiatrist and an invaluable consultant for this book.)

Here are twenty-four causes of injury and illness:

1. BIOMECHANICAL: WEAK FEET AND UNEQUAL LEG LENGTH

Many runners have biomechanically weak feet. This means that the foot has some basic physical flaw that, aggravated by running, leads to foot, leg or knee injuries. A distance runner's foot strikes the ground over 1,000 times during every mile of running. The force of impact on each foot is approximately three to four times the runner's weight. With weak feet, the force exerted upon footstrike causes an

9. Have you made any sudden changes in the quantity or quality of your runs: mileage, speed, hills, surface?
10. Has running on snow or ice changed your running pattern or form?
11. Are you undertrained for the races you are running?
12. Are you racing too frequently?
13. Are you taking time to recover from races and hard workouts?
14. Have you changed running shoes, or are they worn down, or have you started wearing racing shoes?
15. Has your weight changed? Are you overweight or underweight?
16. Is your diet adequate for your training level?
17. Are you taking proper care of your feet?
18. Have you changed any daily habits, such as driving or sitting more?
19. Are you under additional stress?
20. Are you getting enough sleep?
21. Have you been doing other sports that might affect your running?
22. Have you changed running surfaces or are you running on uneven or slanted terrain?

abnormal strain on the supporting tendons, muscles and fasciae of the foot and leg. Arch supports (orthotics), either commercially made or custom fitted by a podiatrist, may help runners with biomechanically weak feet.

If your legs are of different lengths, you may experience pain in your back, knee or hips. In many cases, unequal leg length causes no injury. When it does, the injury often occurs first on the long leg. Structural shortages may occur anywhere in the leg: the upper leg, the lower leg and below the ankle. Heel lifts or orthotics to balance leg length may help; placed inside the shoe, they should never exceed half an inch. Exercises to stretch and strengthen the affected area are also beneficial.

If you experience back, hip or knee problems, have a sports-medicine expert check for leg-length discrepancy before you spend a lot of money for other treatment. This is one of the most neglected causes of running injuries and one of the easiest to repair.

2. OLD INJURIES

Running may create a new problem from an old, forgotten injury. A person who suffered a severe ankle injury or had a childhood disease may have latent weaknesses that existed prior to running and which may be reactivated with the extra stress of running. The site of a previous injury may also prove to be a vulnerable area for a stress fracture. Scar tissue also develops from muscle tears caused by running or other sports, and you may experience recurring problems after you think the injury is healed. Bob Glover's old ankle sprains from his youthful basketball-playing days, and the big toe he once dropped a steel plate on, make periodic "comebacks" to trouble his running—even though the original injuries occurred twenty years ago!

3. POOR FLEXIBILITY AND OVERSTRETCHING

The vast majority of runners do not allow enough time for stretching. Ask any runner how much he or she stretches and the most common reply is, "Not as much as I should." From laziness or lack of discipline, we set ourselves up for injuries due to a lack of flexibility. Tight or shortened muscles are more easily injured than stretched muscles, and cause a variety of biomechanical problems.

In a few cases, runners can be too flexible. You may be naturally too flexible in the ankles, for example, which would make them more liable to pronate too much. Flexibility in the calf muscles can also lead to injury. In these cases, you may not benefit from stretching.

Overzealous or careless stretching can do more harm than good, and it has been blamed for many injuries. The fact is that stretching isn't to blame, but rather straining. Do not stretch injured muscles. Stretching an injured muscle will only aggravate it and delay healing. Leave it alone until tenderness and swelling disappear, then work gradually to improve its flexibility. If you have a recurring problem such as back pain, don't do any exercise that aggravates it.

4. MUSCLE IMBALANCE

It is important that muscles be strong and that opposing muscles have a proper balance of strength. The prime contracting or agonist muscles (buttocks, hamstrings and calf muscles) become overdeveloped and tight with running. Stretching exercises for these muscles coupled with strengthening exercises for the opposing antagonist muscles are essential to restore muscle groups to proper balance. Otherwise, imbalances lead to injury. Strengthening exercises to prevent injuries include those for the abdominal muscles (easing back pain), shin area muscles (shin splints), and quadriceps in the thigh (hamstring and knee pain).

The competitive runner who regularly includes speed work, especially hill training, in his or her routine has less need for supplemental exercises for the quadriceps, buttocks and other muscle groups because these types of runs build strength. But the competitive runner who runs aerobically, mostly on the flat, using the same muscle groups repetitively, is often prone to injury from muscle imbalance.

5. IMPROPER INJURY AND ILLNESS REHABILITATION

Take your time! Allow an injury to heal before running hard or long again, and don't resume training too soon after illness. Relapses are common, resulting in even more training time lost. Many serious injuries result from ignoring or favoring a minor injury. It is always wise to back off. Take your time off; you've earned it.

6. ERRORS IN RUNNING FORM

Technique is important for both fast running and healthy running. A pronounced forward lean will result in extra pressure on the lower leg. Leaning backwards, "braking," will cause pressure on the back and hamstring muscles. Swaying side to side and running too "tight" may also cause injury. Overstriding—when your foot hits in front of your center of gravity—causes the surface to push your body back, and this stress often causes shin splints and stress fractures.

Heel-ball footstrike allows for increased shock absorption, but excessive hitting on the heel causes jarring and sometimes leg and back injury. Videotapes of leading runners in long-distance races reveal that most of these elite runners land ball-heel instead of heel-ball. Most of the "back-of-the-packers," however, land heel-ball. Videotapes of injured average runners at the George Washington University Clinic and Sports Medicine Center reveal that they often cannot tolerate this ball-heel footstrike and tend to develop overuse injuries such as shin splints, calf tightness and stress fractures.

When concerned about preventing injury, run heel-ball.

When concerned about improving speed, run ball-heel; but be alert to warning signs of injury.

7. OVERTRAINING—TOO MUCH MILEAGE, SPEED OR HILL WORK

Too much mileage too soon may be the leading cause of injury to all runners. In his studies, Dr. David Brody, medical director of the Marine Corps Marathon and an orthopedic surgeon, has found that injuries are most frequent among beginner runners and among all other runners who are trying to increase their mileage. Even if you build up your mileage gradually, beyond a certain point you may be unable to handle more. Dr. Lyle Micheli, director of the Division of Sport Medicine at Children's Hospital in Boston, adds that he sees "a real increase in injuries when people get beyond 50 miles a week in running. It's like a medical barrier. All kinds of problems develop, from tendonitis of the heels to irritation of the soles of the feet, to knee problems." The solution may be orthotics, or holding the mileage at a level below that which causes problems until the body is ready to accept more mileage. Most mileage-related injuries are minor and treatable. Risks can be minimized by using common sense and moderation—in getting started, in increasing distances and in judging how much running is enough for you.

Pete Schuder is a frequent victim of what he calls "memory running." Good weather often finds him thinking about the good old days when he was a national class quarter-miler, and he finds himself training at higher mileage than his rusty chassis can handle. The "too much too soon" dilemma applies to both the runner on the way up and the runner coming back—or in Pete's case, over the hill.

Speed work helps you race faster. Unfortunately, it also increases your chance of injury. There is a very fine line between speed work that produces physiological benefits and that which causes injury. With experience, you will develop a feel for what is safe for you and still provides training benefits.

Be careful not to increase the speed of your training pace too rapidly. Sudden changes in the speed of your daily runs may result in fatigue and injury. Also, be careful when your pattern of training changes as, for example, where you find yourself regularly running with a group or individual much faster than you. Run the pace that is best for you.

Hill work is a specialized type of speed training. Sprints uphill place a severe stress on the lower leg and can cause low-back and hamstring injury. Keep away from hill workouts when your Achilles tendons, shins or calves are troubling you or you are recovering from hard races or long runs.

Ease into this type of speed training, whether you are new at it or returning to it as preparation for a key race. Also, beware that sudden changes in the difficulty—hilliness—of your daily runs may cause injury. Be especially careful if you're ordinarily a flatlander and find yourself in a hilly section of the world while traveling.

Safety Note: Beware of the urge to train harder and harder after a few successful races. Restraint and common sense are as important as desire and hard work.

---

8. DOWNHILLS

Running downhill puts a severe strain on the body. According to Dr. David Costill, it "forces the leg muscles to do eccentric work. They stretch out much farther than normal. This causes a lot of minute tears in all the connective tissues." Much more shock is absorbed by your body at impact when running downhill. If you "brake" going downhill, you may cause the muscles along the backs of your legs and in your back to fight against gravity, creating additional stress. Downhill running, therefore, is especially hard on runners with knee or back problems. You should be relaxed and roll downhill with good form. Run ball-heel to minimize shock.

Racing downhills makes strain and stress that much more pronounced. In addition, the racer is prone to blisters and jammed toes caused by the foot sliding forward in the shoe. Stitches are another problem. After a race such as the Boston Marathon, known for its many downhills, you will find that your quads will be very sore due to the straining they take racing downhills. If you're racing or training on downhills, wear well-cushioned shoes. Avoid practicing downhill racing technique unless you really need it to improve your position in races.

9. UNDERTRAINING

You must have the mileage base and speed training to be prepared for races. If you put in only 20 miles a week and then run a marathon, you are asking for injury. If you do all your running at nine-minute miles and then race at six-minute miles, you're asking for injury. You may get away with it and reach the finish line, but the toll on your body could be serious. The collapse-point theory refers not only to falling apart in the race in terms of ability to keep pace, but also to risking musculoskeletal collapse by pushing the body beyond endurance levels for which it was prepared. Overtraining often causes you to break down before you reach the starting line. Undertraining often causes you to break down before you reach the finish line.

10. GREED: OVERRACING

You can stress yourself physically and mentally with too much racing. "Going to the well" once too often will cause injury or illness. Select your races wisely, space them wisely, and allow yourself to recover before applying the race stress again.

11. INADEQUATE RECOVERY

The training effect won't take place if you don't allow your body to recover from stress. Follow the hard-easy system of training. You may need additional easy days or even days off following stressful workouts and races. Allow much more time to recover from marathons.

12. SURFACES AND TERRAIN

Ideally, your runs should take place on slightly rolling courses, without too many steep uphills or downhills. The rolling terrain gives more muscle groups a workout while not taxing them.

It is generally good to change surfaces frequently; however, this may cause problems for some runners. In your daily routine, don't make sudden changes in surface. A medium-hard synthetic path, a dirt trail, or even level grass fields are the best training surfaces. But if you intend to run in road races, you're going to have to run the roads for training. Force yourself to train on pavement two or three times a week. (Conversely, if you run on roads a lot, try to take a break on a softer surface occasionally.)

Cement or concrete are harder than asphalt; you'll get less shock on the road than on the sidewalk. Switching from a very hard to a very soft surface late in a run, or the reverse, may cause injury. If possible, do your speed workout on soft trails with good footing or on a track where you'll get more shock absorption.

Also, beware of obstacles—ruts, rocks, loose or uneven turf, or holes—that may cause injury. They are just as dangerous as potholed streets. On paved surfaces, you face at least three dangers. First, running along sidewalks requires you to leap off the curbs, which increases the shock on the body. A fatigued runner may injure himself or herself; stress fractures occur this way. Second, most roads and sidewalks are banked or crowned for drainage. When you run on them, you are running along an incline; your upper foot is twisting inward with every step, and you're giving yourself a short leg. If possible, run in the middle of the road where it is more level, or cross over the road every mile or so. Strangely, some runners find that they can run on roadbeds slanted one way but not the other. If you go for a postrace run, don't go in the same direction as you raced. Your muscles will be tired and you'll be prone to injury running on the same slant. Third, vehicles. Common sense tells you to run facing traffic. But to alter your impact on a slanted road, you'll have to change that idea. Look for extra-wide aprons where you can safely do some running with the traffic.

Always run defensively. Watch every car, and be alert for zooming bikers, roller skaters, skateboarders, even other runners. Watch out for dogs—on and off leashes. Your best bet to avoid bumping into one of these dangers is to run only in the early morning in crowded parks or meridians popular with other activists.

Beach running may look tempting. Avoid it. In soft sand, your heels sink in and pull your Achilles tendons. On the firm, damp sand you run on a slant. Then there are seashells, broken glass, and driftwood to avoid.

Indoor running can be a blessing in the winter months, but it can also cause more trouble than it is worth. Since you are running around sharp turns, often on a slanted, hard surface, you are severely stressing the inside leg. Ideally, you would minimize injury by changing direction every five minutes, but this is usually impossible, since most tracks are crowded. Therefore, you should limit your indoor runs to 30 to 45 minutes.

Speed work can be helpful indoors if you really must sharpen for a race and all the roads are full of ice and snow. When confined indoors for your speed training, cut back on the intensity and number of repetitions to minimize stress on your legs. One of the leading causes of injury to top college athletes is intense training on indoor tracks with tight turns. Competitive road runners, unaccustomed to such tracks, are even more prone to injury. Save your hard track work for spring, when you can run more safely outdoors as you sharpen for key races.

Some injuries require that you run on certain surfaces. Achilles tendon problems, for example, require even, hard surfaces that don't create a pull on the damaged tendon. Knee injuries, on the other hand, are aggravated by hard surfaces. Running on trails or grass may lessen the shock to your body and strengthen muscles not used on hard surfaces. This may alleviate fatigue and injury. However, don't run on soft, uneven surfaces when injured, or you may aggravate a leg injury: the soft surface puts the leg through a greater range of motion than a hard surface.

For most of us, it is impossible to avoid the roads, and thus we must learn to adjust to them, especially since that is where we race. Using an efficient stride and well-cushioned shoes, the runner with good flexibility who follows a sensible training program should not worry about the hardness of the road ahead. Just pack in the injury-free miles.

13. WEATHER

Cold

The cold-weather runner is less flexible and thus more vulnerable to injury. The main weather-related cause of injuries is poor footing during winter months. According to Dr. Paul Taylor, winter running injuries most often come from being tight when trying to guard against slipping. Tense muscles, whether consciously or unconsciously tightened, are more prone to strains and other overuse injuries. The runner usually alters his running form to increase traction, which leads to further problems. Lateral foot slippage also occurs on icy spots, and if the foot slips, a pulled muscle or tendon may result. Running in a few inches of snow forces you to work muscles normally not taxed. If your quadriceps become fatigued, knee injury could result. Beware of the obvious—if you slip and fall, try to land lightly and then immediately stop your run and put ice on the injured area.

The most common winter running injuries are groin and hamstring pulls caused by slipping and sliding through the snow. These nagging injuries require rest, or they will still be with you when the snow has melted.

Training must go on, with or without dry surfaces. The best prevention is to make sure you warm up well, maintain good flexibility, and run relaxed, not allowing yourself to tense up out of fear of falling. When running on slippery surfaces shorten your stride slightly and shuffle along, maintaining good balance. Be especially careful on downhills, turns and when running in the dark, when you can't see where your feet are landing. Don't attempt fast running under slippery conditions. Studded shoes that aren't overly worn are the best in snow—just like the snow tires you put on your car for better traction. In the fall, be wary of wet leaves, which can be just as slippery as ice.

Cold weather brings the danger of frostbite and hypothermia. To prevent frostbite, keep covered, keep dry, keep moving. Frostbite can result in the loss of fingers or toes and has even caused death. Frostbitten skin is cold, pale and firm to hard to the touch. The first step in treatment is to warm rapidly without excessive heat. Use water at about body temperature. Do not massage or, in the case of toes, walk on the injured area. Do not rub with snow. Take the frostbitten runner immediately to where he or she can get medical aid.

The danger of cold includes the wind, which when combined with air temperature produces the "windchill factor." Running into the wind lowers the windchill factor, while running with the wind may speed you along to produce a sweat. Therefore, begin your runs into the wind on out-and-back courses. Otherwise you'll build up a good sweat with the wind at your back and then turn into the biting wind for the return, which may cause frostbite or at least extreme discomfort.

Hypothermia is the lowering below normal of the central or core temperature of the body. As the temperature falls, the body responds with shivering, which is the muscles' attempt to produce heat. If not attended to, the runner could next become incoherent and then lapse into a coma, even die. Hypothermia usually strikes when you are wearing wet clothing. If your clothes are soaked from getting splashed with slush or if you sweat too much due to overdressing, you should change immediately rather than keep going. Take off wet clothing immediately after running, or hypothermia may strike you.

Follow these guidelines for training and racing in the cold:

• It's never too cold to train, but exceptionally cold weather makes racing times slower and is very uncomfortable.

• Let someone know where you are going and when you expect to return.

• Dress in layers that can be easily adjusted. You can always remove a layer if you get too warm and tie it around your waist. The key is to trap the heat naturally produced by the body. Wear up to three layers, four if it is extremely cold. Two layers are enough for most racing conditions. The innermost layer should be absorbent and nonirritating, such as a cotton T-shirt. Polypropylene undergarments are very lightweight and transmit moisture away from the body, allowing your inside layer, and you, to remain dry and warm. The second insulating layer is usually a long-sleeved turtleneck or a hooded wool sweatshirt, or long underwear. The outer shell is usually designed to break the wind. A nylon Windbreaker or the newer Gore-Tex fabrics, which "breathe" better than nylon and repel water as well as wind, are most often used. Most of the time, the inner layer plus a turtleneck are enough for racing.

The legs usually stay warm with one layer of clothing. If two layers are needed, try tights, long wool underwear or polypropylene bottoms under sweat pants or nylon Windbreakers. For racing, tights or long underwear covered by shorts to help protect the privates are preferred.

• Keep the extremities covered. Mittens are warmer than gloves. An old pair of wool socks will do just fine. Make sure the wrists are covered. Ears should be protected by a ski cap or wool headband. The most important area to keep warm is the head. As much as 50 percent of body heat is lost through your head, as through a chimney. In extremes of cold, a ski mask may be used to keep the face and nose warm. Coating your face with petroleum jelly will also help.

• Feet endure best. Wool running socks are excellent and all you need. If you keep moving and don't get wet, your feet won't get cold.

• If you get hot when training or racing, remove your hat first (tuck it in your shorts), then your mittens, then unzip your outer layer, and then remove it and tie it around your waist. As you cool, replace this clothing in opposite order.

• Be prepared—dress properly. Be flexible. On a single run the conditions may change several times. Don't toss away your gloves and hat when you are racing unless you are positive you won't need them again.

• There is great danger not only in underdressing, but also in overdressing. You should open your clothing as soon as sweat starts to build up. You will get cold much more quickly in sweat-soaked clothing.

Heat

Running in hot weather can be trouble; racing in it can be dangerous. The effects of heat on long-distance running mustn't be taken lightly. Problems you face may include muscle cramps, blisters and fatigue. The symptoms of heat exhaustion include profuse sweating, dizziness, weakness and dehydration. With a further increase in body temperature, often exceeding 105°F, heat exhaustion may be followed by heat stroke, which can be fatal. Listen to the warning signs of heat: headache, dizziness; disorientation; nausea; decrease in sweat rate; pale, cold skin. Don't try to run through these symptoms. Stop, walk or rest. Find shade and pour water on you immediately, and seek medical help. If these symptoms develop after the race, lie down, raise your legs and ask for help.

Air temperature is one factor to consider when running. Humidity is another. The key to regulating body temperature in hot weather is sweat evaporation, which accounts for as much as 90 percent of heat removal. Under very humid conditions, little sweat can vaporize; it is difficult for the body to lose heat. An air temperature of 60°F with 95 percent humidity could be more dangerous than a temperature of 90°F in a dry climate. A headwind facilitates evaporation, but a tailwind eliminates most of the air flow over the skin and therefore reduces sweat evaporation and heat loss. The position of sun and clouds is also a factor. Direct sunlight at high noon results in a rapid rise of body heat; cloud cover, of course, shields the runner.

The runner must understand that he or she can only partially adjust to heat. You cannot run faster in heat, so the next choice is to prepare yourself to be more competitive in the heat than the other runners. Heat affects some runners more than others and even affects the same runner differently on different days. Since serious runners must train in the heat and often are forced to race in it, they should make adjustments in their training and racing in order to achieve their goals. The following guidelines to running in the heat apply to all runners, regardless of level of ability:

Be in Shape. An unconditioned runner places an extra burden on his or her body by running in the heat.

Avoid the Heat. If you don't plan to race in it, don't train in it. Run during the cool of the early morning or late evening. Look for running paths that are shaded, and run on the shady side of the road.

Run in the Heat. Acclimate yourself to the heat. Allow 10 to 14 days of slowly progressive training to get used to new heat conditions. Run at least a few times a week in the heat of the day if you intend to race in the heat. If you live in a cool area and must race in a warmer area, you can "heat train" by running three or four times a week for several weeks in double sweats to create an artificial heat stress. Don't run in a rubber suit, however, since it is not properly ventilated.

Adjust Your Pace. Start out slower and run a steady pace in both training runs and races. You may need to adjust your starting pace for races by as much as a minute and make further reductions in pace along the way. Run within yourself and try to outsmart your opponents rather than trying to outrace them *and* the heat. The result is likely to be disastrous if you challenge the heat.

Adjust Your Distance. On a hot, muggy day, forget your planned long run—cut it short and reschedule it for a cooler day. In the summer months, choose shorter races, preferably 10 km and less.

Keep Your Body Wet. During runs and races, pour water over your head. Use sponges to douse your body with water. During workouts, dunk your shirt in water and drape it over your head and shoulders. Ice is great on hot days. Put it under your hat, and just let it melt. Or rub it across the base of your neck and under the arms.

Drink Plenty of Liquids. Do this before, during and after your workouts and races.

Run on Cool Surfaces. Hot pavement burns your feet, and the heat from the road pushes your temperature up. Try running on the dirt shoulders. Search for dirt or grass surfaces. Pavement sprinkled with water is cooler.

Keep Cool Before and After Your Race. Warm up and cool down in the shade. Try to keep your body temperature as low as possible before racing, and bring it down as quickly as possible after.

Dress Carefully. In direct sunlight, provide the body with shade. Wear white or other bright colors that reflect the sun. A hat should protect your head and shoulders. It should be white, lightweight and well ventilated.

On exceptionally sunny days, wear a full loose-fitting T-shirt, not a tank top, to protect your shoulders. Cotton is better than nylon because it absorbs water and "breathes" more readily.

14. SHOES AND ORTHOTICS

Running shoes designed to prevent injury often contribute to it. While the competitive runner owes his and her existence to the remarkable advances made by shoe manufacturers, and the massive running boom has been made possible by well-cushioned, flexible and comfortable running shoes, it's also true that runners of all types are made to serve as guinea pigs for the shoe business.

According to Dr. Richard Schuster, running injuries vary year to year in response to the latest advances in running shoes. Changes in the flexibility of the shoe and the rigidity of the heel counter, for example, may help some runners but cause problems for others. As shoes get lighter with the use of new materials, the most common breakdown is due to weak heel counters. The wide-flared heel, designed to prevent injury, caused widespread knee problems. The air shoe was a great improvement in increasing shock absorption, but it also aggravated knee problems because it allowed runners to pronate or supinate more than usual. The softer-soled running shoes created a similar problem and wore out faster doing it. Also, the heel sinks further down in the shoe, causing potential cases of Achilles tendonitis and shin splints.

To minimize injury, running shoes must offer flexibility, cushioning, support—and they must fit your feet. Monitor the wear of your shoes daily. Uneven wear of the soles will cause injury, as this affects the angle of your footstrike, causing your foot to roll abnormally. Also check for loss of support in the upper shoe.

When buying shoes, always purchase from a dealer who specializes in running shoes and can help you make the right selection. Always have two pairs of training shoes going at all times to minimize injuries. This way you won't get hurt trying to get a few extra miles out of an aging shoe as you break in a new one, or get blisters from having to rush a new shoe into service if your trusty shoes are lost or destroyed. If you try to resole your shoes or use shoe-saving devices, be careful that you don't overcompensate and cause injuries.

Should you own a pair of racing flats? A common mistake among runners is to wear racing flats when they are not necessary. The average competitor should use the same shoe for both racing and training. This is especially true for the heavy runner. A racing shoe gives less shock absorption and is designed for running on the ball of the foot. It also has less heel lift, and can lead to Achilles tendon injuries. Racing shoes should be worn only for shorter races at first, and then for races beyond ten kilometers when you will be running at a pace much faster than your training pace. Use your racing shoes for occasional short runs and speed workouts to minimize the risk of injury when you switch to them for races. Many training shoes are now made light enough to be used for both racing and training.

Sudden switches to spikes can also cause injury, since they have very low heels, little cushioning, and force you to run on the balls of your feet. Many college cross-country coaches, including Columbia's Pete Schuder, prefer studded flats for cross-country events. Pete also recommends them for 10 km races on tartan tracks because he feels they are safer. Since most road racers would wear spikes only once or twice a year in competition; they're seldom worth the expense and injury risk.

The type of shoe you purchase may be determined by the kind of injury you are susceptible to. You may need a firm heel counter if you pronate and have a knee problem, or a flexible shoe if you have shin splints, or a very well-cushioned shoe if you have heel spurs, and so forth. Your sports-medicine specialist will guide you in a selection of shoes that will minimize your particular problem.

Faults in shoes may also cause injury. Look for good quality and check for bad: stitching that isn't properly secured, parts in the wrong position, heels that lean to one side, improper placement of the studs or waffles on the sole. In the shoe industry, unfortunately, a good thing isn't left alone. You can be certain that as soon as you've found your perfect running shoe, the manufacturer will stop making it. Or a good model will be "upgraded" next year, and at a higher price. Old, trusty models don't stick around long.

Orthotics have become a status symbol. Glover was a running cripple when he was saved by a series of orthotic devices developed by Dr. Schuster. However, he has also seen runners with mild problems which became much worse after wearing orthotics. Before submitting to the expense of custom-made orthotics and the agony of adjustments—you must follow your doctor's advice for easing into them or you'll cause additional injury—first try exercise and commercial arch supports. Our friend in Vermont, Jack Shepherd, suffered from excruciating back and leg pain for a while. He bought a pair of ready-made orthotics, tried one, tried 'em both, the pain disappeared, and he wore the things until they wore out. Then he threw them away, and the pain never returned. You figure it out.

Dr. George Sheehan claims there are several reasons why orthotics fail to work: they are difficult to fit and mold; they impair the runner's flexibility; rear-foot correction is sometimes excessive; they need adjusting and runners don't bother following up with the adjustments. Badly fitted orthotics, Dr. Sheehan says, "can make you worse as well as better."

Pay attention as well to the shoes you wear when not running. Wearing training shoes all day, or even another pair of the same model, may make you susceptible to injury due to the lack of variety of stress. Wearing street shoes that have a hard surface may hurt your feet if you are used to wearing well-cushioned shoes. Dr. Hans Kraus, author of *The Causes, Prevention, and Treatment of Sports Injuries*, solves this problem by painting his running shoes black so he can wear them at the office. High-heeled shoes, for both men and women, are very bad for runners. Constantly wearing these shoes will shorten your Achilles tendon or create ankle problems. The competitive runner who wants to dress up and go dancing in high heels takes chances with his or her Achilles tendons and ankles. Wear lower heels—or dance barefoot. (Just be careful not to get stomped on by a nonrunner wearing spike heels.)

15. BODY WEIGHT

Many competitive runners, when in superb shape, weigh as much as 20 percent less than the average person of the same height. A very fit runner often looks very gaunt, but there is a fine line between looking underweight and feeling underweight. Your bone structure, metabolism and personal preference will dictate what is too little or too much weight for you. Losing weight too rapidly may make you weak and ill; being underweight may have the same effect. However, says Dr. Edward Colt, an endocrinologist at New York City's St. Luke's Hospital, "the lighter you are, within certain limits, the less likely you are to become injured. The limits are set by your own constitution—each individual has an optimum weight below which he or she feels tired and becomes susceptible to infections." Dr. Colt considers excessive weight loss "a running injury" similar to the overtraining syndrome.

Overweight is a well-known and well-documented problem. If you are 20 percent or more over your "ideal" weight, you must get your weight down before racing, to prevent injury. The overweight runner stresses the cardiovascular and musculoskeletal systems and isn't able to handle heat as well as slimmer running friends. The runner who is 30 pounds overweight slams the ground with 20 percent more force than normal. The heavier runner, whether overweight or just big boned, needs well-cushioned training shoes.

Bulimia and anorexia nervosa are psychiatric disorders which are becoming increasingly serious health problems in our stress-filled society. Bulimia is a fear of getting fat, for which the solution is to eat large amounts of food and then induce vomiting. Anorexia is a refusal to eat almost anything at all, even though the individual is hungry and obsessed with food. The anorexic desires to achieve extreme thinness. Bulimia often leads to anorexia, or follows it once the anorexic has returned to eating.

These disorders mainly strike adolescent women from middle- to upper-class homes, but older women and men of all ages are also susceptible. According to Dr. David Herzog of the Eating Disorders Clinic at Massachusetts General Hospital in Boston, as many as one in five college students is believed to have bulimia. Sherrye Henry, Jr., a top cross-country runner at Yale University, conducted a survey in 1981 at the Women's Ivy League Track and Field Championships. She found that women who ran 45 miles a week or more showed anorexic-type behavior, according to an Eating Attitudes Test (EAT) developed at the University of Toronto. Since sprinters and field-event athletes scored very low on the test, the survey suggests that long-distance runners are more prone to this illness than the average person and most other athletes.

As Sherrye Henry, who dropped from 120 to 90 pounds, concludes in an article in *The Runner*: "While there is no conclusive evidence that links anorexia nervosa to long distance running, as runners, we ought to remember that while thin is good, thinner is not always better. And in the case of a runner with anorexia, perfection can kill."

Most runners will find a good racing weight, however, and will have little trouble staying at that level.

16. INADEQUATE DIET

The well-balanced diet of fresh fruits, raw vegetables and protein (but not too much meat) is recommended for runners. Some top runners, however, are notorious junk food addicts, but they pack that stuff in on top of a reasonably balanced diet.

Poor diet will cause immediate problems. The runner who doesn't eat enough carbohydrates and essential vitamins and minerals may find himself or herself feeling weak. Women runners are prone to anemia (for known medical reasons) and should take iron supplements as a precaution. A one-a-day general vitamin and mineral supplement may also be of value to all runners, even if they follow a good diet.

Avoid—and beware of—"special diets." Nothing that you ingest will make you faster. A lot of things you eat, or don't eat, may make you slower, however. Frances Sheridan Goulart noted in *The Jogger* that a low-calorie diet reduces your overall nutrient intake as well as your weight. Fewer calories means less A, D, E, C, and B complex vitamins as well as sports-specific minerals like iron. A low-carbohydrate diet, by contrast, may produce fatigue, calcium depletion, dehydration, and/or hypoglycemia (low blood sugar).

If you eat and compete on a low-fat diet, you run the risk of depleting key fatty acids and may suffer impaired cellular function because of low levels of vitamins A, D, and E. On the other hand, if you reduce protein and emphasize carbohydrates, your body may go into negative nitrogen balance. The result is fatigue, from depletion of B vitamins. High-protein diets, however, may cause excessive losses of sodium and water and of whole-body energy reserves.

Dr. Edward Colt warned runners at a New York Road Runners clinic: "The healthy diet does not cause obesity, heart attack, colon cancer, diabetes, spastic colitis or appendicitis. The unhealthy diet does cause these disorders—at least there is much evidence to implicate it." Eat a balanced diet, and don't fool around with fads.

17. IMPROPER FOOT CARE

Treat your feet like good friends. Wash them daily in warm water, dry them thoroughly, and sprinkle them with antifungus powder. Fungus also feeds on dead skin tissue, so clean your feet with a nail brush, emery board or pumice stone. It is also important to wear dry, clean socks. Corns, warts, infections, slivers, ingrown toenails and the like should be taken care of immediately by your podiatrist.

Take care of blisters, and catch 'em when they're small. Blisters are caused by something rubbing—shoes that are too big or too small, abrasive socks, faults in shoe or sock stitching, downhill running, etc. Friction can be minimized by using a petroleum jelly (but don't destroy your leather orthotics with it), friction-reducing insoles or talcum powder. If the blister is small and not painful, leave it alone. If it is large and painful and interferes with your running, stop running until you no longer favor it. Favoring a blister has been known to cause many knee and other injuries. Dr. Murray Weisenfeld knows his way around blisters, and in his book, *The Runner's Repair Manual,* suggests the following operation (for those with a surgeon's hands):

Sterilize a razor blade, nail clippers or scissors with antiseptic (usually alcohol). Make a small slit in the blister and press out the fluid. Clean the opening with antiseptic. With cotton, soak up the fluid. Cover the blister. Dr. Weisenfeld doesn't like Band-Aids because they are usually plastic and keep air out. He prefers a square of gauze with tape at the edges; at night, remove the gauze and let the blister air. Don't peel the cap off the blister. Let it wear off.

For basic foot care, Dr. Weisenfeld suggests talcum powder between the toes to absorb moisture and reduce friction (protecting against blisters). He suggests cream on your heels in fall and winter to prevent cracking, which can be very painful. Keep your toenails short; long nails jam into the front of your shoes, causing black toenail or ingrown toenails. Dr. Weisenfeld suggests cutting the nails straight across, not in a curve, to prevent ingrown toenail. Rub calluses with an emery board to reduce them. Very thick calluses should be removed by your podiatrist.

All of this will benefit your two friends down there. Treat your feet well and listen to 'em hum while you run.

18. POOR DAILY HABITS

A sudden change in daily habits can cause the runner problems, especially back pain or sciatica. You should be careful lifting heavy objects; always use your powerful legs to do the work and not your back. Sleeping on your back or stomach may also cause problems, and a pillow under your knees or hips respectively may help. Comfort is the key to sleeping correctly, but the preferred position is on your side, knees flexed—the fetal position. The bed should be very firm, and a bed board should be placed under the mattress. Lifting and carrying around a baby may cause back pain in both men and women. There are also occupational hazards: standing or sitting too much, reaching or lifting. A change in posture at home or office may be the cause of pain. If you spend a lot of time sitting, make sure you have good back support. If possible, elevate your feet regularly, too.

Driving can cause tightened muscles, strains in the back, and tension. Pushing the gas pedal or clutch for long periods can cause leg, knee and back pain for some runners. You may want to put a small pillow behind the small of your back for support, or move the driver's seat forward or back to find the most comfortable position. Not all runners find driving troublesome, but some do, and others don't realize that this can be the source of leg or back pain. Remember not to drive (or ride) for too long a period just before a race. Atalanta's Jean Whiston, an Olympic prospect from Ireland, rode in a car for ten hours to a race, which aggravated an old sciatica problem and caused her to drop off her pace during the race. The lesson? If you have pain, always look for a change in personal habits as a possible cause.

19. STRESS

Stress is essential to life, but a cause of death. It is everywhere in our daily lives. It may be pleasant, damaging or helpful. Its negative effect on our bodies may be long last-ing, even occurring after the stressful event itself has ceased. What causes it? Work pressures, social readjust-ment, geographical change, a sudden surprising event. "Stress," says Dr. Hans Selye, author of *Stress Without Distress* and *The Stress of Life*, "is essentially the wear and tear in the body caused by life at any one moment."

There are various kinds of stress: emotional (from a fam-ily argument, the death of a loved one), environmental (from excessive cold or heat), and physiological (from an outpouring of the steroid hormones from the adrenal glands, which are extremely sensitive indicators of stress). Stress changes us physically and may cause a variety of medical ills, some imagined and some very real, painful, even lethal. Each period of stress, Dr. Selye says, especially from frustrating, unsuccessful struggles, leaves some irre-versible chemical scars. When we are burdened beyond our stress tolerance, we become ill, or develop emotional problems, or suffer the physical breakdowns of athletes. Stress takes its physiological toll. Our emotions affect our muscles, and our muscles reflect our emotional problems. Dr. Selye and other medical authorities believe that most ailments, especially back pain, are the result of too much stress.

Some runners run with stress, carrying their tensions vis-ibly during a workout. They run with tight muscles, tense and high shoulders, and short, choppy strides. They are too busy to relax, warm up, stretch and begin running slowly before beating their bodies into the hard-paved roads. They think cooling down is for other runners and risk serious injury by forgoing that series of exercises, too. They often pay the penalty of tight calves and hamstrings, as well as back pain.

In the beginning, as you take up the sport of running, the exercise helps you cope with stress. But after you get into competitive racing, it can become an additional stress which may overwhelm you. Stress, whether caused by the drive to become a better runner or by external factors, makes you vulnerable to illness and injury.

Dr. Hans Kraus, author of *Backache, Stress and Tension*, notes that "tension is the root of all evil." When faced with such stresses as marriage, a baby, lack of sleep, final exams, pressures at work, etc., the runner must adjust his training—back off the mileage and speed work and maybe skip the big race. Take a "time out," and just run for relaxation and stress management rather than for competitive training. Otherwise you risk not only poor performances but serious injury or illness.

20. INADEQUATE SLEEP

Beginning runners often find that they sleep better; perhaps they even need less sleep than the average of about seven-and-a-half hours. But as you start training competitively, you may find just the opposite: that you require more sleep than average, perhaps up to ten hours a day. Many elite runners take regular naps between daily workouts.

The average runners can't do this because running isn't their job. They often find themselves saving time for other duties by stealing sleep time with late-night runs—which may leave them too tired to get to sleep—or they may awaken very early in order to pack in miles before work. If you lose sleep, remember: you can't burn the candle at both ends. You will destroy yourself if you don't back off for a few days until your body recovers.

Sleep patterns are important. You develop a regular rhythm of sleeping and waking. If this rhythm is disrupted, stress results and you will be more susceptible to injury and illness.

Some runners require more sleep than others. Some require much more when training hard. When a runner overtrains, he or she frequently develops insomnia. He gets to sleep easily, but wakes up often during the night and frequently has trouble getting back to sleep. When the warning signs of overtraining hit you, take a break and get some rest. Fatigue tends to accumulate quickly if you don't sleep enough, leaving you susceptible to illness and injury and feeling stale. If you can't get enough sleep, back off your training. Sleepless nights, for whatever reason, must be followed by easy days and lots of sleep. Otherwise you'll end up having plenty of time to sleep, because you won't be running at all.

If you keep accumulating a sleep deficit night after night, warns Dr. Julius Segal of the National Institute of Mental Health, you are in for serious physical and psychological consequences. Adequate sleep is essential. "We sacrifice it," notes Segal, "at considerable peril to our bodies and minds."

21. OTHER SPORTS

Runners sometimes injure themselves playing other sports. For example, a member of a New York Road Runner class once complained of a pain in his chest. Remembering a similar problem he faced in the past, Bob Glover asked if he had been playing other sports recently. Sure enough, the cause was identified. He had caught a few elbows playing basketball, which never bothered him in his prerunning days, but running and breathing hard aggravated the otherwise undetectable injury. The beating you take in other sports is magnified by the pounding of running.

When you reach the competitive level of running, you have to decide which other sports you want to do and what the benefits and risks might be. Downhill skiing, basketball, soccer, tennis, handball and other activities, while fun, carry the risk of sprains and breaks that may take months to heal. And besides such obvious risks of injury, these activities may contribute to injuries in a way you may not readily identify.

Atalanta's Maddy Harmeling, a 2:48 marathon runner, is a physical education teacher. She was having knee problems but didn't know why until she realized that she had been playing a lot of paddleball with her kids, and the lateral movement was straining her knees. Marcy Schwam, one week before her second assault on the world record for 50 miles, decided to take a break and go cross-country skiing with her Atalanta teammates. A few days later, the abductor muscles in her legs started aching. On race day, she flew through 20 miles at 2:14, well ahead of the world record pace for 50 miles. But she soon dropped out because of a leg injury caused by the pulling action of skiing on muscles not used to that strain. Marcy couldn't run for two weeks and learned a hard lesson: When you plan to enter major running competition, don't experiment with other sports which use different muscles.

When combining running with other sports, follow the basic principles discussed in Chapter 2. Don't forget your warm-up and cool-down routine. Many runners who faithfully stretch before running neglect this important principle before playing sports such as tennis, and end up straining muscles. Never do hard workout days in other sports and then race or do speed workouts the next day. Also, don't play other sports in running shoes—they are not made for lateral movement, and you can easily turn your ankles and put strain on your knees. If you want to participate in other sports as well as maximizing your potential as a runner, be very moderate in your activity. You should do much *less* of another sport than you can handle in terms of heart and lung conditioning because your muscles will not tell you that you have overdone it until it is too late—a day or two later.

22. AGE AND SEX

As we age, our bodies betray us. We recover more slowly from long or hard runs, and we require more easy days. If the aging runner—even in his or her 30's or 40's—doesn't adjust, injury results. As we age, we become more brittle, more inflexible, and gradually lose muscle strength—thus, we are more injury prone. The gradual loss of bone mass—especially in women—increases the risk of fractures and retards the healing of bone injuries. Our ability to regulate body temperature also decreases, which makes us more susceptible to heat stroke and frostbite. Dr. Murray Weisenfeld finds that his older patients are more prone to heel spur formation but generally have fewer injuries than younger runners. Maybe they are wiser. Older newcomers are usually more cautious, and wily veterans of the roads have experienced every possible injury and know how to hold them off.

Young runners are susceptible to disease where tendons attach to bones at the heel and the knee. These soft plates—called apophyses—are involved with growing. The plates gradually close with adolescence, but serious damage to them can stunt growth. Some medical people are concerned that very young runners who try long-distance running can be seriously injured; others find little scientific justification for that concern. Dr. Weisenfeld has found that 10–12-year-olds often develop a separation at the heel bone, usually because they hit too hard on their heels, or their shoes lack proper cushioning in the heels. Girls 11 to 14, and slightly older boys, are prone to Osgood-Schlatters disease, which is a separation of the epiphyseal line where the head of the tibia meets the shaft of the tibia.

The incidence of injuries to women is no greater than to men. As Dr. Leslie S. Matthews of Baltimore's Union Memorial Hospital Sports Medicine Center joked, "Women are equally entitled to athletic injury." Most injuries women suffer are sports related, not gender related, he said. Common female-related injuries are pelvic fractures—due to the fact that women have a broader pelvis—and groin injuries. Dr. Weisenfeld also sees a lot of injuries from wearing high-heeled shoes. Besides the Achilles tendon and calf injuries which one would expect, these women often develop calluses and pain under the ball of the foot. When you wear high heels, your weight is placed on the ball instead of the padded heel, which results in the wearing down of the padding under the ball of the foot. Running hard, especially when you have to get up on the balls of the feet, can then cause injury.

23. POOR ADVICE

Everyone gives medical advice to runners. You can go to an orthopedist, podiatrist, chiropractor, physical therapist, osteopath, running coach, trainer, or running buddy. You can be Rolfed, have your foot held and massaged, join a group standing on its head. Your running friends and enemies, even your sedentary grandmother, will freely offer advice.

Beware. There are no quick cures. Sports-medicine experts pop up everywhere. Instant coaches are a national nuisance. Remember: if you ask people for advice, they will give it. A coach's job is to keep you healthy, not to help you run faster at all costs. A running friend may mean well but know nothing. Every runner and every coach has his or her own system. You need to develop your own system, gradually, through your own experiences. In the meantime, follow the commonsense guidelines of highly recognized experts.

A competent medical person will refer you to another source if he or she has been unable to help you or feels that your specific problem should be handled by a specialist. Beware of doctors who don't run, or who have all the answers, or who set up running programs for you. Doctors shouldn't coach, and coaches shouldn't doctor. In the long run, follow any advice only after thinking about it carefully.

24. MARATHONITIS

> WARNING: THE SURGEON GENERAL HAS DETERMINED THAT MARATHON RUNNING IS DANGEROUS TO YOUR HEALTH!

This statement, like those on cigarette packages, should be stamped across the toes of every running shoe. Too many people are training for and running in marathons before they are prepared. Hundreds of men, women and children each year take up running after watching or hearing about a marathon. They take it up specifically to run a marathon. Incredible, but true! For most, there is no in-between. It is all or nothing—26.2 miles or bust. For many of them, it's bust. Very few who take up running and racing can escape the lure. It's like a magnet. You are driven to meet the ultimate challenge—as hyped by the media and all those veterans of the marathon wars.

We constantly urge beginner runners to wait several years before running a marathon. But too many runners attempt the distance during their first year of training. Patience! We prefer a much longer period of build-up and adjustment.

Actually, marathons themselves cause few injuries. But overmileage or improper preparation wipes out thousands of runners. At the New York Marathon, more than 2,000 runners out of the 16,000 accepted for the prestigious race in 1981 never got to the starting line even though their racing numbers were worth their weight in gold. They were injured. Any sports-medicine person in a city with a big marathon will acknowledge the increase in patients for several weeks before and after a marathon. Those who get injured during the marathon are mostly undertrained runners or those who ran with injuries against their doctor's advice and aggravated them. An additional problem is that injuries developed or aggravated en route are most often ignored during the marathon. In a shorter race the runner would probably drop out, but the marathoner feels obligated to suffer, since it is part of the glory.

The majority of veteran marathoners would be best off limiting their marathons to two or three a year—two or less for less experienced racers. This event is not a joke. It hurts. Proper training and preparation are essential. For some, their body type precludes running a marathon. But for too many, the pressure from their friends proves too much to resist. They should heed the above warning. Or take the advice of a running friend who was undertrained for his first New York Marathon and finished in pain. "All I looked forward to those last torturous miles was having a warm bath and a cold beer," he notes. His solution the following year: "I watched it on TV and then had a warm bath and a cold beer."

By the way, why didn't Pheidippides "listen to his body" and stop at ten kilometers?

25. PREVENTION AND MANAGEMENT OF INJURY AND ILLNESS

Prevention of injury and illness means eliminating their causes and reacting to their warning signs. Most injuries and illnesses can be prevented, but once they occur you must treat the cause, treat the injury, and rehabilitate your body in order to return to competitive fitness.

WARNING SIGNS

Many running-related injuries and illnesses can be prevented, either by minimizing the causes or by adjusting to the warning signals our body sends us. The physical and mental symptoms of overstress and impending injury or illness warn us to take heed. As Dr. George Sheehan preaches, "Listen to your body, it will tell you when you are doing too much, when you are close to injury."

Here are some of the warning signs your body may give you:

1. Mild tenderness or stiffness that doesn't go away after a day of rest or after the first few miles of your daily run. Any indications that your musculoskeletal system has been overtaxed.

2. A desire to quit or an unexplained poor perfor-

mance in workouts and races. Also, an uncharacteristic lack of interest in training, racing and life in general.

3. A tired feeling after a full night's sleep or a sluggish feeling that continues for several days. You may also have difficulty falling asleep, or may wake up often in the night and find it difficult to go back to sleep.

4. An increase in your morning pulse rate. Record your pulse in your diary each morning—take it when you first wake up. Note significant increases as a sign that you haven't recovered from the previous day or days of stress. A pulse ten or more beats higher for the average runner and five or more beats higher for the highly trained runner is an indication of trouble.

5. A continued thirst despite replacement of fluids lost after your run. Check your urine. Normal urine is almost clear and odorless. A runner who is dehydrated will pass a darker urine.

6. A significant loss of body weight as measured each morning. A temporary loss of a few pounds due to sweating is normal. Check your weight daily and record it in your diary. A sudden loss of two or more pounds is not normal—fluid weight loss should be replaced by morning.

7. The feeling of a sore throat, fever, or a runny nose coming on, which may indicate your susceptibility to a cold or flu. Any signs that your body is fighting infection. Also, skin blemishes and cold sores.

8. Muscle cramping (due to mineral depletion).

9. Upset stomach, diarrhea, constipation or loss of appetite.

10. Increased irritability, feelings of tension, depression and apathy—a sure sign of the overtraining syndrome.

Respond to any of these warning signs by cutting back your mileage, minimizing or eliminating your speed work, getting more sleep, and taking off a day or two. If the symptoms persist, seek medical attention as a precaution. Don't be cheap here: you'll save on medical bills in the long run by seeking help early.

The most obvious warning sign is *pain*. Pain is a sure

warning of something wrong. Pain should be heeded. Your body yells at you for a reason—without pain signals you would continue to train and more serious injury would result. Runners can push through *discomfort.* There's a difference. Injury and illness cause pain. Oxygen debt and muscle fatigue are discomfort barriers that runners can push through. But pain is the early warning of injury and must not be ignored. Try to push through the discomfort of hard training and racing, but not through the pain signals of injury and illness. While training and racing, runners should listen to their bodies, not try to prove toughness by running through an injury or attempting to ignore it. To prevent injuries, therefore: (1) eliminate the causes; (2) back off your training and racing when warning signs appear.

Most early warning signs will be mild. Don't ignore them. Too many runners—especially men—feel that cutting back, resting, taking time off makes them seem weak. Don't stop running at every muscle twitch, but balance your observation. Watch for what troubles you or gives you pain. Act wisely. Sometimes you can run through the stresses of competitive training and racing. But if you err, err on the side of caution. When in doubt—back off.

One helpful device is the running diary. Enter into it all of your discomforts and pains, your warning signs, plus the training and racing information. This record will not only help you train in a consistent and injury-free pattern, but it will also help you note when pain or discomfort lasts a long time. Our memories on these matters are unreliable. A detailed diary will often reveal the cause of injury and illness. Rereading your past experiences will help prevent future problems.

Perhaps the wisest way to prevent injury is occasionally to take a few days or even weeks off from serious training before major warning signs appear. By choosing to take time off, rather than being forced to by injury, you are giving your body a well-deserved rest without having to suffer physical and mental pain. You will have made an investment in your health by heading off an injury "at the pass."

FOUR SPECIAL ILLNESSES

1. Colds

Running won't protect you from the common cold, which is transmitted by hand contact with an infected person or object. You are more likely to catch a cold by shaking hands than by kissing. The cold is also one of the early warning signs of overtraining and emotional stress: during the 1976 Olympic Games, most of the visits to physicians by the athletes were for treatment of the common cold. Stress, poor nutrition and contact with an infected person all lead to colds. At the Olympic Games, colds easily spread through the village filled with fatigued, highly stressed runners. Moral: Olympians should kiss more, shake hands less.

Easy running at a slow pace may break up the symptoms of a minor cold. Vigorous exercise during infection or fever, however, is not a good idea. If your temperature is more than 100°F, you are better off not exercising at all. After the fever breaks, wait for the sore throat phase to pass before resuming your running. It usually takes five to seven days for the cold to run its course. Remember, when you have a cold, cut back your mileage, slow down your pace, and run within the limitations of your energy.

When you resume, if you don't notice any daily improvement in your health and running, stop and rest more. Do not train hard until you have completely recovered. However coughing after you run is normal, doctors tell us, a reaction to deep breathing that can help clear your lungs.

Don't force yourself to return to running too soon. After Alberto Salazar won the 1980 New York Marathon, he was so pumped up that he went right into training for the prestigious Fukuoka Marathon. He came down with a cold the week before leaving for Japan. He continued to train anyway, and got a strep throat, lost several days of training, and had to cancel his well-earned trip.

You'll be surprised how quickly you can lose your endurance. After a cold or flu, the results may be even more discouraging than after a layoff due to injury. A University of Uppsala (Sweden) study shows that colds with muscle pain often keep competitors from regaining full strength for more than four months. Remember: if you don't take time off and care for that cold, your layoff period will be much longer, or you may injure yourself in other ways. Sometimes you should look upon a cold as a blessing: since you probably caught it from overtraining, it will force you off your feet and into bed, where you cannot injure yourself—at least not from running.

A cold is a virus. Antibiotics will not help: they kill bacteria, not viruses. Medications—sprays, "tiny time capsules," cold remedies—may do more harm than good. They may provide temporary relief, but may also delay return to full health. There are lots of healthful and well-meaning remedies that many runners swear by and that may offer various benefits: chicken soup, peppermint and elder flower tea, wheat germ oil, vitamin C, Mexican food, bee pollen, even acupuncture. We suggest rest, little or no running, lots of natural fruit juices or water, aspirin, a humidifier to increase moisture in the room (if your nose is feeling stuffed up) and even a nice steam bath. Remember the three R's here: rest, relax, recover.

2. The Flu

Fever and flu are more dangerous than the common cold. The body is weak and cannot tolerate the stress of running. When the flu bug hits, your only interest is, and should be, survival. You won't want to run. Running with fever and flu, says Dr. Sheehan, can be dangerous. "Sudden death can occur if the virus is also affecting the heart muscle, which it frequently does."

The rule of thumb is to expect to feel terrible as long as your fever lasts, and then take twice that time to overcome the flu symptoms. Take your time getting out to run. In fact, a walk-run program for a week or so might be wise until your strength returns. Then start your runs slowly and return gradually. When you come back, it is often difficult to determine if you feel tired from physical reasons or mental, because you still *think* you are sick. Dr. Sheehan advises testing yourself to see if you are ready to run yet: "Start your runs very slowly until you reach the point where you start to sweat. This usually takes about six minutes. At this point, you should feel like running no matter how you felt in the beginning. If you don't and five more minutes confirms it, pack it in." Relapses from the flu are common, and weakness caused by the flu can also lead to other injuries.

The body weakened by heavy training may be more vulnerable to the flu virus. Despite your high level of fitness, it can still knock you off your feet. Flu viruses spread rapidly, and many strains are highly contagious. Treatment is similar to that of a cold; antibiotics may be necessary to fight off related infections.

3. The Stitch

There may be no other pain that strikes the runner with the suddenness and devastation of the stitch—a.k.a. the dreaded side stitch. Sometimes it feels like a knife jabbed into the edge of your rib cage, your hips or shoulders; almost always it occurs when you're running hard and ceases when you slow down or stop. The stitch can be both prevented and treated on the run.

The actual cause of the stitch remains unknown. Dr. Gabe Mirkin theorizes that the stitch occurs "when the diaphragm is deprived of oxygen supply due to an obstruction of blood flow caused by pressure from the lungs above and the abdomen below." The result is a spasm in the diaphragm. Another theory is that the diaphragm is forced downward as the lungs and heart work hard, distending the ligaments that connect the diaphragm to the skeleton.

The cause, however, may be traced to one of the following possibilities:

Faulty Breathing. "Belly breathing" is the proper way of

breathing on the run. Improper breathing often results in a strain on the diaphragm. You should practice "belly breathing" in your workouts.

Sometimes stitches occur in races when you start "panic breathing"—pushing hard to catch another runner, or to hold one off. Even when you strain harder, you must learn to breathe relaxed, belly out.

Weak and Tense Abdominal Muscles. Diaphragm cramps can be prevented with strengthening and stretching exercises. These should be done daily, not just when the stitch strikes. Here are three exercises that will help:

A. Bent-knee Sit-ups. Or for advanced sit-ups, put your feet against a wall, cross your arms, and grasp opposite elbows. Exhale, pull your chin to your chest so your head lifts off the floor, contract the stomach to lift your upper chest; release by laying one vertebra at a time back down on the floor.
B. Wall Push-ups. Stand several feet from the wall; lean forward, put hands on the wall and do ten or more push-ups against it.
C. Backward Bend. Cup hands behind head; raise elbows as high as possible; bend slowly backward to the point of maximum extension of torso. Repeat 30 times.

Exercises should be repeated daily. It will take several weeks to condition the diaphragm and stomach properly.

Running Too Soon After Eating. Food in your stomach requires blood to be pumped to the intestinal tract to aid digestion. When running, your muscles need more oxygen and blood supply to the intestines may be diminished, resulting in intestinal cramps. Each person's system dictates how long before running he or she can eat and avoid stitches. The range is from two to six hours.

Gas. According to Dr. Mirkin, the lower intestine forms gas during the breakdown of food. Exercise speeds up intestinal contractions and pushes the gas toward the rectum. If the gas cannot be passed because hard stools are in the way, the colon stretches like a balloon and a stitch occurs.

Diet and Constipation. Improper diet can lead to constipation and belly pains. Too much sugar and starches may contribute to a stitch; some people have an intolerance for milk or wheat products. Greasy foods, such as bacon or french fries, can also burden you.

Fluid Intake. Drinking very cold water during strenuous exercise has been known to cause a stitch. Also, commercial drinks may cause stitches in some runners. During the 1981 Avon International Women's Marathon in Ottawa, Atalanta's Marilyn Hulak charged from 30th place to a few yards out of 10th place late in the race, and then got a side stitch. It may have been caused by the tension of pushing toward the top, but Coach Glover theorized that it was something other than Marilyn's race that did her in. Race officials had put out water cups with plastic lids and straws, and while this made drinking more efficient, pulling water through a straw draws in more air—and thus produces gas. This, together with pushing on downhills, Glover feels, caused the problem.

Downhills. Stitches often appear when you pick up the pace or after a hard downhill stretch which jars the tight muscles in your abdomen. Some runners are very prone to stitches when they drink cold water and then race downhill. Running downhill, you should not let your arms come up, or lean back, or land too hard on your heels. All of these movements put more pressure on, and cause jarring of, fatigued abdominal muscles. Relax running downhill and remember to belly breathe.

Improper Warm-up. Before your hard runs, stretch your abdominal muscles and jog easily. Then do some pickups to prepare your body for the sudden heavy breathing.

Starting Too Fast. This may put you into oxygen debt and place an added burden on your diaphragm muscles. Start within your fitness level and gradually build to your race pace.

Fitness Level. Stitches are more common among beginner runners and racers than among veterans, due to the vets' stronger cardiorespiratory systems and abdominal muscles. The competitive runner, however, often finds himself or herself undertrained—trying to run longer or faster than he or she has trained for. The result is often a stitch. These runners should run at race pace or faster once or twice a week to minimize stitches caused by the stress of competitive racing on their bodies. You are most prone when race day tension and excitement is combined with hard running.

Dr. Mirkin adds that if you develop a stitch, you should decrease the pressure on the lungs and abdomen enough to let blood flow back into your diaphragm. To do this, he suggests that you stop running and empty your lungs by pursing your lips and blowing hard. This should release air trapped in your lungs. To relieve abdominal pressure, bend over and raise your knee on the stitch side while pressing your fingers deep into the painful area. The pain will usually disappear, and you can continue running.

If you get a stitch during a race, however, you may not want to stop. You might try several options:

• As you run, bend over as much as you can and press the stitch with the fingers of your hand. This sometimes relieves the pain.

• Or try the George Sheehan–Ted Corbitt method. They suggest breathing out against a slight resistance—belly breathing—even if you groan a little. Listening to Sheehan and Corbitt, a former Olympic marathoner, during a race is unpleasant, but they claim it works, and they pass other runners as they moan and groan, grasping at their sides. Try breathing in very deeply and noisily. Exhale deeply with a groan. Don't be shy. Your PR may be at stake.

Some runners find that doubling their rate of breathing rids them of the dreaded stitch. Others raise their arms overhead, breathe deeply, expand their stomachs, and, as they lower their arms, exhale loudly and contract their stomachs. (This is no time to worry about appearances!) Still other runners slow their pace until the pain subsides or stop running and lie on their backs, raising arms overhead.

• A few runners get away with not thinking about the pain, and continuing. Try thinking about something else or talking to the runner next to you. A magical minority do something bizarre: Jim Ferris, a former training mate of Bob Glover and ex-University of Oregon runner, used to cure his side stitches by doing a quick somersault in the middle of a race. It worked—and really psyched out the opposition.

Toughing it out may be the option of last resort. Just remember that no one has ever died from a side stitch, although you may feel you are going to be the first. If you have tried all the treatments and eliminated all the causes and are still troubled by the stitch—check with a doctor. You may have internal problems that should be handled medically.

4. The Overtraining Syndrome, and the Blahs

Competitive running involves stress, and stress involves a three-step process. Step One is the stress of training. Step Two is the build-up of resistance (training effect) as a response to the stress. This will not take place unless stress is balanced with recovery. Step Three must be avoided: over-stress and exhaustion.

The overtraining syndrome may be the biggest medical problem doctors see from competitive runners. The basic symptom is a breakdown of some kind: cold, flu, nagging injury, running performance. Overtraining lowers resistance to disease; the runner may lose interest in training, have trouble eating or sleeping, find it difficult to work or study, become irritable. Fatigue or sluggishness may envelop him or her, sometimes accompanied with constipation, diarrhea, or loss of weight. With overly enthusiastic competitive runners, the coach's biggest task is not making them run harder but convincing them to cut back when they should.

The best solution is to cut both mileage and pace sharply, eat carbohydrates and sweets to replace lost glycogen, get plenty of rest (including afternoon naps), and relax. Do something else for a while. Veteran racers, who call this problem "breaking down," are usually much more adept at recognizing the warning signs and remedying the situation.

The Blahs are a bad case of apathy. We often find runners with this problem. They are usually victims of overtraining and often appear before us one or two months before a big marathon when the training is getting routine, tough and boring. Sometimes they are victims of overracing. There are two other types of "Blah" runners. One is the depressed runner who has just finished the big race, usually a marathon, and is suffering from postrace blues: the big event is over. What's next? The other is the runner without goals, whose training has no purpose. This runner needs to focus on something, even a simple race, or else take a break and do something different.

The overtraining syndrome and the blahs can usually be cured by the above methods. If they persist, however, do not overlook them. See your doctor to make sure the symptoms don't become too severe. Competitive runners, especially young ones, who attempt to train through these stages often experience "burnout" and never return to their previous level of racing. Serious cases of mononucleosis are also common among overtrained athletes.

RUNNING THROUGH AN INJURY

The competitive runner cannot lay off every time he or she gets a minor blister, ache, pain or sniffle. Yet by forcing yourself to continue at a high level of training, or any training at all, you may make things worse. Often a day or two off to allow a bad blister to heal, for example, will let you return sooner to quality training than if you had continued, and aggravated the injury. However, total rest beyond two or three days will not help many injuries. You may as well continue to run, but within certain limits. Gentle exercise will help you heal and will also help you maintain a base of fitness. The trick is to train enough to provide these benefits while allowing the injured area to rest by doing relatively less work that does not aggravate the injury. More serious injuries or illness will require good judgment by you and your doctor about whether or not you should continue training or rest. Absolute rest from the stress of running for a few weeks (but not necessarily from other forms of exercise) may be required to allow some injuries to heal properly.

We use the following dozen rules to guide those who decide to run through their injury:

1. Be aware of pain and other warning signals. Pain should protect you from overdoing.

2. Unless you can walk briskly with little or no pain for a mile, don't run.

3. Don't run if your pain makes you limp or otherwise alters your form. You may cause another injury, and it may be far worse than the one you already have. Bravely limping through a run is stupid!

4. You can run with discomfort, but not with pain. If the pain worsens as you run, stop. Beware! Your body produces its own pain-killing drugs, which may allow you to run or race and forget your pain. But after the run, you will be in agony and may have further aggravated your injury. There is danger in pushing hard through workouts and races when you started in pain which disappeared after a few miles.

5. Never use pain-killing drugs to allow you to run. You must feel the pain to adjust to it—either to continue or stop.

6. Avoid hills, speed work, races, long runs and slanted or soft surfaces that aggravate your injury and intensify your pain.

7. Analyze and treat the cause of your injury. Pain is a signal. If your pain lessens when you change shoes, for example, or when you switch to the other side (and slope) of the road, you have learned its cause and can treat it.

8. After running, treat your injury by applying ice, and take aspirin.

9. Warm up thoroughly and cool down thoroughly with each run.

10. Do specific exercises to strengthen or improve flexibility, if it helps heal your injury. Do not overstretch or stretch injured parts until they have recovered.

11. Adjust your training if need be. You may try running twice a day for less time or distance in order to get in the miles with less continuous pounding; this will minimize aggravation of the injury. Injury-prone runners may need to run for three or four days and then take a day off to allow the body to rebuild and keep ahead of the breakdown. Alternate forms of training may be used on these off days. In more extreme cases, alternate days of running with days off, or alternate running with walking for each exercise session. You may find that you can't run more than a mile without having to stop. This is too frustrating. Try alternately running up to the edge of your capacity and then, before you feel pain, walking briskly. With this form of training you can cover four or five miles, which is psychologically satisfying and can help maintain minimal fitness. These same rules can apply when coming back from a lay-off due to injury.

12. Be patient, and persevere.

The key to running through your injury is to develop a feel for your limits. If during a training run you aggravate an injury or develop one which causes you to change your form and/or is painful, stop and take a cab home or call for a ride. Don't force yourself to get a few more miles in so you can keep on schedule. During a race or speed workout, if you feel an injury or tightness coming on, stop. Don't be foolish and feel you have to finish—you'll be a hero today and a painful fool tomorrow.

Distance runners sometimes develop high levels of tolerance for pain. This probably means that they are good at putting up with the discomfort of low-level pain, but are aware of it and adjust or train accordingly. All runners must develop a sense of their limits. This may mean, for example, running up to five miles before the knee acts up and later increasing to seven miles, as the knee strengthens. Since you are the one experiencing the pain, only you can determine the limits of training you can handle. You must balance the need to continue in order to build or maintain fitness with the need to prevent the destruction of your health—and thus your training. Better to play the limits wisely than to challenge those limits and risk long-term setback.

TREATMENT

When you are injured, you can respond in one of four ways: ignore it and run through it, often making it worse; quit running and pray that it will go away; attempt self-treatment; seek medical help. Most runners deal with an injury in that order: ignoring it, quitting for a few days, attempting self-treatment, and finally seeing a doctor. Runners usually injure tissue, bone, tendon or muscles. As Dr. Joan Ullyot describes in *Women's Running*, "the immediate response of the body to the damage is the same: a local outpouring of fluids and cells release substances that cause an inflammatory response, with more leakage of blood cells and lymph—and the results are the classic five signals: heat, redness, pain, swelling and loss of function."

As most runners already know, disability can be minimized by keeping the swelling down. This is done with ICE (ice, compression, elevation), which are used immediately after the injury occurs and continued for a day or two. After 48 hours or so, you should start promoting circulation, because increased blood flow to the injured area will help remove waste products and fluid, which speeds healing. Heat, massage, gentle exercise and even ultrasound will hasten this healing process. Relaxation of the injured area is itself beneficial because much of the pain around the injury is caused by muscle spasms.

Dr. Murray Weisenfeld prepared the following table to aid runners in the treatment of common minor injuries. Extended treatment of all ailments, and early treatment of serious injury, should be administered by a medical doctor.

DR. WEISENFELD'S SUGGESTED TREATMENT FOR COMMON INJURIES TO THE COMPETITIVE RUNNER

INJURY	TREATMENT
Runner's Knee	—Ice after running (10 minutes). —Check training paths for banked surfaces. —Try commercial arch supports. —Strengthen quadricep muscles. —Try pointing toes slightly inward while running. —Improve flexibility of calf and hamstring muscles.
Achilles tendonitis	—Ice after running (10 minutes). —No stretching until pain is gone, then stretch calves, hamstrings and Achilles tendons. —No hill work or speed work. —Run more erect, heel-ball. —Elevate heels.
Shin splints	—Ice after running (10 minutes). —Elevate heels. —Run more erect, heel-ball. —No hills or speed work. —Make sure shoes are flexible at ball. —Do strengthening exercises for muscles in shin area; stretching exercises for the Achilles tendons, calves and hamstrings. For tenderness at inner side of the leg also: —Try commercial arch supports. —Try changing shoes; soft-soled shoes may cause trouble. —Check for leg-length discrepancy. —Avoid banked surfaces.
Stress fracture	—Rest. No running for 6 weeks. —Use alternate exercises.
Back pain/sciatica	—Avoid hills. —Check for leg-length discrepancy. —Check for banked surfaces. —Shorten stride. —Strengthen abdominals; stretch hamstrings, calves and back muscles. —Do relaxation exercises. —Take frequent warm baths, massage.

INJURY	TREATMENT
Black toenail	—If out to end of toe, slit with sterile blade, soak and use antiseptic. —Have podiatrist drill a hole to relieve pressure and drain the blood. —Use longer shoes, tighter laces; pad the tongue. —Put a slit in shoe over injured area.
Heel spurs or bruise	—Ice for 10 minutes after run. —Use soft sponge or Sorbothane heel lifts in both shoes. —Do wall push-ups.
Ankle sprains	—Immediately pack in ice, 15 minutes on, 15 minutes off, and repeat; in between gently rotate ankle. —Elevate. —If pain and swelling persist, seek medical attention.
Arch pain	—Try commercial arch supports. —Raise heels. —Do wall push-ups. —Ice for 10 minutes after run.
Hamstring pain	—Shorten stride. —Don't stretch until pain subsides. —Apply ice for 10 minutes after run. —Raise heels; check for leg-length discrepancy. —No hills; check for soft-soled shoes.
Calf Pain	—If there is sharp, sudden pain—indicating torn muscle—elevate the heel and rest. —If pain comes on gradually, raise heels. —Don't stretch muscle. —Ice after running. —No hills; run erect and heel-ball. —Make sure shoes are flexible across the ball of the foot.
Pain in ball of foot	Usually a bruise of metatarsal head or heads: —Ice after running. —Pad behind bruise. —No speed or hills. —Run heel-ball.

Continued on page 410

INJURY	TREATMENT
Groin pain	—Check for leg-length discrepancy.
	—Run with sore groin as the long leg (closer to curb).
	—Rest.
	—Don't stretch area.

DETRAINING

When you are unable to train, you lose your conditioning fast. After three days' layoff, loss of fitness takes place; according to various studies, it is generally lost two to three times as fast as it was gained. Further studies show that a healthy marathoner who loses ten days of training will lose ten percent of his or her endurance. Whether injured or ill, you will need two or three days of rehabilitation training for every day lost. Even if you were in racing shape when you stopped, it generally takes two weeks of aerobic endurance training plus a week of sharpening for every week lost before you can return to combat-level fitness. If you're out a month, you may need nine to twelve weeks to return to your level of conditioning. If you are concerned about keeping the racing edge, you will shorten the time required to return to preinjury condition if you replace your running time minute for minute with an aerobic equivalent and by doing some anaerobic work.

When you lay off, you will feel a sense of loss. You may be cranky. A layoff may be a blessing in disguise: you will appreciate the joys of being able to run, and it will stimulate you to set new goals and go out and attain them. In fact, establish two goals for yourself: a return to your old PR level, and improving your time.

COMING BACK

Coming back depends on how long you were off, what alternative workouts you have done, and what put you out in the first place. Each injury or illness has its own special road to recovery. A minor cold, for example, may go away soon and allow you light running at a slow pace within a day or so. A more serious flu, or injury, will obviously take longer. When you are better, put together a recovery plan (see below), and start without any pain or changes in form. Losing a week or two may only require a week or two of gradually progressive training starting at one half to one third the preinjury distance. Longer layoffs for more serious injuries require a more conservative comeback. Return after long layoffs by following a program of alternating running and walking, just like a beginner's program except that you can progress more quickly since you can return in less time than you needed to build up the first time. Also take days off between running days. Start slowly: you'll feel side stitches, wobbly knees, muscle soreness, weakness. Beware: veteran runners often find that their heart and lungs can return much faster than the musculoskeletal system; you may be more vulnerable to muscle strain and injury than you realize.

After a long layoff, you might start with a three-to-five-mile distance covered either with three minutes of walking, three minutes of normally paced running or a half mile of walking and a half mile of running. Jogging very slowly may aggravate your injury or cause another. Thus, it may be better to run a fairly normal pace and take walk breaks to prevent continuous pounding. Slowly increase the running period and decrease the walking until you can run nonstop comfortably. Then slowly build back up to your normal training base; never increase your distance by more than ten percent a week. Don't attempt hills and speed work until you've run at least two weeks at your previous distance level.

Here are some further guidelines:

• Reach the base your body can tolerate, and stay there until you feel strong. That might be 40 miles a week instead of the 60 miles that caused the breakdown. Learn your limits and gradually increase your base.

• If you lost a day or two to minor injury or a cold, don't

try to make them up. So what if you don't get in your 60-mile week? Proceed "at the rate of," and pick up where you can on your normal schedule as soon as it is safe. Making up may only set you back instead of getting you back on schedule.

• Since so many runners feel better going uphill, it can be part of rehabilitation. It is therapeutic because the body absorbs only about two-thirds the stress of running on the flat and only half the stress of downhill running. It is safer than doing speed work on a track and gives a similar training effect. But avoid hills if you suffer from lower-leg injury.

• You should also set goals well below your threshold of further injury. Avoid frustration. Give yourself the sensation—and the fact—of making slow and steady progress.

• Approach your racing goals differently. Run the first few races after your layoff only for "reexperience." Just get the feel again. Next, aim to approach your prelayoff times, and then match and exceed them. But don't be in a hurry.

• Reanalyze again and again the *cause* of your injury or illness. The Chinese say: "Fool me once, shame on you; fool me twice, shame on me." Learn from your mistakes and don't repeat them.

Most runners stop running when they are injured, and those who don't often become ex-runners. When you can't run, you need an alternative way to stay fit. It is your choice how active you want to be. If you are patient and disciplined during your alternative training period, you will return to running with a toughened mental attitude about your ability to cope with training obstacles.

Injury, in fact, may be helpful. It can force you to back off and rest. It may also encourage you to condition neglected parts of your body, which in turn will help you to perform at a higher level later. The enforced rest may make you mentally hungry for competition and serve as a means of avoiding the blahs that often accompany overracing and overtraining.

GUIDELINES FOR ALTERNATIVE TRAINING WHEN YOU CAN'T RUN

You have four options when you are injured:

1. Take Off

Do nothing, simply rest. This may be the best choice for a few days while a minor injury mends or an illness such as the flu runs its course. For the first few days, you need exercise only to satisfy your head—you won't lose that much in fitness, and it may be wiser to take a complete break. Even when an injury persists beyond a few days, some runners may choose to take time off if they don't enjoy alternative forms of exercise. In case of serious injury or illness, this is probably the option your doctor will insist upon.

2. Maintain Absolute Minimal Fitness

If you know it will be more than a few days before you'll be able to run again—especially if you have to lay off for two weeks or more—you may, if your doctor agrees, choose to do some type of aerobic workout (swimming, biking, cross-country skiing, or race walking) three to five times a week for 30 consecutive minutes each time. This will maintain minimal cardiovascular and musculoskeletal fitness and prepare you to come back sooner. You may also find the easier schedule a mental relief. You may lose considerable fitness from the competitive level, so don't press too hard during your return.

3. Replace Running with an Alternative Exercise

In order to maintain near-normal fitness when forced off the running trails, you should try to replace the running minute for minute with alternative aerobic exercise. Check with your doctor to make sure you can safely do the new activity. Build gradually to the same amount of *time* you had spent running: for example, one hour a day. If possible, this training should be done at the same vigorous level of exertion as running to achieve aerobic benefit. This option will allow you to psychologically replace the running habit, and although you'll lose some fitness, you will also be able to return to running in good shape.

4. Impersonate a Competitive Runner

If you really *have* to be ready for a big race, then only lack of imagination and discipline need stop you. This is the top level and one for the serious runner who has to lay off for a while but can still exercise vigorously. Build up slowly, follow the hard-easy system, and include training specific to your goals. The same principles that apply to competitive running apply here. If you are in a build-up stage, long bike rides or swims will build strength. Build up to the time you would spend on your long runs, or longer. All types of speed workouts can be done on a bike or in the pool if you need to sharpen close to a race.

Part VI
SUPPLEMENTAL
EXERCISES

26. WEIGHT TRAINING AND SUPPLEMENTAL EXERCISES

A supplemental program of weight training will improve both your strength and your running times. Runners who compete in distance races need upper-body strength and muscular endurance. Just holding up your arms during the long races or finding that extra leg power through those last few miles requires added muscular strength.

Strength-training runs such as *fartlek*, rolling hills, fast continuous runs and rhythm workouts over hills will develop specific muscle groups such as the hamstrings, calves, quadriceps and buttocks. Weight training generally strengthens all the muscle groups of your body when properly selected lifts are included in a weight-training program.

Proper weight training can also help prevent injury due to imbalanced muscle groups and strengthen your body for better performance. Increased overall strength will help a runner drive up hills and continue running fast even during the latter stages of a long-distance run.

A strength-training program will also benefit the runner who needs to increase the drive in his or her arms to help propel the body forward to the finish line. Some runners train with weighted gloves two to three times a week to improve strength and arm drive. In the late stages of the marathon, when attacking hills or the finishing line, the runner with a stronger arm drive will do better. And that arm drive comes from weight training; running itself does little to strengthen your upper body.

Weight training is especially valuable to women runners, who usually have less well-developed muscles than men. Their arms and shoulders may be underdeveloped. Dramatic improvements in running performance are possible for women who develop some upper-body strength, usually through a weight program.

You should design a specific weight-training program and routine, similar to the one you follow for your running workouts. The three-step approach for weight training is as follows: (1) the warm-up; (2) the workout; (3) the cool-down.

THE WARM-UP AND THE COOL-DOWN

The warm-up for lifting weights is basically the same as that for preparing to run. You should do about 15 minutes of stretching exercises, using the four groups of stretching exercises outlined in Chapter 27. These exercises will loosen up the muscles connecting tissues and joints, and allow you to work all areas with little danger of damaging yourself because of tightness.

You should do some warm-up lifting, 10 to 12 relaxed repetitions using very light weights. This will allow your muscles to warm up and loosen.

The cool-down, as with running, is the warmup in reverse. Walk or swim five to ten minutes, and then do your stretching and relaxation exercises.

THE WORKOUT

Several books give detailed theories on weight training. There are a few general rules everyone adheres to:

- Heavy weights with few repetitions build strength and bulk.
- Light weights and many repetitions increase muscular endurance.
- Medium weights lifted about 10 to 15 times build both muscular strength and endurance while increasing bulk very little, if at all.

The Universal and Nautilus machines are the easiest and safest weight-lifting apparatus to use. The weights are connected to the main housing, which prevents you from dropping them on the floor or on your running toes. Weights can be changed quickly and easily by moving small levers or rods. Working out with a basic set of barbells or dumbbells, however, is also worthwhile, and they may be more easily accessible. Be careful if you have not lifted weights before. If possible, start weight training under the supervision of a professional instructor.

The following routine is one we have used successfully with our athletes. It can be done with any equipment, is simple to follow and requires only about 15 to 20 minutes twice a week. We select a medium weight workout to build stamina. Each weight-training routine consists of the following steps:

1. Select the exercise and the weight to be lifted.

2. Do the specified number of repetitions, exhaling as you lift the weight, inhaling as you release the weight.

3. Rest one minute at the completion of the first set to recover, and do some flexibility exercises to keep your muscles and joints loose.

4. Do the second set the same way as the first set.

5. Rest one minute at the completion of the second set, doing flexibility exercises to maintain looseness and complete range of motion.

6. Do the third set (if possible) the same way as the first two sets.

7. Rest one minute at the completion of the third set, do flexibility exercises, and set up your next exercise.

8. Continue with the next exercise following the above seven steps.

SELECTING WEIGHTS AND MAKING PROGRESS

The difficult part of weight training is knowing how much weight to lift and when to increase the weight for each particular exercise.

Rule One: Start Light

You should always start off working with a very light weight. Allow your body to adapt to the increased resistance. Do only a small number of repetitions. We recommend one set of 10 to 15 reps.

Rule Two: Increase the Weight Gradually

You should increase the amount of weight you lift for a particular exercise after you can do three sets of the recommended repetitions easily. Then increase the weight, but only by five to ten pounds. Reduce the number of sets to two, and gradually work your way back up to three sets at the recommended number of repetitions.

THE EXERCISES

The Bench Press

Lying flat on your back, face up, press the weight straight up from your body. This exercise strengthens your arms, chest and upper torso.

Do three sets of 15 repetitions.

Sit-Ups with Weights

Lying on the floor, knees bent and feet hooked under an immovable object, put your hands behind your head and bring your upper body, bent at the waist, to your knees. Place a weight behind your head as you become stronger. This exercise strengthens your abdominal muscles.

Do three sets of 20 repetitions without weights.

Do three sets of 10 repetitions with weights.

Step-Ups

Standing, holding the weight with both hands behind your neck, put one foot on a stationary box about 18 inches high, and step up with the other. A set is complete when the recommended number of repetitions is done with each leg. This exercise strengthens the Achilles tendons, calves and quadriceps.

Do three sets of 10 repetitions with each leg.

Toe Raises

Standing, holding the weight behind your neck (as with step-ups), raise yourself up onto your toes. This exercise strengthens your calf muscles, Achilles tendons and ankle joints.

Do three sets of 15 repetitions.

Reverse Curls

Standing, hold the bar with the weights palms down in front of you, resting the bar on your quadriceps. Keep your back straight, thus not allowing your body to swing, and bring the bar up to your chest. This exercise develops the forearm for better arm swing.

Do three sets of 15 repetitions.

GENERAL RULES FOR WEIGHT TRAINING

• Weight training is progressive, just like running. You begin with low weights and gradually increase the weights as you become stronger.

• You lift twice a week, allowing two to three days between each lifting session to let your muscles rebuild themselves. Weight workouts should be separate from your runs; or, lift first and run second, taking it easy.

• Limit the number of repetitions to 10 to 15 and the number of sets to two or three in order to build muscle strength without building bulk.

• Begin each weight-training session by exercising the large muscle groups first and then the smaller muscles. Alternate upper-body lifting with lower-body lifting.

• Do flexibility exercises before, during and after each repetition lift.

• All lifts should be done through a full range of motion to work the muscles completely.

• Lifting is done to a four-count pace: count to four as you lift the weight, and count to four as you release the weight.

For more complete guidelines, see *Weight Training for Runners* by Ardy Friedberg.

SUPPLEMENTARY EXERCISES WITHOUT WEIGHTS

Important muscles can also be strengthened without the aid of weights. Here are some special exercises that you might add to your running program for specific purposes—to prevent injury and to make your running stronger:

Abdominals

Weak abdominals contribute to poor form and to back pain. Do bent-knee sit-ups.

Upper Body

Weak arms and chest muscles can be strengthened to improve arm drive. Do push-ups.

Quadriceps

Weak quads, especially in relation to strong hamstrings, can cause imbalance, which affects the pull on your kneecaps. These muscles also help pick up your legs and are important in the late stages of long runs and for running uphill. Some supplementary exercises:

• Sit in a chair, straighten the leg and tighten it, holding the kneecap parallel to the floor. Hold for 20 to 30 seconds in isometric contraction. Repeat 10 to 20 times.

• Sit on a table and lift any type of weight suspended from the legs, with legs straight. (One leg at a time.)

• Walk up several flights of stairs regularly.

• Walk in water, emphasizing knee lift.

• Hike or run on hills.

• Tuck your toes under a desk or couch and try to lift it with your toes. Your knees can be either bent or straight. Hold for ten seconds. Relax. Repeat 10 times.

• Stand with your back to the wall. Lift one leg as high as you can, keeping the knee straight. Hold for a five-count. Now bend the knee to relax for the count of five. Straighten the knee again. Do each leg five times, increasing to ten.

Adductor Muscles

These muscles contribute to inner leg pain and groin pull. For strengthening the adductors, try the following:

Lie on your right side with your right hand supporting your head. Your left hand is placed on the floor in front of you for support. Your left foot is flat on the floor in front of your right leg. Your right leg should be slightly ahead of your body. Now, flex your right foot so that the toe points up toward the knee. Keep the knee firm and straight throughout the exercise. Then lift the right leg as high as you can, and then lower it. Start with 5 to 10 repetitions and work up to 20. When you lower the leg each time, do not touch the floor with your foot and do not relax your leg. Keep it firm throughout this exercise. This can also be done with a one-pound weight on your ankle. Turn on your left side, and repeat with your left leg.

Hamstrings

Here is a strengthening exercise to prevent pulls.

Attach a one-pound weight to each ankle. Lie on your back on the floor, arms at your sides. Your knees are bent, feet flat on the floor. Stretch your right leg up as straight as you can. Then put your foot back on the floor. Repeat 10 times. Now repeat with the other leg. Your aim is to straighten the leg so that it is almost at a 90-degree angle to the floor. Start with three sets of 10 extensions for each leg. At first, do this without the weights.

Arch

The following exercises may relieve arch pain.
- Pick up marbles with your toes.
- Roll a bottle under your foot.
- Stand on a towel with your toes over its edge and pick up the towel with your toes.

Postural Muscles

These muscles are important for good running form. The following exercises should strengthen the abdominals, the gluteal muscles (fanny) and the erector spines (back muscles along your spine).
- Lying on your back, tilt your pelvis toward the floor, tighten your buttocks and stomach, and push the lower back into the floor. Hold. Count to 10. Relax. Repeat two more times.
- Stand with your back against a wall, push your lower back towards the wall as you tighten the buttocks and stomach. Count to 10. Relax. Repeat two more times.

Shins

These exercises will strengthen the anterior leg muscles to minimize shin splints.
- Lying down or sitting in a chair, put your right foot on

top of your left foot. Now try to pull your lower foot toward your body as your upper foot pushes it away. Hold for 10 seconds. Switch feet and push-pull for 10 seconds. This is one set. Do five sets.

• Sit on a table with your legs hanging freely over the sides. Flex one foot to lift a weight, perhaps a bucket of pebbles or a sandbag or other weight suspended over the foot. Do not try to lift too much. Do 10 lifts with each foot. Repeat once.

• Attach a rubber bicycle inner tube to a board. Standing, slip your toes under the tube and lift them against it. Hold for a ten-count and switch legs. Do two or three sets.

• Turn your feet inward while standing and make a rolling motion. Do for a few seconds with each leg. Repeat.

• Stand on the edge of a towel and curl your toes to pull the towel under your feet.

SUPPLEMENTAL AEROBIC EXERCISES

Alternative aerobic exercises such as swimming, biking, cross-country skiing and race-walking are beneficial to the competitive runner. They can be used to replace running when you are injured, but they can also be used along with running to help prevent injury. A competitive runner needs to train specifically by running, but supplemental aerobic exercises and weight training can enhance an overall fitness program.

Here are some areas where supplemental aerobic exercise will prove useful:

Balance Musculoskeletal Development

Running primarily strengthens the antigravity muscles along the back and the back of the legs. This creates a muscle imbalance, and most runners need to strengthen the opposing muscle groups: abdominals (stomach), quadriceps (thighs), and shins. Running does little for the upper body; therefore you need exercises to strengthen the chest and arms. Here are the key muscle areas, with alternative exercises that will develop them:

- Ankles: swimming
- Shins: biking (with toe clips)
- Quadriceps: biking, race-walking
- Upper body: swimming, cross-country skiing, race-walking
- Buttocks: cross-crountry skiing, race-walking
- Abdominals: cross-country skiing

Increase Aerobic Fitness

Maintaining a high level of aerobic fitness is important to the competitive runner. Similar aerobic benefits can be obtained with swimming, biking, cross-country skiing, or vigorous race-walking, which can supplement your running.

Many runners would break down physically or mentally if they tried to increase their mileage beyond a certain level. However, a novice marathoner, for example, who runs 40 miles a week can increase his or her aerobic level to the approximate equivalent of 50 plus miles a week by swimming 30–60 minutes a day, three times a week. An experienced marathoner might add, for example, three bike rides of one to two hours each to his or her 80-mile training weeks; this would add up to 90-plus-mile weeks without the extra pounding that that additional amount of running would entail.

Be aware, however, of drawbacks. You may be able to simulate the cardiovascular value of running, but no other activity uses the same specific muscle groups: you still have to get out there and pack in the miles. Hour for hour, running is the best training for the runner. Cross-country skiing, biking, swimming and race-walking are the best alternative aerobic choices. But in these supplemental exercises you must keep up your intensity and not cheat. Because running forces you to pick up your body weight and push it, it is the hardest activity to cheat at. Also, to give yourself a broader range of activities, you may want to combine alternatives: biking and weight training, for example, provide good overall workouts for the upper body, legs and cardiorespiratory systems.

Relax and Recover

Walking, swimming or biking after a hard workout or race will help the competitive runner relax and promotes sleep. These activities also help him or her to recover better from hard effort, and thus minimize injury. They can be used in the evening and the days following a marathon to ease sore muscles back into running shape. Swimming is particularly good for relaxation and postrace recovery, since it provides aerobic work without the trauma of weight-bearing exercise. The water also has a massaging effect on tired muscles.

Bad Weather

Your running paths are buried in snow? Try cross-country skiing. Too hot and muggy outside? Jump in the pool or lake. Too cold for you? Try an indoor bike or treadmill. Don't give up; look for an alternative to running.

Travel

Always take your running shoes along when you travel, whether for business or pleasure. For many reasons, however, it may not be possible to run, or you may prefer to enjoy another aerobic activity while traveling. Stuck in a hotel in a strange city at night? Try the hotel pool or exercise equipment. Check out pools and indoor exercise equipment at local YMCA's or health clubs.

Atalanta's national class masters runner Patty Lee Parmalee faced a dilemma. She was on a sailboat in the Virgin Islands for a vacation, missing the team training runs in the cold, icy month of January. What to do? Glover convinced her to jump overboard and train daily in the ocean, just as she would have on the roads of Central Park. She built up to swimming for half an hour a day and twice a week simulated her team speed workouts by "running in the water" using a life jacket or by flutter kicking holding on to the boat rope ladder. Since she isn't a skilled swimmer, she found that she felt more tired, especially in the upper body, than if she had run. But she proved she could stay in shape under very unusual conditions, and returned to the roads and racing in fine shape.

Every year her teammate Nancy Tighe, winner of the 1981 Long Island Marathon in the 50–59 age group, spends two to three weeks traveling by bike with her husband, John. Although they make it a "fitness vacation" away from career work, she gives up running entirely during this time. They tour the countryside in such places as Ireland, Austria, England, Vermont and Kentucky at a rate of about 50 miles a day. Upon her return, she looks forward to running again. Besides maintaining aerobic conditioning, the bicycling has also strengthened her quads considerably.

Change of Pace

Hard competitive training is not always fun. It can become tiring and boring. Give yourself some time off without guilt. Taking a day off for another, supplemental exercise is an excellent idea. If you are not training for a race, try taking several weeks to learn another exercise, and add it to your training program.

GUIDELINES FOR SUPPLEMENTAL TRAINING

Don't just jump into a supplemental exercise. You must plan your nonrunning exercise as carefully as your program of running. Here are some guidelines for adding exercise to your running schedule:

1. Whatever you select as an alternative exercise for a *change of pace*, continue to run a few times each week to

keep your "running legs." This will ease the transition when you return to running full-time.

2. If you select an alternative exercise to *increase your aerobic fitness base*, don't over do it. You should not exceed approximately 25 percent of your total training equivalency doing alternative exercise. Thus, if you are running 75 miles a week at about 7:30-per-mile pace (8 miles per hour), don't do more than the equivalent of an additional 25 miles a week (such as three hours a week of vigorous swimming in your training heart-rate range) in another activity. Don't think you are running 100-mile weeks—it is *not* the same. Remember, you are training to be a runner, not a swimmer, cyclist or race-walker. The activity supplements your running, it doesn't replace it.

3. If you wish to cut back your running in order to rest or treat an injury and wish to *maintain approximately the same level of aerobic fitness*, try to cut back by no more than one third of your running time. The runner doing 75 miles a week would cut back up to 25 miles of running and replace it with approximately three hours a week of alternative activity in his heart-rate range.

4. Ease into the activity. Treat your new exercise just as you did running during your first few months: Don't overdo it. Too much is worse than too little.

5. If new techniques are required, take lessons (for example, cross-country skiing). Start the new exercise slowly, and do it every other day, alternating with running if possible.

6. Training principles that apply to running (as explained previously) also apply to your alternate activity—especially the principle of alternating hard and easy days and training without overstraining.

7. Your alternative exercise should be performed at a training heart rate, or perceived exertion, equivalent to your rate during running.

8. If your exercise is less demanding than running, do it longer. The rule of thumb is: if you can't reach your training heart rate, exercise for twice as long.

Marilyn H____ 1981 Metropolitan Athletics Congress

Co-Runner of the Year, is a good example of a runner who uses supplemental training to improve running performance. She gradually replaced her first love, tennis, with running and ran the 1980 New York Marathon in 3:11. She then increased her training to 100–110 miles a week along with twice-a-week speed workouts with her Atalanta teammates. But that wasn't all. She also biked the five miles each way to and from work—which strengthened her quads—and swam an hour every evening after her second run of the day—which strengthened her upper body. These supplemental activities also gave her increased aerobic conditioning without the trauma of pounding out more miles on the road. Her program was the equivalent of at least 130-mile running weeks.

Her secret for staying injury-free is the evening swim. This relaxes her and massages her tired muscles. She also tries to swim right after all races, and after long runs will add a few laps in the pool backstroking to relieve pressure in the lower back. The bike ride to work helps to loosen up muscles which are always stiff in the morning following a rigorous day of training. In six months, this combination enabled her to cut her marathon time by 26 minutes—a minute per mile—as she recorded a national class 2:45 in the 1981 Boston Marathon.

The average runner has neither the time nor the desire to utilize supplemental exercise to this extreme, but a minimal amount of alternate forms of exercise will help round out your training program and make you a more complete athlete.

27. THE WARM-UP AND COOL-DOWN ROUTINES

Every workout should follow the 1-2-3 approach: warm-up, run, cool-down. A proper warm-up and cool-down of relaxation, stretching and easy running is essential for most runners. The key is to follow the routines properly. Since running strengthens muscles at the back of the legs and back and makes them stronger and less flexible than the opposing, or antigravity, muscles in front, a balanced program of stretching tight muscles and strengthening opposing muscles should be followed to minimize injury. The warm-up and cool-down routines help you prepare for and recover from each run in three ways:

1. Relaxation exercises calm you down so that you don't carry tension with you on your run. The cool-down relaxation leaves the run behind and makes you feel surprisingly fresher. These routines are transitions allowing body and mind to move safely from your hectic life into running and calmly back again.

2. Walking and easy running at the start help your breathing and heart rate respond to exercise gradually. This permits a safe transition into running. For speed work and racing, "pickups" put your cardiorespiratory systems in tune with the demand of the workout. Following your

runs, you need to slow your heart rate down and allow that extra blood needed to bring fuel to your legs to return to your heart and other vital organs.

3. Stretching increases your athletic ability and efficiency. Runners lengthen their stride and increase their fluidity with less muscle tightness and leg cramping.

The first requirement for increasing your flexibility is to learn how to relax. A few minutes of relaxing and limbering exercise releases tension so that muscles can be stretched properly. Stretching exercises should condition the muscle and connecting tissues. A muscle works best when at its maximum length. Static stretching should be done, which involves slow and rhythmic movements, stopping and holding at the point of first discomfort.

It is important to perform about ten to fifteen minutes of static stretching exercises before vigorous activity. The time you spend here will save time that would be lost to injury. At least ten minutes of stretching and relaxation should be done after your workouts to prevent muscle tightness. The exercises are also of value performed during the day whenever you can, perhaps while you're on the phone. It all adds up to increased flexibility and a more fit body.

GUIDELINES FOR STRETCHING

- Easy does it. Don't force it!
- Don't bounce or swing your body freely against a fixed joint—such as forcing a toe-touch with knees locked.
- Avoid overstretching. Too much is worse than too little. You can be injured by overstretching.
- Don't stretch injured muscles. Stick to easy limbering movements until the muscle is healed and ready to be stretched.
- Don't overdo stretching after a hard workout or race.
- Avoid exercises that aggravate a preexisting condition—especially knee or back pain.
- Don't try advanced exercises too soon. Ease into each stretching routine just as you do with your running.

• Breathe properly. Do belly breathing while stretching, just as you do when running. Take a deep abdominal breath and let it out slowly as you reach forward with your stretch.

• Warm the muscles. A muscle can be stretched safely only when it is relaxed and warm. Do relaxation exercises before starting. Some experts suggest that you run a few minutes first to warm up the muscles before stretching. We advise this before speed workouts and races, but not before your daily runs. Runners aren't likely to start their daily run and then after a mile stop to stretch. Start your daily run with easy relaxation and limbering exercises, and then some gentle stretches. Then stretch more thoroughly after you run.

• Include all major joint movements in your stretching.

• Include stretching for specific areas: hamstrings, calves, Achilles tendons. This is especially good when doing speed work.

• Older runners should work especially hard to remain flexible.

• Stretching in the morning, when you are stiff, can be a problem, especially the day after a hard race or workout. Try easy limbering and walking, followed by an easy run. A hot bath or shower first may help. Stretch more thoroughly upon returning.

• In cold weather, warm up thoroughly indoors, especially for speed work and races. Perhaps a bath or shower would help, or an indoor stationary bike ride before your run.

• In warm weather, don't let feeling warm fool you into thinking you are warmed up and stretched. Be sure to stretch thoroughly.

• Don't be in a hurry. Take your time, and do the stretching step by step and thoroughly. Use the same basic routine every day so you feel comfortable with it; know it, and stay with it. You should never cut short your stretching just to get in an extra mile.

• Add to your stretching routine exercises for other parts of your body: sit-ups for your abdominals, push-ups for your arms and upper body. You may even add a few special exercises to your routine for specific strengthening or stretching: leg extensions for your quadriceps, for example, or additional stretches for your groin area.

Remember: when a muscle is jerked into extension, it tends to "fight back" and shorten. When the muscle is slowly stretched and held, it relaxes and lengthens. Reach easily and hold; do not tug and pull. The relaxed, lengthened muscle is more efficient, less prone to injury, and recovers sooner from stress. Reach to the point of first discomfort, and hold for a count of ten. Then relax for a count of ten before repeating.

THE ROUTINES

Use the same basic exercises for your warm-up and cool-down, and the same exercises before each type of run that you do. Here is a basic sample program for you to follow for all your runs. If you want variety or need to add a few specialized stretching exercises for specific problems to your program, refer to the book *Stretching* by Bob Anderson and *The Runner's Handbook* by Glover and Shepherd.

The basic exercises are the same for your three types of workouts—daily endurance runs, speed workouts, races—although your total warm-up and cool-down routine will change to prepare you for faster running. Here is the sample warm-up and cool-down routine used for daily training endurance runs, plus guidelines for adapting that routine to speed work and races.

The warm-up consists of three steps: relaxation exercises, stretching and strengthening exercises, and the cardiorespiratory build-up. You begin with relaxation to "break" muscle tension that frequently causes muscular strain, especially back pain. These exercises also warm up muscles that are tense and difficult to stretch.

Here is a sample 15-minute warm-up routine. Lie on the floor with your knees bent. (You should always have your knees flexed when lying on your back, to relieve pressure on the lower back.) Do the following exercises in order:

Relaxation Exercises

1. *Belly Breathing*. Close your eyes. Take a deep breath and concentrate on letting your stomach rise as you breathe in. Let go slowly and breathe out. Repeat two more times. To be certain you are breathing properly, place your hands on your stomach. They should rise as you inhale.

2. *Head Roll*. Same position. Roll head slowly to one side and let it relax there and go limp. Roll head slowly back to the center, and then roll to the other side. Let go. Repeat three full rolls, right to left and left to right being one roll.

3. *Shoulder Shrug*. Same position. Relax, and as you take a deep breath, slide your shoulders up toward your ears and hold for a few seconds. Exhale, letting your shoulders drop limply to a relaxed position. Repeat two more times.

4. *Arm Limbering*. Same position. Raise your right arm ten inches off the floor, clench the fist tightly for ten seconds, then let the arm drop limply to the floor. Repeat with your left arm.

5. *Leg Limbering*. Same position. Slowly slide one leg forward until it is stretched flat on the floor, and let it go limp. Raise the leg ten inches off the floor, and flex all the leg muscles for ten seconds. Let the leg drop and relax, and slowly return it to the flexed position. Repeat with the opposite leg.

Lying-Down Stretches

1. *Double Knee Flex*. Same position. Pull both knees to your chest as far as you can without raising your hips. Then hug your knees with your arms, and bring your head to your knees. Let go, bring your arms back down to your sides. Lower your legs slowly to the flexed position with feet on floor. Repeat at least three times, up to twenty.

2. *Double Knee Roll*. Same position—arms outstretched, palms down. Roll both knees together to one side until the outside knee touches the floor. At the same time, turn your head to the opposite direction, and hold. Remain in this position for a few seconds. Then roll to the opposite side. Do one complete set three times.

3. *Lying Hamstring/Calf Stretch*. Same position. Bring one knee to your chest and slowly straighten the leg towards the ceiling, pointing the toe (hamstring stretch). Slowly lower the leg to the floor and relax. Return to the flexed position. Alternate legs, and repeat for a total of two full sets. Then repeat the process, pointing the heel toward the ceiling (calf stretch), for a total of two full sets.

4. *Back Arch*. Same position, but with feet as close to buttocks as possible with heels on floor. Grasp your heels with your hands, and as you take a deep breath, arch your back, lifting your bottom off the floor but keeping your heels flat and shoulders level. Hold; exhale as you return. Repeat twice.

5. *Cobra*. Lie on your stomach, arms at your side. Arch your back and look towards the ceiling. Hold, relax, and repeat.

Sitting Stretches

1. *Ankle Rolls*. Sit cross-legged. Grasp right foot with both hands and rotate ankle. Reverse direction. Repeat with left ankle.

2. *Groin Stretch*. Same position. Place the soles of your feet together. Push down on your knees. Gently bend your head toward your feet. Hold the position with head down for a few seconds. Sit up; repeat two more times.

3. *Sitting Hamstring, Calf and Back Stretch*. Sit with legs straight and spread, both hands overhead. Inhale, and then exhale slowly, and slide your arms along your left leg toward your left toe (keep the back of your knee flat against the floor). Reach as far as you can comfortably, and hold for a ten-count. Inhaling, bring arms back overhead; sit up straight. Exhale as your arms reach toward your right toe,

and hold at the point of first discomfort. Don't worry if you can't reach your toes. Repeat twice for each leg.

4. *Sitting Quadriceps Stretch*. Tuck your legs under you, sit on them, and lean back on your hands. Push your hips gently forward. Hold to a count of ten. Repeat two more times.

5. *Hip Stretcher*. Sit with your legs straight out. Bend your left leg across the right and hug it with your arms, knee to chest. Hold; count ten; repeat with your other leg. Repeat twice with each leg.

Standing Stretches

1. *Total Body Stretch*. Stand with legs apart, arms extended toward the ceiling. Grab air with your right hand, then your left, alternating as you rise on your toes. Do this for ten seconds, then let your upper body slowly bend forward at the hips, breathing out, and hang loosely as you slightly flex your knees. Slowly rise to a standing position as you inhale.

2. *The Wall Push-Up*. Stand about three feet from a wall, tree or lamppost. Place your hands on the wall, keeping your hips and back straight, heels firmly on the ground. Now slowly allow your straight body to lean close to the wall. Drop your forearms toward the wall so that you touch it with your hands and elbows. Keeping your back straight and heels flat, now tuck your hips in toward the wall. Then straighten your arms and push your body back to the starting position. Repeat twice. Hold to a ten-count.

Next, stand close to the wall, feet together, hands on the wall. Bend at the knees, keeping your feet flat on the ground. (This is good for your Achilles tendon.) Hold for a ten-count. Repeat two more times.

3. *Standing Quadriceps Stretch*. Lean against the wall with your right hand. Reach behind you with your left hand and grasp the top of your right foot. Gently pull your heel toward your buttocks. Hold for a count of ten. Do twice with each leg.

4. *Upper Back, Arm and Hamstring Stretch*. Stand with legs

apart, hands clasped behind your back. Bend forward, bringing your arms overhead, tucking your chin into your chest. Hold for ten seconds. Slowly rise back to a standing position.

5. *Side Stretches.* Stand with legs apart, right hand on the side of your right leg, left hand overhead. Bend to the right at the waist, also stretching overhead arm to the right. Look up to outstretched hand. Hold for ten seconds, and alternate stretch to the other side. Repeat each side one more time.

Strengthening Exercises

1. *Push-ups.* Lie on floor on your stomach. Then rise off the floor, back straight, so only your hands and toes touch. Form is important. Do five and work up to fifteen or so with good form. Back straight, fanny high, touch only your chest to the floor.

2. *Sit-ups.* Lie on back, knees bent. Have someone hold your feet, or anchor them under a chair, bed or bleacher. Put your hands behind your head and roll up smoothly to a sitting position with your head close to your knees. Exhale slowly as you roll up and inhale while rolling down. Start with a few and work up to more. Do as many as you comfortably can with good form.

Safety Note: If you do not have the time to do the whole series of exercises properly, select as many of them as you can do without rushing. It is better to do a few well than to do none at all or do all of them haphazardly.

The Cardiorespiratory Warm-Up

After stretching, begin a five-minute brisk walk. Pick up your pace as you near the starting point of your run. Or start jogging slowly for five minutes, and then ease into your training pace. Don't go full throttle as soon as you

SAMPLE 15-MINUTE WARM-UP AND COOL-DOWN ROUTINES

RELAXATION EXERCISES
1. Belly Breathing
2. Head Roll
3. Shoulder Shrug
4. Arm Limbering
5. Leg Limbering

LYING-DOWN STRETCHES
1. Double Knee Flex
2. Double Knee Roll
3. Lying Hamstring/Calf Stretch
4. Back Arch
5. Cobra

SITTING STRETCHES
1. Ankle Rolls
2. Groin Stretch
3. Sitting Hamstring, Calf and Back Stretch
4. Sitting Quadriceps Stretch
5. Hip Stretcher

STANDING STRETCHES
1. Total Body Stretch
2. The Wall Push-up
3. Standing Quadriceps Stretch
4. Upper-Back, Arm and Hamstring Stretch
5. Side Stretches

STRENGTHENING
1. Push-ups
2. Sit-ups

Note: For cool-down, do the exercises in reverse order, from standing stretches to relaxation, ending with belly breathing. Then close your eyes and rest for two minutes.

start your run. Allow your pulse to move up gradually and settle into your training range.

The Cool-Down

This is the warm-up in reverse: cardiorespiratory cool-down, stretching, relaxation exercises. It is also the easiest step to skip. But runners who miss their cool-down get injured because they haven't stretched and relaxed their muscles after a run.

After your workout, slowly walk for above five minutes. Follow this walk with the same stretching exercise routine as above, in reverse order, perhaps skipping a few stretches to make it a ten-minute routine. Don't do any push-ups or sit-ups. The purpose of the cool-down is to return the body to its preexercise level, insuring the return of normal blood flow from the extremities to the heart and preventing muscle tightness. It is also important to slow your heart rate; your recovery pulse should be under 100 beats per minute at the conclusion of your cool-down. Take your pulse after your cool-down walk and stretch.

SPEED WORKOUTS AND RACES

The Warm-Up Routine

Before any fast runs, prepare your body for the stress. Bring your heart rate and breathing up to your aerobic exercise level, and prepare your muscles and joints for hard work. Your warm-up includes the following:

1. *Relaxation and Easy Stretching.* Loosen up. Follow relaxation and lying-down stretches in sample on page 439.

2. *Warm-Up Run.* Continue your prespeed workout routine with a slow 10-to-30 minute jog before stretching further. For long races like the marathon, jog only about five minutes. This is a slow, leisurely, warming-up jog. The purpose is to loosen the body and warm it so that you can stretch more thoroughly. Some runners also find that easy runs of two to four miles in the morning before an early-afternoon speed workout, or a run at noon before an evening workout, helps loosen them.

3. *Stretch.* Continue with the sitting and standing stretches in sample on page 439.

4. *Pickups.* Run a set of six-to-twelve "pickups" or "strides" of about 60 yards on grass (if smooth) or on the road or track, at increasing speeds. These should be brisk but not all-out. Do the first two or three slowly, concentrating on warming up your body and moving easily. Pick up the speed as you become loose; concentrate on good running form. This routine is specific dynamic stretching for the muscles and joints used in speed work and racing, and brings your heart and breathing up to the rates used during the hard work ahead.

5. *Relax and Limber Up.* Now do a two-or-three-minute period of light exercises, including head rolls, leg shakes, Achilles tendon and groin stretches, and any other relaxed stretching you may need. Do specific stretching for any area you feel is tight. Do not, however, perform these stretches in a nervous, haphazard manner. You are now ready for your speed workout or race.

6. *Ease into It.* If you are doing a continuous strength-training run, start at an easy pace to get your heart rate up into your training range and your muscles warmed before stepping on the gas. For intermittent track work or hills, run your first repetition conservatively, as a continuation of the warm-up. Jog into each start—never use a standing start.

For races, if the start is delayed after your carefully planned warm-up (begun 30 minutes before race time), keep moving, jogging easily and walking briskly. Avoid last-minute nervous stretching, which can be dangerous. Try to do a few more pickups right before the start, to bring your heart rate closer to race level. For the marathon, however, keep calm and try to conserve energy.

The Cool-Down Routine

This is perhaps the most important—and often most neglected—part of your routine. It helps you recover from your workout and be ready for the next day.

1. *Walk or Jog.* After your workout or race, walk around or jog easily to cool down. An easy jog of one to four miles will help you recover from the stress of the run. Next, walk around slowly for a few minutes until your heart rate returns close to normal. Novices, or those running marathons, probably will be too tired to do any more running. They should walk; do not sit or lie down. If you do, you'll tighten up.

2. *Stretch.* Follow your daily run routine. If your muscles are very tired and tight, do fewer stretches and don't force them. You may not be able to work your muscles as thor-

oughly, since they are fatigued. Be careful. Overstretching here can lead to injury.

3. *Relax*. End your routine with easy relaxation exercises. An easy swim, walk or bike ride may help you recover from your workout—now, later in the evening, or the next morning. Afterwards, of course, there is the runner's reward: the postworkout beer!

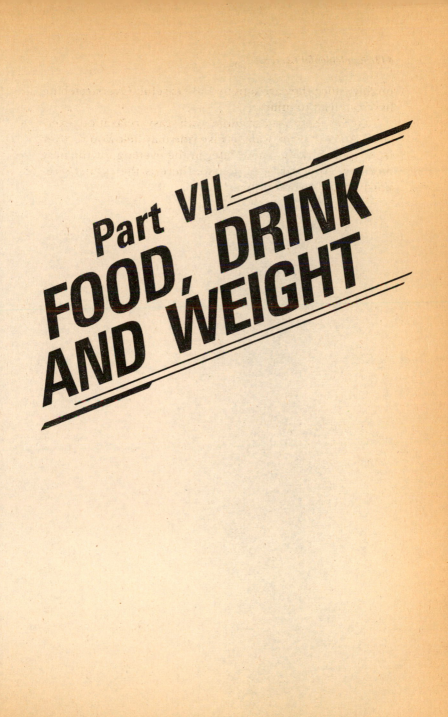

Part VII
FOOD, DRINK AND WEIGHT

28. EATING AND RUNNING

The competitive runner doesn't need any special diet, just a healthy one based on sound nutrition. Food is a fuel and a source of nutrients. Proper nutrition means that essential nutrients—carbohydrates, fats, proteins, vitamins, minerals and water—are both consumed and absorbed for optimal health. A runner's basic needs aren't very different from those of other healthy people, although the high-mileage runner may need to consume more calories and carbohydrates. The runner training in hot weather will need to make some important adjustments to preserve the body's fluid and mineral balance. Some alterations are also advisable during the final days before a marathon.

What we eat depends on many factors—most of them related to our habits and culture, along with taste. Generally, the runner should keep away from saturated fats and excess protein, sugar and highly processed foods. Concentrate on more complex carbohydrates: fruits, vegetables and grains (simple carbohydrates include "nasty junk food").

Dr. David Costill is a noted authority on exercise physiology for runners. He is director of the Ball State University Human Performance Laboratory and author of *A Scientific Approach to Distance Running*.

According to Dr. Costill, the ideal diet for the average person who runs 20–30 miles a week should contain 50 percent carbohydrates, 30 percent fat and 20 percent protein. The runner who logs high mileage—more than 70 miles a week—needs more than 1,000 additional calories a day, consisting of 70 percent carbohydrates, 20 percent fat and 10 percent protein. This high-mileage runner finds that "junk food" adds carbohydrates on top of a sound diet; it cannot replace them. You will need complex carbohydrates for fuel to run long distances. In summary, eat in moderation and eat what you are accustomed to as long as it is nutritious.

FASTING AND VEGETARIANISM

Some runners argue for fasting and against eating meat. Fasting is thought to cleanse and detoxify your body and prepare its metabolism for the demands of running long races after its glycogen supplies are low. In a *Runner's World* survey, some 13 percent of all distance runners said that they fasted regularly for one to three days at a time on water and juices. Some runners periodically fast up to two weeks at a time, drinking only water or fruit and/or vegetable juices, to condition their bodies to live off their own resources. Fasting may be used both during training and before and during competition.

Fasting has its dangers, however. Ideally, it should be done only with your doctor's approval and in moderation. When fasting, blood acidity can become abnormal, muscle and body organs can be adversely affected, excessive amounts of minerals can be lost, and glycogen supplies may be reduced below safe levels. You may feel tired and weak. Fasting before a marathon is the opposite of carbohydrate loading. But if it makes you faster and is safe for you, do it. We don't recommend it, however, for the average runner.

Vegetarianism has grown in popularity with the natural foods movement of the 1970s. Vegetarian restaurants are thriving, and many of their customers are runners. According to vegetarians, meat is full of impurities that cause disease and disrupt digestion. Studies have shown that vegetarians are leaner, have less cholesterol and a lower incidence of heart disease than their meat-eating friends. Several top runners, including 1968 Boston Marathon winner Amby Burfoot and 1978 Avon International Marathon winner Marty Cooksey, are vegetarian runners.

Vegetarianism is a complex issue. Some vegetarians eat no animal products at all. Others, the ovo-lacto vegetarians, exclude all flesh foods—meats, poultry and fish—but eat eggs, milk and cheese. A reduced intake of all meats would probably be a sound idea for every American, runner or nonrunner. Nonmeat sources of protein are better for you (and it is vital to get the right kind of needed protein) and are easily found in nuts, soybeans, whole grains, and other sauces. Vegetarians sometimes go in for exotic diets that ignore elementary essentials of nutrition, especially the minerals and vitamins.

MINERALS AND VITAMINS

Runners who eat a well-balanced diet often take vitamin and mineral supplements, but they may only be passing expensive urine and getting no additional benefits. A good diet supplies all the essential vitamins and minerals; however, a competitive runner who may not be following the best diet may indeed benefit from a moderate amount of supplements. Most are harmless even in excess; the body passes out what it doesn't need in urine. Some vitamins, such as A, D and K, in high concentrations can cause toxic side effects, but others taken as supplements may be useful to the competitive runner. A Russian study indicated that daily doses of important vitamins and minerals, along with a nutritionally adequate diet, would aid physical and mental performance for athletes undergoing strenuous training.

Natural vitamins are found in plants and animals as organic food substances. Because our bodies cannot synthesize vitamins (with few exceptions), we must supply them through our diet or with supplements. For the stresses of long-distance running, we recommend a daily multivitamin, 500 milligrams to one gram of vitamin C, and some vitamin B complex. The B complex vitamins aid in the metabolism of fat, which could be helpful in endurance events. The multivitamin protects you against deficiencies in diet. Vitamin C may protect you against colds, other illness and injury, and help you recover from injury.

Minerals aid in warding off fatigue and cramps, and they maintain the body's delicate water balance. Potassium and magnesium are especially important to minimize cramping—they are lost in body sweat and can be depleted while training in hot weather. Iron supplements may also be important for women during menstruation. Excessive fatigue in both men and women runners may be due to running-related anemia. Iron assists in the oxygen-carrying capacity of the blood. A 1981 study at Canada's Simon Fraser University concluded that iron deficiency may be common in male and female distance runners and that "the presence of latent iron deficiency without anemia may reduce work capacity and impair race performance." If you are prone to cramping during hot weather, you may wish to take potassium and magnesium supplements. Potassium is available naturally in fruits and vegetables (especially cantaloupes, strawberries, oranges, bananas, apricots, dates and tomatoes) and magnesium is found in various nuts and grains. Iron is obtained from leafy green vegetables, lean meats and dried fruits.

Contrary to popular belief, you should not take salt tablets or add salt to your diet to replace that lost in sweat. You have plenty of salt in your diet already, although most of it is hidden.

A well-balanced diet is important for the runner going into competition. A few weeks before the race, some runners neglect their diets. This is a mistake. As you begin to taper your mileage, *do not* taper your food intake as well.

But don't increase it, either. You should maintain the balance of essential foods. For races of more than 20 miles, you may want to consider carbohydrate loading.

CARBOHYDRATE LOADING

Glycogen is a stored carbohydrate made from simple sugar. It is stored in the muscles and liver. Glycogen serves as the body's basic fuel and converts into sugar for the bloodstream when you need more energy. Carbohydrates create glycogen, which aids endurance. The average runner can store enough glycogen to last about 20 miles—the point at which you "hit the Wall" by literally running out of energy.

In the late 1960's, Swedish exercise physiologist Eric Hultman developed the idea of "carbohydrate loading," a means of manipulating the diet in order to increase glycogen stores. The classic seven-day diet based on his studies worked this way:

1. Seven days before the race, go for a long run of two to three hours in order to help deplete glycogen stores in your muscles.

2. For the next three days, eat a diet high in protein and fats and low in carbohydrates in order to deplete your glycogen stores further. Regular running is maintained during this phase to burn off still more glycogen.

3. For the last three days before the race, the diet is reversed. The runner "loads" on carbohydrates and minimizes running in order to store up glycogen levels.

This diet was based on tests that showed that athletes who followed this regimen would be able to improve their performances because the depleted muscles would soak up more glycogen during the loading period than nondepleted muscles. The athlete would increase glycogen storage by as much as 100–300 percent.

This carbo-loading technique was popularized by the dominant marathoner of the 1960's—Great Britain's Ron Hill. It was the craze of the 1970's, and most runners' times improved using it. Dr. Paul Milvy reported that the average marathon time for those who followed this diet for the 1977 New York Marathon was four minutes faster than the average for those who didn't use it, based on a sample of 2,000 runners.

The diet seemed to work better for the average runner than for the faster runner. Costill wrote in *The Runner*: "The difference between elite and average marathoners is that even if both started out with the same amount of glycogen, the elite marathoner would spare it by burning a higher ratio of fat. Although more oxygen is required to burn fat, the highly developed oxygen transport system of the elite runner allows this. Furthermore, he moves more economically, which means that he uses less oxygen to accomplish the same task. The average runner, on the other hand, depletes his glycogen supply sooner and doesn't have an efficient oxygen transport to burn fat. That's why hitting the wall is so devastating and why carbohydrate loading is more important for the average runner than for the elite runner."

We do not, however, recommend the classic regimen. The depletion phase is too taxing physically and psychologically. For instance:

1. The runner becomes very irritable, depressed and tired. He or she runs the risk of seriously upsetting family and coworkers. When the body doesn't have carbohydrates to burn, fat is burned instead, which can upset your hormones and acid-alkaline balance. The condition, called "ketosis," results in your feeling very cranky.

2. Runners who have followed the program have sometimes fared worse in a race because of leg cramps, diarrhea and fatigue.

3. The program places a severe strain on the kidneys. The high-fat/high-protein diet is not good for you.

4. You are experimenting with a system that is unpredictable. It may work for you once, while another time it may cause gastrointestinal problems. When you are mentally and physically keyed up for a race, messing with your metabolism can be risky.

5. The depletion stage makes you vulnerable to colds and flu and can result in loss of sleep.

6. You can't enjoy your runs while depleting—you are very weak, and running is a struggle. Then resting for three days can disturb your feel for running. The average runner loses enjoyment. The serious runner loses a sense of fine tuning.

Never use this system for your first marathon, but if you are a veteran runner and feel that for a big race it will help you both physically and mentally—go ahead. It works for many runners. However, don't overdo it or attempt it more than twice a year. Experiment with it for a low-key race or a long training run before trying it for a major race.

Many runners have experimented with modifying the diet. They find that they can skip the unpleasant depletion stage and just load up for three days before the race with good results. This has led to further research on the potentially dangerous and unpredictable depletion phase. Dr. Costill found that runners who loaded but didn't deplete had nearly the same amount of stored glycogen as the runners who suffered through the difficult depletion phase of the classic diet.

Dr. Costill's conclusion is the program we recommend: there is no advantage to be gained from depleting. Stick to your normal diet until three days before the marathon, and then eat foods high in carbohydrates. Also rest—with minimal running—for those three days in order to build energy reserves. There is no advantage to be gained by building up glycogen reserves for nonmarathon events; if you are running a 10 km event, follow your normal diet.

Some runners complain of extra weight and a feeling of stiffness when "loaded." This is because about three grams of water are stored with each gram of glycogen; be sure to drink plenty of fluids during the loading period to allow proper body functioning. This extra water and weight will not slow you down but will help you avoid dehydration and electrolyte imbalance late in the race. A key point: Don't overeat. The idea is to increase the *percentage* of carbohydrates in your total food intake. When Bob Glover first heard of "loading," he really got loaded. He ate several loaves of bread and many of those nasty chocolate chip cookies—too many. He fertilized the course on race day in several key places. Eat a normal diet, including some protein, but with the emphasis on carbohydrates. Some runners develop digestive problems with this loading program and are unable to follow it. Dr. Costill suggests eating both simple and complex carbohydrates, although some nutritionists discourage the former. Liquid carbohydrate supplements may help those with digestive problems. Studies show that some liquid supplements may increase glycogen storage faster than the normal heaping plates of pasta.

THE LAST SUPPER

The most important meal obviously comes the night before a race rather than on race day. You should eat a major meal in the early evening (about 6 p.m.) before race day. This meal should be high in carbohydrates, especially before a marathon, and include some protein. The typical "last supper" would be a spaghetti dinner with meat or clam sauce, and bread. Spaghetti is 100 percent carbohydrate and digests easily; other pastas such as lasagna and ziti may be substituted.

Not all premarathon meals need be Italian, however. Chinese and Japanese food, primarily rice and vegetables, would be of benefit. Salads and leafy vegetables or fruits are another excellent choice. Beware: Don't stuff yourself. A snack around ten will pack in a few more carbohydrates, but don't overdo it. Some runners like a candy bar or cookies, while others prefer bananas, oranges or apples.

Select with care where you eat the night before a marathon. Make reservations, or, if dining out free at the pre-race feed, get there early. Don't upset your stomach by standing in line for an hour or so before eating. And don't attend that huge spaghetti feast for the racing masses if the scene makes you nervous. A meal in your hotel room may be your best option.

RACE DAY

The race-day meal may do more harm than good. At this last moment, you cannot eat your way to a better time; you can, however, eat your way out of the race. Follow two important rules: Don't eat anything you haven't eaten before a previous race, or you may be unpleasantly surprised; and don't eat too close to the starting time.

By eating too close to race time, you are asking your body to compete with itself. Extra blood is pumped to the stomach to aid in the digestive process. But when you run, extra blood is required by the working muscles to provide fuel. Combining these two demands weakens both processes. You have less energy for running, and you are also likely to have gastrointestinal problems such as diarrhea, nausea and perhaps vomiting and stitches.

Generally, digestion requires three to five hours; that should also be the length of time between your last food and the start of the race. (The actual time it takes to digest food depends on when you eat, what you eat, and your emotional state.) You should enter competition with an empty colon and stomach.

According to Dr. Marvin Brooks, an assistant professor of clinical medicine at the University of California at San Francisco, "Gastrointestinal problems occur during a race because the colon is not completely empty before the start. As the race progresses, the residue in the large intestine is propelled along, and cramps result. Ignoring the cramps won't help—they'll only get worse, and even if your stomach is empty, a full colon can cause nausea or dry heaves. To reduce your chances of cramping and nausea, you should make sure to have an empty colon (large intestine) before the race. A fairly simple diet can achieve this." The diet for two to three days going into the race should contain a minimum of roughage.

Digestion is also affected by your emotional state. Stress may prolong digestion, and a large, exciting race, or an important one, may create special digestive problems. Do yourself a favor: Eat less when under stress, and eat only foods that you have previously eaten when under stress and digested without difficulty.

William Gottlieb, managing editor of *Prevention* health books, suggests: "Any event that takes an hour or more of constant activity, such as a marathon, calls for a specific type of prerace food: carbohydrates. Lots of them. And there are three reasons why:

"First, protein doesn't burn clean. It's a dirty fuel, and the kidney has to excrete the waste products. But during an event your kidneys are benched; the muscles are the first string. That means the wastes stay in your blood—and you feel wasted.

"Second, protein is an oxygen hog. To move a high-protein meal out of your stomach takes 10 to 15 percent more oxygen than a meal of carbohydrates.

"And third, fat is no better. Unlike carbohydrates, fat doesn't burn fast; it's beaten by carbos before it's even out of the starting blocks. For some people, the problem isn't that fat digests slowly; it's that it hardly digests at all."

For those without digestive problems, a good carbohydrate breakfast can be of great value before a marathon. But for other than long events, the prerace meal offers only psychological advantages—it makes runners feel more comfortable. For shorter events, the meal is not critical—eat defensively if at all. If you eat for the marathon, eat some carbohydrates but don't overindulge. It is very easy for the nervous runner to compulsively eat his or her way to a poor performance.

According to Dr. Jean Mayer, sweets before a race stimulate overproduction of insulin, which in turn depletes the body's stores of glycogen. Since this is your fuel, eating sweets can actually decrease your available energy for the race.

In general, as we've said, don't eat anything three to five

hours or less before a race. You may shorten this time for your training runs. Also, use your training for just that: to find out what foods you can eat before running that will be beneficial, and that you won't end up either fighting or flinging out on the road.

One other item. Some runners find that they have to sit down to dinner with their families before going out on a training run. Nibble away at light, very easily digestible foods while the rest of the family enjoys their meal. Then go for your run an hour later, and eat another light meal when you return. If you plan speed workouts, don't eat anything. Because of their intensity, speed workouts may be harder than races on your gastrointestinal system.

Most races are held in the morning. This presents both training problems—if you are used to running at the end of the day—and eating problems. Most veteran runners eat little—coffee and toast—or nothing before a race. Most novices eat more, and eat it closer to competition, because they think they need the energy—a misconception. To insure a high-glycogen level in your liver if you are carbohydrate loading for a marathon, you should, according to Dr. Costill, combine a carbohydrate-packing meal the night before with a smaller meal three to five hours before a marathon. Dr. Costill notes that "the final meal also will trigger peristalsis and help empty any solid waste still in the lower intestine. Some walking around or a light prerace warm-up may help the emptying process and prevent pit stops."

So what should the typical runner eat on marathon morning? Your meal should be high in carbohydrates, low in sugar, fat and protein. It should ward off hunger pains and be easily digestible. Adequate fluids should accompany your meal, which may consist of toast, or even pancakes (watch the butter and syrup), and perhaps coffee or tea. Some runners drink orange juice, others react badly to it; some cannot hold down milk, wheat products or too much fruit. The basic rule: Experiment before your workouts to find out what you can eat and tolerate before your races.

Second, watch your starting time. Subtract three to five

hours, and eat no later than that time. Don't be absurd about this, however, and eat breakfast at 4 a.m. for an 8 a.m. race. It would be better to skip the meal. A 10 a.m. race allows you to eat lightly around six or seven, while a noon start, as in the Boston Marathon, leaves plenty of time to eat and digest your food. If you have problems, take only fluids on race mornings. Avoid sugar: it may cause a low blood-sugar level later.

When you find the right combination of foods and time before races, write it down. Stick to it. Don't try to become a prerace gourmet. Some runners have goats' stomachs and can train and race after eating. Others can eat before training, but never before a race. When in doubt, drink but don't eat.

EATING AFTER THE RACE

Runners obsessed with proper diet before a race often ignore it afterwards. But what you eat and drink for several days after your race, especially a marathon, will affect your recovery; a proper diet will help minimize injury and illness and allow you to return to a normal training and racing routine sooner.

You may be tired of pasta and long for steak and eggs. But besides eating what you want—and your body will often tell you what it needs—you should follow your prerace diet for several days after a long race. A marathon will especially deplete your glycogen stores. To recover, and replace lost glycogen, you should eat plenty of carbohydrates afterwards as well as before. In effect, this is a carbohydrate-reloading to get glycogen back into your muscles and liver. Dr. Costill says, "Probably the first meal after the marathon should be like the last big meal before. If the night before you have spaghetti or some other heavy carbohydrate, the meal after competition should be very much the same. You want to recover as much of that used up glycogen as possible. It often takes three to five days to recover the glycogen. That's part of the problem of recovering from a marathon. A lot of people don't go after the carbohydrates hard enough and that is part of the cause for the fatigue and difficulties in getting back to running form again."

Here's a chance to expand your intake and knowledge of carbohydrates. Go beyond mere pasta. Nancy Clark, author of *The Athlete's Kitchen: A Nutrition Guide and Cookbook*, suggests rice pilaf, stuffing, sweet potato, winter squash, corn, split pea soup, banana bread, corn muffins, biscuits with jam, apple crisp, date squares, fruit cup/sherbert.

The extra amount of protein you need to replace after a long race is not significant. Your normal American diet— which usually includes two to three times the amount of protein needed—will be more than adequate. Two containers of yogurt after the race will take care of your protein needs. Eating fatty foods isn't recommended either, despite the fact that you have burned fat as a fuel during the race. Fat supplies are plentiful in your body. Sodium, a component of salt, is an electrolyte lost when you sweat. But the average American diet contains 10 to 60 times the required amount; you don't need to replace it. If your body craves it, try pretzels, popcorn or cheese as a snack to satisfy your urge. Salt losses are best replaced by foods rather than fluids. The clear conclusion of all this is that a balanced diet, perhaps with an emphasis on carbohydrates, will replenish all the energy stores of fat and glycogen plus other essential vitamins and minerals. Fluid intake is important and should be maintained and watched carefully. Remember, the balanced, healthful diet is all any runner needs.

29. DRINKING AND RUNNING

Drinking enough fluids is essential for the competitive runner. On race day, in fact, fluids are more important than food. Runners don't die of hunger pangs, but dehydrated runners can, and have, died from lack of fluids.

1. WHAT TO DRINK IN YOUR DAILY DIET

Your body is mostly water; thus, it needs a good fresh supply of water every day to maintain its balance and function normally. There is little danger of consuming too much water; any excess is flushed away by your kidneys. Chronic dehydration causes an increase in appetite, and thus could cause weight gain.

Your body requires at least six glasses of fluid every day; some fluid replacement will come from the foods you eat. When you exercise, you need much more fluid, at least two to three quarts daily, and half of this should be water. Drink water before and during your meals. Also remember that fluids are important during carbohydrate loading to prevent dehydration.

Water is the main compont of our cells, urine, sweat and

blood. When you are dehydrated, your cells become dehydrated and chemical reactions are impaired. The cells can't build tissues or utilize energy efficiently. You don't produce urine, and consequently toxic products build up in your bloodstream. You don't sweat, so your temperature rises. Your blood volume decreases, and you have less blood to transport oxygen and nutrients through your body. The result is that your muscles become weak, and you are soon in danger of collapse.

Runners, of course, drink other beverages besides water. Two popular but controversial ones are coffee and beer.

Coffee

Coffee contains caffeine, which is a drug. Excessive intake of caffeine causes irregular heart beats, and in some people may aggravate conditions such as ulcers, gout or high blood pressure. It is a stimulant and can cause hyperactivity and even stomach spasms. It should be cut back in or eliminated from our diets.

Americans consume a lot of caffeine unintentionally. It is commonly added to foods, beverages (coffee and the colas), and over-the-counter drugs. Adverse effects—including headaches, sleeplessness and anxiety—may result from drinking four or five cups of brewed coffee daily, ten to twelve cups of instant coffee, or fifteen 12-ounce servings of caffeinated soft drinks. This may seem like a lot, but it's not exceptional; according to the American Council on Science and Health, some 11 million Americans consume this much caffeine daily. Too much coffee or cola late in the evening after a workout when your body may already be jittery can result in troubled sleep.

Beer

Nectar of the gods, ambrosia of those who seek fast times—beer may be the runner's fuel. It doesn't take a scientific study to know that a majority of competitive runners, including those of world class, drink a lot of beer and argue (sometimes loudly) that it helps them. Dr. Peter Wood, of the Stanford University Disease Prevention Program, discovered that runners outdrank nonrunners by two to one. We're still trying to find out if that's cans or pitchers.

A quart of beer supplies about 450 calories, which will quickly replenish depleted energy reserves. That quart contains about the same amount of carbohydrates as a quarter pound of bread, but goes down much faster and is metabolized quickly. Beer also contains B complex vitamins and other nutrients. Studies indicate, however, that one beer lowers heat tolerance for as long as three days. Alcohol promotes urination, and can thus help cause dehydration. If you have a slow metabolic rate or if you don't keep your mileage up, beer consumption will add weight; many runners prefer the low-calorie beers.

We recommend as part of your daily diet, if you wish, two or three glasses of beer. But that's it! If you're knocking down a six-pack a day, you not only have a weight problem but also a drinking problem. We do not recommend beer to excess. A beer or two in the evening may help you relax and promote sleep, especially the night before a big race. Before one Boston Marathon, a top level marathoner couldn't get to sleep because he was so nervous. Bob Glover suggested he have a couple of beers. He drank two—and became quite dizzy. He woke up on the floor with a hangover, and ran a terrible race. He didn't tell Glover that he had never had a drink before in his life. However, the postrace, postworkout beer will replace lost fluids and minerals and help you relax. Whoever heard of a runner's party without beer?

Whatever you drink—water or juice—drink more of it the day before a race in hot weather. If you drink too much, you will urinate more, but you want to have a full tank of fluids prior to race day.

2. DRINKING BEFORE RUNNING AND RACING

Some runners argue that caffeine ingested before a race improves their times. The evidence on this is still inconclusive. About an hour before the race, these runners drink a cup of unsweetened tea or coffee or swallow two caffeine pills. The theory is that the caffeine releases fatty acids into the bloodstream as fuel, thus sparing and slowing the use of muscle glycogen and on the onset of fatigue until much later in the race than normally.

Dr. Costill's work shows that caffeine intake may increase the ability to perform work by as much as 16 percent in some people. He warns, however, that caffeine is a drug, and that some people do not benefit from it; in fact, about 20 percent of the population has a negative reaction. Some runners have found that caffeine before a race produces jitters and diarrhea. Studies have also shown that caffeine can increase heat production, which is bad on a hot race day.

If you want to see what caffeine might do for, or to, you, practice drinking one to three cups of tea or coffee before a long training run and see how your body reacts. Don't experiment on race day. We would prefer to see you improve your race times by following the training guidelines in this book, however, rather than by experimenting with a drug that may harm you as much as help you.

Avoid sugared drinks for one to three hours before a race. You may have an insulin reaction that will temporarily lower your blood sugar, leaving you with less fuel for energy. Dr. Costill has determined that runners who drink sugared beverages a few hours before exercising become prematurely exhausted.

You should drink very little fluid in the two hours before you race. It takes one to one-and-a-half hours for your body to eliminate excess fluids through urination. So if you drink fluids between a half hour and one-and-a-half hours before the race, you may have to urinate at the starting line or shortly after the race begins. The world's largest urinal, *over 200 feet long*, near the start of the New York Marathon draws plenty of business because nervous runners drink too much in the hours immediately before the start.

The American College of Sports Medicine recommends that runners drink 13–17 ounces of fluids 10–15 minutes prior to racing (or for that matter prior to long runs). Normally the kidneys shut down as you start running so that your last-minute fluid intake that doesn't reach the kidneys will remain in your body. Thus, you are actually "fluid loading." This extra fluid will be immediately available for sweat, which helps cool the body on a hot day. The extra fluids will help prevent or delay dehydration and overheating.

Look for water stations at the starting area. Water is your safest bet before the race. Avoid fruit juices, sweetened athletic drinks, alcoholic beverages and anything you aren't used to.

3. DRINKING ON THE RUN

In warm or hot weather, especially during long runs, it is important to drink on the run. There are at least three basic reasons:

1. As you run, your body temperature rises as body fluids are depleted. This loss dehydrates you and can cause serious damage to your circulatory system. Fluid intake on hot days especially is essential to your health because it minimizes dehydration and helps cool the body.

2. Important minerals and chemicals known as electrolytes (sodium, potassium, magnesium) are lost through the pores in perspiration. Fluids containing these minerals can be ingested before and during the race to replace those lost. Electrolyte depletion could result in fatigue or leg cramping, or upset the body's water balance.

3. Sugar solutions supply glucose (used for energy) to the body, offsetting that lost during exercise, especially late in a long run.

The body loses fluids more rapidly than they can be absorbed through the stomach. On hot days, you should drink more than you think is necessary. Don't rely upon your thirst: you could be down one to two quarts of sweat before your mouth even feels thirsty. Drink as much as you can without upsetting your stomach—a further reason for drinking mainly water. Dr. Costill says: "During the marathon, you can't even come close to replacing the fluids you lose. Drinking at aid stations may replace only one tenth of the fluids you lose. But this 10 percent is important."

In general, a weight loss of two percent or more of one's body weight by sweating affects performance. A loss of five to six percent affects health. A weight loss of five to seven pounds is not uncommon during long runs. A runner may lose about three or four pounds per hour during a marathon, but he or she can only absorb about 1.8 pounds of water from the stomach in the same period. Obviously, regardless of how much a runner drinks, he or she cannot keep up with the weight loss from sweating. Thus, a runner will dehydrate twice as fast as he or she can replace fluids during a race and will finish dehydrated.

You can lose a pound of sweat in as little as two miles. Dehydration also affects your body's ability to control body temperature. The combination of dehydration, heat build-up generated by work, and warm air temperatures can dramatically increase your body temperature. Your normal body temperature is 98.6°F. Commonly, it can rise as high as 106°F on hot days, which is extremely dangerous if prolonged. Temperatures as high as 108°F might be fatal, so it is critical to keep the body temperature down by replacing lost fluids. In studies by Costill, it was shown that rectal temperatures in runners were two degrees (F) cooler when the runners drank fluids during a two-hour run than when they did not.

So start drinking about 10 to 15 minutes before the start of the race, and then drink about every 15 minutes during the race on hot days (somewhat less often on cool days). Fluid stations should be located about every two miles.

Your body can absorb about six ounces of fluid every 15 to 20 minutes. Therefore you should take a full cup of fluid every two to three miles. More than two cups at one time may distend your stomach and cause problems with proper breathing. Remember: it takes up to 20 minutes for the fluid to be absorbed and take effect, so don't wait until you feel hot and thirsty to begin drinking. By then it will be too late. Fluids taken during the last two or three miles may not help in your race but will aid in your recovery.

You don't have to wait to reach fluid stations before you drink. Some runners carry their drinks with them and don't stop at the water stops at all. In most major marathons, spectators line the course and supply you with fluids. Just be careful of what you take. Water is the safest to accept from a stranger. By supplementing the official fluid stations, you don't need to down as much fluid each time—downing a full cup at once without spilling it isn't easy. Some races don't supply fluids often enough to meet your demands. Also, in some big races it is very hard to get fluids without literally standing in line and fighting for them. So it is helpful to have a backup system of fluid supply.

A good choice then is to have friends stationed along the course with plastic squeeze bottles of your favorite road-tested beverage. This will involve forming a team—friends, kids, relatives—and making them part of your racing success. This way you know what you are getting, and you're getting it from encouraging supporters.

Fluid replacement is critical in short races, too. Even in 5 km races, the slower runner will benefit from drinking fluids. The faster runners will only waste time because they will finish before the fluids are absorbed. Prerace fluid intake, however, is still essential in short races. As a rule of thumb, if you are racing longer than 30 minutes, it is important to drink fluids during the race as well as before. And don't neglect fluids on a cold day. Running will raise your body temperature and deplete fluids even when the spectators are wearing fur coats.

Drinking in a race can be tricky. Most runners try to grab

a cup of liquid and throw it down quickly as they run. This is difficult to accomplish and hard on your stomach; it may spoil your rhythm more than stopping altogether. Some runners will try to carry the drink and finish it off in a few mouthfuls. The easiest way to drink on the run is to use a plastic squeeze bottle with a nozzle. You can control your intake, and you don't have to worry about spilling a drop. Of course, you need someone to hand the bottle to you and take it back.

The surest way to make sure that you get that needed full cup is to stop and drink it or drink it while walking. For some, this is a good excuse to take a break. You may find that you will lose less time overall if you pause for a drink rather than trying clumsily to drink on the run.

Race directors should tell you before the race starts where the water stations are located—at which mile marks and on which side of the road—and they should post warning signs (or have someone calling out) when stations are coming up. Slower runners should take their time, drink a cup of fluid, and then move along. Faster runners, however, may limit their stops to avoid losing ground to competitors. Sometimes, in an effort to break away, a runner will skip a fluid station if he or she sees an opponent take a drink. Some races have been won this way. But others have been lost by competitors who suddenly fall apart from failing to replace lost fluids.

When in doubt, be cautious. Drink. Research shows that time lost drinking is more than made up for in performance by the average long-distance runner. He or she doesn't slow down from dehydration and overheating.

Fluids are also essential for your long training runs whatever the temperature. On hot days, drink often. In New York City's Central Park, for example, runners break up their six-mile loop by stopping at a water fountain every three miles. On longer runs on humid days, they stop more often. If there are no handy drinking fountains along your route, trying running an out-and-back course and stashing a plastic squeeze bottle in the grass along the way. Or scout out a friendly gas station, school or home along your route. Never think that not drinking during training runs will toughen you for hot weather racing.

4. WHAT DRINKS ARE BEST ON THE RUN

Should you drink water, juice, soda or commercial athletic drinks? Some prefer to make up their own concoction. For the most part, however, plain water is best. Here are some of the other options available to runners:

Special Athletic Drinks

These fluids—such as ERG, Gatorade, Body Punch—make a lot of claims and have avid supporters, who argue that when we sweat, we lose more than water. We lose electrolytes—minerals such as sodium, potassium, magnesium, calcium and phosphate. These losses may cause cramping and impair your body's normal functioning. Despite advertising claims for these special drinks—and their use in marathon events and by athletic teams—they may not be all that is claimed for them. Dr. Costill's research indicates that we may not need to replace electrolytes lost through sweat during competition because the loss is very small. These drinks also contain sugar.

Sugared Drinks

Some runners and competitive cyclists drink sugared fluids—in athletic drinks, soda and other beverages. The cyclists claim that these drinks eliminate "bonking"—running out of liver glycogen—which causes dizziness, hypoglycemia and confusion. You can recover from bonking by consuming sugar immediately. But runners are mostly concerned with muscle—not liver—glycogen losses. Some studies indicate that sugar taken during competition goes into the bloodstream and is used by our muscles to delay the burning of stored glycogen, thus prolonging endurance. Others indicate that the glycogen stored previously in the muscles is the determining factor in "hitting the Wall"—not the circulating glucose (sugar) in the bloodstream.

Sugar may or may not help you beat the Wall, but it may help you feel less fatigued, especially if you aren't a highly trained marathoner. According to Dr. Joan Ullyot, author of *Women's Running*: "The blood sugar level is kept up mainly by metabolism of liver glycogen and to some extent by what you ingest. That's why I think things like ERG are so important during a race. They keep your blood sugar up which makes you feel better. Blood sugar doesn't do anything for the muscles, though. The brain needs sugar. The brain is the only organ in the body that needs sugar all the time. If the mind perceives that the blood sugar is low, you are going to feel fatigue whether or not you have plenty of fuel. But the trained marathon runners who have been tested during the marathon all had very high blood sugar levels. The ability to maintain blood sugar level is developed through training." Thus, the average runner and the novice need sugar during the race more than the well-trained runner does. Sugar intake, however, delays the absorption of fluids. On a cool marathon day, sugar solutions may be helpful, but on a hot day, play it safe and stick to cool water.

The American College of Sports Medicine advises race sponsors to mix fluids and small amounts of sugar—less than 2.5 grams glucose per 100 ml water—to help absorption. Some runners down cola during races. Cola should be defizzed and diluted with water. Frank Shorter used defizzed cola en route to his 1972 Olympic Marathon victory. Others take both water and the race fluid and drink half of each to dilute the drink further, aid absorption and lessen the chances of getting an upset stomach. Some runners take sugared iced tea, which packs the water, sugar and the supposed "boost" of caffeine.

Your choice of drinks depends on:

Your Preference and Needs. Sugared drinks or drinks high in citric acid may upset your stomach, but you may benefit from them. Whatever you drink, practice drinking it on your long training runs and in low-key races—noting both its effect on you and how easily it can be consumed while you run. Your best bet is to choose a drink based on your own experience with it. For some runners, dehydration is more of a problem than for others. Some of us run well in the heat, others need all the fluids we can get just to survive.

Heat. Studies show that water is absorbed 50 percent faster than a sugar solution, which means it works faster to prevent dehydration or overheating. Anything mixed with water delays its absorption. Your preferred drink on a hot day should be water: it is more important to get fluids quickly into your system than to worry about replacing lost energy substances. Cold water absorbs faster than warm fluids. Cold drinks—contrary to the old myth—will not cause cramps. The ideal fluid temperature for absorption is 40°F. In cooler weather, water isn't as necessary, but some fluid intake is always advisable. You may wish to drink more sugared drinks, but switch to water if the weather warms up during the race.

Distance. Under ten miles, water is all you need. For the marathon, sugared drinks *may* help you through the last miles—through the Wall—but if you dehydrate, you are in worse trouble. The Wall doesn't kill—dehydration does. Alberto Salazar had to be given emergency fluids intravenously when his body temperature dropped to 88°F after winning the 1982 Boston Marathon on a hot, sunny day. He had lost an enormous amount of body fluids and was dangerously dehydrated.

5. WHAT TO DRINK AFTER YOU RUN

After your workout or race, you should replace lost fluids, electrolytes and energy reserves. Studies show that sweat loss may result in an 8 percent loss of body weight and a 13 to 14 percent reduction of body water. Marathoners often lose 6 to 12 pounds, or the equivalent of as much as 1 to

1.5 gallons of fluids. This is not a weight loss, but a fluid loss, and is not permanent. You'll actually burn off only enough calories to lose less than a pound of body fat.

To rehydrate adequately takes between 24 and 48 hours. Weigh yourself before and after every workout and race to see how much fluid weight you are losing. You should replace lost body weight by drinking plenty of fluids after long, hot runs—twice as much as you feel is necessary. One gallon of water equals about 8.5 pounds. That works out to more than a pint of fluids to replace each pound of weight loss.

Start replacing fluids as soon as you finish your run. Sip, if you cannot gulp fluids. When your stomach settles, pour them in. In hot weather, consume cold drinks to bring down your body temperature as well as replace the fluid loss. Studies show that runners who drink two cups of ice water absorb half of it in 20 minutes—twice the amount of those who drink warm water. In cold weather, also drink some cold water to replace lost fluids, but then add something warm to prevent chill—hot chocolate, tea, coffee or soup.

You should drink plenty of fluids throughout the day in proportion to the amount of weight you lost. Dr. Jack Scaff, former director of the always hot Honolulu Marathon, advises runners to keep drinking until they have clear urine. Dark urine is a symptom of dehydration. Dr. Costill warns: "The human thirst mechanism is quite slow. As a result, you may be eight pounds dehydrated and have a couple of glasses of fluid and feel satisfied. But an hour later you will be thirsty again. You have to just force yourself to drink some extra. Watch your body weight for the next 24 hours. Generally this is enough time to get your fluids back."

Beware of chronic dehydration caused by going several days without properly replenishing lost fluids. This is a dangerous condition that is frequently overlooked. It lowers a runner's tolerance to fatigue, reduces his ability to sweat, elevates his rectal temperature, and increases the stress on his circulatory system. "Probably the best way to guard against chronic dehydration," says Dr. Costill, "is to check your weight every morning before breakfast. If you note a two or three pound decrease in body weight from morning to morning, efforts should be made to increase your fluid intake. You need not worry about drinking too much fluid, because your kidneys will unload the excess water in a matter of hours." Better too much fluid for the kidneys than not enough. According to Dr. Edward Colt, "There is a lot of evidence that runners are suffering from chronic dehydration which becomes even more severe during long runs or marathons. The evidence for this is the sixfold increase in kidney stones among marathon runners which Paul Milvy, John Thorton and I reported in the *Journal of Sports Medicine and Physical Fitness*. Kidney stones occur much more frequently in people who are dehydrated. Susceptibility to urine infections also results."

But what should you drink after your long run or race? You need to replace what you lost—sweat. The fastest, simplest and safest way to do that is by drinking cold water. But you have also sweated out electrolytes which help your body function properly. Shortages in these minerals will affect your recovery. However, the mineral loss isn't high. A few normal well-balanced meals and a few glasses of orange, pineapple or tomato juice should easily replace most lost minerals. Soda pop has very little potassium, and the special athletic drinks have even less. The athletic drinks are more valuable during your race than after, since they are diluted to enable your body to absorb them better while exercising. Soda pop will help you replace lost fluids, supply sugar to help replace depleted glycogen reserves, perhaps satisfy your taste. We do not recommend coffee or milk, wines or liquor as fluids after running. Alcohol makes you urinate more frequently and thus causes you to lose fluids when you are trying to replenish your supply. Before celebrating with a postrace beer, drink several glasses of water, and then eat something nutritious with the beer.

What do the researchers say about the postrace beer? Comments Dr. Costill in *The Runner*: "My preference for a postrace drink is a cold beer, since I seem to be able to recover fastest with this drink. Also, I seem to be able to drink relatively large quantities of this alcoholic beverage and remain sober following a marathon, although I have never tested the reason why in a laboratory."

30. RUNNING AND YOUR BODY WEIGHT

Elite runners are lean and mean, but most runners need to work at reducing body fat and weight. We need only essential fat (about four percent for men and ten percent for women) and enough weight for muscle strength to power us through training and races. We should strive for stronger engines, lighter chassis and good health.

To determine your best weight, consider the following list and then consult the chart estimating the best racing weight for you. Remember: estimates are generalizations; you alone (perhaps together with your doctor) can determine your best weight.

WHAT DID YOU WEIGH AT 18–25?

During these years most of us were light: we were too active to get fat. Theoretically, we stop growing in our early twenties. According to Dr. Irwin Maxwell Stillman, author of *The Inches-Off Diet*, no one should weigh more than he or she did at age 25. Life-insurance weight charts—which show that people weigh more as they age—merely reflect what is happening, not what should be happening. As we age, our metabolism slows. To counteract this slowdown, we should eat less and exercise more, and level off our weight instead of continuing to gain. Your weight at age 25, therefore, should be a first goal.

HOW DO YOU LOOK AND FEEL?

Dr. Ken Cooper, the author of *Aerobics*, suggests that you stand nude in front of a full-length mirror and look at yourself critically. If you *look* fat, you are. Now the unfair test: try running in place and look for jiggles, especially the thighs and stomach. Very fit runners are often gaunt in the face because their body fat percentage is so low.

A runner may lose inches from the waist but weigh the same, because muscle weighs more than fat, although it takes up less space. With proper weight training, you may actually gain weight, but lose body fat. If you are running to control your weight, you need to run and diet at the same time to reach the level you wish. If your goal is to run faster, you need to weigh as little as you can and still feel strong.

HOW DO YOU PERFORM?

Generally, you will pick your ideal weight by the process of self-selection. As your mileage approaches a high, consistent level, you will find a comfortable and efficient weight for you. Veteran runners can tell what they weigh by how their training is going. Bob Glover is 6'1" and weighs 160 pounds when running very little. He weighs 157 at 50 miles a week, 155 at 70 a week, and 152 at 100 a week. He can guess his weight within a pound by feeling how his body reacts to training.

Check your diary to see what you weighed when you ran your best workouts and races. Weigh yourself daily (but not after runs, when you have temporarily lost body fluids), and record your weight.

Some runners perform poorly when just a few pounds over their ideal body weight; others, when a few pounds under. Being too much overweight can dramatically slow your race time. But you can also perform poorly and be prone to injury and illness if you are underweight. You can actually burn away essential muscle and thus lose strength in key muscle groups, which can make you more vulnerable to injury.

WHAT ARE YOUR GOALS?

You may wish to race lighter for marathons than for other races. Often marathoners will train at a comfortable weight and then, as the marathon approaches, bring the weight down a little. Some choose to improve upper body strength, and will thus gain some weight to help them perform better at shorter distances. Don Paige, the USA's top half miler, was a skinny high schooler. But after an extensive weight training program, he gained a powerful upper body and a few more pounds, which resulted in one of the most feared kicks of middle distance racers in the world.

BODY FAT PERCENTAGE

Your body consists of two types of tissues: fat and lean body tissue—bone, organ and muscle. The amount of fat you carry is called your body fat percentage. It is determined by dividing your total body weight by the weight of your fat. Body fat percentage is commonly estimated by using calipers to measure the fat under the skin (skinfolds) or by an underwater weighing technique. The latter is more accurate, but both are estimates. You can have a skinfold estimate taken at your local YMCA.

Body weight and body fat percentage are closely linked. According to Dr. David Costill, each pound of fat added or lost can result in an increase or decrease in body fat percentage of as much as half a point, which will affect performance. Some runners may weigh within the standard limits, while having a high percentage of body fat. They are underweight and overfat. Big-bodied runners and some other athletes, such as professional football players, may be heavier than the weight charts suggest, but low in body fat percentage. They are overweight, but "underfat." For some of them, losing weight is equated with losing strength—an undesirable result. Consequently, when predicting your best weight, you need to consider several things. The most important is how lean you are. Here are normal body fat ranges:

	MEN	WOMEN
Elite marathoner	4%–8%	10%–12%
Advanced and champion competitive runners	6–10	15–20
Novice and basic competitive runners	15	20
Overweight	20 +	25 +

DETERMINING RACING WEIGHTS FOR MEN

The Elite Runner

The most widely used rule of thumb for determining racing weight for men is the 2:1 ratio—two pounds of body weight for every inch of height. We have tested this theory on hundreds of runners, and it is very accurate for runners around the average height for male marathon runners, 5'10" (70 inches), where the average weight is around 140 pounds. (To determine your best running weight, multiply height in inches by two). Elite runners at the 1980 U.S. Olympic Trials averaged 70 inches and 139 pounds. The chart on page 476 for elite marathoners follows the 2:1 ration for heights from 5'7" to 6'2" in men. Adjustments are made below 5'7" (or the runner has it too easy) and above 6'2" (or the runner has it too hard).

You should not aim for this 2:1 ratio unless you can do it without sacrificing strength. Weighing what an elite runner weighs will not by itself make you fast; and it could, by weakening you, make you slow. Most elite runners weigh

RACING WEIGHTS FOR MALE ELITE RUNNERS

HEIGHT	WEIGHT IN POUNDS
5'4" (64")	119
5'5" (65")	125
5'6" (66")	129
5'7" (67")	134
5'8" (68")	136
5'9" (69")	138
5'10" (70")	140
5'11" (71")	142
6'0" (72")	144
6'1" (73")	146
6'2" (74")	148
6'3" (75")	153
6'4" (76")	158

Note: As with all charts, consider each of the charts in this chapter as estimated guidelines only. The charts have been proven to be quite accurate for most runners; they are most likely to be inaccurate at the extremes. Shorter people or those with very small frames perhaps weigh a little less. Taller people or those with very big frames may weigh a little more. The bottom line is your body fat percentage, not your total weight.

what they do because their high training mileage (100–140 miles per week) burns up enormous amounts of calories (more than 5,000 a day); they have small frames on average heights, and a very low body fat percentage (four to eight percent).

If your times and mileage are approaching those of the elite runner, you might benefit from being within two pounds either way of the weights shown on the chart above. For the lighter-weight elite, the loss of only two pounds going into a race might result in improved performance, although others may find even that much loss weakening. The elite runner, through experience, can tell what weight is best for him or her, and generally it will be close to what is listed on this chart.

Pete Schuder has found that most—but not all—of his top runners fit this chart. For example, All-Ivy League cross-country performers Charlie Miers from England

(5'9" and 125 pounds) and Wally Collins (5'8" and 130) are well under the 2:1 ratio.

Advanced and Champion Competitors

These runners are serious about their training and wish to be as efficient as possible by running as light as they can and still maintain enough strength for both their running and their work day (most elite runners have to worry only about their running). They should weigh within ten percent of the elite runner's weight at the same height. (See chart below.) By bringing their weight closer to five percent of the elite runner—perhaps for important races— they may get into even better shape. Reaching the elite weight may be impossible; it may require both taking the time to run 100 or more miles a week and not getting injured doing it.

These runners usually compete at about 10 percent body fat on a small-to-medium frame. It is essential to watch the diet; extra weight will affect performance. This formula has proven accurate: Bob Glover used it in 1980

RACING WEIGHTS FOR MALE ADVANCED AND CHAMPION COMPETITORS

HEIGHT	WEIGHT IN POUNDS
5'4" (64")	131
5'5" (65")	137
5'6" (66")	142
5'7" (67")	147
5'8" (68")	149
5'9" (69")	152
5'10" (70")	154
5'11" (71")	156
6'0" (72")	158
6'1" (73")	160
6'2" (74")	163
6'3" (75")	168
6'4" (76")	174

and 1981 to set weight standards for several executives who competed in the New York Marathon. Most were over-weight novice runners and workaholics. Those who came closest to their weight goals as determined by Glover from these charts also came closest to their time goals.

By way of comparison with yourself, the average height for serious male competitors in the 1981 Boston Marathon (who had to qualify with times of 2:50 or better, 3:10 for masters) was 69 inches. Using the height-in-inches-times-two formula and adding ten percent, we predict a weight of 152 pounds. Their average weight was 148 pounds.

Novice and Basic Competitors

These runners' weight range is listed on the chart below, for men over age 25. Note that the ranges are listed by body frame type. Since all such charts are merely guide-lines, you may be better off using the lower figure in your range; when in doubt, select the lighter frame. These are minimal fitness standards. The closer you come toward the weight of the competitive runner, the better you will look, feel and run. The runners have a body fat percentage of about 15 percent.

RACING WEIGHTS FOR MALE NOVICE AND BASIC COMPETITORS*

HEIGHT	SMALL FRAME	MEDIUM FRAME	LARGE FRAME
5'4"	118–126 pounds	124–136	132–148
5'5"	121–129	127–139	135–152
5'6"	124–133	130–143	138–156
5'7"	128–137	134–147	142–161
5'8"	132–141	138–152	147–166
5'9"	136–145	142–156	151–170
5'10"	140–150	146–160	155–174
5'11"	144–154	150–165	159–179
6'0"	148–158	154–170	164–184
6'1"	152–162	158–175	168–189
6'2"	156–167	162–180	172–194
6'3"	160–171	167–185	178–199
6'4"	164–175	172–190	182–204

*Developed by the Metropolitan Life Insurance Company.

DETERMINING RACING WEIGHTS FOR WOMEN

Unfortunately, the formula that works so well for men doesn't work for women. They have a different body fat/body muscle makeup. And since women are new to competitive racing, large numbers of highly trained women have yet to be studied. We have, however, arrived at a formula that has so far proven accurate for most women runners. Note, however, that women's weights may increase slightly during menstruation. Also, women should be careful not to place too much value on thinness and loss of weight at a sacrifice to health and strength. Each runner type has similar characteristics to men, and should follow the same guidelines listed for her male counterpart in this chapter.

The Elite Runner

The elite female runner, who runs about 80 to 100 miles a week, has a body fat percentage of 10 to 12 percent. Grete Waitz, for example, has a body fat percentage of 9 percent. The average elite female runner is 5'6" tall and weights 108 pounds. To determine the weight of the elite runner, subtract 10 percent from the weight listed for your height for the advanced and champion competitive runner on page 480.

RACING WEIGHTS FOR FEMALE ELITE RUNNERS

HEIGHT	WEIGHT IN POUNDS
5'0"	81
5'1"	86
5'2"	90
5'3"	95
5'4"	99
5'5"	104
5'6"	108
5'7"	113
5'8"	117
5'9"	122
5'10"	126

The elite female runner may weigh a little more, on the average, than the chart on page 479 indicates.

Advanced and Champion Competitors

The average runner in this category is 5'6" and weighs 120 pounds. She has a body fat percentage of 15 to 20 percent. Dr. Joan Ullyot's theory for the proper weight for women runners is used as the formula here: start with five feet in height and 90 pounds in weight; add five pounds for each additional inch. A five percent reduction in weight from this will improve times for many women runners.

All of the dozen or so sub-three-hour marathoners that Bob Glover coaches with his Atalanta team fall at or just below this figure. Jean Whiston, however, at 5'6" and 110 pounds is the team's only runner at elite runners' weight—and she is an elite runner. She was 10 pounds overweight and running local class, but not elite-level times. After losing weight, she made NCAA college All-America in cross-country for the University of Maryland. Sharon Barbano, Atalanta's cofounder, is 5'5" tall and weighs 114 pounds. After losing 15 pounds when she took up running, and then another 10 when she wanted to become a top mara-

RACING WEIGHTS FOR FEMALE ADVANCED AND CHAMPION COMPETITORS

HEIGHT	WEIGHT IN POUNDS
5'0"	90
5'1"	95
5'2"	100
5'3"	105
5'4"	110
5'5"	115
5'6"	120
5'7"	125
5'8"	130
5'9"	135
5'10"	140

thoner—her times came down from 3:30 to 2:53 and then—at her lowest weight—to 2:46. For her, the increase in mileage to 90–100 a week made the difference; before, she starved herself and couldn't get off those extra pounds.

Novice and Basic Competitors

These runners run 20 miles a week or more and have a body fat percentage of 20 to 25 percent. The weights, listed on the chart below are for women over age 25. Note that the range is listed by body frame type, and use the chart only as a guideline. The closer you come to the weight of the advanced and champion competitive runners, the better you are likely to run.

RACING WEIGHTS FOR FEMALE NOVICE AND BASIC COMPETITORS*

HEIGHT	SMALL FRAME	MEDIUM FRAME	LARGE FRAME
5'0"	96–104	101–113	109–125
5'1"	99–107	104–116	112–128
5'2"	102–110	107–119	115–131
5'3"	105–113	110–122	118–134
5'4"	108–116	113–126	121–138
5'5"	111–119	116–130	125–142
5'6"	114–123	120–135	129–146
5'7"	118–127	124–139	133–150
5'8"	122–131	128–143	137–154
5'9"	126–135	132–147	141–158
5'10"	130–140	136–151	145–163

*Developed by the Metropolitan Life Insurance Company.

THE BIG-BODIED RUNNER

This runner isn't fat, just overweight. His or her body wasn't designed for running. It is usually large-framed, with large muscle mass and average or higher body fat percentage. He or she is a victim of heredity. A seven-foot basketball player will never be a great marathoner no matter how fit; he is too tall. But then, Bill Rodgers will never do a whirling, in-your-face, slam-dunk in the Boston Garden either.

Unfortunately, not all running problems are physical. The large-bodied man or woman may never try running, or may quit after a short effort because the sport does not offer him or her enough satisfaction. Even races, which provide incentive and focus for training, do not reward these runners. We think they should.

Realistic goals are needed. Most of us have had to adjust our goals in some ways. You can't be what you weren't born to be. Races should offer prizes in weight divisions for the overweight (but not the overfat), based on the percentage of weight over those weights listed for competitors at their height and sex. For example, the 6'1" big-bodied runner who should weigh 160 pounds but weighs 10 percent more (176 pounds) could compete against runners of all heights with a similar 10 percent weight handicap.

RUNNING, CALORIES AND WEIGHT

The runner burns off one calorie per kilogram (2.2 pounds) of body weight for every kilometer (.62 miles) run. This is approximately 100 calories per mile—3500 calories equals one pound. Thus, you have to run 35 miles to run off one pound of permanent fat; how fast you run that mile means little. Running twice as fast will only increase your caloric expenditure by 10 percent. A heavier person will burn a few more calories per mile than a lighter person. Fortunately, you don't have to run 35 miles to burn one pound of fat. According to Dr. Gabe Mirkin, medical editor of *The Runner*, "There are three mechanisms activated by regular exercise that control weight gain. First of all, with regular running exercise, you will find that you eat less. This is because the 'appestat'—the mechanism that is in your brain—tells you when and how much to eat. As a beginner, you will eat less. Later, as a competitor, you may eat more, but the appestat helps prevent you from overeating. However, for some runners it doesn't do a good job. Second, you burn extra calories after you stop exercise. For four to six hours after exercising, your pulse rate and temperature continue to increase. During the course of a year, the extra calories that are burned from increased metabolism after exercising can amount to a weight loss of five to ten pounds. Third, you absorb less food.

"It is quite easy for a runner who eats too much and doesn't watch the scales to balloon up quickly. Some runners have a slower metabolic rate than others, or their appestat may be set too high. Those with a low metabolic rate can eat like a sparrow and still have a weight problem. For these runners, the solution is often higher mileage when the body can handle it."

When Bob Glover was the physical director at the Rome, New York, YMCA, he used to run with Pat Merola, a big-boned Italian with a high appestat, slow metabolism and a weakness for his wife's Italian cooking. If Pat cut his mileage back even slightly, he would gain as much as 20 pounds in two weeks. According to Dr. William Haskell, professor of medicine at Stanford University, although active, slim people take in about 600 calories a day more than their inactive, overweight friends, their appestat prevents them from consuming more than they will run off. This is why some people can eat twice as much and not gain weight.

Runners eat much more than the average person, who consumes and burns 1500 calories a day on an inactive schedule. Studies show that marathon runners consume and burn as much as 5,000–6,000 calories a day. This is why many of them munch on junk food all day long—they need more energy to keep their weight up, and their appestat tells them to eat.

Losing Weight

Improper or fad dieting can result in too low a level of calories, fat, carbohydrates or protein, resulting in health impairment. Just a few calories added or not burned per day will, in time, allow fat to creep up on you. Here are some tips for the runner trying to lose weight:

- The key is to run more, eat less; burn more calories, consume less.
- Watch what you eat. Try to switch to lower-calorie alternatives—water instead of soda, an apple instead of a candy bar.
- Eat smaller amounts, more often. Research shows that you can gain more on one big meal than on six smaller ones. Or eat the same foods in smaller proportions. Cut out desserts.
- Be disciplined. Keep a weight diary to force yourself to stick with your goal. Set a reasonable goal, such as five to ten pounds off before your next big race. Then more for your next race, and so on.
- Don't reduce liquid intake—you must replace lost fluids from sweat.
- Forget spot reducing gimmicks! Running combined with some weight training should take care of specific contours. Spot reducing is a myth.
- Run long and slow. Runners who run at a comfortable aerobic pace burn more fat than those who train at a higher heart-rate level.

You can't follow both a strict diet and a strict training program. One runner we know was determined to lose weight. He lost over fifty pounds and completed the 1981 New York Marathon. Then he tried to shave off a few more pounds by combining a diet of only 1000 calories a day with an 80-mile training week. Both were extremes that should have been avoided. The result was that he became extremely weak in the middle of one of his runs to work (due to glycogen depletion) and was forced to call a taxi. After that experience, he upped his caloric intake slightly and reduced his mileage slightly, along with the extra pounds.

Problems Caused by Being Overweight

Weight works against the runner. Every excess pound is an extra burden. Try running with ten pounds of weight strapped in your backpack. Here's how weight affects running:

- The runner hits the ground at a force of impact three times his or her body weight; the more you weigh, the harder you hit. Thus, you are more prone to injury.
- Heavier runners do not handle heat well. Body fat works as an insulator, trapping in heat built up while running. Heavier runners lose more fluids and risk dehydration. Drink extra fluids.
- Extra weight makes the heart work harder, possibly overtaxing it.
- Excess weight affects performance by lowering your aerobic capacity.

Aerobic Capacity and Weight

As mentioned previously, aerobic capacity is the ability to take in and use oxygen to do the work: running. Since your aerobic capacity (maximum oxygen uptake or consumption) is measured by dividing the amount of oxygen you can consume per minute by your body weight, each pound or kilogram of extra weight reduces your aerobic capacity and thus your race times. There are three ways to improve this capacity:

1. Increase your ability to consume oxygen by improving your aerobic fitness level.

2. Decrease your body weight, making you more efficient at your present ability to consume oxygen.

3. Or both—increase aerobic fitness as you lose weight. As you increase your mileage, you gain by increasing cardiovascular fitness and by losing weight.

According to exercise physiologist K. J. Cureton at the University of Georgia, tests on runners showed that their aerobic capacity declines by one milliliter of oxygen per kilogram of weight per minute for every one percent of added weight. Studies of marathoners show that a five percent drop in body weight results in a five percent improvement in performance.

The bigger and stronger your engine and the lighter your chassis, the faster you can race—up to the point where loss of weight would make you weaker.

WEIGHT AND RACE TIMES

We have developed the following formula, which has proven to be fairly accurate at estimating how much faster you could run if you lost weight and kept your level of fitness and lean body weight (muscle and bone) the same.

Men

Consult the racing weight charts on pages 476–78 and find the weight recommended for your height. To calculate your race times, add or subtract minutes according to this formula:

- For the 10 km, add approximately 2½ minutes per 10 pounds of extra weight above the figure listed.
- For the marathon, add approximately 10 minutes per 10 pounds.

For example, take a 6'1", 160-pound competitive runner who runs about 42 minutes for the 10 km and a 3:20 marathon. If he were to weigh 20 pounds more, he would run approximately 47 minutes for 10 km and 3:40 for the marathon.

At the top of the opposite page is a chart showing comparisons for this particular size male runner—6'1" and about 160 pounds. You can see how excess weight may limit his potential.

MEN—WEIGHT AND RACE TIMES

WEIGHT	10 KM TIME (+2:30 PER 10 LBS.)	MARATHON TIME (+10 MIN. PER 10 LBS.)
150	39:30	3:10
160	**42**	**3:20**
170	44:30	3:30
180	47	3:40
190	49:30	3:50

Women

Consult the racing weight charts on pages 479–81 and find the weight recommended for your height. Calculate your race times by adding or subtracting minutes according to this formula:

• For the 10 km race, add approximately 4 minutes per 10 pounds of extra weight above the figure listed.

• For the marathon, add approximately 20 minutes per 10 pounds.

For example, take a 5'4", 110-pound woman competitor who runs the 10 km in 40 minutes and the marathon in 3:05. If she were to weigh 20 pounds more, her times would be 48 minutes and 3:45. Here's a chart on her potential:

WOMEN—WEIGHT AND RACE TIMES

WEIGHT	10 KM TIME (+4 MIN. PER 10 LBS.)	MARATHON TIME (+20 MIN. PER 10 LBS.)
100	36	2:45
110	**40**	**3:05**
120	44	3:25
130	48	3:45
140	52	4:05

Note: For both men's and women's formulas, improvements by weight loss cannot be expected beyond ten pounds less than the starting weight: the weight of the competitive runner of your height. Weight loss below the starting figure may not result in faster times without increased training and a certain amount of inherited talent. The charts are only guidelines to show you how excess weight slows you down. With time and training, you will find the best weight for your height and competitive level.

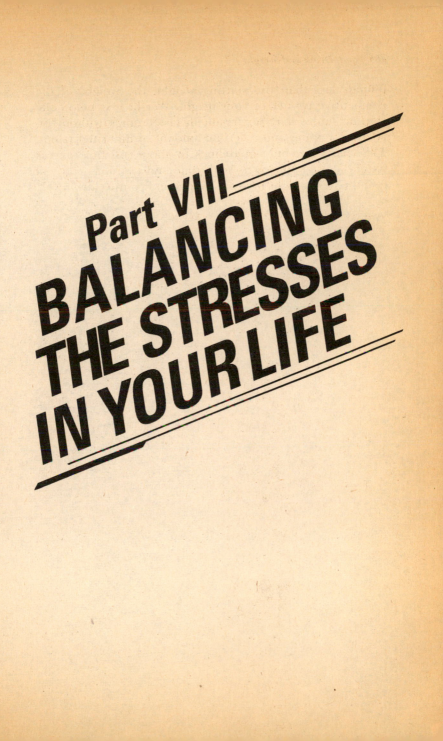

Part VIII
BALANCING THE STRESSES IN YOUR LIFE

31. THE RUNNER'S TRIANGLE

When the running boom first spread across America, one of the popular clichés of the time was that running itself created a positive addiction. It was an excellent way of overcoming the stress in our lives and of adding purpose and direction. Many of us found running to be, indeed, a positive force in our lives. But when we cross over into competitive running, for some of us, that can change. Competitive running can become too all-encompassing; it can become our primary reason for living. Competitive racers at the top make running their way of life and accept the commitment, pain and failure with the success and, often, financial rewards. For them, the addiction to running has tangible benefits. But for most of us who run races and train hard but also have lives away from running, becoming too dedicated, too committed to running can create a very real problem: negative addiction.

Bob Glover, seeing the wreckage of bodies and dreams after the hot 1978 New York Marathon, coined the phrase "the runner's triangle of life." He was distressed that so many competitive runners had invested too much of their emotional, as well as their physical, being into that race, only to lose it all against the heat and the sun. The runner must balance the triangle of life: body, mind, and soul. He or she must balance the physical side of running, the intellectual and career side of life, and the spiritual and emotional side.

Running can be the central focus in our lives and can give us a positive reward, something we succeed at. But we need to balance it with other parts of our lives or running will become negative, draining the good in us. The runner who puts virtually his or her entire reason for living into running a race, or a series of races, is probably psychologically wounded. He or she is missing the point. Running must be fun; it must balance your life (making you more fit, less sedentary); it should bring you new friends, goals, a fresh sense of who you are and where you are going. It should not damage your career, family, love life; it should not make you into something you are not meant to be.

If you are under pressure at work, back off the running. Exercise for stress management, and cut the distance, speed and structure of your runs until the stress eases. Open yourself up and talk to other runners about stress. Don't take out the stresses of your life on your running. You will make yourself more tense and injury-prone. Pounding out your tension on hard pavement is a one-sided battle.

One middle-aged woman we know went through an emotional divorce, precipitated in part by her new independence as a runner, which her husband didn't understand. She turned all her frustrations loose on her running, and improved her times and filled her trophy case. But she was obsessed. She was showing him—she was having an affair with running. When she finally crashed—a cold led to pneumonia and bed rest—she realized that she had lost perspective; she had neglected her children and herself. She put running into perspective, reassembled her family and modified her career goals. She rebuilt her triangle, but not without pain and hard-learned lessons.

Dr. Edward Colt believes that many running-related injuries are caused by overuse due to blind addiction to running. "Running addiction cannot be gauged by mileage. Some runners who run 140 miles per week know exactly when they should ease back or stop their training. Some runners who run as little as twenty miles per week may be strongly addicted. Running addiction is predictable. The addictive personality is a lifelong disorder and an afflicted individual will have shown unmistakable signs before he ever starts to run. Overindulgence in one or more of the following: food, alcohol, drugs, sex, gambling, cigarettes and so forth is usually evident in the past history of the running addict. Often running is used as therapy for these more harmful addictions. If you are a running addict, face it and be careful. If you are not a running addict, you are a most unusual person."

Runners think that because they are running they are automatically mentally healthy. The sport does indeed help us improve our self-image, and that carries over into other activities. It is false, however, to believe that running by itself will make us happy, healthy or emotionally balanced.

One of the better New York City runners jumped out of a window to his death not long ago. His running didn't save him from other stresses. A 45-year-old British executive died from an overdose of aspirin. In his suicide note, he said that life was not worth living: he couldn't run because of a knee injury. That man had lost his perspective; running had become an obsession, a distortion of reality.

Putting running ahead of living soon distorts our runner's triangle. Noel Carroll, a former Irish Olympic runner, wrote in *The Runner's Book*: "The reality of the runner's life is that somebody else is always affected by his running. It may be a spouse, or a girlfriend, or a boyfriend, or a mother and father, or the children. To ignore the fall-out is to court disaster. It can create an atmosphere that does nobody any good—and certainly not the runner."

What runners need is balance. Sacrifices do need to be made, but these should be balanced with the whole of one's life. With good scheduling, you can balance your triangle: keep running (body), job or school (mind), and family or friends (soul) in perspective.

WORK

According to William P. Morgan, director of the Sports Psychology Laboratory at the University of Wisconsin: "As the individual becomes more aware of self, he starts losing interest not only in his relationships, but also in such matters as vocational achievement. Promotions are, in fact, often a bother. They can mean increased responsibility, additional stress, the possibility of relocation and less time and attention for self. . . . Needless to say, such a point of view not only can limit 'professional growth,' but it can jeopardize one's actual employment."

Some serious runners hold running-related jobs which carry limited responsibility and flexible hours, but also limited income. Bill Rodgers and Frank Shorter sacrificed for years to become the best in their sport and became financially independent only after achieving a certain status. Sacrifices must be balanced with the possible payoff. If you have only limited ability, but work in a running-shoe store to have time out to train, perhaps your should reevaluate your situation.

If both partners work and there are no children, the couple may have some flexibility. One may be able to work less in order to be able to train more. Sacrifices are balanced with realistic payoffs. To throw away a potential in sport is a waste. But to throw away your life to chase a futile dream is a greater waste.

Success in a running program, as in business, often depends on developing a routine. It is much easier to plan your running time if your work hours are consistent and regular than if your hours are constantly changing. You may find your lunch hour to be a convenient time to run as long as there is a place to sponge and change when you are done. If you are within distance, running to and from work, using a small backpack to carry your clothes, will let you make good use of your commuting time and interfere less with family and work.

FAMILY AND FRIENDS

When you start a running program or build for a big race, you should make your family circle or friends into allies, a support group. It takes skill to handle family members. The best way to win at the game is to be flexible, sharing your running interest with your family and friends and accommodating household duties and babysitting in your schedule.

The Glovers learned all about planning when baby Christopher arrived in 1981. Bob, like so many new fathers, suddenly found himself in many roles: husband, father, breadwinner, coach, author and sometime runner. He started jogging with his wife to help her get back into shape, pushing Christopher in his carriage as they jogged. They became quite an attraction in Central Park: "Awwww, look at that *family*!"

But are running and marriage compatible? In 1980, *Parade* magazine, in an article titled "Running Out of Marriage," stated: "The more runners run, the more conflicts they experience with spouses or close relatives. A poll taken in the Boston area indicated that runners who averaged more than 70 miles a week were far more likely to have marital problems than occasional or moderate runners.

"Nearly half the full-time runners admitted that their partners felt neglected. In 40 percent of the cases, the friction from running was serious enough to lead to divorce."

Forty percent of married runners putting in more than 70 miles a week got divorced! Is it difficult to train seriously and keep others happy? You must work at keeping others happy as much as you do at running. Running can become an affair—it can become a demanding lover that breaks you apart from your friends, family or loved ones. The divorce rate, for example, among New York Marathon runners is 3.5 times the national average.

Let's talk about partners. A "partner" here is the other person in your life who means a lot to you. There are two types of running partnerships: both partners run together; one runs but the other doesn't. When both run, they have a shared interest; running together adds time together. Many romances begin as runners meet—both of us got "caught" this way.

The biggest problem, we have found, occurs when the woman (especially if she is the wife) runs and the man doesn't. Or where both run, and the woman runs better (faster, more competitively). Held back by our society both as an athlete and in her career, she now finds more self-confidence and becomes more independent. She may rebel against some of the traditions of marriage imposed by her husband (who does the shopping, who cooks, who tends the kids?) or lose respect for him if he is overweight and underexercised. He, in turn, may become jealous of her new independence and her new running friends. Small issues lead to larger ones: dinner is late while she runs; she postpones having a baby as her running increases in importance.

She might try making him into a cheerleader; he could supply her with liquids at spots along the way during races. But she should never try to make him into a coach, and he must never try to coach her (particularly if he doesn't run himself). Coaching and marriage make a volatile mixture.

The woman runner carries more pressures than a man. She oftentimes balances a career, running and marriage, and then must decide whether to accept the physical limitations of pregnancy and the time limitations of motherhood. Some women runners postpone all of these choices except running. Linda Schreiber, on the other hand, wrote *Marathon Mom*, which details how she took up running after becoming the mother of five (including quadruplets arriving in one fast finish) and reached the sub-three-hour marathon level. Her husband and kids cheer along her routes.

Most runners view their running as well integrated with

other aspects of their lives and even making a positive contribution to their nonrunning side. But the line between positive and negative addiction is thin. Some ten out of twelve runners interviewed by Michael Sachs and David Pargman of Florida State University said that they had a psychological or physiological dependence on running; they were placing running first in their lives. Some runners lose perspective altogether. Running becomes an end, not a means. The final stages of this negative addiction occur when running becomes your job and your job is viewed avocationally, when loved ones and friends are placed second, when the exercise addict (like the alcoholic or heroin addict) will not stop running even when faced with serious injury.

When most runners move over the line from dedication to obsession, Dr. Brent Waters, a clinician and researcher in exercise psychology at Royal Ottawa Hospital, says, it is a transient overindulgence. "Nevertheless, obsession with running appears to be becoming a more serious problem. Avoidable overuse syndromes are becoming all too frequent, and the families of some runners are becoming more vocal in their justified complaints that they are being relegated to a secondary role in the runner's life."

Scary? Look around you. Look inside yourself. Don't let the runner's triangle collapse on you and your loved ones in exchange for more mileage and faster times.

APPENDICES

BASIC PHYSIOLOGY TERMS

1. *Aerobic:* Running "with oxygen" at a conversational pace well within your training heart-rate range. All easy endurance runs are done aerobically.

2. *Aerobic capacity:* The ability to supply oxygen to the muscle tissues. Highly conditioned runners have higher aerobic capacities and can race at a faster pace more comfortably than less-conditioned runners. A runner with a higher aerobic capacity may fail to beat another runner, however, since performance is affected by such things as form, style, mental toughness, ability to run with lactic acid, proper pacing, natural speed, muscle strength, endurance, and so forth.

3. *Cardiorespiratory systems:* Endurance running improves the efficiency of both your ability to transport blood and oxygen by the heart and blood vessels (cardiovascular system) and your ability to breathe in air and exchange oxygen and carbon dioxide through the lungs and pulmonary arteries (circulorespiratory system). We combine these systems into the term "cardiorespiratory systems."

4. *Anaerobic:* This means "running without oxygen." When this happens, oxygen debt occurs, lactic acid accumulates, breathing becomes heavy, and "the Bear" may

jump on your back. Anaerobic running is running above your training heart-rate range. All racing includes some anaerobic and some aerobic running. The shorter and faster the race, the more you will run (and thus need to train) anaerobically. Fast speed-training runs will condition you to this.

5. *Aerobic-anaerobic borderline:* This is running at the edge of being out of breath, near 85 percent of your maximum heart rate, the top of your training heart-rate range. As you become better conditioned, you will be able to run at a faster pace before reaching this point; thus, you can extend your aerobic-anaerobic borderline and race faster. Some training runs are done at this borderline in order to push it back—condition you—so you can run at this intense pace. It is also called the "anaerobic threshold."

6. *Lactic acid:* A chemical substance released in the bloodstream when you run very fast—anaerobically, or in oxygen debt—that leads to muscle fatigue.

7. *Oxygen debt:* When you can't supply enough oxygen by normal aerobic means, you borrow energy, chemically causing a build-up of lactic acid in your muscles. When you slow down or stop running, you repay the debt—recover—and continue to function aerobically.

8. *Glycogen:* A starchlike substance stored in muscle tissues which is created from carbohydrates and used as the principal fuel for long-distance runners.

9. *The Bear:* The feeling of extreme fatigue and tightness caused by a build-up of lactic acid. The Bear will "jump on your back" when you try to sprint very hard or during short, fast races, because you cannot supply the needed oxygen to meet the demand. You go into oxygen debt.

10. *The Wall:* The point during a long run or race at which your body is running out of glycogen and shifts more to fat as an energy source. This happens at about 20 miles. You feel weary, heavy-legged because you can't supply your muscles with energy fast enough to keep working efficiently. The result is often a dramatic slowdown in pace

as you "hit the Wall." You may be able to push back the Wall by carbohydrate loading—which supplies extra glycogen storage—and taking long training runs, which condition the body to burn fat more efficiently.

11. *Fast-twitch muscle fibers:* One of two types of fibers. These contract rapidly and exhaust glycogen quickly during fast sprinting. Track sprinters have a predominance of these fibers. If you lack leg speed, it is largely because you weren't born with enough of these fibers in proportion to slow-twitch fibers.

12. *Slow-twitch muscle fibers:* These fibers burn glycogen slowly and efficiently during long-distance runs. Runners with approximately 70 percent slow-twitch fibers and 30 percent fast-twitch are usually better at the 5 km–10 km distances. Most marathon runners have a higher proportion of slow-twitch fibers, 80 to 90 percent.

13. *Training effect:* The pace you must train at to benefit from your exercise (at least 60 to 70 percent of maximum heart rate). The upper limit of your training heart-rate range for aerobic endurance running is 85 percent of maximum heart rate.

RHYTHM AND POWER WORKOUT GUIDES

The rhythm and power workout guides are only estimates of what you should and can do. In some cases the suggested ranges of quantity may be too hard or too easy for you. Adjust to fit your specific needs.

ONE MILE TRAINING

INEXPERIENCED MILER

DISTANCE	FAST RHYTHMIC PACE			MED RHYTHMIC PACE			SLOW RHYTHMIC PACE		
	Quant	Inten	Rest	Quant	Inten	Rest	Quant	Inten	Rest
220	6–10	880	2 min.	8–12	1 mile	1 min.	10–15	5 km	1 min.
440	4–6	880	3 min.	6–10	1 mile	2 min.	8–10	5 km	2 min.
880	—	—	—	3–4	1 mile	3 min.	4–6	5 km	3 min.
1 MILE	—	—	—	—	—	—	3–4	5 km	3 min.
SHORT HILLS	—	—	—	—	—	—	—	—	—
LONG HILLS	—	—	—	—	—	—	—	—	—

EXPERIENCED MILER

DISTANCE	FAST RHYTHMIC PACE			MED RHYTHMIC PACE			SLOW RHYTHMIC PACE		
	Quant	Inten	Rest	Quant	Inten	Rest	Quant	Inten	Rest
220	10–15	880	1 min.	8–16	1 mile	¾ min.	10–20	5 km	¾ min.
440	6–10	880	3 min.	6–12	1 mile	2 min.	8–16	5 km	1½ min.
880	—	—	—	3–6	1 mile	3 min.	6–10	5 km	2 min.
1 MILE	—	—	—	—	—	—	3–5	5 km	3 min.
SHORT HILLS	—	—	—	—	—	—	6–12	5 km	*
LONG HILLS	—	—	—	—	—	—	—	—	—

*Hill Rest Periods: The time required to run back down the hill at your normal endurance training pace.

5 KM TRAINING

NOVICE COMPETITOR

DISTANCE	FAST RHYTHMIC PACE			MED RHYTHMIC PACE			SLOW RHYTHMIC PACE		
	Quant	Inten	Rest	Quant	Inten	Rest	Quant	Inten	Rest
220	—	—	—	6–10	5 km	1 min.	8–12	10 miles	1 min.
440	—	—	—	4–8	5 km	2 min.	6–8	10 miles	2 min.
880	—	—	—	3–4	5 km	4 min.	4–6	10 miles	3 min.
1 MILE	—	—	—	—	—	—	2–3	10 miles	4 min.
SHORT HILLS	—	—	—	—	—	—	5–8	10 miles	*
LONG HILLS	—	—	—	—	—	—	—	—	—

BASIC COMPETITOR

DISTANCE	FAST RHYTHMIC PACE			MED RHYTHMIC PACE			SLOW RHYTHMIC PACE		
	Quant	Inten	Rest	Quant	Inten	Rest	Quant	Inten	Rest
220	6–10	1 mile	1½min.	8–12	5 km	1 min.	10–14	10 miles	½ min.
440	4–8	1 mile	2 min.	6–10	5 km	2 min.	8–10	10 miles	1 min.
880	2–3	1 mile	3 min.	4–6	5 km	3 min.	4–6	10 miles	2 min.
1 MILE	—	—	—	2–4	5 km	3 min.	3–4	10 miles	3 min.
SHORT HILLS	—	—	—	—	—	—	8–10	10 miles	*
LONG HILLS	—	—	—	—	—	—	—	—	—

ADVANCED COMPETITOR

DISTANCE	FAST RHYTHMIC PACE			MED RHYTHMIC PACE			SLOW RHYTHMIC PACE		
	Quant	Inten	Rest	Quant	Inten	Rest	Quant	Inten	Rest
220	8–12	1 mile	1 min.	10–16	5 km	¾ min.	12–20	10 miles	½ min.
440	6–10	1 mile	2 min.	8–12	5 km	1½min.	10–14	10 miles	1 min.
880	3–4	1 mile	3 min.	6–8	5 km	2 min.	6–8	10 miles	2 min.
1 MILE	—	—	—	3–4	5 km	3 min.	4–5	10 miles	2 min.
SHORT HILLS	—	—	—	8–10	5 km	*	10–14	10 miles	*
LONG HILLS	—	—	—	5–7	5 km	*	—	—	—

CHAMPION COMPETITOR

DISTANCE	FAST RHYTHMIC PACE			MED RHYTHMIC PACE			SLOW RHYTHMIC PACE		
	Quant	Inten	Rest	Quant	Inten	Rest	Quant	Inten	Rest
220	10–16	1 mile	1 min.	12–20	5 km	¾ min.	14–25	10 miles	½ min.
440	8–12	1 mile	1½min.	12–16	5 km	1½min.	12–20	10 miles	1 min.
880	4–6	1 mile	3 min.	8–10	5 km	2 min.	8–10	10 miles	2 min.
1 MILE	—	—	—	4–5	5 km	3 min.	5–6	10 miles	2 min.
SHORT HILLS	—	—	—	8–12	5 km	*	12–18	10 miles	*
LONG HILLS	—	—	—	6–8	5 km	*	—	—	—

*Hill Rest Periods: The time required to run back down the hill at your normal endurance training pace.

10 KM TRAINING

	DISTANCE	FAST RHYTHMIC PACE			MED RHYTHMIC PACE			SLOW RHYTHMIC PACE		
		Quant	Inten	Rest	Quant	Inten	Rest	Quant	Inten	Rest
NOVICE COMPETITOR	220	—	—	—	—	—	—	—	—	—
	440	—	—	—	6–10	10 km	2 min.	6–10	½ mar	1 min.
	880	—	—	—	4–8	10 km	3 min.	4–8	½ mar	2 min.
	1 MILE	—	—	—	3–4	10 km	4 min.	4–5	½ mar	3 min.
	SHORT HILLS	—	—	—	4–6	10 km	*	—	—	—
	LONG HILLS	—	—	—	2–4	10 km	*	—	—	—
BASIC COMPETITOR	220	—	—	—	—	—	—	—	—	—
	440	6–10	5 km	2 min.	8–12	10 km	1½ min.	10–15	½ mar	1 min.
	880	4–6	5 km	3 min.	6–8	10 km	2 min.	6–10	½ mar	2 min.
	1 MILE	2–4	5 km	3 min.	4–5	10 km	3 min.	5–7	½ mar	3 min.
	SHORT HILLS	—	—	—	8–10	10 km	*	10–12	½ mar	*
	LONG HILLS	—	—	—	4–6	10 km	*	—	—	—
ADVANCED COMPETITOR	220	—	—	—	—	—	—	—	—	—
	440	8–12	5 km	1½ min.	12–16	10 km	1½ min.	12–20	½ mar	¾ min.
	880	6–8	5 km	2 min.	8–10	10 km	2 min.	8–10	½ mar	1 min.
	1 MILE	3–4	5 km	3 min.	4–6	10 km	3 min.	5–8	½ mar	2 min.
	SHORT HILLS	8–10	5 km	*	10–15	10 km	*	12–15	½ mar	*
	LONG HILLS	5–7	5 km	*	6–8	10 km	*	—	—	—
CHAMPION COMPETITOR	220	—	—	—	—	—	—	—	—	—
	440	12–16	5 km	1½ min.	12–20	10 km	1 min.	16–20	½ mar	½ min.
	880	8–10	5 km	2 min.	8–12	10 km	1–2 min.	10–12	½ mar	½–1 min.
	1 MILE	4–5	5 km	3 min.	5–8	10 km	2–3 min.	6–8	½ mar	1–2 min.
	SHORT HILLS	8–12	5 km	*	12–18	10 km	*	16–20	½ mar	*
	LONG HILLS	6–8	5 km	*	8–10	10 km	*	—	—	—

* Hill Rest Periods: The time required to run back down the hill at your normal endurance training pace.

MARATHON TRAINING

NOVICE COMPETITOR

DISTANCE	FAST RHYTHMIC PACE			MED RHYTHMIC PACE			SLOW RHYTHMIC PACE		
	Quant	Inten	Rest	Quant	Inten	Rest	Quant	Inten	Rest
220	—	—	—	—	—	—	—	—	—
440	—	—	—	6–10	10 km	2 min.	8–10	mar	1 min.
880	—	—	—	4–8	10 km	3 min.	5–8	mar	2 min.
1 MILE	—	—	—	3–4	10 km	4 min.	4–5	mar	3 min.
SHORT HILLS	—	—	—	4–6	10 km	*	—	—	—
LONG HILLS	—	—	—	2–4	10 km	*	—	—	—

BASIC COMPETITOR

DISTANCE	FAST RHYTHMIC PACE			MED RHYTHMIC PACE			SLOW RHYTHMIC PACE		
	Quant	Inten	Rest	Quant	Inten	Rest	Quant	Inten	Rest
220	—	—	—	—	—	—	—	—	—
440	4–6	5 km–4 miles	2 min.	8–12	10 km	1½min.	10–15	mar	1 min.
880	3–4	5 km–4 miles	3 min.	6–8	10 km	2 min.	6–10	mar	2 min.
1 MILE	2–3	5 km–4 miles	3 min.	4–5	10 km	3 min.	5–8	mar	3 min.
SHORT HILLS	—	—	—	8–10	10 km	*	10–12	mar	*
LONG HILLS	—	—	—	4–6	10 km	*	—	—	—

ADVANCED COMPETITOR

DISTANCE	FAST RHYTHMIC PACE			MED RHYTHMIC PACE			SLOW RHYTHMIC PACE		
	Quant	Inten	Rest	Quant	Inten	Rest	Quant	Inten	Rest
220	—	—	—	—	—	—	—	—	—
440	8–12	5 km–4 miles	2 min.	12–16	10 km	1½min.	12–20	mar	¾ min.
880	6–8	5 km–4 miles	3 min.	8–10	10 km	2 min.	8–10	mar	1 min.
1 MILE	3–4	5 km–4 miles	3 min.	4–6	10 km	3 min.	5–8	mar	2 min.
SHORT HILLS	8–10	5 km–4 miles	*	10–15	10 km	*	12–15	mar	*
LONG HILLS	5–7	5 km–4 miles	*	6–8	10 km	*	—	—	—

CHAMPION COMPETITOR

DISTANCE	FAST RHYTHMIC PACE			MED RHYTHMIC PACE			SLOW RHYTHMIC PACE		
	Quant	Inten	Rest	Quant	Inten	Rest	Quant	Inten	Rest
220	—	—	—	—	—	—	—	—	—
440	10–15	5 km–4 miles	1½min.	12–20	10 km	1 min.	16–20	mar	½ min.
880	6–8	5 km–4 miles	2 min.	8–12	10 km	1–2 min.	10–12	mar	½–1 min.
1 MILE	4–5	5 km–4 miles	3 min.	5–8	10 km	2–3 min.	6–8	mar	1–2 min.
SHORT HILLS	8–12	5 km–4 miles	*	12–18	10 km	*	16–20	mar	*
LONG HILLS	6–8	5 km–4 miles	*	8–10	10 km	*	—	—	—

*Hill Rest Periods: The time required to run back down the hill at your normal endurance training pace.

POWER WORKOUT GUIDE

NOVICE COMPETITOR

DISTANCE	Quantity	Intensity	Rest
220			
440			
880	Not Recommended		
1 MILE			
SHORT HILLS			

BASIC COMPETITOR

DISTANCE	Quantity	Intensity	Rest
220	Not Recommended		
440	Not Recommended		
880	2–3	90% effort	6–10 min.
1 MILE	1–2	90% effort	6–10 min.
SHORT HILLS	Not Recommended		

ADVANCED COMPETITOR

DISTANCE	Quantity	Intensity	Rest
220	6–8	90% effort	4–6 min.
440	4–6	90% effort	5–8 min.
880	3–4	90% effort	6–10 min.
1 MILE	2–3	90% effort	6–10 min.
SHORT HILLS	4–6	90% effort	5–8 min.

CHAMPION COMPETITOR
EXPERIENCED CROSS-COUNTRY RUNNER / EXPERIENCED MILER

DISTANCE	Quantity	Intensity	Rest
220	6–8	90% effort	4–6 min.
440	4–6	90% effort	5–8 min.
880	3–4	90% effort	6–10 min.
1 MILE	2–3	90% effort	6–10 min.
SHORT HILLS	4–6	90% effort	5–8 min.

90% EFFORT GUIDE

ESTIMATE OF YOUR ALL-OUT TIME/ MILE	90% EFFORT/ MILE	90% EFFORT/ 880	90% EFFORT/ 440	90% EFFORT/ 220
4:00	4:24	1:55	52	26
4:10	4:35	2:00	54	26
4:20	4:46	2:05	56	27
4:30	4:57	2:10	58	27
4:40	5:08	2:15	60	28
4:50	5:19	2:20	62	28
5:00	5:30	2:25	64	29
5:10	5:41	2:30	66	29
5:20	5:52	2:35	68	30
5:30	6:03	2:40	70	30
5:40	6:14	2:45	72	31
5:50	6:25	2:50	74	31
6:00	6:36	2:55	76	32
6:10	6:47	3:00	78	32
6:20	6:58	3:05	80	33
6:30	7:09	3:10	82	33
6:40	7:20	3:15	84	34
6:50	7:31	3:20	86	34
7:00	7:42	3:25	88	35
7:10	7:53	3:30	90	35
7:20	8:04	3:35	92	36
7:30	8:15	3:40	94	36

Note: This chart is keyed to your all-out mile time. Estimate that time as your reference mark, then you can refer to the columns to estimate your 90% power effort for each distance, 220 to 1 mile. Example: if you can run a mile all-out in 6:00, you would run your power workouts as follows: 6:36 for 1 mile, 2:55 for 880, 76 for 440, 32 for 220. *Safety Note:* This chart is meant to be a flexible guide. Don't set too high a time goal. Be conservative.

RACE-TIME COMPARISON AND PREDICTOR CHART

5 KM	10 KM	10 MI	HALF MARATHON	MARATHON
14:00	29:00	48:20	1:02:30	2:15:00
14:15	29:30	49:10	1:03:45	2:17:30
14:30	30:00	50:00	1:05:00	2:20:00
14:45	30:30	50:50	1:06:15	2:22:30
15:00	31:00	51:40	1:07:30	2:25:00
15:15	31:30	52:30	1:08:45	2:27:30
15:30	32:00	53:20	1:10:00	2:30:00
15:45	32:30	54:10	1:11:15	2:32:30
16:00	33:00	55:00	1:12:30	2:35:00
16:15	33:30	55:50	1:13:45	2:37:30
16:30	34:00	56:40	1:15:00	2:40:00
16:45	34:30	57:30	1:16:15	2:42:30
17:00	35:00	58:20	1:17:30	2:45:00
17:15	35:30	59:10	1:18:45	2:47:30
17:30	36:00	60:00	1:20:00	2:50:00
17:45	36:30	60:50	1:21:15	2:52:30
18:00	37:00	61:40	1:22:30	2:55:00
18:15	37:30	62:30	1:23:45	2:57:30
18:30	38:00	63:20	1:25:00	3:00:00
18:45	38:30	64:10	1:26:15	3:02:30
19:00	39:00	65:00	1:27:30	3:05:00
19:15	39:30	65:50	1:28:45	3:07:30
19:30	40:00	66:40	1:30:00	3:10:00
19:45	40:30	67:30	1:31:15	3:12:30
20:00	41:00	68:20	1:32:30	3:15:00
20:15	41:30	69:10	1:33:45	3:17:30
20:30	42:00	70:00	1:35:00	3:20:00
20:45	42:30	70:50	1:36:15	3:22:30
21:00	43:00	71:40	1:37:30	3:25:00
21:15	43:30	72:30	1:38:45	3:27:30
21:30	44:00	73:20	1:40:00	3:30:00
21:45	44:30	74:10	1:41:15	3:32:30
22:00	45:00	75:00	1:42:30	3:35:00
22:15	45:30	75:50	1:43:45	3:37:30
22:30	46:00	76:40	1:45:00	3:40:00
22:45	46:30	77:30	1:46:15	3:42:30
23:00	47:00	78:20	1:47:30	3:45:00

5 KM	10 KM	10 MI	HALF MARATHON	MARATHON
23:15	47:30	79:10	1:48:45	3:47:30
23:30	48:00	80:00	1:50:00	3:50:00
23:45	48:30	80:50	1:51:15	3:52:30
24:00	49:00	81:40	1:52:30	3:55:00
24:15	49:30	82:30	1:53:45	3:57:30
24:30	50:00	83:20	1:55:00	4:00:00
24:45	50:30	84:10	1:56:15	4:02:30
25:00	51:00	85:00	1:57:30	4:05:00
25:15	51:30	85:50	1:58:45	4:07:30
25:30	52:00	86:40	2:00:00	4:10:00
25:45	52:30	87:30	2:01:15	4:12:30
26:00	53:00	88:20	2:02:30	4:15:00
26:15	53:30	89:10	2:03:45	4:17:30
26:30	54:00	90:00	2:05:00	4:20:00

Note: To predict your marathon time from your half-marathon time, multiply it by 2 and add 10 minutes. The predicted marathon times based on the 10 km and half-marathon times may be inaccurate (slower) by as much as five minutes for women.

PACING CHARTS

PACE PER MILE

How to Use

This chart explains what pace you race per mile for the most common racing distances—both in miles and kilometers. It can be used these ways:

1. *As a guide to even pacing.* For example, if you wish to run an even pace at 7 minutes per mile for a marathon race, your "splits" should be: 5 miles—35:00, 10 miles—70:00, half marathon—1:31:42, 15 miles—1:45:00, 20 miles—2:20:00, and at the marathon finish—3:03:32. If your course is marked in kilometers, your splits should be: 5 km—21:45, 10 km—43:30, 15 km—1:05:15, 20 km—1:27:00, 25 km—1:48:45, 30 km—2:10:30, and marathon—3:03:32.

2. *To help you select a starting pace.* If you wish to break 3½ hours for the marathon, for example, you can refer to the chart and find that this means you must average 8 minutes per mile. Thus you may choose to go out right at 8:00 pace, or perhaps at 7:50 per mile.

3. *To determine your average pace per mile for the race after you have finished.* If you ran 45:21 for 10 km, for example, the chart indicates that you averaged 7:18 per mile

(Times on this chart are in minutes:seconds or hours:minutes:seconds. Example—49:43, 3:29:45.)

MILE PACE	5 KM	5 MI	10 KM	15 KM	10 MI	20 KM	13.1 MI	15 MI	25 KM	30 KM	20 MI	MARATHON 26.219
4:30	13:59	22:30	27:58	41:57	45:00	55:55	58:57	1:07:30	1:09:55	1:23:54	1:30:00	1:57:59
4:31	14:02	22:35	28:04	42:06	45:10	56:08	59:10	1:07:45	1:10:10	1:24:12	1:30:20	1:58:25
4:32	14:05	22:40	28:10	42:15	45:20	56:20	59:23	1:08:00	1:10:25	1:24:30	1:30:40	1:58:52
4:33	14:08	22:45	28:16	42:25	45:30	56:33	59:36	1:08:15	1:10:41	1:24:50	1:31:00	1:59:18
4:34	14:11	22:50	28:23	42:34	45:40	56:45	59:49	1:08:30	1:10:56	1:25:08	1:31:20	1:59:44
4:35	14:14	22:55	28:29	42:43	45:50	56:58	1:00:03	1:08:45	1:11:12	1:25:26	1:31:40	2:00:10
4:36	14:17	23:00	28:35	42:52	46:00	57:10	1:00:16	1:09:00	1:11:27	1:25:46	1:32:00	2:00:36
4:37	14:21	23:05	28:41	43:02	46:10	57:22	1:00:29	1:09:15	1:11:43	1:26:04	1:32:20	2:01:03
4:38	14:24	23:10	28:47	43:11	46:20	57:35	1:00:42	1:09:30	1:11:59	1:26:22	1:32:40	2:01:29
4:39	14:27	23:15	28:54	43:20	46:30	57:47	1:00:55	1:09:45	1:12:14	1:26:42	1:33:00	2:01:55
4:40	14:30	23:20	29:00	43:30	46:40	58:00	1:01:08	1:10:00	1:12:30	1:27:00	1:33:20	2:02:21
4:41	14:33	23:25	29:06	43:39	46:50	58:12	1:01:21	1:10:15	1:12:45	1:27:18	1:33:40	2:02:48
4:42	14:36	23:30	29:12	43:48	47:00	58:25	1:01:34	1:10:30	1:13:00	1:27:36	1:34:00	2:03:14
4:43	14:39	23:35	29:18	43:58	47:10	58:37	1:01:47	1:10:45	1:13:16	1:27:56	1:34:20	2:03:40
4:44	14:42	23:40	29:25	44:07	47:20	58:49	1:02:00	1:11:00	1:13:31	1:28:14	1:34:40	2:04:06
4:45	14:45	23:45	29:31	44:16	47:30	59:02	1:02:13	1:11:15	1:13:47	1:28:32	1:35:00	2:04:32
4:46	14:49	23:50	29:37	44:26	47:40	59:14	1:02:27	1:11:30	1:14:03	1:28:52	1:35:20	2:04:59
4:47	14:52	23:55	29:43	44:35	47:50	59:27	1:02:40	1:11:45	1:14:19	1:29:10	1:35:40	2:05:25
4:48	14:55	24:00	29:50	44:44	48:00	59:39	1:02:53	1:12:00	1:14:34	1:29:28	1:36:00	2:05:51
4:49	14:58	24:05	29:56	44:54	48:10	59:52	1:03:06	1:12:15	1:14:50	1:29:48	1:36:20	2:06:17
4:50	15:01	24:10	30:02	45:03	48:20	1:00:04	1:03:19	1:12:30	1:15:05	1:30:06	1:36:40	2:06:44
4:51	15:04	24:15	30:08	45:12	48:30	1:00:16	1:03:32	1:12:45	1:15:20	1:30:24	1:37:00	2:07:10
4:52	15:07	24:20	30:14	45:22	48:40	1:00:29	1:03:45	1:13:00	1:15:36	1:30:44	1:37:20	2:07:36
4:53	15:10	24:25	30:21	45:31	48:50	1:00:41	1:03:58	1:13:15	1:15:51	1:31:02	1:37:40	2:08:02
4:54	15:13	24:30	30:27	45:40	49:00	1:00:54	1:04:11	1:13:30	1:16:07	1:31:20	1:38:00	2:08:28
4:55	15:17	24:35	30:33	45:50	49:10	1:01:06	1:04:24	1:13:45	1:16:23	1:31:40	1:38:20	2:08:55

MILE PACE	5 KM	5 MI	10 KM	15 KM	10 MI	20 KM	13.1 MI	15 MI	25 KM	30 KM	20 MI	MARATHON 26.219
4:56	15:20	24:40	30:39	45:59	49:20	1:01:19	1:04:38	1:14:00	1:16:39	1:31:58	1:38:40	2:09:21
4:57	15:23	24:45	30:45	46:08	49:30	1:01:31	1:04:51	1:14:15	1:16:54	1:32:16	1:39:00	2:09:47
4:58	15:26	24:50	30:52	46:18	49:40	1:01:43	1:05:04	1:14:30	1:17:10	1:32:36	1:39:20	2:10:13
4:59	15:29	24:55	30:58	46:27	49:50	1:01:56	1:05:17	1:14:45	1:17:25	1:32:54	1:39:40	2:10:39
5:00	15:32	25:00	31:04	46:36	50:00	1:02:08	1:05:30	1:15:00	1:17:40	1:33:12	1:40:00	2:11:06
5:01	15:35	25:05	31:10	46:45	50:10	1:02:21	1:05:43	1:15:15	1:17:56	1:33:30	1:40:20	2:11:32
5:02	15:38	25:10	31:17	46:55	50:20	1:02:33	1:05:56	1:15:30	1:18:11	1:33:50	1:40:40	2:11:58
5:03	15:41	25:15	31:23	47:04	50:30	1:02:46	1:06:09	1:15:45	1:18:27	1:34:08	1:41:00	2:12:24
5:04	15:44	25:20	31:29	47:13	50:40	1:02:58	1:06:22	1:16:00	1:18:42	1:34:26	1:41:20	2:12:51
5:05	15:48	25:25	31:35	47:23	50:50	1:03:10	1:06:36	1:16:15	1:18:58	1:34:46	1:41:40	2:13:17
5:06	15:51	25:30	31:41	47:32	51:00	1:03:23	1:06:49	1:16:30	1:19:14	1:35:04	1:42:00	2:13:43
5:07	15:54	25:35	31:48	47:41	51:10	1:03:35	1:07:02	1:16:45	1:19:29	1:35:22	1:42:20	2:14:09
5:08	15:57	25:40	31:54	47:51	51:20	1:03:48	1:07:15	1:17:00	1:19:45	1:35:42	1:42:40	2:14:35
5:09	16:00	25:45	32:00	48:00	51:30	1:04:00	1:07:28	1:17:15	1:20:00	1:36:00	1:43:00	2:15:02
5:10	16:03	25:50	32:06	48:09	51:40	1:04:13	1:07:41	1:17:30	1:20:16	1:36:18	1:43:20	2:15:28
5:11	16:06	25:55	32:12	48:19	51:50	1:04:25	1:07:54	1:17:45	1:20:31	1:36:38	1:43:40	2:15:54
5:12	16:09	26:00	32:19	48:28	52:00	1:04:37	1:08:07	1:18:00	1:20:46	1:36:56	1:44:00	2:16:20
5:13	16:12	26:05	32:25	48:37	52:10	1:04:50	1:08:20	1:18:15	1:21:02	1:37:14	1:44:20	2:16:47
5:14	16:16	26:10	32:31	48:47	52:20	1:05:02	1:08:33	1:18:30	1:21:18	1:37:34	1:44:40	2:17:13
5:15	16:19	26:15	32:37	48:56	52:30	1:05:15	1:08:47	1:18:45	1:21:34	1:37:52	1:45:00	2:17:39
5:16	16:22	26:20	32:44	49:05	52:40	1:05:27	1:09:00	1:19:00	1:21:49	1:38:10	1:45:20	2:18:05
5:17	16:25	26:25	32:50	49:15	52:50	1:05:39	1:09:13	1:19:15	1:22:04	1:38:30	1:45:40	2:18:31
5:18	16:28	26:30	32:56	49:24	53:00	1:05:52	1:09:26	1:19:30	1:22:20	1:38:48	1:46:00	2:18:58
5:19	16:31	26:35	33:02	49:33	53:10	1:06:04	1:09:39	1:19:45	1:22:35	1:39:06	1:46:20	2:19:24

MILE PACE	5 KM	5 MI	10 KM	15 KM	10 MI	20 KM	13.1 MI	15 MI	25 KM	30 KM	20 MI	MARATHON 26.219
5:20	16:34	26:40	33:08	49:43	53:20	1:06:17	1:09:52	1:20:00	1:22:51	1:39:26	1:46:40	2:19:50
5:21	16:37	26:45	33:15	49:52	53:30	1:06:29	1:10:05	1:20:15	1:23:06	1:39:44	1:47:00	2:20:16
5:22	16:40	26:50	33:21	50:01	53:40	1:06:42	1:10:18	1:20:30	1:23:22	1:40:02	1:47:20	2:20:43
5:23	16:44	26:55	33:27	50:11	53:50	1:06:54	1:10:31	1:20:45	1:23:38	1:40:22	1:47:40	2:21:09
5:24	16:47	27:00	33:33	50:20	54:00	1:07:06	1:10:44	1:21:00	1:23:53	1:40:40	1:48:00	2:21:35
5:25	16:50	27:05	33:39	50:29	54:10	1:07:19	1:10:58	1:21:15	1:24:09	1:40:58	1:48:20	2:22:01
5:26	16:53	27:10	33:46	50:39	54:20	1:07:31	1:11:11	1:21:30	1:24:24	1:41:18	1:48:40	2:22:27
5:27	16:56	27:15	33:52	50:48	54:30	1:07:44	1:11:24	1:21:45	1:24:40	1:41:36	1:49:00	2:22:54
5:28	16:59	27:20	33:58	50:57	54:40	1:07:56	1:11:37	1:22:00	1:24:55	1:41:54	1:49:20	2:23:20
5:29	17:02	27:25	34:04	51:06	54:50	1:08:09	1:11:50	1:22:15	1:25:11	1:42:12	1:49:40	2:23:46
5:30	17:05	27:30	34:11	51:16	55:00	1:08:21	1:12:03	1:22:30	1:25:26	1:42:32	1:50:00	2:24:12
5:31	17:08	27:35	34:17	51:25	55:10	1:08:33	1:12:16	1:22:45	1:25:41	1:42:50	1:50:20	2:24:38
5:32	17:11	27:40	34:23	51:34	55:20	1:08:46	1:12:29	1:23:00	1:25:57	1:43:08	1:50:40	2:25:05
5:33	17:15	27:45	34:29	51:44	55:30	1:08:58	1:12:42	1:23:15	1:26:13	1:43:28	1:51:00	2:25:31
5:34	17:18	27:50	34:35	51:53	55:40	1:09:11	1:12:55	1:23:30	1:26:29	1:43:46	1:51:20	2:25:57
5:35	17:21	27:55	34:42	52:02	55:50	1:09:23	1:13:08	1:23:45	1:26:44	1:44:04	1:51:40	2:26:23
5:36	17:24	28:00	34:48	52:12	56:00	1:09:36	1:13:22	1:24:00	1:27:00	1:44:24	1:52:00	2:26:50
5:37	17:27	28:05	34:54	52:21	56:10	1:09:48	1:13:35	1:24:15	1:27:15	1:44:42	1:52:20	2:27:16
5:38	17:30	28:10	35:00	52:30	56:20	1:10:00	1:13:48	1:24:30	1:27:30	1:45:00	1:52:40	2:27:42
5:39	17:33	28:15	35:06	52:40	56:30	1:10:13	1:14:01	1:24:45	1:27:46	1:45:20	1:53:00	2:28:08
5:40	17:36	28:20	35:13	52:49	56:40	1:10:25	1:14:14	1:25:00	1:28:01	1:45:38	1:53:20	2:28:34
5:41	17:39	28:25	35:19	52:58	56:50	1:10:38	1:14:27	1:25:15	1:28:17	1:45:56	1:53:40	2:29:01
5:42	17:43	28:30	35:25	53:08	57:00	1:10:50	1:14:40	1:25:30	1:28:33	1:46:16	1:54:00	2:29:27
5:43	17:46	28:35	35:31	53:17	57:10	1:11:03	1:14:53	1:25:45	1:28:49	1:46:34	1:54:20	2:29:53
5:44	17:49	28:40	35:38	53:26	57:20	1:11:15	1:15:06	1:26:00	1:29:04	1:46:52	1:54:40	2:30:19

MILE PACE	5 KM	5 MI	10 KM	15 KM	10 MI	20 KM	13.1 MI	15 MI	25 KM	30 KM	20 MI	MARATHON 26.219
5:45	17:52	28:45	35:44	53:36	57:30	1:11:27	1:15:19	1:26:15	1:29:19	1:47:12	1:55:00	2:30:46
5:46	17:55	28:50	35:50	53:45	57:40	1:11:40	1:15:33	1:26:30	1:29:35	1:47:30	1:55:20	2:31:12
5:47	17:58	28:55	35:56	53:54	57:50	1:11:52	1:15:46	1:26:45	1:29:50	1:47:48	1:55:40	2:31:38
5:48	18:01	29:00	36:02	54:04	58:00	1:12:05	1:15:59	1:27:00	1:30:06	1:48:08	1:56:00	2:32:04
5:49	18:04	29:05	36:09	54:13	58:10	1:12:17	1:16:12	1:27:15	1:30:21	1:48:26	1:56:20	2:32:30
5:50	18:07	29:10	36:15	54:22	58:20	1:12:30	1:16:25	1:27:30	1:30:37	1:48:44	1:56:40	2:32:57
5:51	18:11	29:15	36:21	54:32	58:30	1:12:42	1:16:38	1:27:45	1:30:53	1:49:04	1:57:00	2:33:23
5:52	18:14	29:20	36:27	54:41	58:40	1:12:54	1:16:51	1:28:00	1:31:08	1:49:22	1:57:20	2:33:49
5:53	18:17	29:25	36:33	54:50	58:50	1:13:07	1:17:04	1:28:15	1:31:24	1:49:40	1:57:40	2:34:15
5:54	18:20	29:30	36:40	54:59	59:00	1:13:19	1:17:17	1:28:30	1:31:39	1:49:58	1:58:00	2:34:42
5:55	18:23	29:35	36:46	55:09	59:10	1:13:32	1:17:30	1:28:45	1:31:55	1:50:18	1:58:20	2:35:08
5:56	18:26	29:40	36:52	55:18	59:20	1:13:44	1:17:44	1:29:00	1:32:10	1:50:36	1:58:40	2:35:34
5:57	18:29	29:45	36:58	55:27	59:30	1:13:57	1:17:57	1:29:15	1:32:25	1:50:54	1:59:00	2:36:00
5:58	18:32	29:50	37:05	55:37	59:40	1:14:09	1:18:10	1:29:30	1:32:40	1:51:14	1:59:20	2:36:26
5:59	18:35	29:55	37:11	55:46	59:50	1:14:21	1:18:23	1:29:45	1:32:56	1:51:32	1:59:40	2:36:53
6:00	18:38	30:00	37:17	55:55	1:00:00	1:14:34	1:18:36	1:30:00	1:33:12	1:51:50	2:00:00	2:37:19
6:01	18:42	30:05	37:23	56:05	1:00:10	1:14:46	1:18:49	1:30:15	1:33:28	1:52:10	2:00:20	2:37:45
6:02	18:45	30:10	37:29	56:14	1:00:20	1:14:59	1:19:02	1:30:30	1:33:44	1:52:28	2:00:40	2:38:11
6:03	18:48	30:15	37:36	56:23	1:00:30	1:15:11	1:19:15	1:30:45	1:33:59	1:52:46	2:01:00	2:38:37
6:04	18:51	30:20	37:42	56:33	1:00:40	1:15:24	1:19:28	1:31:00	1:34:15	1:53:06	2:01:20	2:39:04
6:05	18:54	30:25	37:48	56:42	1:00:50	1:15:36	1:19:41	1:31:15	1:34:30	1:53:24	2:01:40	2:39:30
6:06	18:57	30:30	37:54	56:51	1:01:00	1:15:48	1:19:55	1:31:30	1:34:45	1:53:42	2:02:00	2:39:56
6:07	19:00	30:35	38:00	57:01	1:01:10	1:16:01	1:20:08	1:31:45	1:35:01	1:54:02	2:02:20	2:40:22
6:08	19:03	30:40	38:07	57:10	1:01:20	1:16:13	1:20:21	1:32:00	1:35:16	1:54:20	2:02:40	2:40:49
6:09	19:06	30:45	38:13	57:19	1:01:30	1:16:26	1:20:34	1:32:15	1:35:32	1:54:38	2:03:00	2:41:15

MILE PACE	5 KM	5 MI	10 KM	15 KM	10 MI	20 KM	13.1 MI	15 MI	25 KM	30 KM	20 MI	MARATHON 26.219
6:10	19:10	30:50	38:19	57:29	1:01:40	1:16:38	1:20:47	1:32:30	1:35:48	1:54:58	2:03:20	2:41:41
6:11	19:13	30:55	38:25	57:38	1:01:50	1:16:51	1:21:00	1:32:45	1:36:04	1:55:16	2:03:40	2:42:07
6:12	19:16	31:00	38:32	57:47	1:02:00	1:17:03	1:21:13	1:33:00	1:36:19	1:55:34	2:04:00	2:42:33
6:13	19:19	31:05	38:38	57:57	1:02:10	1:17:15	1:21:26	1:33:15	1:36:34	1:55:58	2:04:20	2:43:00
6:14	19:22	31:10	38:44	58:06	1:02:20	1:17:28	1:21:39	1:33:30	1:36:50	1:56:12	2:04:40	2:43:26
6:15	19:25	31:15	38:50	58:15	1:02:30	1:17:40	1:21:53	1:33:45	1:37:05	1:56:30	2:05:00	2:43:52
6:16	19:28	31:20	38:56	58:25	1:02:40	1:17:53	1:22:06	1:34:00	1:37:21	1:56:50	2:05:20	2:44:18
6:17	19:31	31:25	39:03	58:34	1:02:50	1:18:05	1:22:19	1:34:15	1:37:36	1:57:08	2:05:40	2:44:45
6:18	19:34	31:30	39:09	58:43	1:03:00	1:18:18	1:22:32	1:34:30	1:37:52	1:57:26	2:06:00	2:45:11
6:19	19:37	31:35	39:15	58:52	1:03:10	1:18:30	1:22:45	1:34:45	1:38:07	1:57:44	2:06:20	2:45:37
6:20	19:41	31:40	39:21	59:02	1:03:20	1:18:42	1:22:58	1:35:00	1:38:23	1:58:04	2:06:40	2:46:03
6:21	19:44	31:45	39:27	59:11	1:03:30	1:18:55	1:23:11	1:35:15	1:38:39	1:58:22	2:07:00	2:46:29
6:22	19:47	31:50	39:34	59:20	1:03:40	1:19:07	1:23:24	1:35:30	1:38:54	1:58:40	2:07:20	2:46:56
6:23	19:50	31:55	39:40	59:30	1:03:50	1:19:20	1:23:37	1:35:45	1:39:10	1:59:00	2:07:40	2:47:22
6:24	19:53	32:00	39:46	59:39	1:04:00	1:19:32	1:23:50	1:36:00	1:39:25	1:59:18	2:08:00	2:47:48
6:25	19:56	32:05	39:52	59:48	1:04:10	1:19:45	1:24:04	1:36:15	1:39:41	1:59:36	2:08:20	2:48:14
6:26	19:59	32:10	39:58	59:58	1:04:20	1:19:57	1:24:17	1:36:30	1:39:56	1:59:56	2:08:40	2:48:41
6:27	20:02	32:15	40:05	1:00:07	1:04:30	1:20:09	1:24:30	1:36:45	1:40:11	2:00:14	2:09:00	2:49:07
6:28	20:05	32:20	40:11	1:00:16	1:04:40	1:20:22	1:24:43	1:37:00	1:40:27	2:00:32	2:09:20	2:49:33
6:29	20:09	32:25	40:17	1:00:26	1:04:50	1:20:34	1:24:56	1:37:15	1:40:43	2:00:52	2:09:40	2:49:59
6:30	20:12	32:30	40:23	1:00:35	1:05:00	1:20:47	1:25:09	1:37:30	1:40:59	2:01:10	2:10:00	2:50:25
6:31	20:15	32:35	40:30	1:00:44	1:05:10	1:20:59	1:25:22	1:37:45	1:41:14	2:01:28	2:10:20	2:50:52
6:32	20:18	32:40	40:36	1:00:54	1:05:20	1:21:12	1:25:35	1:38:00	1:41:30	2:01:48	2:10:40	2:51:18
6:33	20:21	32:45	40:42	1:01:03	1:05:30	1:21:24	1:25:48	1:38:15	1:41:45	2:02:06	2:11:00	2:51:44
6:34	20:24	32:50	40:48	1:01:12	1:05:40	1:21:36	1:26:01	1:38:30	1:42:00	2:02:24	2:11:20	2:52:10

MILE PACE	5 KM	5 MI	10 KM	15 KM	10 MI	20 KM	13.1 MI	15 MI	25 KM	30 KM	20 MI	MARATHON 26.219
6:35	20:27	32:55	40:54	1:01:22	1:05:50	1:21:49	1:26:15	1:38:45	1:42:16	2:02:44	2:11:40	2:52:37
6:36	20:30	33:00	41:01	1:01:31	1:06:00	1:22:01	1:26:28	1:39:00	1:42:31	2:03:02	2:12:00	2:53:03
6:37	20:33	33:05	41:07	1:01:40	1:06:10	1:22:14	1:26:41	1:39:15	1:42:47	2:03:20	2:12:20	2:53:29
6:38	20:37	33:10	41:13	1:01:50	1:06:20	1:22:26	1:26:54	1:39:30	1:43:03	2:03:40	2:12:40	2:53:55
6:39	20:40	33:15	41:19	1:01:59	1:06:30	1:22:39	1:27:07	1:39:45	1:43:19	2:03:58	2:13:00	2:54:21
6:40	20:43	33:20	41:25	1:02:08	1:06:40	1:22:51	1:27:20	1:40:00	1:43:34	2:04:16	2:13:20	2:54:48
6:41	20:46	33:25	41:32	1:02:18	1:06:50	1:23:03	1:27:33	1:40:15	1:43:49	2:04:36	2:13:40	2:55:14
6:42	20:49	33:30	41:38	1:02:27	1:07:00	1:23:16	1:27:46	1:40:30	1:44:05	2:04:54	2:14:00	2:55:40
6:43	20:52	33:35	41:44	1:02:36	1:07:10	1:23:28	1:27:59	1:40:45	1:44:20	2:05:12	2:14:20	2:56:06
6:44	20:55	33:40	41:50	1:02:46	1:07:20	1:23:41	1:28:12	1:41:00	1:44:36	2:05:32	2:14:40	2:56:32
6:45	20:58	33:45	41:57	1:02:55	1:07:30	1:23:53	1:28:25	1:41:15	1:44:51	2:05:50	2:15:00	2:56:59
6:46	21:01	33:50	42:03	1:03:04	1:07:40	1:24:06	1:28:39	1:41:30	1:45:07	2:06:08	2:15:20	2:57:25
6:47	21:04	33:55	42:09	1:03:13	1:07:50	1:24:18	1:28:52	1:41:45	1:45:22	2:06:26	2:15:40	2:57:51
6:48	21:08	34:00	42:15	1:03:23	1:08:00	1:24:30	1:29:05	1:42:00	1:45:38	2:06:46	2:16:00	2:58:17
6:49	21:11	34:05	42:21	1:03:32	1:08:10	1:24:43	1:29:18	1:42:15	1:45:54	2:07:04	2:16:20	2:58:44
6:50	21:14	34:10	42:28	1:03:41	1:08:20	1:24:55	1:29:31	1:42:30	1:46:09	2:07:22	2:16:40	2:59:10
6:51	21:17	34:15	42:34	1:03:51	1:08:30	1:25:08	1:29:44	1:42:45	1:46:25	2:07:42	2:17:00	2:59:36
6:52	21:20	34:20	42:40	1:04:00	1:08:40	1:25:20	1:29:57	1:43:00	1:46:40	2:08:00	2:17:20	3:00:02
6:53	21:23	34:25	42:46	1:04:09	1:08:50	1:25:33	1:30:10	1:43:15	1:46:56	2:08:18	2:17:40	3:00:28
6:54	21:26	34:30	45:52	1:04:19	1:09:00	1:25:45	1:30:23	1:43:30	1:47:11	2:08:38	2:18:00	3:00:55
6:55	21:29	34:35	42:59	1:04:28	1:09:10	1:25:57	1:30:36	1:43:45	1:47:26	2:08:56	2:18:20	3:01:21
6:56	21:32	34:40	43:05	1:04:37	1:09:20	1:26:10	1:30:50	1:44:00	1:47:42	2:09:14	2:18:40	3:01:47
6:57	21:36	34:45	43:11	1:04:47	1:09:30	1:26:22	1:31:03	1:44:15	1:47:58	2:09:34	2:19:00	3:02:13
6:58	21:39	34:50	43:17	1:04:56	1:09:40	1:26:35	1:31:16	1:44:30	1:48:14	2:09:52	2:19:20	3:02:40
6:59	21:42	34:55	43:24	1:05:05	1:09:50	1:26:47	1:31:29	1:44:45	1:48:29	2:10:10	2:19:40	3:03:06

MILE PACE	5 KM	5 MI	10 KM	15 KM	10 MI	20 KM	13.1 MI	15 MI	25 KM	30 KM	20 MI	MARATHON 26.219
7:00	21:45	35:00	43:30	1:05:15	1:10:00	1:27:00	1:31:42	1:45:00	1:48:45	2:10:30	2:20:00	3:03:32
7:01	21:48	35:05	43:36	1:05:24	1:10:10	1:27:12	1:31:55	1:45:15	1:49:00	2:10:48	2:20:20	3:03:58
7:02	21:51	35:10	43:42	1:05:33	1:10:20	1:27:24	1:32:08	1:45:30	1:49:15	2:11:06	2:20:40	3:04:24
7:03	21:54	35:15	43:48	1:05:43	1:10:30	1:27:37	1:32:21	1:45:45	1:49:31	2:11:26	2:21:00	3:04:51
7:04	21:57	35:20	43:55	1:05:52	1:10:40	1:27:49	1:32:34	1:46:00	1:49:46	2:11:44	2:21:20	3:05:17
7:05	22:00	35:25	44:01	1:06:01	1:10:50	1:28:02	1:32:47	1:46:15	1:50:02	2:12:02	2:21:40	3:05:43
7:06	22:04	35:30	44:07	1:06:11	1:11:00	1:28:14	1:33:01	1:46:30	1:50:18	2:12:22	2:22:00	3:06:09
7:07	22:07	35:35	44:13	1:06:20	1:11:10	1:28:27	1:33:14	1:46:45	1:50:34	2:12:40	2:22:20	3:06:36
7:08	22:10	35:40	44:19	1:06:29	1:11:20	1:28:39	1:33:27	1:47:00	1:50:49	2:12:58	2:22:40	3:07:02
7:09	22:13	35:45	44:26	1:06:39	1:11:30	1:28:51	1:33:40	1:47:15	1:51:04	2:13:18	2:23:00	3:07:28
7:10	22:16	35:50	44:32	1:06:48	1:11:40	1:29:04	1:33:53	1:47:30	1:51:20	2:13:36	2:23:20	3:07:54
7:11	22:19	35:55	44:38	1:06:57	1:11:50	1:29:16	1:34:06	1:47:45	1:51:35	2:13:54	2:23:40	3:08:20
7:12	22:22	36:00	44:44	1:07:06	1:12:00	1:29:29	1:34:19	1:48:00	1:51:51	2:14:12	2:24:00	3:08:47
7:13	22:25	36:05	44:51	1:07:16	1:12:10	1:29:41	1:34:32	1:48:15	1:52:06	2:14:32	2:24:20	3:09:13
7:14	22:28	36:10	44:57	1:07:25	1:12:20	1:29:54	1:34:45	1:48:30	1:52:22	2:14:50	2:24:40	3:09:39
7:15	22:31	36:15	45:03	1:07:34	1:12:30	1:30:06	1:34:58	1:48:45	1:52:37	2:15:08	2:25:00	3:10:05
7:16	22:35	36:20	45:09	1:07:44	1:12:40	1:30:18	1:35:12	1:49:00	1:52:53	2:15:28	2:25:20	3:10:31
7:17	22:38	36:25	45:15	1:07:53	1:12:50	1:30:31	1:35:25	1:49:15	1:53:09	2:15:46	2:25:40	3:10:58
7:18	22:41	36:30	45:22	1:08:02	1:13:00	1:30:43	1:35:38	1:49:30	1:53:24	2:16:04	2:26:00	3:11:24
7:19	22:44	36:35	45:28	1:08:12	1:13:10	1:30:56	1:35:51	1:49:45	1:53:40	2:16:24	2:26:20	3:11:50
7:20	22:47	36:40	45:34	1:08:21	1:13:20	1:31:08	1:36:04	1:50:00	1:53:55	2:16:42	2:26:40	3:12:16
7:21	22:50	36:45	45:40	1:08:30	1:13:30	1:31:20	1:36:17	1:50:15	1:54:10	2:17:00	2:27:00	3:12:43
7:22	22:53	36:50	45:46	1:08:40	1:13:40	1:31:33	1:36:30	1:50:30	1:54:26	2:17:18	2:27:20	3:13:09
7:23	22:56	36:55	45:53	1:08:49	1:13:50	1:31:45	1:36:43	1:50:45	1:54:41	2:17:38	2:27:40	3:13:35
7:24	22:59	37:00	45:59	1:08:58	1:14:00	1:31:58	1:36:56	1:51:00	1:54:57	2:17:56	2:28:00	3:14:01

MILE PACE	5 KM	5 MI	10 KM	15 KM	10 MI	20 KM	13.1 MI	15 MI	25 KM	30 KM	20 MI	MARATHON 26.219
7:25	23:03	37:05	46:05	1:09:08	1:14:10	1:32:10	1:37:09	1:51:15	1:55:13	2:18:16	2:28:20	3:14:27
7:26	23:06	37:10	46:11	1:09:17	1:14:20	1:32:23	1:37:23	1:51:30	1:55:29	2:18:34	2:28:40	3:14:54
7:27	23:09	37:15	46:18	1:09:26	1:14:30	1:32:35	1:37:36	1:51:45	1:55:44	2:18:52	2:29:00	3:15:20
7:28	23:12	37:20	46:24	1:09:36	1:14:40	1:32:47	1:37:49	1:52:00	1:55:59	2:19:12	2:29:20	3:15:46
7:29	23:15	37:25	46:30	1:09:45	1:14:50	1:33:00	1:38:02	1:52:15	1:56:15	2:19:30	2:29:40	3:16:12
7:30	23:18	37:30	46:36	1:09:54	1:15:00	1:33:12	1:38:15	1:52:30	1:56:30	2:19:48	2:30:00	3:16:39
7:31	23:21	37:35	46:42	1:10:04	1:15:10	1:33:25	1:38:28	1:52:45	1:56:46	2:20:08	2:30:20	3:17:05
7:32	23:24	37:40	46:49	1:10:13	1:15:20	1:33:37	1:38:41	1:53:00	1:57:01	2:20:26	2:30:40	3:17:31
7:33	23:27	37:45	46:55	1:10:22	1:15:30	1:33:50	1:38:54	1:53:15	1:57:17	2:20:44	2:31:00	3:17:57
7:34	23:31	37:50	47:01	1:10:32	1:15:40	1:34:02	1:39:07	1:53:30	1:57:33	2:21:04	2:31:20	3:18:23
7:35	23:34	37:55	47:07	1:10:41	1:15:50	1:34:14	1:39:21	1:53:45	1:57:48	2:21:22	2:31:40	3:18:50
7:36	23:37	38:00	47:13	1:10:50	1:16:00	1:34:27	1:39:34	1:54:00	1:58:04	2:21:40	2:32:00	3:19:16
7:37	23:40	38:05	47:20	1:10:59	1:16:10	1:34:39	1:39:47	1:54:15	1:58:19	2:21:58	2:32:20	3:19:42
7:38	23:43	38:10	47:26	1:11:09	1:16:20	1:34:52	1:40:00	1:54:30	1:58:35	2:22:18	2:32:40	3:20:09
7:39	23:46	38:15	47:32	1:11:18	1:16:30	1:35:04	1:40:13	1:54:45	1:58:50	2:22:36	2:33:00	3:20:35
7:40	23:49	38:20	47:38	1:11:27	1:16:40	1:35:17	1:40:26	1:55:00	1:59:06	2:22:54	2:33:20	3:21:01
7:41	23:52	38:25	47:45	1:11:37	1:16:50	1:35:29	1:40:39	1:55:15	1:59:21	2:23:14	2:33:40	3:21:27
7:42	23:55	38:30	47:51	1:11:46	1:17:00	1:35:41	1:40:52	1:55:30	1:59:36	2:23:32	2:34:00	3:21:53
7:43	23:58	38:35	47:57	1:11:55	1:17:10	1:35:54	1:41:05	1:55:45	1:59:52	2:23:50	2:34:20	3:22:19
7:44	24:02	38:40	48:03	1:12:05	1:17:20	1:36:06	1:41:18	1:56:00	2:00:08	2:24:10	2:34:40	3:22:46
7:45	24:05	38:45	48:09	1:12:14	1:17:30	1:36:19	1:41:32	1:56:15	2:00:24	2:24:28	2:35:00	3:23:12
7:46	24:08	38:50	48:16	1:12:23	1:17:40	1:36:31	1:41:45	1:56:30	2:00:39	2:24:46	2:35:20	3:23:38
7:47	24:11	38:55	48:22	1:12:33	1:17:50	1:36:44	1:41:58	1:56:45	2:00:55	2:25:06	2:35:40	3:24:04
7:48	24:14	39:00	48:28	1:12:42	1:18:00	1:36:56	1:42:11	1:57:00	2:01:10	2:25:24	2:36:00	3:24:30
7:49	24:17	39:05	48:34	1:12:51	1:18:10	1:37:08	1:42:24	1:57:15	2:01:25	2:25:42	2:36:20	3:24:57

MILE PACE	5 KM	5 MI	10 KM	15 KM	10 MI	20 KM	13.1 MI	15 MI	25 KM	30 KM	20 MI	MARATHON 26.219
7:50	24:20	39:10	48:40	1:13:01	1:18:20	1:37:21	1:42:37	1:57:30	2:01:41	2:26:02	2:36:40	3:25:23
7:51	24:23	39:15	48:47	1:13:10	1:18:30	1:37:33	1:42:50	1:57:45	2:01:56	2:26:20	2:37:00	3:25:49
7:52	24:26	39:20	48:53	1:13:19	1:18:40	1:37:46	1:43:03	1:58:00	2:02:12	2:26:38	2:37:20	3:26:15
7:53	24:30	39:25	48:59	1:13:29	1:18:50	1:37:58	1:43:16	1:58:15	2:02:28	2:26:58	2:37:40	3:26:42
7:54	24:33	39:30	49:05	1:13:38	1:19:00	1:38:11	1:43:29	1:58:30	2:02:44	2:27:16	2:38:00	3:27:08
7:55	24:36	39:35	49:12	1:13:47	1:19:10	1:38:23	1:43:43	1:58:45	2:02:59	2:27:34	2:38:20	3:27:34
7:56	24:39	39:40	49:18	1:13:57	1:19:20	1:38:35	1:43:56	1:59:00	2:03:14	2:27:54	2:38:40	3:28:00
7:57	24:42	39:45	49:24	1:14:06	1:19:30	1:38:48	1:44:09	1:59:15	2:03:30	2:28:12	2:39:00	3:28:26
7:58	24:45	39:50	49:30	1:14:15	1:19:40	1:39:00	1:44:22	1:59:30	2:03:45	2:28:30	2:39:20	3:28:53
7:59	24:48	39:55	49:36	1:14:25	1:19:50	1:39:13	1:44:35	1:59:45	2:04:01	2:28:50	2:39:40	3:29:19
8:00	24:51	40:00	49:43	1:14:34	1:20:00	1:39:25	1:44:48	2:00:00	2:04:16	2:29:06	2:40:00	3:29:45
8:01	24:54	40:05	49:49	1:14:43	1:20:10	1:39:38	1:45:01	2:00:15	2:04:32	2:29:26	2:40:20	3:30:11
8:02	24:58	40:10	49:55	1:14:53	1:20:20	1:39:50	1:45:14	2:00:30	2:04:48	2:29:46	2:40:40	3:30:38
8:03	25:01	40:15	50:01	1:15:02	1:20:30	1:40:02	1:45:27	2:00:45	2:05:03	2:30:04	2:41:00	3:31:04
8:04	25:04	40:20	50:07	1:15:11	1:20:40	1:40:15	1:45:40	2:01:00	2:05:19	2:30:22	2:41:20	3:31:30
8:05	25:07	40:25	50:14	1:15:20	1:20:50	1:40:27	1:45:53	2:01:15	2:05:34	2:30:40	2:41:40	3:31:56
8:06	25:10	40:30	50:20	1:15:30	1:21:00	1:40:40	1:46:07	2:01:30	2:05:50	2:31:00	2:42:00	3:32:22
8:07	25:13	40:35	50:26	1:15:39	1:21:10	1:40:52	1:46:20	2:01:45	2:06:06	2:31:18	2:42:20	3:32:49
8:08	25:16	40:40	50:32	1:15:48	1:21:20	1:41:05	1:46:33	2:02:00	2:06:21	2:31:36	2:42:40	3:33:15
8:09	25:19	40:45	50:39	1:15:58	1:21:30	1:41:17	1:46:46	2:02:15	2:06:36	2:31:56	2:43:00	3:33:41
8:10	25:22	40:50	50:45	1:16:07	1:21:40	1:41:29	1:46:59	2:02:30	2:06:51	2:32:14	2:43:20	3:34:07
8:11	25:25	40:55	50:51	1:16:16	1:21:50	1:41:42	1:47:12	2:02:45	2:07:07	2:32:32	2:43:40	3:34:34
8:12	25:29	41:00	50:57	1:16:26	1:22:00	1:41:54	1:47:25	2:03:00	2:07:23	2:32:52	2:44:00	3:35:00
8:13	25:32	41:05	51:03	1:16:35	1:22:10	1:42:07	1:47:38	2:03:15	2:07:39	2:33:10	2:44:20	3:35:26
8:14	25:35	41:10	51:10	1:16:44	1:22:20	1:42:19	1:47:51	2:03:30	2:07:54	2:33:28	2:44:40	3:35:52

MILE PACE	5 KM	5 MI	10 KM	15 KM	10 MI	20 KM	13.1 MI	15 MI	25 KM	30 KM	20 MI	MARATHON 26.219
8:15	25:38	41:15	51:16	1:16:54	1:22:30	1:42:32	1:48:04	2:03:45	2:08:10	2:33:48	2:45:00	3:36:18
8:16	25:41	41:20	51:22	1:17:03	1:22:40	1:42:44	1:48:18	2:04:00	2:08:25	2:34:06	2:45:20	3:36:45
8:17	25:44	41:25	51:28	1:17:12	1:22:50	1:42:56	1:48:31	2:04:15	2:08:40	2:34:24	2:45:40	3:37:11
8:18	25:47	41:30	51:34	1:17:22	1:23:00	1:43:09	1:48:44	2:04:30	2:08:56	2:34:44	2:46:00	3:37:37
8:19	25:50	41:35	51:41	1:17:31	1:23:10	1:43:21	1:48:57	2:04:45	2:09:11	2:35:02	2:46:20	3:38:03
8:20	25:53	41:40	51:47	1:17:40	1:23:20	1:43:34	1:49:10	2:05:00	2:09:27	2:35:20	2:46:40	3:38:29
8:21	25:57	41:45	51:53	1:17:50	1:23:30	1:43:46	1:49:23	2:05:15	2:09:43	2:35:40	2:47:00	3:38:56
8:22	26:00	41:50	51:59	1:17:59	1:23:40	1:43:59	1:49:36	2:05:30	2:09:59	2:35:58	2:47:20	3:39:22
8:23	26:03	41:55	52:05	1:18:08	1:23:50	1:44:11	1:49:49	2:05:45	2:10:14	2:36:16	2:47:40	3:39:48
8:24	26:06	42:00	52:12	1:18:18	1:24:00	1:44:23	1:50:02	2:06:00	2:10:29	2:36:36	2:48:00	3:40:14
8:25	26:09	42:05	52:18	1:18:27	1:24:10	1:44:36	1:50:15	2:06:15	2:10:45	2:36:54	2:48:20	3:40:41
8:26	26:12	42:10	52:24	1:18:36	1:24:20	1:44:48	1:50:29	2:06:30	2:11:00	2:37:12	2:48:40	3:41:07
8:27	26:15	42:15	52:30	1:18:46	1:24:30	1:45:01	1:50:42	2:06:45	2:11:16	2:37:32	2:49:00	3:41:33
8:28	26:18	42:20	52:37	1:18:55	1:24:40	1:45:13	1:50:55	2:07:00	2:11:31	2:37:50	2:49:20	3:41:59
8:29	26:21	42:25	52:43	1:19:04	1:24:50	1:45:26	1:51:08	2:07:15	2:11:47	2:38:08	2:49:40	3:42:25
8:30	26:24	42:30	52:49	1:19:13	1:25:00	1:45:38	1:51:21	2:07:30	2:12:02	2:38:26	2:50:00	3:42:52
8:31	26:28	42:35	52:55	1:19:23	1:25:10	1:45:50	1:51:34	2:07:45	2:12:18	2:38:46	2:50:20	3:43:18
8:32	26:31	42:40	53:01	1:19:32	1:25:20	1:46:03	1:51:47	2:08:00	2:12:34	2:39:04	2:50:40	3:43:44
8:33	26:34	42:45	53:08	1:19:41	1:25:30	1:46:15	1:52:00	2:08:15	2:12:49	2:39:22	2:51:00	3:44:10
8:34	26:37	42:50	53:14	1:19:51	1:25:40	1:46:28	1:52:13	2:08:30	2:13:05	2:39:42	2:51:20	3:44:37
8:35	26:40	42:55	53:20	1:20:00	1:25:50	1:46:40	1:52:26	2:08:45	2:13:20	2:40:00	2:51:40	3:45:03
8:36	26:43	43:00	53:26	1:20:09	1:26:00	1:46:53	1:52:40	2:09:00	2:13:36	2:40:18	2:52:00	3:45:29
8:37	26:46	43:05	53:32	1:20:19	1:26:10	1:47:05	1:52:53	2:09:15	2:13:51	2:40:38	2:52:20	3:45:55
8:38	26:49	43:10	53:39	1:20:28	1:26:20	1:47:17	1:53:06	2:09:30	2:14:06	2:40:56	2:52:40	3:46:21
8:39	26:52	43:15	53:45	1:20:37	1:26:30	1:47:30	1:53:19	2:09:45	2:14:22	2:41:14	2:53:00	3:46:48

MILE PACE	5 KM	5 MI	10 KM	15 KM	10 MI	20 KM	13.1 MI	15 MI	25 KM	30 KM	20 MI	MARATHON 26.219
8:40	26:56	43:20	53:51	1:20:47	1:26:40	1:47:42	1:53:32	2:10:00	2:14:38	2:41:34	2:53:20	3:47:14
8:41	26:59	43:25	53:57	1:20:56	1:26:50	1:47:55	1:53:45	2:10:15	2:14:54	2:41:52	2:53:40	3:47:40
8:42	27:02	43:30	54:04	1:21:05	1:27:00	1:48:07	1:53:58	2:10:30	2:15:09	2:42:10	2:54:00	3:48:06
8:43	27:05	43:35	54:10	1:21:15	1:27:10	1:48:20	1:54:11	2:10:45	2:15:25	2:42:30	2:54:20	3:48:33
8:44	27:08	43:40	54:16	1:21:24	1:27:20	1:48:32	1:54:24	2:11:00	2:15:40	2:42:48	2:54:40	3:48:59
8:45	27:11	43:45	54:22	1:21:33	1:27:30	1:48:44	1:54:38	2:11:15	2:15:55	2:43:06	2:55:00	3:49:25
8:46	27:14	43:50	54:28	1:21:43	1:27:40	1:48:57	1:54:51	2:11:30	2:16:11	2:43:26	2:55:20	3:49:51
8:47	27:17	43:55	54:35	1:21:52	1:27:50	1:49:09	1:55:04	2:11:45	2:16:26	2:43:44	2:55:40	3:50:17
8:48	27:20	44:00	54:41	1:22:01	1:28:00	1:49:22	1:55:17	2:12:00	2:16:42	2:44:02	2:56:00	3:50:44
8:49	27:24	44:05	54:47	1:22:11	1:28:10	1:49:34	1:55:30	2:12:15	2:16:58	2:44:22	2:56:20	3:51:10
8:50	27:27	44:10	54:53	1:22:20	1:28:20	1:49:47	1:55:43	2:12:30	2:17:14	2:44:40	2:56:40	3:51:36
8:51	27:30	44:15	54:59	1:22:29	1:28:30	1:49:59	1:55:56	2:12:45	2:17:29	2:44:48	2:57:00	3:52:02
8:52	27:33	44:20	55:06	1:22:39	1:28:40	1:50:11	1:56:09	2:13:00	2:17:44	2:45:18	2:57:20	3:52:29
8:53	27:36	44:25	55:12	1:22:48	1:28:50	1:50:24	1:56:22	2:13:15	2:18:00	2:45:36	2:57:40	3:52:55
8:54	27:39	44:30	55:18	1:22:57	1:29:00	1:50:36	1:56:35	2:13:30	2:18:15	2:45:54	2:58:00	3:53:21
8:55	27:42	44:35	55:24	1:23:07	1:29:10	1:50:49	1:56:49	2:13:45	2:18:31	2:46:14	2:58:20	3:53:47
8:56	27:45	44:40	55:31	1:23:16	1:29:20	1:51:01	1:57:02	2:14:00	2:18:46	2:46:32	2:58:40	3:54:13
8:57	27:48	44:45	55:37	1:23:25	1:29:30	1:51:14	1:57:15	2:14:15	2:19:02	2:46:50	2:59:00	3:54:40
8:58	27:51	44:50	55:43	1:23:34	1:29:40	1:51:26	1:57:28	2:14:30	2:19:17	2:47:08	2:59:20	3:55:06
8:59	27:55	44:55	55:49	1:23:44	1:29:50	1:51:38	1:57:41	2:14:45	2:19:36	2:47:28	2:59:40	3:55:32
9:00	27:58	45:00	55:55	1:23:53	1:30:00	1:51:51	1:57:54	2:15:00	2:19:58	2:47:46	3:00:00	3:55:58
9:10	28:29	45:50	56:58	1:25:27	1:31:40	1:53:56	2:00:11	2:17:30	2:22:25	2:50:54	3:03:20	4:00:22
9:20	29:00	46:40	58:00	1:27:00	1:33:20	1:56:00	2:02:22	2:20:00	2:25:00	2:54:00	3:06:40	4:04:44
9:30	29:31	47:30	59:02	1:28:33	1:35:00	1:58:04	2:04:33	2:22:30	2:27:35	2:57:06	3:10:00	4:09:06
9:40	30:02	48:20	60:05	1:30:07	1:36:40	2:00:10	2:06:44	2:25:00	2:30:12	3:00:15	3:13:20	4:13:28
9:50	30:33	49:10	61:07	1:31:40	1:38:20	2:02:14	2:08:55	2:27:30	2:32:47	3:03:21	3:16:40	4:17:50
10:00	31:05	50:00	62:09	1:33:14	1:40:00	2:04:18	2:11:07	2:30:00	2:35:23	3:06:27	3:20:00	4:22:13

PACE CHART FOR TRACK RACES AND WORKOUTS

How to Use

This chart can be used to select even-paced splits for races or speed workouts on a quarter mile (440 yard) track:

1. If you wish to run a 6-minute mile, for example, you can determine that your splits should be: 45 seconds at 220 yards, 1:30 after one lap (440 yards or a quarter mile), 2:15 at 660 yards, and 3 minutes after two laps (880 yards or a half mile). To find your splits at 220-yard or 440-yard intervals beyond 880 yards, add the time under those columns to the 880-yard time. Example: the split for ¾ mile for a 6-minute mile is 4:30 (3:00 + 1:30).

2. If you did a speed workout on the track and wish to determine your pace-per-mile average, locate your average time for that distance and refer to the left-hand column for your average pace per mile. Example: 8 × 440 yards averaging 1:40 each is a pace of 6:10 per mile.

Note: Since 400 meters is very close to 440 yards, this chart can also be used for approximate pacing for 200 meters, 400 meters, 600 meters, 800 meters and 1600 meters.

(Times on this chart are in minutes:seconds.tenths of seconds. Example—1:07.5)

1 MILE	220 YDS (1/8)	440 YDS (1/4)	660 YDS (3/8)	880 YDS (1/2)
4:30	33.75	1:07.5	1:41.25	2:15
4:40	35.0	1:10.0	1:45.0	2:20
4:50	36.25	1:12.5	1:48:75	2:25
5:00	37.5	1:15.0	1:52.5	2:30
5:10	38.75	1:17.5	1:56.25	2:35
5:20	40.0	1:20.0	2:00.0	2:40
5:30	41.25	1:22.5	2:03.75	2:45
5:40	42.5	1:25.0	2:07.5	2:50
5:50	43.75	1:27.5	2:11.25	2:55
6:00	45.0	1:30.0	2:15.0	3:00
6:10	46.25	1:32.5	2:18.75	3:05
6:20	47.5	1:35.0	2:22.5	3:10
6:30	48.75	1:37.5	2:26.25	3:15
6:40	50.0	1:40.0	2:30.0	3:20
6:50	51.25	1:42.5	2:33.75	3:25
7:00	52.5	1:45.0	2:37.5	3:30
7:10	53.75	1:47.5	2:41.25	3:35
7:20	55.0	1:50.0	2:45.0	3:40
7:30	56.25	1:52.5	2:48.75	3:45
7:40	57.5	1:55.0	2:52.5	3:50
7:50	58.75	1:57.5	2:56.25	3:55
8:00	1:00.0	2:00.0	3:00.0	4:00
8:10	1:01.25	2:02.5	3:03.75	4:05
8:20	1:02.5	2:05.0	3:07.5	4:10
8:30	1:03.75	2:07.5	3:11.25	4:15
8:40	1:05.0	2:10.0	3:15.0	4:20
8:50	1:06.25	2:12.5	3:18.75	4:25
9:00	1:07.5	2:15.0	3:22.5	4:30
9:10	1:08.75	2:17.5	3:26.25	4:35
9:20	1:10.0	2:20.0	3:30.0	4:40
9:30	1:11.25	2:22.5	3:33.75	4:45
9:40	1:12.5	2:25.0	3:37.5	4:50
9:50	1:13.75	2:27.5	3:41.25	4:55
10:00	1:15.0	2:30.0	3:45.0	5:00

MILE-KILOMETER TIME COMPARISONS

How to Use

It is easy to figure out what your pace per mile is for an odd racing distance in miles, such as 7 miles. Just divide your time by your mileage—in this example, 7. But for odd racing distances in kilometers, it isn't as easy. This chart shows you what a pace per mile is equivalent to per kilometer. If you race an 8-kilometer race, for example, in 48 minutes, divide this time by 8 to determine the pace per mile for one kilometer. Then look to the left-hand column to see what your pace per mile was for 8 kilometers. Forty-eight divided by 8 equals a pace of 6 minutes per kilometer, which is a pace of 9:40 per mile. You can also figure it the other way. If your goal is a 9:40-per-mile pace, you should hit each kilometer split in slightly over 6 minutes—for example you would hit two kilometers in 12 minutes.

(Times on this chart are in minutes:seconds.tenths of seconds. Example—2:47.80)

MILE	KILOMETER	MIN/ MILE	MIN/ KILOMETER
4:30	2:47.80	7:20	4:33.46
4:40	2:54.02	7:30	4:39.67
4:50	3:00.23	7:40	4:45.89
5:00	3:06.45	7:50	4:52.10
5:10	3:12.66	8:00	4:58.32
5:20	3:18.88	8:10	5:04.53
5:30	3:25.09	8:20	5:10.75
5:40	3:31.31	8:30	5:16.96
5:50	3:37.52	8:40	5:23.18
6:00	3:43.74	8:50	5:29.39
6:10	3:49.95	9:00	5:35.61
6:20	3:56.17	9:10	5:41.82
6:30	4:02.38	9:20	5:48.04
6:40	4:08.60	9:30	5:54.25
6:50	4:14.81	9:40	6:00.47
7:00	4:21.03	9:50	6:06.68
7:10	4:27.24	10:00	6:12.90

RACING-DISTANCE CONVERSIONS

ENGLISH TO METRIC		METRIC TO ENGLISH	
ENGLISH	METRIC	METRIC	ENGLISH
220 yards	201.168	200	218y, 2'2" (0.124 mi)
440 yards	402.336	400	437y, 1'4" (0.249 mi)
880 yards	804.672	800	874y, 2'8" (0.497 mi)

RACE	CONVERSION	RACE	CONVERSION
1 mile	1,609 meters	1,500 meters	0.93 miles
2 miles	3,219 meters	3,000 meters	1.86 miles
3 miles	4,828 meters	5,000 meters	3.11 miles
5 miles	8,047 meters	8,000 meters	4.97 miles
6 miles	9,656 meters	10,000 meters	6.21 miles
10 miles	16,193 meters	15,000 meters	9.32 miles
Half marathon	21,098 meters	20,000 meters	12.43 miles
15 miles	24,140 meters	25,000 meters	15.53 miles
20 miles	32,187 meters	30,000 meters	18.64 miles
Marathon	42,195 meters	Marathon	26.22 miles
30 miles	48,280 meters	50,000 meters	31.07 miles
50 miles	80,467 meters	100,000 meters	62.14 miles

Note: The English measurements and the metric ones beside them are the standard races and are approximately the same distance.

RECOMMENDED READING

SPORTS MEDICINE

Kraus, Dr. Hans. *The Causes, Prevention and Treatment of Sports Injuries.* New York: Playboy Press, 1981. A general guide for all athletes by the man who helped create the President's Council on Physical Fitness and Sports.

Sheehan, Dr. George. *Dr. George Sheehan's Medical Advice for Runners.* Mountain View, California: World Publications, 1978. The running doctor's answers to dealing with "the diseases of excellence."

Weisenfeld, Dr. Murray F., with Barbara Burr. *The Runner's Repair Manual.* New York: St. Martin's Press, 1980. The best listing available in down-to-earth language to help the runner treat his or her own injuries.

PHYSIOLOGY FOR RUNNERS

Costill, David L. *A Scientific Approach to Distance Running.* Los Altos, California: Track and Field News, 1979. Based on probably the most extensive running studies yet conducted by exercise physiologists on runners, by the director of the Human Performance Laboratory at Ball State University and contributing editor for *The Runner* magazine.

Dare, Bernie. *Running and Your Body: Applying Physiology to Track Training.* Los Altos, California: Tafnews Press, 1979. Perhaps the best source for the runner who wishes to better understand the physiology behind his or her training.

SPECIAL TOPICS

Anderson, Bob. *Stretching.* Bolinas, California: Shelter Publications, 1980. A complete illustrated guide to hundreds of stretches.

Edwards, Sally. *Triathlon: A Triple Fitness Sport.* Sacramento, California: Fleet Feet Press, 1982. Perhaps the first guide to this increasingly popular sport by a top ultramarathoner and triathlon athlete.

Friedberg, Ardy. *Weight Training for Runners.* New York: Fireside Books, 1981. A simplified guide for the runner who wishes to become a more complete, stronger athlete.

Gardner, James B., and J. Gerry Purdy. *Computerized Running Training Programs.* Los Altos, California: Tafnews Press, 1970. A computerized guide to setting your own workouts. Used by track coaches around the country.

Shapiro, James. *Ultramarathon.* New York: Bantam Books, 1981. A guide to the world beyond 26.2 miles by a runner-writer who ran across the USA.

Ullyot, Dr. Joan. *Running Free: A Guide for Women Runners and Their Friends.* New York: G. P. Putnam's Sons, 1980. Includes the best available answers to the special sociological, physiological and psychological questions women runners ask. Dr. Ullyot writes regular columns for *Women's Sports* and *Running* magazine and is a sub-three-hour marathoner.

RUNNING PUBLICATIONS

National Masters News
P.O. Box 2372
Van Nuys, CA 91404
   The bible of the masters (veterans) movement. Contains race results, upcoming masters races, stories of interest for the age-30-plus runner. A must if you are a masters runner who wants to keep abreast of what's happening in your sport.

New York Running News
International Running Center
9 East 89th Street
New York, NY 10028

The official magazine of the 25,000-member New York Road Runners Club. Includes regular articles from founding editor Ted Corbitt, pioneer Joe Kleinerman and president Fred Lebow.

The Runner
One Park Avenue
New York, NY 10016

Includes general running information and race results, and articles from such big names as Dr. David Costill, Hal Higdon, Nina Kuscsik, Marty Liquori, Dr. Gabe Mirkin, Bill Rodgers, Dr. Richard Schuster, Frank Shorter and Craig Virgin.

Runner's World
P.O. Box 366
Mountain View, CA 94040

Includes general running information and results, and articles from such big names as Amby Burfoot, Derek Clayton, Dr. George Sheehan, Arthur Lydiard, Brooks Johnson, Bill Dellinger and Dr. Steve Subotnik.

Running
P. O. Box 10990
Eugene, OR 97440

The Nike-owned magazine contains longer feature stories of more general interest than the other running magazines, and isn't full of race results. Includes regular running tips from Senior Editor Joe Henderson, plus articles from Don Kardong and Dr. Joan Ullyot.

Running Commentary
2011 Kimberly Drive
Eugene, OR 97405

A "newsy" newsletter written twice a month by Joe Henderson. It keeps you up to date on the latest running gossip as well as the latest research findings and training methods.

Running and Fitness
2420 K Street NW
Washington, DC 20037
The official publication of the 35,000-member American Running and Fitness Association. Includes articles and information of interest to the casual runner and average competitor, with regular medical articles by Dr. Gabe Mirkin and training articles by Bob Glover.

Running Times
14416 Jefferson Davis Highway
Suite 20
Woodbridge, VA 22191
"The National Calendar Magazine for Runners" includes races from all over the country and the world, along with very comprehensive race results—from even local races—and feature articles. Published by top ultramarathoner Ed Ayres and edited by top marathoner Phil Stewart.

Track & Field News
Box 296
Los Altos, CA 94022
"The bible of the sport." Interviews with top athletes from track and field plus road-racing and comprehensive track-meet results.

RUNNING
ORGANIZATIONS

American Running & Fitness Association (ARFA)
   Formerly called the National Jogging Association, this membership organization promotes running and fitness. Membership includes the newsletter *Running and Fitness*. For information call (202) 965-3430 or send a s.a.s.e. to:

American Running & Fitness Association
2420 K Street, NW
Washington, DC 20037

The Athletics Congress (TAC)
   The national governing body for track and road racing. All competitors racing internationally or in national events sanctioned by TAC are expected to be members. For information on your regional TAC office call (317) 638-9155 or send a s.a.s.e. to:

The Athletics Congress
P.O. Box 120
Indianapolis, IN 46206

The International Running Center
   Home of the New York Road Runners Club and an international running library. Contact for international running events.

International Running Center
9 East 89th Street
New York, NY 10028
(212) 860-2280

National Running Data Center (NRDC)
   Publishes books, newsletters and rankings of all distances by age group. *NRDC News* is issued monthly to subscribers.

NRDC
Box 42888
Tucson, AZ 85733

Road Runners Club of America (RRCA)
   The most active organization in the road-racing field, with over 200 member clubs. For the address of your local RRC organization or for information on starting a chapter in your area, send a long s.a.s.e. to:

Sanford Schmidt
Road Runners Club of America
732 Linden Place
Alton, IL 62002

Robert H. Glover and Associates, Inc.
46 West 71st Street
New York, NY 10023

   Corporate fitness consultants; running classes of all levels from beginner to advanced competitor.

INDEX

Aaken, Dr. Ernst Van, 31
addiction to running, 491–97
advanced competitor category,
    29, 75, 82, 143, 144–45,
    203, 205, 207, 243, 255
body weight for men in,
    477–78; body weight for
    women in, 480–81; cross-
    country training, 255. *See
    also* cross-country:
    inexperienced competitor,
    experienced competitor;
    distance training, 59;
    5 km—4-mile race training,
    234, 238; marathon
    training, 212–13, 220–21;
    mile training, 243. *See also*
    mile, the: inexperienced
    miler, experienced miler;
    power-training runs, 134;
    race-time ranges, 34–35;
    rhythm workout, 122; speed
    workout, 88–89; 10 km—
    half marathon training,
    194–95, 199
Aerobics (Cooper), 473

American College of Sports
    Medicine, 462, 467
American Council on Science
    and Health, 459
Anderson, Bob, 434
Atalanta marathoners, 75, 138,
    208, 284, 285, 305, 385,
    388, 401, 427, 480
*Athlete's Kitchen: A Nutrition
    Guide and Cookbook, The*
    (Clark), 457
average competitor. *See* basic
    competitor
Avon International Marathon,
    139, 177, 208, 284, 305,
    401, 447

Backache, Stress, and Tension
    (Kraus), 387
Ball State University, 445
Bannister, Roger, 240
Barbano, Sharon, 480
basic competitor category
    (average), 29, 45, 76, 78,
    82, 143, 144, 188, 203,
    205, 207, 243, 255

basic competitor category (*cont.*)
  body weight for men in, 478;
    body weight for women in,
    481; cross-country training,
    255. *See also* cross-country:
    inexperienced competitor;
    5 km—4-mile race training,
    233–34, 237; marathon
    training, 211–12, 218–19;
    mile training, 243. *See also*
    mile, the: inexperienced
    miler; power-training runs,
    133; race-time ranges,
    33–34; rhythm workout,
    122; speed workout, 88; 10
    km—half marathon
    training, 193–94, 198
"Bear, the," 276, 295, 355–56
Benson, Herbert, 295
body weight, 472–88
  based on looks, 473; big-
    bodied runners, 481–82,
    compared with weight at
    age 18 to 25, 472–73;
    dieting and, 482–86; fat,
    percentage of, 474–75;
    goals for, 474; men's racing
    weights, 475–78; and
    performance, 473; and race
    times, 486–89; women's
    racing weights, 479–82
Boston Bonne Bell 10 km, 285
Boston Marathon, 22, 41, 45,
    96, 139, 282–83, 284, 325,
    369, 430, 447, 456, 460,
    468, 478
British Medical Journal, 30
Brody, Dr. David, 367
Brooks, Dr. Marvin, 453
Bottinger, Dr. L. E., 30
Bowerman, Bill, 315, 317, 328
Burfoot, Amby, 325, 447

California, University of, at San
    Francisco, 453
Carroll, Noel, 493

*Causes, Prevention, and Treatment
    of Sports Injuries, The*
    (Kraus), 380
Cavanagh, Dr. Peter, 315, 328,
    333
Cerutty, Percy, 332–33
champion competitor category,
    29, 143, 144–45, 203–204,
    205, 207, 243, 255
  body weight for men in,
    477–78; body weight for
    women in, 480–81; cross-
    country training, 255. *See
    also* cross-country:
    experienced competitor;
    5 km—4-mile race training,
    235, 239; marathon
    training, 213–14, 222–23;
    mile training, 243. *See also*
    mile, the: experienced
    miler; power-training runs,
    135; race-time ranges,
    36–37; rhythm workout,
    123; speed workout, 89; 10
    km—half marathon
    training, 195–96, 200
Chodes, John, 276
Clark, Nancy, 457
Clayton, Derek, 317–18, 325,
    336, 337
Coe, Sebastian, 240
"collapse point," 79, 205
Collins, Wally, 477
Colt, Dr. Edward, 381, 383,
    470, 492–93
Columbia University, 125, 138,
    255, 260, 268, 379
competition against oneself,
    19–21
competitive running:
  and age, 59–60; and body
    weight, 472–88; categories
    in, 29; competition against
    oneself, 19–21; cross-
    country, 254–68;
    confidence, build-in of, in,

53, consistency, principle of, in, 42–44; dedication to, 19–25; distance training, 50, 56–67; and drinking fluids, 458–71; endurance-training runs, 74–80; environmental limitations in speed workouts, 89–94; experience in, 54; extended goals in, 54–55; first marathon, 176–86; first race, 167–75; 5 km—4-mile race, 229–39; flexibility in, 51–53; foundation training and sharpening, 40–42; frequency of training, 70–73; form, 50, 315–35; goal-setting for, 281–87; and heart rate, 67–70; heat, training for running in, 51; individuality in, 51–53; ingredients to success in, 25–26; injury and illness, common causes of, 361–93; injury and illness, prevention and management of, 394–414; marathon, the, 201–15; mental preparation for, 292–311; mile, the, 240–53; moderation and balance in, 55; and nutrition, 445–57; obstacles to, overcoming of, 21–25; pace training, 67–70; patience in, 54; power-training runs, 124–34; predicting race times, 287–91; progressive stress, adaptation to, in, 44–46; race-time ranges, 32–38; racing technique, 342–57; recovery principle, 46–48; rhythm-training runs, 108–23; and "runner's triangle," 491–97; specificity of training for, 48–51; speed, training for, 50, 81–97; strength-training runs, 98–107; style, 336–41; supplemental exercises for, 422–30; 10 km—half marathon, 187–200; terrain training, 50–51; time of day for training, 72–73; training principles, basic, 39–55; training schedules, 135–51; training schedules, writing of, 152–64; ultramarathon, the, 269–77; warm-up and cool-down routines for, 431–42; weight training for, 417–22

Computerized Running Training Programs (Gardner and Purdy), 288

Comrades Marathon (South Africa), 270

confidence, building of, in training, 53

consistency, principle of, 42–44

Cooksey, Marty, 356, 447

cool-down routines. *See* warm-up and cool-down routines

Cooper, Dr. Ken, 473

Corbitt, Ted, 270, 276–77, 402

Corbitt (Chodes), 276–77

Costill, Dr. David, 368, 445–46, 450, 451, 452, 455, 456–57, 461, 463, 469, 470, 471, 474

cross-country, 254–68
  build-up schedules for, 262–65; experienced competitor, 255, 256–57, 260–62, 264, 265; fitness category, 257; individual workouts, 259–62; inexperienced competitor, 255–56, 259–60, 263; long-run goals, 258; rebuilding phase, 262; selection of

cross-country (cont.)
    race, 257; time goals, 257;
    tips for, 266–68; training
    cycle and phases, 258;
    weekly mileage goals, 258
Cureton, K. J., 31, 486

Darr, Flip, 294
Davis, C. T., 20
"Death Grip, the," 276
d'Elia, Toshi, 22
deVries, Herbert, 98
distance training, 50
    cutting down on, 66; high
        mileage in, 66–67;
        increasing mileage in, 59;
        minimum for "survivors,"
        58; as related to time,
        60–61; tips for, 64–65
Down, Linda, 176–77
drinking fluids and running,
        458–71
    after running, 468–71; before
        running and racing,
        461–62; on the run,
        462–66, 466–68; what to
        drink, 458–60

eating. See nutrition
Eating Attitudes Test, 382
elite competitor category
        (national class), 37–38, 41,
        75, 76
    body weight for men in,
        475–77; body weight for
        women in, 479–80; race-
        time ranges, 37
Elliott, Jumbo, 97
endurance-training runs, 74–80
    long-distance, 75–79;
        medium-distance, 79; short-
        distance, 79–80
exercises, supplemental, for
        competitive running,
        422–30

aerobic, 425–28; guidelines
    for, 428–30; without
    weights, 422–25
experience, as aspect of
    training, 54
experienced competitor. See
    advanced competitor

Fairmount Park (Philadelphia),
    255
fartlek training, 83–84, 95,
    101–102, 104–105, 109,
    151, 190, 192, 193, 194,
    208, 211, 213, 214, 233,
    255, 258, 261, 417
Ferris, Jim, 403
Fisher, Garth, 100
5 km—4-mile race, 229–39
    build-up schedule, 12-week,
        235–39; fitness category,
        230; individual workouts
        for, 232–35; long-run goals,
        231; rebuilding phase, 235;
        selection of race, 230; time
        goals, 230; training cycle
        and phases, 230; weekly
        mileage goals, 231
flexibility in training, 51–53
Florida State University, 497
food. See nutrition
form, running, 315–35
    arm action, 330–33; body
        angle, 328–30; footstrike,
        317–24; forward stride,
        324–28; total, 334–35;
        training for, 50
Fox, Terry, 23–24, 25
foundation training and
        sharpening, 40–42
frequency of training, 70–73
Friedberg, Ardy, 422
Fukuoka Marathon, 397

Galloway, Jeff, 48
Gardner, James B., 288

George Washington University, 366

Georgia, University of, 31, 486

Gertsch, Guy, 96

Glover, Bob, 18, 19, 20, 21, 22, 23, 24, 25, 43, 47, 53, 75, 138, 271, 276, 282, 305, 318, 341, 347, 364, 380, 388, 401, 403, 427, 434, 452, 460, 473, 477–78, 480, 483, 491, 495

Glover, Christopher, 495

goal-setting, 281–87

goals, extended, for training, 54

Gottlieb, William, 454

Goulart, Frances Sheridan, 383

group running, 78, 95–96, 110, 182

Harmeling, Maddy, 388

Haskell, Dr. William, 483

Hearn, Angella, 284–85

heart rate:
   maximum, 68; recovery, 69; resting, 67–68; training, 68–69

heat, training for running in, 51

Henderson, Joe, 39, 42

Henry, Sherrye, Jr., 382

Herzog, Dr. David, 382

Hill, Ron, 449

hill training, 51, 102–103, 110, 112, 113, 194, 210, 213, 258, 260, 261, 417

Honolulu Marathon, 469

Hulak, Marilyn, 282–83, 308, 401, 429–30

Inches-Off Diet, The (Stillman), 472

individuality in training, 51–53

injury and illness in competitive running, common causes of, 361–93

age and sex, 389–90; biomechanical, 363–64, body weight, 381–82; down-hills, 368–69; errors in running form, 366–67; greed: overracing, 369–70; heat, 375; improper foot care, 383–84; improper rehabilitation, 366; inadequate diet, 382–83; inadequate sleep, 387–88; marathonitis, 391–93; muscle imbalance, 365–66; old injuries, 364; other sports, 388–89; overtraining, 367–68; poor advice, 391; poor daily habits, 385; poor flexibility and overstretching, 364–65; shoes and orthotics, 378–81; stress, 385–87; surfaces and terrain, 370–72; undertraining, 369; weather, 372–75

injury and illness in competitive running, prevention and management of, 394–414

alternative training, 413–14; colds, 397–98; coming back, 410–12; flu, 398–99; overtraining syndrome and the blahs, 403–404; running through an injury, 404–407; stitch, the, 399–403; treatment, 407–410; warning signs, 394–96

injury, questions to ask when sustained, 362–63

Jacobson, Dr. Edmund, 295

Jensen, Clayne, 100

Jogger, The magazine, 383

John F. Kennedy 50-Mile-Run (Maryland), 270

Johnson, Brooks, 329
Journal of Sports Medicine and Physical Fitness, 470

Kraus, Dr. Hans, 380, 387

Lebow, Fred, 17, 19
L'Eggs Mini-Marathon, 21
London Marathon, 285, 298
London School of Hygiene and Tropical Medicine, 20
Long Island Marathon, 428
Lydiard, Arthur, 317
Lynch, Dr. Jerry, 292, 293–94, 295–96, 297

Manufacturers Hanover Corporate Challenge (New York City), 229
marathon, the, 201–15
  build-up schedules, 18-week, 214–23; endurance-training pace, 207; fitness category, 202; individual workouts for, 207–14; long-run goals, 204–205; rebuilding phase, 214; selection of race, 202–203; time goals, 202–203; tips for, 224–28; training cycle and phases, 203–204; weekly mileage goals, 204–206
"marathon fever," 17–18, 176
marathon, first, 176–86
  four-month training for, 178–79; selection of, 177; six-month training for, 180, 181; three-month training for, 180, 181; tips for, 182–86; training for, 177–81
Marathoning (Steffny), 288
Marathon Mom (Schreiber), 496
Marine Corps Marathon, 367

marriage, stress placed on by competitive running, 495–97
Maryland, University of, 480
Matthews, Dr. Leslie S., 390
Mayer, Dr. Jean, 454
mental preparation for racing, 292–311
  analysis of race, 310–11; anxiety, prerace, dealing with, 300–301; confidence, 293–94; motivation, 293; prerace checklist, 298–300; relaxation, 294–96; strategy, 301; visualization, 296–98
Merola, Pat, 483
Micheli, Dr. Lyle, 367
Miers, Charlie, 476–77
mile, the, 240–53
  build-up schedules, 248–51; experienced miler, 244, 248, 250, 253; fitness category, 244–45; individual workout, 247, 249–50; inexperienced miler, 243–44, 247, 249, 251–52; long-run goals, 246; pace progression, 251; rebuilding phase, 248; selection of race, 245; time goals, 245; tips for, 251–53; training cycle and phases, 245–46; weekly mileage goals, 246
Milvy, Dr. Paul, 449–50, 470
Mirkin, Dr. Gabe, 317, 399, 400, 402, 482
Mittleman, Stu, 277
moderation and balance in training, 35
Moore, Alicia, 285
Morgan, William P., 494

national class competitor. *See* elite competitor

National Running Data Center, 57, 288

Nett, Toni, 287

New York Marathon, 21, 23, 24, 25, 41, 176–77, 208, 284, 285, 317, 325, 356, 392, 397, 430, 450, 462, 478, 484, 491, 495

New York Road Runners Club, 17, 19, 21, 23, 285, 316–17, 383, 388

New York Running News, 17

Nike Team Challenge, 139

1974 Marathon Handbook, The (Young), 57

North Jersey Masters Track Club, 19, 317

novice competitor category, 29, 40, 45, 76, 78, 82, 115, 143, 144, 188, 203, 205, 207, 243, 255
  body weight for men in, 478; body weight for women in, 481; distance training, 58–59; 5 km—4-mile race training, 232–33, 236; marathon training, 210–11, 216–17; race-time ranges, 32–33; rhythm workout, 121; speed workout, 87–88; 10 km—half marathon training, 190–93, 197

nutrition for runners, 445–57
  carbohydrate loading, 449–52; fasting and vegetarianism, 446–47; last meal before race, 452–53; minerals and vitamins, 447–49; postrace eating, 456–57; race-day eating, 453–56

older runners, 30

Olympic Marathon, 46, 467

On the Road: The Marathon (Shapiro), 273

Oregon, University of, 315, 403

Osler, Tom, 269

Ovett, Steve, 240

Oxford University, 255

pace training, 67–70

Paige, Don, 474

Pargman, David, 497

patience in training, 54

Parmalee, Patty Lee, 20–21, 427–28

Parade magazine, 495

Pennsylvania State University, 315, 328

Pepsi Challenge 10 km series, 187

Personnelmetrics, 24

Physician and Sportsmedicine, The magazine, 300

power-training runs, 124–34
  charting for, 132–34; guidelines, 132; intensity of, 127–28; planning, 126–29; quantity of, 126–27; rest in, 128–29; speed, control of, 129–131; speed, increasing, 131–32

predicting race times, 287–91
  analyzing results, 290; goal setting, 289–90; pace, establishment of, 290; speed workout guidelines, 291; system for, 289–91

Prevention magazine, 454

Progressive Relaxation (Jacobson), 295

pulse, taking of, 69–70

Purdy, J. Gerry, 288

race, first, 167–75
  eight-week training program for, 169–70; progression toward, 175; recovery from,

race, first (cont.)
174; selection of, 168; tips
for, 170–74; training for,
170–74
race-time prediction. See
predicting race times
racing technique. See technique,
racing
recovery, principle of, 46–48
Relax and Win (Winter), 295
Relaxation Response, The
(Benson), 295
rhythm-training runs, 108–23
charts for, 120–23; general
guidelines for, 119–20;
intensity, determination of,
113–15; pace, control of,
116–17; quantity selection,
111–12; rest, determination
of, 112–13; speed,
increasing of, 117–19;
writing a rhythm workout,
110–17
Road Runners Club (national),
268
Rodgers, Bill, 25, 38, 315, 317,
482, 494
Rodriguez, Mary, 21–22
Roe, Allison, 38, 81, 103, 317
Rome Marathon, 308
Rothfarb, Ruth, 177
Run Farther, Run Faster
(Henderson), 42
Runner, The magazine, 293, 382,
450, 471, 482
Runner's Book, The (Carroll), 493
Runner's Handbook, The (Glover
and Shepherd), 18, 341,
434
Runner's Repair Manual, The
(Weisenfeld), 363, 384
Runner's World magazine, 24,
315, 325, 336
running boom, 17–18
running form. See form, running
Running Free (Ullyot), 32

Running On (d'Elia), 22
running style. See style, running

Sachs, Michael, 497
Salazar, Alberto, 38, 81, 317,
325, 397, 467
Sanders, Odis, 47
Scaff, Dr. Jack, 469
Scientific Approach to Distance
Running, A (Costill), 445
Scientific Basis of Athletic
Conditioning, The (Jensen
and Fisher), 100
Schlein, Mort, 23
Schreiber, Linda, 496
Schuder, Pete, 43, 54, 125, 138,
255, 260, 268, 318, 320,
329, 354, 367, 379, 476
Schuster, Dr. Richard, 378, 380
Schwam, Marcy, 22–23, 270,
276, 277, 388–89
Segal, Dr. Julius, 388
Selye, Dr. Hans, 386
Shapiro, Jim, 273
Sheehan, Dr. George, 362, 380,
394, 398, 402
Shepherd, Jack, 18, 355, 380,
434
Shorter, Frank, 38, 201, 336,
337, 467, 494
Simon Fraser University
(Canada), 448
Singer, Dr. Robert N., 300–301
Southern California, University
of, 98
specificity of training for
running, 48–51
speed training, 50, 81–97
environmental limitations in,
89–93; factors influencing,
86–94; fitness and
experience levels, 87–89;
goals for, 86–87; in groups,
95–96; 1-2-3 approach in,
84–86; physical,
psychological limitations,

94; tips on, 96–97; variety in, 94–95

Spiridon Magazine, 288

Sport Psyching: Playing Your Best Game All of the Time (Tutko), 296

Squires, Bill, 317

Stanford University, 460

Steffny, Manfred, 287–88

Stillman, Dr. Irwin Maxwell, 472

strength-training runs, 98–107 advanced *fartlek*, 104–105; fast continuous, 103–104; modified *fartlek*, 101; rolling hills, 102–103; tempo, 105–106

stress, progressive, adaptation to, 44–46

Stress of Life, The (Selye), 386

Stretching (Anderson), 434

style, running, 336–41 breathing, 340–41; light feet, 338–39; relaxation, 339–40; rhythmic flow, 337–38

Subotnik, Dr. Steve, 351

supplemental exercises. *See* exercises, supplemental

Taylor, Dr. Paul, 372

technique, racing, 342–57 downhill, 348, 350–54; finish, the, 354–57; in the race, 343–44; passing, 344–45; starting, 342–43; uphill, 345–48, 349

10 km—half marathon, 187–200 build-up schedules, 12-week, 196–200; fitness category, 188; individual workouts for, 190–96; long-run goals, 189; planning build-up races, 188; time goals, 188; training cycle and phases,

188–89; weekly mileage for, 189–90, 191

terrain, training for, 50–51

Thorton, John, 470

Tighe, Nancy, 428

Toronto, University of, 382

training schedules, 135–51 blending phases in, 150–51; cycles, 136–39, 149; endurance (foundation) phase, 140–41; guide for scheduling, 155–59; phases, 139–47, 149; race spacing, 147–48; rebuilding phase, 145–47, 148–49; sample, 163–64; sharpening phase, 142–43; strengthening phase, 141; tapering phase, 143–45; writing of, 152–64

Traum, Richard, 24, 176

Tutko, Dr. Thomas, 296, 297

Ullyot, Dr. Joan, 32, 407, 467, 480

ultramarathon, the, 269–77 faster ultras, tips for, 273–77; first ultra, tips for, 270–73; racing ultras, 273; training program for, 277

Uppsala, University of (Sweden), 398

Vahlensieck, Christa, 288

Van Cortlandt Park (New York City), 255, 268

Villanova University, 97

Virgin, Craig, 81

Waitz, Grete, 38, 81, 317, 479

"Wall, the," 57, 205, 227, 276, 295, 355–56, 468

Wanamaker Mile, 240

warm-up and cool-down routines, 431–42 basic exercises, 434–40; guidelines for stretching,

warm-up and cool-down
routines (*cont.*)
432; sample, 15-minute,
439; for speed workouts,
440–42
Washington University (St.
Louis), 30
Waters, Dr. Brent, 497
weight training for competitive
running, 417–22
exercises, 420–21; general
rules, 421–22; selecting
weights progressively, 420;
warm-up and cool-down,
418; workout, 418–20
Weight Training for Runners
(Friedberg), 422
Weisenfeld, Dr. Murray, 363,
384, 390, 407–10

West Side YMCA (New York
City), 24
Whiston, Jean, 385, 480
Winter, Bud, 295
Wisconsin, University of, 494
women runners, 31–32
Women's Ivy League Track and
Field Championship, 382
Women's Running (Ullyot), 407,
467
Wood, Dr. Peter, 460
World Masters Championship,
22

Yale University, 382
Young, Ken, 57
younger runners, 30–31

Zatopek, Emil, 81